CLASS, SEX AND REVOLUTIONS

Gunnar Olofsson & Sven Hort
(eds.)

Class, Sex and Revolutions

Göran Therborn – a critical appraisal

Arkiv Academic Press

Arkiv Academic Press is an imprint of

Arkiv förlag
Box 1559
SE-221 01 Lund
Sweden

STREET ADDRESS Lilla Gråbrödersgatan 3 c, Lund
PHONE +46 (0) 46 13 39 20

arkiv@arkiv.nu
www.arkiv.nu

A list of Arkiv Academic Press titles can be found in the
last pages of this book. For up-to-date information on
distribution and available titles, please visit:

www.arkivacademicpress.com

Cover design with inspiration from Leif Thollander by David Lindberg

© The authors/Arkiv förlag
First edition by Arkiv förlag 2016
Arkiv Academic Press international edition 2016
For print information, see the back page of this copy
ISBN: 978 91 980854 8 8

Göran Therborn at 75

Tabula Gratulatoria

Ola Agevall
Göran Ahrne
Risto Alapuro
Elmar Altvater
Heine Andersen
Perry Anderson
Gunnar Andersson
Jan Annerstedt
Dominique Anxo
Göran Arnman
Håkan Arvidsson
Inga-Lill Aspelin
Lars Bengtsson
Margot Bengtsson
Mats Benner
Christian Berggren
Paavo Bergman
Ylva Bergström
Boel Berner
Margareta Bertilsson
Ulf Bjereld & Marie Demker
Ulla Björnberg
Anders Björnsson
Robin Blackburn
Agneta Bladh
Raimo Blom
Thomas P. Boje
Thomas Brante

Claus Bryld
Christine Buci-Glucksmann
Michael Burawoy
Margareta Bäck-Wiklund
Mattias Börjesson
Jan Carle
Chang Kyung-sup
Thomas Coniavitis
Einar Dahlin
Per Dannefjord
Göran Djurfeldt
Charles Edquist
Hedda Ekerwald
Gabriella Elgenius
Rosmari Eliasson-Lappalainen
Aant Elzinga
Emma Engdahl
Filipe Faria
Gary Fine
Daniel Fleming
Sven-Erik Forsell
Tomas Forser
Denis Frank
Mats Franzén
Barbara Fritz
Björn Fryklund
Bengt Furåker
Anna G. Jónasdottir
Per Gahrton
Ian Gough
Claes-Göran Green
Jukka Gronow
Göran Gustafsson
Rolf Å. Gustafsson
Sverker Gustavsson
Christina Gynnå Oguz

Anita Göransson
Elina Haavio-Mannila
Bernt Hagtvet
Anna Hallberg & Jörgen Gassilewski
Lars Hansson
Sten Henriksson
Urban Herlitz
C.H. Hermansson
Christer Hogstedt
Rebecca & Sven Hort
Hans Isaksson
Urban Janlert
Per H. Jensen & Annick Prieur
Britt-Marie Johansson & Nikolaos Tzampazis
Ingvar Johansson
Stefan Jonsson
Claes-Göran Jönsson
Ingrid Jönsson
Daniel Kallós & Lisbeth Lundahl
Bernt Kennerström
Pauli Kettunen
Abdulhadi Khalaf
Habibul Haque Khondker
Lisa Kings
Markku Kivinen
Anders Kjellberg
Barbro Klein
Juha Koivisto
Zhanna Kravchenko
Eva Kärfve
Jörgen Elm Larsen
Aliaksei Lastouski
Åsa Christina Laurell
Lena Lavinas
Hilda Lennartsson
Rolf Lidskog

Sven-Eric Liedman
Boel Lindberg & Gunnar Olofsson
David Lindberg
Mats Lindberg
Staffan Lindberg
Anna-Lisa Lindén
Gerd Lindgren
Sven-Åke Lindgren
Kent Lindkvist
Svante Lundberg
Åsa Lundqvist
Bengt-Åke Lundvall
Anders Löfqvist
Johan Lönnroth
Alan Mabin
Lars Magnusson
Harri Melin
Kina Meurle-Hallberg & Hans Hallberg
Lars Mjöset
Anders Molander
Anne-Marie Morhed
Diana Mulinari
Karin Månsson
Per Månsson
Sven-Axel Månsson
Ilkka Mäkinen
Hannu Nieminen
Ann Nilsen
Jan Nilsson
Kjell Nilsson
Tommy Nilsson
José Pacheco
Joakim Palme
Apostolis Papakostas
Sonia Camara Perena
Anders Persson

Karl Gunnar Persson
Abby Peterson
Tomas Peterson
Olof Petersson
Ellinor Platzer
Carlos Prieto del Campo
Anna-Sofia Quensel
Rune Romhed
Hans-Edward Roos
Jeja Pekka Roos
Lennart Rosenlund
AnnChristin & Bo Rothstein
Malena Rydberg
Helge Rönning
Tapio Salonen
Åke Sandberg
Tom Sandlund
Glenn Sjöstrand
Sten-Åke Stenberg
Anders Stephanson
Mikael Stigendal
Göran Sundqvist
Sune Sunesson
Stefan Svallfors
Richard Swedberg
Mats Svegfors
Olle Svenning
Levi Svenningsson
Lennart Svensson
Marta Szebehely
Sonia Therborn
Thomas & Marie Therborn
Thomas Thomell
Håkan Thörn
Per Arne Tjäder
Catta & Sven-Erik Torhell

Torbjörn Tännsjö
Immanuel Wallerstein
Dick-Urban Vestbro
Denny Vågerö
Gunnar Wetterberg
Karin Widerberg
Tony Wood
Eric Olin Wright
Nikolay Zakharov
Rune Åberg
Gunnar Ågren
Ulf Öhlund
Elisabeth Özdalga

Department of Social Studies, Linnaeus University
Department of Sociology, Lund University
Department of Sociology, Uppsala University

ANNA HALLBERG
tomogram

att det. i rundeln om honom. kindbenen och armbenen
rakryggen. ändå är böljande. ett ängsull osynligt. vara nära det
ljusfjunet. aldrig säga. snudda det varma vattnet. forsa runt i
gladskrattet. det blir stort om honom. folk börjar flytta runt. saker
och skålar. stöter emot en axel. helt försiktigt. nästan som
oavsiktligt. att förlåt mig som är så klumpig. och det där lugna.
vänliga som rätar ut. så att också vi. liksom lättar. ljusnar.

om så bara en enda. och att hon blev som tokig. lämnade allt ifrån
sig. att det var en våg. hon sa det. att den kastade sig över och att
hon inte kunde. motstå. och här gick väl åsikterna isär. redan då. att
nog kunde man. att hon då med den blicken. så man vart tyst. vågen
som fanns kvar där inne. och rullade. fast det var så länge sedan.
och bara en pingsthelg. om det var värt allt det för så lite. och att
man ändå ville. några skvalp från den vågen. så man skrapade.
tiggde fram det. rös. och ruskade. och såg ner på sina händer.

det var det att alla såg. utom de två som skulle. och givet var ju att
det var de som. och när något skulle lyftas eller bäras. eller hämtas
eller skickas. hur de följde i varandra som ingenting. och ändå. var
kom hon ifrån. den som klev emellan. att det inte gick att göra
ogjort sedan.

att så stora avstånd. mellan människorna. och orden. och himlen.
fast så litet. i samma jävla grop. att det måste gnagas och hånas och
hållas stången. så att inte. och att då. som nåden. likt förbannat
rämnar. och att det enda. om kroppen kan förlåta. inte vem som
helst men att. i den hundvalpens ludna öra. innan allt har förbenats.
om så bara några timmar. på ett liv. veta det. långt innanför huden.
att det kan räcka. långt. och att gå. jämte därefter. sida vid sida.
härda ihop.

Contents

SECTION II. Sex, Gender and Power

SECTION III. Global Modernities

Acknowledgements

Sweden and the Far North are perhaps not the most suitable sites to launch a critical appraisal of the works of Göran Therborn. No local library has a full collection of his global output. However, in the winter months of 2015 we started out from southern California and Korea respectively and approached some 50 senior scholars around the world and on all continents, inviting them to enlist in a serious intellectual exchange with Göran's key contributions to social theory and research. Our preferred model article already existed: Perry Anderson's 'Atlas of the Family', first published in *The Nation* in May 2005, which made possible a comparison with Eric J. Hobsbawm's 'Retreat of the Male', published in *London Review of Books* in August the same year.

The great majority of Göran's friends and colleagues enthusiastically jumped on the bandwagon, agreed that the book was a great idea and presented the most fascinating proposals. Less than a handful did not reply, our email addresses probably being wrong. Close to a dozen more or less immediately said NO, due to other commitments or because they were now working in fields far from Göran's concerns. No big deal. Representation from four out of five continents looked possible. Closer to deadline one after the other – most often with very good reasons – found their possibility to finalize a serious manuscript lacking due to various well-known difficulties in academic or private life. However, we were able to replace seniors with juniors, and younger students of his work from the walks of life we knew. They were eager to join (almost at the last minute), which we as editors are very grateful for. Unfortunately we were not able to reach and enlist some of his most gifted recent students from later years (e.g. among those listed in *The World*).

We ended up with a book with two introductions – one international by Robin Blackburn, the other with a slightly more narrow generational focus by yours truly, and three thematic sections consisting of a handful of chapters each. Some of the authors take issue with a certain aspect of Göran's work, from gender and inequality to politics and revolutions, others develop themes that are or have been central to him: globality, modernity, solidarity, space. There are also articles that offer a long view of a career that began close to Petrograd, moved towards Saigon and continued forwards in the direction of Latin America and the Far South.

Apart from contributors and advisors, we would like to thank all those who helped us in making this book not only possible but also real. Two Swedish Sociology Departments – Lund and Linnaeus – generously supported this endeavour. Göran began his academic career at the Department of Sociology at Lund University in the 1960s and 1970s and he is now affiliated to Linnaeus University. Many thanks as well to the publisher, Arkiv förlag, for all their efforts in transforming this large set of articles into a book and for their endurance with our style of work. This also applies to our wives, Rebecca and Boel.

We are also grateful to all those who have supported this volume by signing up for the *Tabula Gratulatoria*, since this book is also a *Festschrift* in the Swedish academic tradition. They represent a wide selection of Göran's old and new friends and colleagues – and some old foes as well. Göran's daughter Anna opens the book with a poem in the local vernacular.

Växjö, June 2016
Sven Hort and Gunnar Olofsson

INTRODUCTIONS

ROBIN BLACKBURN

Göran Therborn and the Old Mole

I know of no other socialist thinker as persistent and perceptive in his analysis of the social contradictions of globalized capitalism as Göran Therborn. This gives him great insight into of the political forces which seek to challenge the social order, whether from the Left or the Right. Therborn uses theory to generate not abstract models but empirical tests, practical insights and provocative puzzles.

Bearing this in mind I hope that he will accept as a tribute to his work a sketch of British politics in the last decade culminating in the election of Jeremy Corbyn, an inveterate leftist, as party leader in September 2015. The new leader did not attend a university but has explained that he picked up an education in the labour movement. He has explained that a seminar at the house of Tony Benn, organized by Ralph Miliband and Leo Panitch, was particularly important.

The New Left in Europe and North America failed until recently in its primary and enduring goal – to found and sustain a party. But it did nourish elements of a collective and cosmopolitan sub-culture, with magazines, publishing houses and a niche in academia. Ralph Miliband was a leading light of this milieu. The Miliband-Poulantzas exchanges raised the question of the tasks of theory, the structural understanding of power, and the scope of bourgeois democracy. There was never to be a Therborn-Miliband debate, nor, sadly, a Therborn-Poulantzas debate, but Therborn's work has supplied an indispensable pole of reference for activists and theorists alike.

The Miliband Panitch seminar, known to those involved as the London Corresponding Society (LCS), certainly took notice of Therborn's work when they decided to focus on unemployment following the appearance of Therborn's *Why Some Peoples Are More Unemployed Than Others* (1986). Those involved in the LCS hoped thereby to be furnishing a sounding board and workshop for a future Labour leader – as indeed they were. Corbyn's win can be seen as a belated victory for Tony Benn, who died in 2013.

I first met Göran at a New Left summer school in the English seaside resort Margate in 1963. The British Labour party had a new – and supposedly more leftwing – leader, as did the largest union, the TGWU. The Campaign for Nuclear Disarmament could mobilize hundreds of thousands of demonstrators. However the real excitements were those on the international scene, associated with Khrushchev, Dubček, Ho Chi Minh, Mao, Fidel Castro, the Italian Communist Party (PCI) or the emergence of a New Left party in France.

Perry Anderson had just published an extended three-part critique of Swedish Social Democracy in *New Left Review* so the youthful Therborn was plied for information and his own appraisal. At this time the Labour Party's modernisers pointed to the Swedish welfare state as their model but without grasping that it required more sweeping reforms and a more hegemonic stance than Labour had been thus far prepared to consider.

In 1963–64 *New Left Review* published Tom Nairn's scathing account of the timidity of Labourism. He supplied an early version of an idea that Göran was to develop later in his work on ideology. Nairn urged that British Labour suffered not from weak class consciousness but from the wrong type of class feeling. Labourism expressed corporate rather than hegemonic class consciousness. Labour was seen as a corporate interest within a given order rather than as a transformational and hegemonic force capable of challenging an unjust social order and offering leadership to other layers of the oppressed.

The Margate summer school was aimed at encouraging a Leftist current inside the Labour Party, with a Trotskyist group furnishing some organizational experience. However the Wilson government moved to the right and its claims to be harnessing the 'white heat' of the technological revolution to socialism seemed empty rhetoric.

May 68 and the student revolts took us in a direction mapped out by Göran in a striking text entitled, 'From Petrograd to Saigon' (*New Left Review* 48, 1968; discussed in this volume by Anders Stephanson). In this text he explained how the peasants and workers of a poor Asian country of medium size could challenge the false equation of West and East in Cold War stereotypes. Communism here was on the side of the wretched of the earth, the weaker-but-stronger force in a struggle for national liberation that had global resonance.

The emergence of a revolutionary student movement in the 1960s and 70s created an appetite for theoretical understandings of imperialism and capitalism. Göran's labour to produce a historical and materialist sociology supplied a vital set of ingredients, brought together in his first major work, *Science, Class and Society* (1976).

As editor of *Zenit* Göran was also able to supply a Swedish component to New Left theory, including the ways in which well-conceived welfare arrangements would anticipate the fiscal crisis of the state and promote 'de-commodification'.

In the 70s and after Göran was a supporter of the Swedish Left Party, a pioneer of Euro-Communism, but he stressed the continuing vitality of European Social Democracy. Attempts to create revolutionary or New Left parties had failed. But, as Göran added, on the plane of social values and ideals the 1960s and 70s had a major impact, helping to inspire movements linked to anti-racism, anti-colonialism, second wave feminism, citizenship, ecology and Green politics. (See his discussion in his fascinating study *European Modernity and Beyond*, 1995.)

The new social movements often had a de facto anti-capitalist impetus but on the basis of alternative ways of life that were quite sketchy. An exception here, as Göran noted, was the controversies and mobilizations prompted by Rudolf Meidner's 'wage-earner fund' proposals. Göran's colleague Jonas Pontusson supplied a detailed account of this ambitious attempt to link the workers' movement to an auxiliary source of finance and 'energy' (as Therborn put it). While traditional welfare pacified its recipients the wage-earner funds would furnish them with new leverage and scope.

One of Göran's most remarkable texts, 'Vorsprung durch rethink', appeared in *Marxism Today* in 1989. Without using the words socialist or capitalist he evoked an alternative vision of social relations by describing how it might look like to some future visitor to planet earth.

A preference for the concrete is a hallmark of Therborn's work, with any singular outcome the effect of a hierarchy of multiple inputs. There are question-begging terms which we should strive to avoid, 'class interest' and 'social narrative' being prominent amongst them. The identification of contradictions lends dynamism to structure but does not abolish it.

Göran's most recent writing on 'Class in the 21st century' and 'New masses?' returns in a new way to themes he engaged in the sixties and seventies of the last century, namely the scope for the eruption of student and youth movements against exclusion from education, housing and/or employment.

Göran has always had an interest in Latin America, which he has visited frequently. He was the keynote speaker at the 2015 conference of Latin American Social Scientists. In 2013 I visited Ecuador with Göran, Nancy Fraser and Eli Zaretsky. We were able to garner first hand information concerning the country's Citizens' Revolution during the presidency of Rafael Correa. The interview with Correa published in *New Left Review* in 2013 gives an idea of the issues covered, with the Ecuadorean president stressing his government's determination to avoid neo-liberal traps and a subservient foreign policy. A new socio-economic model had reduced economic equality and identified new ways of confronting climate change. We met the minister in charge of tax collection, Carlos Marx, who explained how he had been able to double the county's revenues simply by ensuring tax compliance on the part of the corporations and rich. If the latter undervalued their assets to avoid taxes then the state would buy them out cheaply.

Given the huge changes that have overtaken the world it is remarkable that there should be continuities and parallels across more than half a century between the British New Left and Göran Therborn's later work, but Göran has detected some in two recent masterly overviews, the above-mentioned 'Class in the 21st century' (*New Left Review* 78, 2012) and 'New masses?' (*New Left Review* 85, 2015). As is always the case with Göran there is an extraordinary ability to spot new patterns and to register the endurance of the status quo.

The Left in Britain mounted a serious challenge in the heyday of 'Bennism' in 1979–83, but this was contained and then reversed by the rise of New Labour in the 1990s and early 2000s. Few formerly Leftwing parties were as thoroughgoing as New Labour in their rejection of the past, in their embrace of financialized capitalism and in their championing of the US White House and its wars.

Tony Blair and Gordon Brown used privatization and debt – especially consumer debt, bank debt, and corporate debt – to finance construction. This was a privatized Keynesianism. Hospitals were saddled with debt that they are still paying off – and will be in twenty years' time.

Blair won three General Elections (1997, 2001, 2006) but with a share of the vote that declined to 38 per cent of the vote cast in 2006, with some doubts about the future of the boom and wars in Iraq and Afghanistan. In 2010 the electorate had the opportunity to register its scathing verdict on Labour in power, saving the banks at the expense of nurses, schoolteachers, students, and the unemployed. Labour's share slumped to 28 per cent.

The workings of capitalist democracy have always been a crucial concern of socialists but Göran has brought to bear his keen eye and professional formation. In *What Does the Ruling Class Do When it Rules?* (1978) he showed how capitalism has been able not just to survive but also to flourish in new ways in periods of Labour or Social Democratic government. In the 1990s and early 2000s Blair and Clinton adopted the Reagan/Thatcher programme and gave it greater scope as they de-regulated and financialised. It was claimed by Margaret Thatcher herself that her revolution was not complete until it had been adopted by the Opposition too.

Against this backdrop recent developments in the British Labour Party are heartening, especially the heavy defeat of the Blairite candidates for the post of party leader in 2015. The victor, with 57 per cent of the vote, was Jeremy Corbyn, chairman of the Stop the War

Coalition and the former aide to Tony Benn. During more than twenty years in parliament Corbyn had voted against the advice of Labour Whips no less than five hundred times.

Corbyn's win was a great surprise to all, including Corbyn himself. Less of a surprise, especially to Corbyn, was the subsequent campaign of attrition by those he had defeated to prevent him from exercising the huge mandate he had acquired from the party's members. Corbyn's campaign had attracted an influx of new members and these will also be puzzled by the animosity and defiance of many Labour parliamentarians.

When Göran developed his account of the structure and dynamics of the bourgeois workers parties he was able to draw on the seminal writings of Ralph Miliband on *Parliamentary Socialism* and of Tom Nairn's *New Left Review* essays on British 'Labourism'. These writers stressed that Labour's deference to the state owed much to the latter's prestige and longevity. But both also came to see that the United Kingdom, with its archaic electoral principles, its House of Lords, Privy Council and Monarchy was vulnerable in new ways, as democratic institutions became a global norm.

Göran has stressed how unsettling waves of democratization have been, and the argument applies to so-called 'mother of parliaments' as well. It is not surprising that these arise in the aftermath of the crises as the Wall Street collapse, the agony of the Eurozone and unending mayhem in the Middle East.

The election of Corbyn as Labour leader can be seen as disproof of classical socialist pessimism concerning British Labour. It is all the more remarkable since Labour in 2015 was far to the right of Labour in 1979, let alone 1945. On the other hand such pessimists would have plenty to say about the tight limits within which Corbyn has had to work since his election. He has often been in a minority in his own Shadow Cabinet and has entered a series of compromises that risk demoralising his supporters (on which more below).

The onset of overlapping crises has encouraging the emergence of new left parties like Syriza in Greece, Podemos in Spain and Five Stars in Italy but yet each of these is subject to ferocious disciplinary pressure, whether from the bond markets, the IMF, the local capitalist media, the regime of party competition or the fracturing of the state. If Corbyn is successful he might hope to do better but the truth is that these new left formations lack the educated support and institutional solidity of the class-based social democratic parties. Therborn's insistence on a rigorous realism as well as a hopeful radicalism will be more important than ever.

January 2016

SVEN HORT & GUNNAR OLOFSSON

A Portrait of the Sociologist as a Young Rebel

Göran Therborn 1941–1981

> As far as Marx in our time is concerned, my impression is that he is maturing, a bit like a good cheese or a vintage wine – not suitable for dionysiac parties or quick gulps at the battlefront.
>
> *From Marxism to Post-Marxism?*, Therborn 2008: ix.

The emergence of a global Swedish intellectual and social scientist

He belongs to the unbeaten, a survivor of a merciless defeat sublimated by many in his generation. This book is an interim report, and the pages to come are an attempt to outline the early years and decades of Göran Therborn's life trajectory, the intricate intertwining of his socio-political engagement and writings with his social scientific work and publications. In this article the emphasis is on the 1960s and early 1970s, on Sweden and the Far North rather than the rest of the world. We present a few preliminary remarks on a career – in the sociological sense – that has not come to a close, far from it, hence still in need of further (re-)considerations and scrutiny. Writing about people you feel an intellectual affinity with, as Perry Anderson (1992) once remarked, is a daunting task.

During the period leading up to 1981, Göran Therborn established himself as a Marxist intellectual, at first in the Swedish setting through his writings in the *Zenit* journal and other publishing activities during the 1960s and the early 70s. Concurrently, he also entered the international scene where *New Left Review* and New Left Books served as his key springboards. This was the time when he published his analysis of the Swedish miner's strike – *Spontaneität und Massenaktion im 'Wohlfahrtsstaat'* – appearing in German (1970), his provocative critique of the Frankfurt school, published as *Critica e rivoluzione: Saggio sulla Scuola di Francoforte* in Italian (1972), and finally his 1974 thesis *Science, Class and Society* in the modern *Lingua franca* of the academic world (1976[1]). Furthermore, during the first part of the 1970s two books appeared in Swedish in a series edited by *Zenit* at Cavefors ('the Swedish Maspéro') publishing house: his M.Phil. dissertation *Klasser och ekonomiska system* (1971) and a pilot study to his dissertation, *Vad är bra värderingar värda?* (1973).[2]

Before Therborn achieved such a high reputation for the quality of his work, he had a period of mixed blessings, where he was recognized as both a leading Marxist theoretician and as an *enfant terrible* in respectable Swedish *öffentlichkeit*. In this text we will sketch some of the major early phases of GThs (his final *Zenit* abbreviation) socio-political activities and engagements which at first came to influence and later to be subordinated to his social scientific intellectual ambitions and projects. Years before Göran in the terminology of Michael Burawoy (2007), became a critical and professional social scientist he was actually a public sociologist, even then with a globalist perspective.

In spring 1960 Göran graduated from the classical Gymnasium, the senior high school in Hanseatic Kalmar, and went to Lund, Scania, for university and an academic life that so far has spanned five and a half decades and an equal number of spatial-territorial worldly continents.

In the pages to come the pre-amble to this double trajectory will be traced in some detail, until 1981. This comprises the zone of engagement between (student) politics and social sciences in Sweden, and the interpenetration of Global-European and Swedish developments in the early writings of Göran Therborn – before 1981 when he left Sweden for a professorship in political science at the

---

1. A first version was printed in Sweden in 1974.
2. Simultaneously a summary of his 1972 Swedish class analysis was included in an English reader together with a fair number of articles by mainstream Swedish social scientists: *Readings in the Swedish Class Structure* (Scase 1976).

Catholic University of Nijmegen in the Netherlands, before his rise to European and international fame in the wider sociological and socio-political community. This was a twenty-year period in which there was a left-wing revival amid continuous changes and transformations in the political arena as well as in the social sciences.

From family to academic life and student politics

Göran Therborn grew up in a rather remote and poor part of Southeast Sweden. He was born in 1941 and the only child in a successful landowning family on the rural countryside to the south of Kalmar. At the age of seven, he went to the local parish primary school. In 1952, after the fourth grade, Göran entered the junior high school in the nearby small town of Kalmar, once one of the major medieval cities around the Baltic with an impressive Vasa-castle.

In one of his self-presentations, Göran states that he received a lot of attention from the grown-ups in the household, and in particular, he focuses on his teenage conversations at the time of Suez and Hungary (1956) with his politically conservative father. Ragnar Therborn was a self-made man and a successful gardener-entrepreneur who married upwards into a larger landowning clan. Göran's mother Karin worked in the office of the family business, and probably had a powerful influence on her only offspring. Culturally, the parental couple shared an interest in the decorative arts, and they built an impressive mansion in a classical style, later inherited and from the new Millennium occupied by their son after his retirement from Cambridge.[3] In brief, this was the atlas of the young Therborn's family.

These social and regional beginnings most likely opened Göran's eyes to existing inequalities,[4] but there was as well a radical literary

---

3. Its exterior is visible on the family digital homepage, www.therborn.com.
4. In the years 1929–1931 a major and long-lasting labour conflict pitted the farm workers against the tightly knit large landowners in exactly this area of Sweden. Moreover, in the late 19th century, Kalmar was the birthplace of the leading Swedish speculative industrial-capitalist, Ivar Kreuger – global match-monopolist and symbol of the 'Second Swedish Great Power era'– who in 1932 dramatically passed away in Paris.

edge to his interests. During his high school years Göran also read contemporary literary works on the ongoing social change in Sweden. In 1956 Göran went from junior high school to the classical gymnasium in Kalmar, where he studied humanities and languages; not only English, German and French but also Latin, which later made his acquisition of Italian, Spanish and Portuguese easier. During the latter part of senior high school Göran took out a subscription to the *New Statesman*, and the young bookworm ordered new volumes from Paris and Germany from the local bookstore.

In 1960 he left rural Ljungbyholm for Lund, the latter still a rather sleepy academic centre with some twelve thousand students and a fairly small number of tenured professors. In what once had been the ecclesiastical centre in Hamlet's kingdom of Denmark later transformed into a Swedish peripheral royal colonial-educational outpost, the newcomer chose to take a course in political science. Göran wrote his first term paper on Spanish anarcho-syndicalism, and his candidate thesis on Gustav Landauer, the German revolutionary anarchist. These were not the typical subjects for political science students of the day. Choosing these themes was a reflection of his political, extra-curricular activities and engagements. After arriving in Lund he almost immediately entered into intellectual and political student activity, staying away from mainstream Swedish politics. Together with a few other like-minded students, he founded a tiny libertarian anarcho-syndicalist study group which within weeks became a recognised student club within the Student Union in Lund, with Göran as chairman.

Why this choice? Göran had, during his high school years, happened to come in contact with the small Swedish syndicalist milieu (SAC), its daily paper (*Arbetaren*, 'The Worker'), the quarterly journal of its youth organisation, *Zenit* – its name was inspired by the Spanish anarcho-syndicalist journal *Cenit* – and the writings of their iconic hero, the celebrated modernist author Stig Dagerman (1922–54).[5] Choosing neither official social democracy and its career-

---

5. Dagerman was a prominent figure in the early post-war generation, once an editor of the cultural page at the anarcho-syndicalist daily *Arbetaren*, and still read and translated into the major languages. He committed suicide in 1954, at the age of 31.

advancing student club at Lund University, nor the left-leaning *Clarté*, with its mix of left-wing social democrats and traditional Communists – and where the latter group was dominant in 1960 – he selected the small syndicalist tradition, having an honourable and 'clean' relation to the Powers of the State, the Swedish and the Soviet. This was an understandable choice for an intellectual rebel coming from a conservative, rural bourgeois background.

The early writings of a political and social science student in *Zenit*

In the spring of 1961, at the age of twenty, a brief version of his thesis on social and economic democracy in civil-war Spain was published in *Zenit*, in an issue which memorized the outbreak of the Civil War in 1936, with a drawing of Picasso on its front page. This was Göran's first major article, appearing in a working class cultural youth journal based in Stockholm, with a limited but nationwide circulation, having less than 1 000 readers. *Zenit* was an open-minded journal advocating human emancipation, equality, and global neutrality between the two geopolitical blocs, against narrow-minded collectivism, militarism, the bomb, and racism (South African Apartheid in particular) and with an interest in modern culture, including cinema, and criticisms of commercialism and mass consumer society.

1961 was Göran's first year as a contributor to *Zenit* and altogether he published two major articles – the second one on 'modern syndicalist experiences', a review of a French syndicalist author Louis Mercier's *Syndicalisme vivante* (translated to Swedish that year). On top of that, one letter to the editors and a few translations (on English anarchism and Polish worker's councils, both signed), plus a joyous note on 'Political literature' in a Stockholm antiquarian bookshop – he had acquired Landauer's *Die Revolution*. At the end of the year he was a member of the editorial committee, representing Lund.[6]

In 1962 Göran served a year of compulsory military service, although with civilian duties, in the capital of Sweden. He came to

---

6. The last issue of the year carried a drawing by Paul Flora, the father of renowned sociologist Peter Flora, on its cover: the Berlin wall and its two non-communicating sides.

live in a small room in Sveavägen 98, Stockholm, the headquarters of Swedish syndicalists, the tiny national trade union federation SAC, an internationalist working class association on the fringe of Swedish working class movement.[7] Moving to Stockholm Göran also left behind political science a period of twenty years. This year he also extended his horizon beyond the European scene and produced a major overview of the anti-colonial revolt in Africa. 1962 was also the year when he established himself as the most productive contributor to *Zenit*; from now on, he wrote editorials, lead articles, polemics, travel reports, book reviews, etc. either under his own name or various signatures such as the *nom de plume* Bernt Land. In 1963, he moved back to Lund and soon the journal's centre of gravidity had shifted southwards. As a side-track he gradually started studying sociology.

Working together with a few friends in Lund,[8] over the coming years Göran took command and produced a journal that attracted new readers on the emerging left of centre but also estranged the die-hard syndicalists. The journal gradually became explicitly socialist, not only anarcho-syndicalist. It connected with a variety of young left-wingers. From now on, Marx and Proudhon were published interchangeably. While the flow from Göran's pen and typewriter continued – on subjects such as alienation and industrial democracy – the review also introduced and translated major European radicals, such as Antonio Gramsci, André Gorz, Ernest Mandel, Herbert Marcuse, Tom Nairn (on Labour's Imperialism) and a young Robin Blackburn on the Cuban revolution. Moreover, important international issues such as the war in Vietnam were covered in the pages of the journal; in the latter case through the first Swedish translation of the program of the National Liberation Front. *Zenit* opened up its pages to a broad spectrum of Swedish society from young left-leaning liberals and social democrats to anti-Stalinist communists, feminists, peaceniks, provies and other youngsters on the outskirts of Swedish politics.

---

7. The SAC building was, located only a few blocks away from the more spacious administrative-political office of the Social democratic party.
8. One of these was Gunnar Olofsson, another his later Swedish translator, Gunnar Sandin.

From an old to a new 'third force' of the Left

The first half of the 1960s witnessed the break-up of the cold war stranglehold on the minds and thoughts of people and nations. The transformation of *Zenit* during this period, and Göran's crucial role in this process fit into the larger international social, cultural and political convulsions. Göran's intense trips to European left gatherings, in particular in the British Isles, but also his honeymoon in Algeria in the summer of 1963 (!), is visible in the pages of the journal.

Through his efforts and those of his close comrades-in-arms *Zenit* became of equal standing to the old left wing student magazine *Clarté*. With a history back to the 1920s, *Clarté* had been the most important journal to promote an ecumenical Left perspective between Social Democracy and traditional communism in a country where no independent and unorthodox party of that kind ever had existed after World War II.

Since the early 1930s Social Democracy had cemented its domination within the working class as the governing national party, while the Comintern-affiliated Communist Party since the late 1930s had been able to occupy a small but stable space to the left of Social Democracy with no other political party in between the two blue-collar organizations. However, in 1964 the CP was shaken by the change of leadership. The old leader belonged to the '1929 generation'[9] and a younger cadre, the editor-in-chief of its national Stockholm daily, C.H. Hermansson, replaced him. He was the party's 'single most important asset' according to a statement by Göran in late 1965. That year Hermansson published *Vänsterns väg* ('The Road of the Left') in a paperback series published by Rabén & Sjögren (a publisher owned by left-of-centre Swedish Coop), which markedly deviated from previous publications from the party. Hermansson opened up for a modernisation of the party's organization as well as policy. In neighbouring Denmark and Norway two independent Left Socialist parties had largely replaced old-time CPs, and intense

---

9. In 1929 the party leadership broke away from the Communist International and formed a 'national' Communist Party. A new Communist Party, affiliated to Comintern, was born in 1929 (Kennerström 1974).

contacts began to evolve across open borders between these parties and the new leadership of the Swedish CP. In Lund *Zenit* organized Nordic meetings and similar events took place in Copenhagen. Also in Helsinki the effects of the splits within the Finnish working class movement were felt among a younger cohort that for a brief moment oriented itself towards the West European scene.

It was in this conjuncture that Göran together with three co-authors in spring 1966 published *En ny vänster* ('A New Left', in the pocket book series of Rabén & Sjögren). This book had an instant and major impact in the Swedish political and cultural debate of the day, and rapidly ran into a second printing. It appealed not only to the nascent broad non-organized left community in Sweden but also to left-leaning social liberals, left-wing social democrats as well as to modernizing communists. It was a book that gave rise to comments and bitter criticisms in journals and in book-form. The Maoists and orthodox Marxist-Leninists, by now dominating *Clarté*, were very hostile; the same applied to the book length critique of the 'new left' from two younger liberals who attacked it in *Den nygamla vänstern* ('A New-Old Left', published by Bonniers 1967).[10]

1965 was the year when the independent and youthful Swedish anti-Vietnam-war movement got on its feet, and the incoming PM Olof Palme, already a member of government and the heir-apparent, began to attack the injustice and immortality of the US occupation. Thus, with Social Democracy there was a generation within reach of New Left thinking, in particular in its student association.[11] But this was also the year when the first Maoist tendency saw the light of day on the fringe of the CP, within the emerging anti-war movement and in particular within the student association Clarté[12] and from

---

10. One of them (Daniel Tarschys) became a professor in political science, MP and Secretary-General of the European Council, while the other (Carl Tham) first became party secretary of the liberal party and then twice a government minister, first for the liberals, and then, after his conversion, for the Social Democrats.

11. In a companion to this book, published simultaneously in Swedish as a *Festschrift*-section of the journal *Arkiv: Tidskrift för samhällsanalys* (no. 6, 2016), Olle Svenning writes about this moment.

12. Publisher of the journal with the same name.

this strand of thought the most critical voices against *En ny vänster* were mounted. While *Zenit* became less attached to anarcho-syndicalism, the majority in *Clarté* moved towards the Marxist-Leninist-Maoist pole while a minority later joined forces with Göran and his collaborators. Apart from publishing, political mobilization at this time became a major activity and concern for Göran.

An organisational interlude – the route into, within and through organized political activity: 1965–1970

Göran Therborn's career over more than 50 years can be summarised as an intricate and dynamic relation between 'the political' and 'the scientific'. 'The Political' has three dimensions: First, a basic and continuous relation to left-wing politics, although with shifting allegiances over time. Secondly, and this is the crucial anchor point, an analytical focus on power and the political struggles and transformations that have shaped not only relations between social classes, and nation states but the world order as a whole. But there is also a third dimension to Göran's relations to the political, a rather brief period of actual organisational involvement in political activism, complementing his posture as a socialist and Marxist intellectual. The social scientific dimensions will be identified later, but throughout the 1960s the Department of Sociology was turned into an 'operation-base' in Göran's words.

In 1965 the political Göran became a member of the (large) governing board of the Social democratic student club in Lund. This student club was an important recruiting ground for the social democratic government – the Prime Minister at the time (Tage Erlander) had made his political debut in Lund and returned annually to meet the student association in a large and open debate in the imposing Student Union building. Erlander was in the early 1960s often accompanied by the club's former chairman Ingvar Carlsson (who in 1986 succeeded Palme as PM). This student club was thus an important springboard for those aiming for a political-administrative career in Sweden at that time. However, in 1965 and 1966, a broad left coalition, including members of the *Zenit* team, was elected to form the new governing board of the Social democratic student club in Lund.

After marrying in 1963 Göran had moved to Malmö but had stayed outside local politics until 1965/66 when he became involved with a group of independent Social Democrats, most of them employed in the city's municipal administration. Simultaneously he joined the Social Democratic party in Malmö. On the cover of the political manifesto *En ny vänster*, Göran was listed as a social democrat. But his period as a *bona fide* social democrat became even shorter than his affiliation with the syndicalist movement.

From late 1966, he took an active part in the creation of the Socialist Association (SF)[13], a small and independent socialist grouping consisting of left-wing social democrats, modernising communists and some unaffiliated left-wing activists, that aimed to launch a 'new left' political vision of and for Sweden.

Zenit had a close relationship to domestic politics in Sweden during the run-up to the 1968 national election. Some members of the editorial committees in Lund and Stockholm were on the lists of the new Socialist Association, founded in 1967, which campaigned in cooperation with the Left Party Communists. This association also produced a programmatic platform outlining a 'new left' radical vision of Swedish society and the steps needed to bring it to reality. Göran was the main author of this document, *Program för socialism* ('A Program for Socialism', published by Bonniers and appearing in the late autumn 1967). This association had its origins in the Stockholm area but also acquired some following in the south of Sweden. It was seen, not without good reason, as a way for the Swedish CP to broaden its political appeal. This had two effects. First, the Social democratic party did not accept double affiliation and some leading members of SF left the social democrats or were expelled; Göran one among the latter. Secondly, in the run-up to the coming election in September 1968 there was an electoral agreement between the small SF and the much larger CP. This made it possible for SF to have leading members topping the ballot paper in a few

---

13. 'Socialistiska förbundet' (SF) in Swedish. For its background see Christer Hogstedt's chapter in *Program för socialism* (1967).

constituencies. Göran Therborn was the first name on the ballot paper in the Lund-Malmö constituency,[14] and was very active in the election campaign. In late August 1968 the Soviet Union and five other Warsaw pact countries invaded Czechoslovakia. In this situation the CP and its affiliate was dealt a severe blow and the CP just barely survived as a parliamentary force. Göran, as many others in SF, later joined the Swedish CP and he also for a period participated actively in the local organisation of the CP in Malmö, e.g. in writing for a workplace sheet – *Kockumknogarn* – together with workers from the city's large shipyard.

The university as a red base: 1962–1981

Göran's incursion into the organisational side of local politics was not successful. However, there is another organizational dimension to his restless activity: the university and its potential mobilization of students. From a sleepy beginning in the early 1960s tertiary mass education became a hallmark of Lund University as the years passed by during this decade. New students arrived, often from families without a traditional academic background and gradually came to dominate the student corpus.[15] Lund was no exception to an international pattern. In the last years of the 1960s the situation in Sweden for a moment became explosive, if in no sense revolutionary in an utterly left-reformist society.

In June 1968, at the end of the May events in Paris, Lund University celebrated its 300th anniversary under the guard of a similar number of riot policemen, and a slightly fewer number of horses, despite that the town was rather empty as the students were on vacations. However, the previous month had seen some violent

---

14. The constituency also included two major industrial towns in the region, Helsingborg and Landskrona. Malmö was the third largest city in Sweden, Helsingborg among the top ten; both heavily industrialized since the late 19th century.

15. Gesser (1971) shows that the number of students in the humanities and social sciences at Lund University had increased fivefold from 1960 to 1968. And it was among these students that the left found its audience.

demonstrations in nearby Båstad where the Davis Cup match between Sweden and Rhodesia caused a lot of criticisms against 'the white game' and had to be moved to the French Riviera.[16] And in Stockholm left-wing students had recently 'occupied' their own Student Union building.

In Lund, part of the tercentennial events was an international multidisciplinary colloquium on scientific research and politics with some 200 participants from more than ten countries under the joint auspices of the University and its student union. Among those present were three sociologists, the North-American Amitai Etzioni, the Latin-American André Gunder Frank and the French-Greek Nicos Poulantzas. Göran was the host and official commentator for this session.

The conference proceedings went wild when the issue of scientific responsibility reached top of the agenda. The Vietnam War fuelled the discussions, and when it became known that the US ambassador to Sweden had been invited to the anniversary in Lund, an overwhelming majority of the conference participants decided to send a telegram in which they expressed their disagreement with this invitation, 'as long as the war continues the US Ambassador is not a welcome guest in our academic community'. At the end of the meeting a proposal was made that the participants should sign the 1967 'Appeal of Havana' to the intellectuals of the world; in this case only a minority did so – 56 out of 200.[17]

Thus, the university and its main campus around the Dome were temporarily turned into a red base for a few days. Otherwise, throughout the 1960s it was the Faculty of Social Sciences, and especially the Department of Sociology, of the University of Lund which

---

16. The Swedish director Bo Widerberg made a documentary about these events together with a large group of young film-workers – *Den vita sporten* ('The White Game') – that was released in the autumn 1968.

17. Göran had participated in the Havana conference but his exact role during these two days of hot and intense debate in Lund is not detectable from the conference proceedings. He may have been 'one of the participants in the symposium' who went forward with either one of these proposals whether it was the telegram or the Havana Appeal (Dencik 1969: 5–6).

provided a room and the necessary facilities from which to operate both on campus and also globally.[18] Sociology may have had its domestic origins in Lund (there seems to have been an association as early as 1901) but from the late 1940s it was first taught there in a homespun Parsons-Lundbergian fashion, and a decade later its first professor was inaugurated. Göran started out as a sociology undergraduate after completing his draft and returning to Lund. In 1965 he wrote his BA-thesis on mass media and the Tonkin incident, which was to appear as an article in *Zenit* the same year. At that time he was already a teaching assistant, soon to become an extra lecturer teaching in particular economic sociology. He introduced Andrew Shonfield's *Modern Capitalism* as well as Karl Polanyi's famous 1957 chapter on 'The economy as an instituted process' to undergraduates eager to learn more about the society they lived in and were supposed to work for.

Göran became a PhD-student under the supervision of Gösta Carlsson who went from Stockholm and joined the tiny Lund department as full professor in 1958. Carlsson was a key member of the first generation of Swedish sociologists, and an active contributor to its Nordic community, visible through its jointly run English-language journal *Acta Sociologica*.[19] Carlsson's significance is overlooked in most chronologies of Swedish sociology, though Göran has stressed his importance as a role model. After a decade in office Carlsson gave up his chair at Lund University in protest against academic bureaucratization and streamlining, as well as the student protest activity.[20] Carlsson's role as supervisor was taken over by his younger co-worker Bengt Gesser, a specialist in the field of sociology of education; 'the only intellectual at the Department', Göran once caustically remarked.

---

18. An overview of the Department of Sociology in Lund in the 1960s and early 1970s is presented in Olofsson (2015).

19. *Acta* was originally published by Munksgaard in Copenhagen and dating back to 1956 (Swedberg 1993).

20. Carlsson later returned to academic work through a special senior research position financed by the National Science Council and located at Stockholm University.

Göran's sociological interventions in *Acta Sociologica* had to wait until the 1970s but his contributions to *Sociologisk Forskning* – the domestic academic journal edited from Uppsala by the rising star Johan Asplund – began already in 1967 with a review of a major theoretical textbook edited by Asplund. Göran did not conceal his critical instincts. This book focused on the sociological canon from Comte to Weber while the young reviewer considered the selection as 'arbitrary' missing such key sociological figures as Spencer and Tönnies. In a characteristic mould Göran concluded that 'viewed as a whole, this book is a fairly uninteresting textbook for students who are and will remain disinterested in sociology. What we need is a textbook for those who are interested in sociology' (quoted from Larsson and Magdalenic 2014: 43–44). Nevertheless, it was soon on the Sociology 101 reading list at the Department of Sociology in Lund.

His first major article in *Acta Sociologica* presented a project initiated in late 1976 after the end of more than four decades of uninterrupted Social democratic rule. In a special supplement of this journal aimed for the 1978 Uppsala International Congress of Sociology Göran together with three collaborators – among them Anders Kjellberg, a future specialist on trade union mobilization, as well as Staffan Marklund, a future social policy expert – outlined a framework for an analysis of the transformation of Sweden as a social formation – 'before and after Social Democracy 1932–1976' (see Olsson 1978 and Hort 2010). Through its critical appraisal of policy and power, this joint article sets itself apart from much more rosy, enthusiastic hopes for the transformative potentials of Swedish social democracy articulated by mainstream Swedish sociologists at the time.[21] The tone was cautious in the *Acta*-article – measured socio-political achievements and shortcomings were far from the idea of the irreversibility of the welfare state later to appear in Göran's writings on the similar Dutch experience. It is pertinent to add that absent among the authors of the *Acta Sociologica* article

---

21. This is visible in the works by e.g. Bengt Abrahamsson and Anders Broström (1980), Ulf Himmelstrand and his collaborators (1981) and in particular Walter Korpi's internationally successful and more solid work, *The Working Class in Welfare Capitalism* (1978).

was the project's only research assistant, Bo Rothstein, who at age 24 may have been too young to be fully included. In the late 1970s, he was still a left-wing student politician in Lund, on his way into editorial work at *Zenit*. However, in this research project he took on, with great success, the jewel in the crown of the Swedish model, the active labour market policy and its high-profile administration.[22] In this volume the nowadays by far the most cited Swedish political scientist – since early 2016 an Oxford don – contributes with an article on corruption, institutions and social trust.

A parallel intellectual universe: the new Nordic *Zenit* 1967–1977

In the aftermath of *En ny vänster*, in late 1966 a new *Zenit* was launched by left-wingers from the four Nordic countries. Ten years after 1956 a major organizational transformation of *Zenit* began as ownership of the journal was transferred to an independent association with individual membership outside the control of the SAC traditionalists. At the end of the year a manifesto for a new Nordic and socialist journal got off the ground. The manifesto was written by the Göteborg literary giant Kurt Aspelin and signed by 43 individuals from four countries who were listed in its first issue; five women, the rest men, most of them in their twenties and thirties, Göran among them.

Hence, intellectuals from the four Nordic countries as well as from various sections of the Left joined forces to create a *New Left Review* of the Far North.[23] In 1966 in the last issue of the 'old' *Zenit* Göran Therborn published the first part of an article entitled 'The crisis of Social Democracy and the possibilities of Socialism'. In the

---

22. See the monograph by Rothstein (1996). It was first published as a Swedish Ph.D. thesis in 1986.

23. *New Left Review* was the most obvious international reference. The nucleus of the *Zenit* group even tried to strike a deal with the *International Socialist Journal* in Rome, to make *Zenit* into a Swedish version of *ISJ*. Other important references were *Les temps Modernes* and *Partisans* in Paris, the German review *neue kritik*, and the US journals *Studies on the Left* as well as *Monthly Review*.

new journal – no. 1, 1967 – its two parts were merged and printed together with the same heading.

The first issue of the new *Zenit* also marked the start of a completely new endeavour, a brief spell of a 'Left Scandinavianism'.[24] From 1967 and for a few years ahead, *Zenit* became a truly Nordic socialist journal with editorial committees in six cities: the four capitals Copenhagen, Helsinki, Oslo and Stockholm plus Göteborg and Lund in Sweden. The Copenhagen committee was dominated by social historians while the Helsinki crew had a tilt towards the country's Swedish minority. In Oslo it included key intellectuals such as the Sartrean philosopher-sociologist Dag Österberg. In Göteborg two senior social science and history lecturers, Lars Herlitz and Rita Liljeström, joined Aspelin, all of them belonging to a pre-1956 generation. In 1967 the October uprising in St Petersburg was 50 years old, and this was highlighted in *Zenit* with a special issue devoted to the Russian Revolution, edited by and with major articles by Aspelin, Herlitz and Agneta Pleijel.

The Lund committee was revitalized and a few new people added,[25] while *Zenit* never gained a foothold in Uppsala where at that time there was still a vibrant Social Democrat cohort dominating the campus left though an emerging Maoist faction soon challenged it from the far left. Nor was the journal able to recruit collaborators in the far north of Umeå – since the early 1960s a new and 'red' Swedish university town. Apart from change of contents and style[26] many at the time well-known Scandinavian intellectuals supported the new journal, the non-Swedish more academic than the large Swedish cohort.

---

24. A variant of the kind of Scandinavianism that on and off had occurred since the coming of the public sphere in the 19th century, whether bourgeois or proletarian.

25. Among the first of these were Lennart Berntson and Gunnar Persson, both of whom were inspired by the American *Monthly Review*. They published a very successful pamphlet on imperialism and aid to the developing countries (*U-hjälp och imperialism*, Bonniers 1968). Gunnar Persson later became an internationally acknowledged economic historian.

26. Including Leif Thollander's advanced modernist design of the journal, in all its aspects. For decades Thollander was a leading designer of books in Sweden, and a member of the Stockholm editorial committee 1967–1973.

Zenit covered culture, history, politics and theory. The centre of gravity moved to Stockholm from which city fifteen issues of the journal were produced during 1967, 1968 and 1969.[27] Despite a considerable input from Göran over these crucial years, he was not alone in putting his mark on the new journal. Although his influence remained strong there were those who took issue with Göran's ambitions, for instance Iréne Matthis – a founding member of Group 8, the Stockholm feminist-socialist avant-garde – and her husband, the late Tomas Gerholm (1942–1995), an anthropologist and former editor of *Clarté*.[28]

At the end of 1969, the main editorial office returned to Lund, and the links to the other Nordic nodes gradually became somewhat diluted.[29] In Norway, the young left became Maoists, in Helsinki Breznevites, while the young student left in Copenhagen turned Hegelian. In Göteborg Aspelin was able to inject new energy into the running of the journal.[30] The Stockholm editorial team never fully recovered. The repercussions of '1968', its deployment and retraction, were felt in many respects within and outside the new journal. The Nordic New Left in early 1967 was not the same as in late 1969 when a two month-long miner's strike shook the Swedish establishment, the newly elected PM Olof Palme included.

Between 1969 and 1971 *Zenit* published a series of reports on wildcat strikes. The first one dealt with the dockworker strike in Göteborg and the second analysed on the three-months-long miners

---

27. The late Eva Adolfsson (1942–2010) was soon a key member of the editorial team. From 1968 she was the managing editor of the journal together with Bernt Kennerström.

28. Matthis together with Dick Urban Vestbro translated and published 'Women – the longest revolution' by Juliet Mitchell, first for the journal *Zenit*, later as a special publication (*Zenit* småskrifter nr 3, 1969).

29. The Oslo group, Österberg an exception, went with the rapidly growing Maoist camp. The Danish left developed their own publishing channels, while the Finnish left began to drift either into a peculiar pro-Soviet 'Breznevite' direction, which had an impact on some members in the Helsinki group, or became prominent Social Democrats, even prominent 'Swedish liberals' (Nils Torvalds, in the EU Parliament from the late 1990s).

30. Elisabeth Özdalga in this volume is a representative of this (1970-) generation.

strike above the Polar circle, in Kiruna, Gällivare and Svappavaara. This report was published in a special issue of the journal, numbered 16½. The latter report was to a large extent written by Göran, and parts of it translated into German, *Spontaneität und Massenaktion im 'Wohlfahrtsstaat'*, appearing half a year after the publication of *Zenit* 16½. The late sixties also saw the Vietnam anti-war movement growing by the day, despite internal fights and quarrels. Into the early seventies these were the years of a triumphalist Left with the coming of new communist parties – even prospective Internationals – in the waiting: Marxist-Leninist-Maoists, Luxemburgians, Trotskyists, workerists, etc. etc.

In retrospect the culmination of Göran's *Zenit* writings is probably the analysis of the Swedish class structure, which completely dominated its 1972 May Day issue. A decade later it was turned into a full-length book, his last written in the local vernacular. Inspired by the works of Nicos Poulantzas, and underpinned by his theoretical criticisms of mainstream stratification research, Göran undertook a major statistical investigation of the historical development of main classes and 'special categories' in Swedish society from the 1930s onwards, their boundaries, and relationship to each other, the state, the forces and modes of productions. The empirical scrutiny of Swedish administrative statistics – job positions and institutional power – proved successful and challenged both academic research and left-wing politics. The Nordic sociological and especially the Swedish level-of-living investigations had caused a lot of unrest within the governing social democratic party. Therborn's intervention in *Zenit* made its impact felt in the intersection of academia and politics, the social and the scientific.[31]

Göran remained on the *Zenit* editorial board for some time but moved to Stockholm for a few years, out of touch with the internal workings of the journal, though contributing with a lengthy article on the Portuguese revolution in 1974.

---

31. In 1979 a new and updated version of his analysis of the Swedish class structure reached an English audience (Fry 1979).

Göran goes international

Neutral Sweden belonged to the Far North and had been cut off from the European scene of the early post-war period, US was the preferred chosen land to the defeated continent – Europe – and an empire – the British – going astray. A younger Swedish generation turned their eyes towards the 'third world' including China. Göran followed in these footsteps, was a subscriber to *Accra Evening News*, and travelled extensively during the first years of the 1960s. On behalf of *Zenit* he soon made contact at first with anarchists and leftists throughout Europe. This was at the birth of the new left of the 1960s. From 1963, in *Zenit* there are reports in a special section developed by Göran: 'Outsides'. This is where for instance Perry Anderson first appeared in the journal, in a report from the Alderstone march. Quite soon, however, Göran's writings also moved beyond the local language. In 1965 he went international with one article – 'Power in the Kingdom of Sweden' – in *International Socialist Journal* edited from Rome by Lelio Basso, assisted by Peter Wollen (at the time also a member of the *New Left Review* editorial committee). At the end of that year another article appeared in the London-based *New Left Review*: 'The Swedish Left'. The *ISJ* was an episode in the history of the European new left, the *NLR* is still going strong – both as a respected non-mainstream journal and from 1970 also a prospering publishing house (New Left Books/Verso) – and has had lasting effects on Göran's life and letters. Altogether he has so far published 26 articles in this journal, three during the 1960s, six in the 1970s, etc. (see the archive on *New Left Review's* homepage).

Power in the Kingdom of Sweden did, according to Göran, not rest with the royal household, but rather, the country's economically successful bourgeoisie. Sweden was an industrial latecomer that overcame the Great Depression and benefitted from closeness to the German market during Nazi rearmament. Thus, the hegemony of the bourgeoisie continued despite an increasingly strong trade union movement and many years of Social Democrats at the helm of cabinets and in other significant state administrative positions.

The *ISJ* article was an overview in Gramscian language of working-class influence under a continuing latent bourgeois dominance, with definite opportunities for an open-minded socialist left to the left of the left in power. The *NLR* article painted a formidable but bleak picture of a ruling national working-class party which after the Petrograd shockwaves and the coming of Swedish Parliamentary rule had never experienced a serious crisis, no moment of fundamental rethinking, no Resistance movement against Fascism, or a 'moment of truth'. Göran ended with a characteristic comparative note: 'the SAP is monolithic to a degree almost unprecedented in (European) Social Democratic history'.

The year 1956 figured pre-eminently in this portrait of Swedish Social Democracy but 'the crisis of NATO, the Bomb and Imperialism were for the Swedes only distant dramas to be viewed from outside, since Sweden was not directly integrated into the imperialist system.' Moreover 'programmatic discussion in the fifties on the whole came down to seeking theoretical ornamentation for the prevailing political routine'.

Göran also noted the parochial intellectual isolation and the integration of fragmented radical intellectuals in the big media 'which has not favoured the development of any coherent social and cultural critique'. After this picture of the established Left, Göran entered with two forces at hand to the left of the established polity: Swedish communism, and – surprisingly given the picture already mentioned – the Social Democratic Left. Traditional communism is 'in a static perspective ... by far the most important force of the Swedish Left', and Hermansson 'its single most important asset'. The latter judgement was not to last long.[32]

---

32. Before the decade had come to a close Göran also took issue with the defeat in Sweden of the modernizers within the Left Party Communists (the formal name of transformed CP) at its Twenty-Second congress: 'Swedish Communism – end of an interlude' (*New Left Review* 58, 1969).

The global breakthrough: Vietnam 1968

Of outmost importance for his international future was, however, another *NLR*-article from the year before. In March–April 1968 Göran published a worldwide survey of the political and theoretical implications of the internal struggle inside the country and global opposition to the War in Vietnam: 'From Petrograd to Saigon'. The *NLR* editors introduced it as a commissioned article saying that 'the Swedish Left has pioneered militant actions against the American War in Vietnam; the quality of Therborn's theses reflects this experience'. Göran is presented as the editor of *Zenit*, 'our Swedish counterpart' – not Nordic! In this volume it is scrutinized separately by Anders Stephanson.

With this article in the *NLR* Göran laid the foundation among young future social science and history professors for his present esteem and established himself as a global revolutionary dialectical thinker and writer. Although this article to our limited knowledge was not published in any other major language in 1968 it established Göran as a fully recognized member of the internationalist new left intelligentsia. His reputation as a dialectician of global revolution would be further reinforced by his critique of the academic delusion of Western Marxism.

During the 1970s Göran published six articles in *NLR*, producing perhaps his most important ones at the start of the decade. The first two of them had already been printed in Sweden in 1969 – a critique of the Frankfurt school in *Häften för kritiska studier* ('Cahiers of Critical Studies') leading to a major setback for the influence of the 'Frankfurt school' among the student radicals in Sweden.

In 1970–71 this article appeared in two issues of *NLR*. They were later to reappear in an edited volume by the *NLR* on New Left Books: *Western Marxism: A Critical Reader*.[33] Therborn's critique was translated into Italian as mentioned at the start of this article.

---

33. This book included contributions by Ronald Aronson, Lucio Colletti, Norman Geras, André Glucksmann, André Gorz, Michel Löwy, John Merrington, Gareth Stedman Jones – and Göran Therborn. Separately, Perry Anderson published its intended introduction (1976).

In 1977, moreover, his remarkable essay 'The rise of democracy and the rule of capital' was printed in *NLR*, to become his most cited article.

As important as the number of articles is the triplet of his major books written from a decidedly Marxist standpoint which were published by New Left Books/Verso between 1976 and 1980. Apart from his reworked dissertation, *Science, Class and Society* (1976), he launched the imaginative *What Does the Ruling Class Do When it Rules?* in 1978. He then took upon himself to investigate the Marxist theme of the day in *The Ideology of Power and the Power of Ideology* (1980), which included a critical discussion of Louis Althusser's conception of ideology.

With these works, which will be scrutinized by other contributors to this volume, he was able to get out of the position as a Swedish civil servant and into the tenured world of the universal academy, far from the limits of the nation-state.

Nijmegen and after – finding a way back to the central concerns of sociology

Göran left Sweden for a chair in political science at the University of Nijmegen in 1981, at a time when his international fame and credentials were already well established.[34] We will not go into any detail about this later and more glorious part of his career – we will only point to some of the major stations on the way.

In this volume Robin Blackburn gives an international account and assessment of Göran's work in particular after the publication *Why Some Peoples Are More Unemployed Than Others* (1986). Moreover, during the 1980s Göran participated in several international research projects, and produced a fair number of articles and papers for numerous journals and conferences visible in the list of his publications, to be found on his homepage (www.therborn.com).

---

34. In Nijmegen he gathered a group of young research students who left their marks on Dutch and Flemish social research and practice but also made an input to Peter Flora's never finished comparative welfare state project *Growth to Limits* (see volume IV, 1987).

In 1987/88 Göran went back to Sweden to take up a chair in sociology at Göteborg University – where he immediately initiated a major research program on social steering.[35] At the end of the decade, two of his papers intended for the international scene were collected into a Swedish volume on *Borgarklass och byråkrati i Sverige* ('Bourgeoisie and Bureaucracy in Sweden'), essays that to our knowledge never appeared in English (or any other language). A little more than a decade later Göran joined SCASSS – Scandinavian Collegium for Advanced Studies in the Social Sciences – in Uppsala from which he retired as a Swedish civil servant only to join Cambridge University for another three years of intense activity as its chair in general sociology. Throughout these decades he travelled extensively: Africa, Asia, Australia, North America, and of course what was to emerge as the new Central and Eastern Europe. Two Swedish institutions of higher learning would again become his base camp from which he reached out to the international social scientific community.

During the 1990s and first decade of the millennium he continued to tour the world but he also managed to publish several articles in many different languages. Organizationally he became heavily involved in the sociological community of the Far North, first as president of the domestic Swedish Sociological Association, the publisher of *Sociologisk Forskning*, later as chairman of its joint Nordic Association, the publisher of *Acta Sociologica*. He was in charge of the annual or bi-annual meetings of these associations, and even managed to invite – and finance its travels – the Board of the International Sociological Association to one of these meetings close to the Polar circle long before he was elected a member of the latter's executive. In the early 1990s, he took an active part in the set-up of the first European Sociological Association, which spanned the previously divided continent; though he never became a board member. Twice, in 1998 and 2002, he tried, but failed narrowly, to become the President of the ISA. However, in 2011 at

---

35. See Therborn and Olsson (1991). The Swedish King came to town to listen to its first major public presentation (through his 'adjutant' his royal highness asked far-sightedly how many beds there were in Sweden).

the age of 70 he agreed to become the editor-in-chief of *European Societies*, the main journal of ESA, for a four years period with the Sociology Department of Linnaeus University as a major node of production.

From the late 1980s in Göteborg he wrote what is now considered his major sociological works, on the one hand *European Modernity and Beyond* (1995), on the other hand *Between Sex and Power* (2004). These books have so far had an impressive impact on the scholarly world (see the appendix below) but they have not been seriously discussed in Scandinavian or Swedish sociology. The exception is the article by Anita Göransson and Karin Widerberg in this volume.[36]

His influential global sociology synthesis *The World: A Beginner's Guide* was published in 2011 and *The Killing Fields of Inequality* appeared in 2013. The impact of these books, especially his continuous work on inequality, can be seen in the articles below, especially in the chapter by the Brazilian scholar Lena Lavinas.

From an intellectual perspective there is peculiar lacuna in this success story. *From Marxism to Post-Marxism?* (2008) – a collection of three previously published essays – is probably the most neglected of all the books Göran has written in the later decades. Despite the book's appearance at a time of soul-searching among traditional macro-economists and a revival for Marx and 'Marxisant economics', and more generally societal crisis theory, no serious international discussion seems to have followed in its footsteps.[37] There was neither a Poulantzas-Therborn exchange, as Blackburn remarks,[38] nor an exchange of ideas similar to the one that came to the fore

---

36. Göransson and Widerberg's article is simultaneously published in Swedish in the above-mentioned *Festschrift*-section of the journal *Arkiv: Tidskrift för samhällsanalys* (no. 6, 2016) – the same journal that in 2014 (no. 3) published Swedish versions of his *NLR*-articles on classes in the 21st century and the new masses.

37. That year (2009), after the Lehmann Brothers crash, *Das Kapital* was a best-seller for instance in Germany.

38. An allusion to the famous debate in *New Left Review* between Ralph Miliband and Nicos Poulantzas on the Marxist theory of the state.

after the publication of *The Ideology of Power and the Power of Ideology*.[39] *From Marxism to Post-Marxism?* is in any case also the book where Göran advanced the idea of a global 'intellectual sociology'. Maybe Burawoy's idea of *a public* sociology had closed the market for another new global sociology? Limited space for competition, or signs taken for wonder of an ideological crisis of the market for post-Marxist thought?

Göran's route from sociology to Marxism – and onwards: his specificity as a social scientist

Especially in the early stages of his career, Göran was regarded primarily as a 'theoretician'. He has certainly made his mark in this field and put forward forceful critiques of different theoretical traditions during his long career, spanning from his M. Phil.-thesis in the early 1970's, criticizing the suppositions of the key stratification theories in American sociology, to his inclusive and incisive overview of the current ideological and theoretical landscape of critical leftist thought in his 2008 book on *From Marxism to Post-Marxism?*. There are thus very good reasons for regarding Göran first and foremost as a social theorist.

This is in our view a too limited assessment of his work. Yes, he certainly masters social theory to an extraordinary degree. But he is not a system-building theorist. He should be regarded and valued as a highly sophisticated and theoretically informed comparatist. He is able to use large masses of data for demonstrating the validity of his theoretical arguments and conceptual elaborations (e.g. family systems, modes of state interventions etc.). His broad comparative approach, underpinned by an astonishing erudition in many languages, combined with inventiveness in finding simple indices for his arguments are central to his key contribution to the social sciences as a comparative and empirical social scientist. Even when he dealt with theories, as in his dissertation, theories were dealt with comparatively and empirically.

---

39. See the exchange in *New Left Review* 142–143 (1983–1984).

He is a methodologically adept social scientist, but has not written methodological recipes or handbooks – they are present in his practice. His use of smart and simple indicators to make his points are visible in definition such as 'a state is a welfare state when more than half of its expenditures are devoted to welfare measures'; or in his empirical argument, in terms of a threshold index, for stating – in his 1977 *NLR*-article 'The rule of capital and the rise of democracy' – that the USA became a full-fledged bourgeois democracy only in the 1960's. This aspect becomes ever more present in his later books and articles.

In the early and mid-1960's we find that Göran was among the first in Sweden to discuss and reflect on the contributions of Herbert Marcuse (*One Dimensional Man*) and Jürgen Habermas (*Strukturwandel der Öffentlichkeit*), as well as deeply well-read in Gramsci's *Prison Notebooks* (the six Italian volumes from Einaudi). Quite early in the 1960s he read and absorbed Marx, not only *Das Kapital*, but also *Grundrisse* (the 1953 edition from Berlin), without falling into the Hegelian and historicist abyss that came to characterize large parts of the Danish and the German intellectual left in the 1970s.

He is, from almost the very beginning, explicitly non-Hegelian in his view of social theory and social reality. His early embrace of the historical Marxist tradition was Sartrean-Gramscian (applied in the useful Nairn-Anderson mode), later his methodological position was sharpened by absorbing Louis Althusser's epistemology for breaking with historicist and unilineal assumptions of historical development and the acceptance of the different forms of social and ideological power in distinct apparatuses and fields of influence, not being subsumed under an overarching historical subject.

Seen from the near outside it could be argued that Göran had two early role models – Perry Anderson and Eric Hobsbawm. Both in terms of their erudition and analytical ambition, broad sweep in terms of languages, sources and materials they mastered – but also as models for a basically respectful attitude towards the inheritance of the revolutionary traditions of the 20th century, at times explicitly Leninist in its formulations and in analytical terms, but later and over time more attenuated and rethought within a broader macrosociological tradition.

In short, Hobsbawm had a much larger attraction than either Hegel or Habermas, (Perry) Anderson and (Louis) Althussser rather than (Theodor W.) Adorno, (Barrington) Moore and later (Michael) Mann a more lasting impact than (Herbert) Marcuse.

His book from 2008, *From Marxism to Post-Marxism?* can be seen as sequel to the dissertation from 1974/76, which in a sense told the history of the life and times of the academic discipline of sociology, seen from the perspective of its eloquent opponent, the Marxist tradition. In this collection of essays he reviews the challenges to the Marxist traditions of the 20th century, coming from an impressive array of new non- and post-Marxist intellectual traditions as well as from revitalized academic disciplines. The Marxism Göran once enthusiastically embraced as the natural alternative to traditional sociology and political science has lost its primacy as the sole challenger in social theory. However, it remains a fertile component in the emancipatory social thought, which has come to the fore in Göran's publications both his later books and most recent important articles in *NLR* on the new global masses of the 21st century and the current state of social progress.

'Before the Eagle ascended' – a preliminary summary

The Swedish ascendancy of an *enfant terrible* has been sketched in some detail above, however, only extremely tentatively the domestic repercussions of the international establishment in a broader republic of letters of a radical global intellectual.

Arriving in Lund at the age of 19, its university and student corpus offered an arena for public involvement which rapidly extended northwards to include the tiny anarcho-syndicalist youth movement in Sweden. However, his early outward activities culminated in 1968 with the publication of 'From Petrograd to Saigon' while his domestic political fortunes ended abruptly a few months later with the failure for his bid to become an MP.

After 1970 his activities and ambitions gradually shifted to critical intellectual work within social sciences, in his case the field of sociology. The balance gradually moved from his activities as a left-wing political intellectual to a role as a critical, *Marxisant* sociologist. This led in a quick turn first (1971) to a M.Phil. thesis that combined an analysis of the post-war stratification debates within sociology and an overview of the literature on economic systems, and then to his impressive doctoral[40] thesis *Science, Class and Society* in 1974, later published by New Left Books in 1976.

Together with a sense of distance from the national culture went his independence of mind. Economics and politics intertwined at the heart of his writings, history always present. Philosophically the 1960s were Sartrean-Gramscian, the 1970s Althusserian. For most of this period, almost from the start, he was close to *New Left Review* and Perry Anderson. Göran was a card-carrying Swedish party Marxist after his own fashion and outside the precincts and prescripts of the domestic CP. In the 1970s academic work took precedence for Göran, in particular after the English release in 1976 of his 1974 dissertation. Two major works followed in due course: *What Does the Ruling Class Do When it Rules?* (1978) and *The Ideology of Power and the Power of Ideology* (1980). In French, together with Christine Buci-Glucksmann he published *Le défi social-démocrate* (1981) which could be considered as a summary of the previously mentioned 'before and after Social Democracy' project in a comparative European perspective.

In Sweden, *Zenit* survived but ran gradually out of steam. By the time the Left Party Communists dropped its 'C' to become simply the Left Party, this journal ceased to exist. Since long ago Göran had disappeared from the streets of Lund to become a political science professor in Nijmegen. However, already in 1987 he returned to Sweden, this time as a tenured professor in sociology at Göteborg University.[41] A decade later he moved to join SCASSS in Uppsala.

Hence, as the final song of a conventional research paper use to end, more research is needed. There are German, Italian, and Spanish publications, at the end maybe also Dutch publications

---

40. The classic Swedish doctoral degree, of which Göran's was one of the last in Sweden, corresponded to a *doctorat d'État* in France or a *Habilitation* in Germany.

41. In the late 1980s he had for a short while become an op-ed columnist in the main Swedish daily (von Platen 1996: 281).

that have eluded us, as have some Chinese, Japanese, Arabic, Korean and other translations. Until 1984 Göran had published twelve articles in *New Left Review*, which together with his three books being published by New Left Books/Verso was his most important forum before the mid 1980s. In 1986 he published *Why Some Peoples Are More Unemployed Than Others*. Through the *New Left Review*/New Left Books he became an institutionalized social scientist. His growing output has increasingly gone into the academic or semi-academic press – into journals and edited volumes. His major books from 1995 were published by Sage, Routledge and Polity Press. At the end of the first decade of the third millennium he returned more frequently to *New Left Review*/Verso with *From Marxism to Post-Marxism?* and comparative articles on social classes and mass revolts around the world.

At the age of 75 he is still going strong, participating in several international social scientific and socio-political endeavours, from Cape Town to New York. Not to speak of Berlin, Cambridge, Kalmar and Ljungbyholm – to and through global modernity.

References

Abrahamsson, B. and Broström, A. (1980) *The Rights of Labor*. Beverly Hills, Calif.: Sage.

Anderson, P. (1976) *Considerations on Western Marxism*. London: New Left Books.

Anderson, P. (1992). 'Foreword', in *A Zone of Engagement*. London: Verso.

Burawoy, M. (2007) 'The field of sociology: Its power and its promise', in Clawson, D., Burawoy, M. et al. (eds.) *Public Sociology*. Berkeley: University of California Press.

Dencik, L. (ed.) (1969) *Scientific Research and Politics*. Lund: Studentlitteratur.

Fry, J. (ed.) (1979) *Limits to the Welfare State: Critical Views on Post-War Sweden*. Westmead: Saxon house.

Gesser, B. (1971) 'Val av utbildning och yrke', in SOU 1971:61, *Val av utbildning och yrke*. Stockholm: Allmänna förlaget.

Himmelstrand, U., Ahrne, G. et al. (1981) *Beyond Welfare Capitalism: Issues, Actors and Forces in Societal Change*. London: Heinemann.

Hort, S.E.O. (2010) 'Deconstructing Göteborg, reconstructing sociology', in Hort, S.E.O. (ed.) *From Linnaeus to the Future(s) – Letters from Afar*. Växjö: Linnaeus University Press.

Kennerström, B. (1974) *Mellan två internationaler: Socialistiska partiet 1929–1937* ['Between two Internationals: The Socialist Party 1929–1937']. Lund: Arkiv förlag.

Korpi, W. (1978) *The Working Class in Welfare Capitalism: Work, Unions and Politics in Sweden*. London: Routledge and Kegan Paul.

Larsson, A. and Magdalenic, S. (2015) *Sociology in Sweden*. London: Palgrave Macmillan.

New Left Review (2010) *Index of Articles and Authors 1960–2010*. London: NLR.

Olofsson, G. (2015) 'Sociologin i Lund under 1960-talet – expansion, växtvärk, omvandling', in Andersson, G. and Jerneck, M. (eds.) *Samhällsvetenskapliga fakulteten i Lund – en vital 50-åring: En jubileumsskrift*. Lund: Lund University.

Olsson, S.E. (1978) 'Välfärden i Norden – och i Sovjet', *Dagens Nyheter*, 22 July.

Rothstein, B. (1996) *The Social Democratic State: The Swedish Model and the Bureaucratic Problem of Social Reforms*. Pittsburgh: University of Pittsburgh Press (original Swedish edition 1986).

Scase, R. (ed.) (1976) *Readings in the Swedish Class Structure*. Oxford: Pergamon Press.

Swedberg, R. (1994) 'Contemporary sociology in Sweden' in Mohan, R.P. and Wilke, A.S. (eds.) *International Handbook of Contemporary Developments in Sociology*. Westport, Conn.: Greenwood Press.

von Platen, G. (1996) *Resa till det förflutna: Minnen, 3, Att få börja ett nytt liv*. Stockholm: Fischer.

Books by Göran Therborn, referred to in the text

(2013) *The Killing Fields of Inequality*. Cambridge: Polity Press.

(2011) *The World: A Beginner's Guide*. Cambridge: Polity Press.

(2008) *From Marxism to Post-Marxism?* London: Verso.

(2006) *Inequalities of the World*, editor and co-author. London: Verso.

(2004) *Between Sex and Power: Family in the World, 1900–2000*. London: Routledge.

(1995) *European Modernity and Beyond: The Trajectory of European Societies, 1945–2000*. London: Sage.

(1991) *Vision möter verklighet* ['Vision Meets Reality'], with Olsson, S.E. et al. Stockholm: Liber.

(1989) *Borgarklass och byråkrati i Sverige* ['Bourgeoisie and Bureaucracy in Sweden']. Lund: Arkiv förlag.

(1986) *Why Some Peoples Are More Unemployed Than Others*. London: Verso.

(1981) *Le défi social-démocrate*, with Buci-Glucksmann, C. Paris: Maspero.

(1981) *Klasstrukturen i Sverige 1930–1980* ['The Class Structure of Sweden 1930–1980']. Lund: Zenit.

(1980) *The Ideology of Power and the Power of Ideology*. London: Verso.

(1978) *What Does the Ruling Class Do When it Rules?* London: Verso.

(1976) *Science, Class and Society*. London: New Left Books.

(1973) *Vad är bra värderingar värda?* ['What is the Value of Good Values?']. Staffanstorp: Cavefors.

(1972) *Critica e rivoluzione: Saggio sulla Scuola di Francoforte* ['Critique and Revolution: the Frankfurt School']. Bari: Laterza.

(1971) *Klasser och ekonomiska system* ['Classes and Economic Systems']. Staffanstorp: Cavefors.

(1970) *Spontaneität und Massenaktion im 'Wohlfahrtsstaat'*. Frankfurt: Neue Kritik.

(1967) *Program för socialism* ['A Program for Socialism']. Stockholm: Aldus/ Bonnier.

(1966) *En ny vänster* ['A New Left']. Stockholm: Rabén & Sjögren.

Journal articles from

Acta Sociologica 1978–2016

Arkiv 1975–2016

European Societies 2011–2014

Häften för kritiska studier 1969–1979

International Socialist Journal 1964–1968

New Left Review 1965–2016

Sociologisk Forskning 1967–2016

Zenit 1961–1966; 1967–1996

Appendix: Göran Therborn's impact as a 'public' and as a 'professional' sociologist

There are a couple of ways to measure the influence world wide of Göran Therborn's books and articles. If we phrase it in the terms of Göran as a 'public sociologist', the number of languages his books and articles have been translated into is a relevant measure. His books and articles have appeared in twenty-four languages (Swedish, Norwegian, Danish, Finnish, English, French, German, Dutch, Portuguese, Spanish, Italian, Greek, Slovene, Serbo-Croat, Hungarian, Polish, Belarussian, Russian, Ukrainian, Turkish, Arabic, Persian, Chinese, and Korean). Using this indicator he has no equal among his Swedish colleagues in the social sciences.

If we turn to Göran Therborn's impact in the academic social scientific community, in the English-speaking world and circles, his impact as a 'professional sociologist', to continue using Burawoy's conceptual scheme, we will have to use a simple measure such as the number of quotations and references counted by Google Scholar. These data are easily available but they are also heavily skewed towards the English-speaking world.[42] According to the counts in Google Scholar, Göran's presence in the scholarly literature is significant but not remarkable. The figures below date from spring 2016.

His most cited book is the book on *Ideology* (totalling 989). It's followed by the book on *European Modernity* (868), *What Does the Ruling Class Do When it Rules?* (521), *Sex and Power* (513), the *Unemployment* book (461).

His first book in English, *Science, Class and Society* has noted 363 in all, while his work *From Marxism to Post-Marxism?* has until now only reached 109. His book on social democracy published in French together with Buci-Glucksmann reached 127 citations in their French and German editions, indicating the Anglo-American bias in the Google Scholar measure.

His most cited article was the text on 'The rule of capital and the rise of democracy' that has been referred to 609 times. He has published many articles that have been cited more than 100 times.

This indicates that his books and articles have been read and used by a large number of people. To put this figures in a proper context we can note that Walter Korpi's book on *The Democratic Class Struggle* (1983) has been quoted more than 2 000 times. Esping Andersen's book on *The Three Worlds of Welfare Capitalism* (1990) has been cited more than 24 000 times. Perry Anderson's *Lineages of the Absolutist State* (1974) reached almost 3 000 citations. But all this is a far cry from the astonishing impact of Bourdieu and Foucault (respectively more than 450 000 and 620 000).

---

42. His 1978 book on the *Ruling Class* was translated into Arabic. According to the translator Abdulhadi Khalaf, this book is still widely used in the Arabic-speaking world. But we have not been able to find a single reference to that edition in the Google Scholar database.

Combining the public and the professional aspects

Most of the impact Göran's books and articles has had in their translations (more than twenty languages outside the English and Scandinavian orbits) is simply not visible when we use an indicator such as Google Scholar.

To get an adequate measure of his impact we must add his accumulated presence in the conference and lecture circuits, his proficiency in many languages, his role as journal editor, as editor of a number of books, his organizational presence within the Sociological associations – the Swedish, the Nordic, the European and other continental as well as the International on sociology and nearby disciplines.

SECTION I
Class, Politics and Revolutions

ANDERS STEPHANSON

On Geopolitics in Therbornism, Early and Late

Immediately after the Tet Offensive in early 1968, Göran Therborn issued a rapturous ode in the *New Left Review* to 'the incredible heroism of the Vietnamese militants' who had shown so clearly 'that revolutionary peoples, not imperialism, are invincible'. Socialists everywhere, he claimed, now felt 'instinctively' the same kind of identification and solidarity with the Vietnamese Revolution as in 1917 with the onset of the Russian Revolution. Hence the title of his panegyric: 'From Petrograd to Saigon' (Therborn 1968).

Therborn, then in his mid-twenties, was certainly right to see the Tet Offensive as a decisive event, if not quite for the right reasons. Victory in Vietnam would take another seven years and even that revolutionary change did not actually signal a world-historical transformation of the magnitude of Red October. Unimaginably from the view of 1968, Richard Millhouse Nixon would visit Beijing a mere four years later and a de facto alliance of sorts was begun; and before the end of the 1970s the newly unified Vietnam would indeed find itself at war, a limited one but a war nonetheless, with said People's Republic of China (and again Hanoi proved 'invincible'). Contrary to contemporary impressions, moreover, the Tet Offensive proved on closer inspection a devastating military setback for the National Liberation Front, decimating it and so opening up for a vastly expanded role for regular North Vietnamese armies in the South. Still, *politically and ideologically*, not least in the United States, the Tet Offensive did reveal in spectacular fashion the utter bankruptcy of the Pentagon version of the war; and it played a significant role in Lyndon B. Johnson's decision the following month to de-escalate the war and not to run for president again.

Radical exuberance notwithstanding, Therborn's notion of an 'instinctive' identification was thus pertinent, part of a larger, original reflection on the importance of Tet and the Vietnamese Revolution for the Left in the west. His historical question was this: why was the sign of anti-communism which the United States used to such good effect two decades ago in destroying the Greek revolution no longer working? The answer was grounded in a contrast between the cold war then and now (i.e. 1968). In the late 1940s and early 50s, the conflict between east and west had made possible 'a massive political and ideological consolidation of capitalism'. Opposition to the bourgeois order had been 'neutralized' – the east, bureaucratic, repressive and far poorer, was no ideological and political match for the US-fuelled advance of western capitalism. World War II for the United States had been a good thing, the Soviet Union conversely paying a horrifically destructive price for the eventual victory. Exacerbating what had always been a vastly unequal starting point, that wartime legacy turned the ensuing cold war into an *unequal conflict that was presented and experienced on both sides as being equal* (emph. in the original). What Therborn meant was that for the US and the USSR alike, it took the form of a symmetrical conflict between two equals, whereas in fact it was nothing of the kind. The would-be 'choice' in the contrast between the two supposed equivalents was thus for the western working class a foregone conclusion. Hence the 'neutralization' (Therborn 1968).

I think he was both right and wrong about this. He was right about the unequal power. He was also right about the presentation, if perhaps not the experience, of an equal competition of 'models', and the advantages that this, on the whole, generated for the US and the west (though we should remember that the Marshall Plan and NATO did not altogether 'neutralize' for instance the Italian communists who increased their votes in 1951 compared to the admittedly sharp setback of 1948). He was wrong, however, to superimpose the cold war in its stabilized form, say, the late 1950s, on the cold war as such. For the cold war was after all a US invention, the answer in a way to the question in 1946–47 as to how to create an unequivocal, peacetime commitment to a global role and to a transatlantic economy and security system in particular. From that angle, it was always much less about actually fighting the would-be world conqueror in Moscow than it was about a limitless license to act wherever and whenever. Stalin's regime, painfully aware of its inferiority, reverted in the face of this to a version of the old anti-fascist matrix, a defensive posture coupled with defensive alliances in the name of national independence.[1] The 'competitive modelling', by contrast, was a product of the Khrushchev period, the heady moment of Sputniks, expanding mass production and the Kitchen Debate, a moment when, with the notable exception of Berlin, the conflict had been mutually territorialized. From about 1963, after the Cuba Missile Crisis the preceding, it took on much more of a typical Great-Power conflict than a cold war, what Therborn in 1968 already refers to as 'detente' (and a fetter).

Therborn's ultimate point was indeed contemporary and two-fold. First, the manifestly *unequal* struggle in Vietnam 'between imperialism and national liberation' – itself the most graphic illustration of the wider conflict between 'the desperately deprived and rebellious workers and peasants in Asia, Africa and Latin America' and western capitalist societies – was reflected in the different planes on which the conflict was taking place. Asymmetry was matched by asymmetry so to speak. Therborn's strategic source of inspiration here was Mao's concept of protracted, guerrilla warfare, where the revolutionary forces avoid frontal combat while slowly and persistently undermining the very social order of the other side, blunting the latter's technological and material superiority and eventually inversing it into an advantage (as the 'people' will readily come to grasp who the enemy is). Second, successful third-world revolution put the very heartlands of comfortable western capitalism into question: ideologically and politically, it was now (again, we are in 1968) becoming clear that the struggle is not about scarcity versus plenitude as the old cold war stipulated but about inequalities and racism, revealing them as integral features of the west itself. Vietnam had thus unblocked the political impasse of the cold war. Indeed, this was a struggle led not by some vaguely nationalist force but by an explicitly Marxist-Leninist one. Thus, in Therborn's paradoxi-

---

1. I have argued this in several places, to no great effect. A condensed version may be found in Stephanson (2005).

cal formulation, '*an unequal struggle waged as unequal equalizes the inequality*' (Therborn 1968).

Vietnam, then, was demonstrating that capitalism even in its bourgeois-democratic form produced imperialist violence. The whole contradiction between capitalism and socialism had returned from its cold war detour, now taking the form of a clear-cut confrontation where radicalized youth across the most advanced western societies were mobilized against capitalism itself. Down the line, 'anachronistic, Cold War anti-communism' would cease to 'mystify' the working class, in turn opening up again for a properly emancipatory dialectic. The line drawn from Petrograd to Saigon was clear.

It is easy to dismiss this as wishful thinking amidst the uproar of 1968. Yet it will be recalled that Therborn's scenario seemed very soon to be confirmed in the massive insurgence in metropolitan France, involving both students and workers; and in fact he was right to detect that Vietnam, along with other struggles such as that over civil rights in the United States (the murder of Martin Luther King, Jr. coincided with the publication of the article) drastically undermined the conventional cold war frame, already fraying, of the 1950s and early 60s. Here, however, I want to pursue another thematic in Therborn's argument, present and operative but not in the conceptual foreground. In passing, he mentioned 'the international system' and dismisses 'bourgeois political science' along with its 'formalistic categories' – a view of political science and certainly the subfield of International Relations I suspect he has maintained ever since. Against it, he proposes 'concrete historical theory' and 'the dialectical concept of contradiction', in other words what he takes to be Marxism. The more *specific* Marxist theory at work here was however Lenin's concept of imperialism.

That theory has not aged well for all manner of reasons but Lenin's provisional attempt to make sense of World War I and its relationship to capitalism (and 'revisionism') became the unshakeable orthodoxy of Marxism-Leninism, whatever its particular incarnation. It served as ultimate foundation for all Soviet theorization of the international system, making perfect sense indeed (long with 'the main contradiction') of the bipolarity of the cold war: the imperialist camp, led by the United states, ably resisted by the democratic, pro-gressive camp, led by the Soviet Union (and so on). In due course, *nevertheless*, Moscow developed a fairly sophisticated understanding of the actual workings of the system which featured 'the correlation of forces' as a homemade version of the balance of power. I leave that aside along with the more precise aspects of Lenin's theory. What interests me here, because its relevance for Therborn, then and now, is instead the notion of a constitutive contradiction between the relations and the forces of production: capitalism develops the latter enormously such that at a certain point ('stage' in Lenin's Hegelian-Marxist terminology, indicating a step – *Stufe* – in a staircase), they begin to mark powerfully and objectively in their very structure and form a social and by extension socialist character. Imperialism and war is one attempted solution to this historic impasse along with 'bribery' of the labour aristocracy; socialist transformation in accordance with the direction of things is the other. Capitalism has become monopoly capitalism, i.e. imperialism; and so, fettered by its private mode of appropriation, it is unable to develop. It is 'mori-bund' in Lenin's term.[2]

The idea, taken from Marx's introduction to the *Contribution to the Critique of Political Economy* (from 1859), is Hegelian through and through. That does make it wrong, far from it; but in this case it happened to be spectacularly wrong. Giant monopolies notwith-standing, there was no *constitutive* contradiction between the private mode of appropriation and the social character of production. Capi-talism has continued to develop the forces of production massively, if unevenly, for a century since Lenin's pamphlet. For it is one thing to say that capitalism produces oligopolies and monopolies whose very form may suggest they could become public property, and quite another to say that the form is a sign of 'moribund capitalism' qua imperialism, the shell objectively outgrown. Indeed, the *Kapital-logische Schule* (however doxological) showed in the 1970s that the

---

2. Cf. Stephanson (1983/84: 25–39). Lenin's text (which should be read together with his interesting reflections on Hegel and Clausewitz in 1915) can be found anywhere on the Internet but authoritatively in the *Collected Works* (Lenin 1964: 185–305).

notion of a stagnating, semi-administered stage of monopoly capitalism separate from capitalism in its classical commodity form made no Marxist sense.[3]

It made a lot of sense, however, to Moscow – the 'unfettered' rise of ever-expanding planned and scientific production against the always-already stagnating and crisis-ridden capitalist system. It made a lot of sense too from a different vantage point to the Therborn of 1968 and one can readily see why: the Vietnamese Revolution, anti-imperialist and Marxist-Leninist, was breaking one of the weakest links in the imperialist chain and so also undoing the mystifications of the cold war, the debilitating, geopolitical bipolarity of the US and the USSR. The aberration was ending, the 'fettered' condition of the cold war was ceasing to exist and so the 'fettered' condition of capitalism itself, private but social, was emerging in its true light across the board.

From Therborn's standpoint, then, the break was not only with the conventional frame of the cold war; it was also with the earlier horizontalization in the position of the Soviet party and the Comintern on the fundamental contradiction, viz. that it was now between the Soviet Union and the outside rather than, vertically, between capital and labour. One recalls here Nicos Poulantzas' withering critique in *Fascism and Dictatorship: The Third International and the Problem of Fascism* (1974 [1970]) – the 'natural' notion that fascism was somehow a sign of stagnating and rotting monopoly capitalism, enchained if you will in its final stages. In the latter part of the 1930s, at any rate, there emerged out of this a strategic and tactical edifice whose basic simplicity ('defend the socialist fatherland') made possible a remarkably flexible range of actual foreign policies, often indistinguishable from the precepts of classical realism. The ultimate version of this logic, following Mao's extensive reflections on contradiction, may be found in the singularly perverse foreign policy of the People's Repub-

---

3. My original source of inspiration many years ago was Anders Molander's 'Monopol och socialism i Lenins imperialismanalys' (1977). This led me to (among other works) Christel Neusüss, *Imperialismus und Weltmarktbewegung des Kapitals* (1972) and Bernd Rabehl, *Marx und Lenin* (1973). On the (understudied) phenomenon of *Kapitallogik* in the Bundesrepublik, see Altvater and Hoffman (1990: 134–155).

lic of China in the late 1960s and early 70s: support for any regime, however reactionary, opposed to the 'New Tsars' in the Kremlin, the now supposedly restored capitalist regime and main enemy of the surviving Marxist camp headquartered in Beijing.

Therborn, at this youthful stage, viewed the geopolitical map differently of course: progressive and revolutionary forces of anti-imperialism in struggle against imperialism and reaction graduating into one for socialism proper. The contradiction involved vertical and horizontal forces on both sides and had no single geopolitical centre, though 'Vietnam' is its focal point and most acute expression. Beyond this, international relations seemed not to require much more *systematic thought*. Marxism itself did not have a lot to say on the subject and in any case Therborn was not interested. His theoretical concerns in the ensuing years lay elsewhere, in an increasingly Althusserian preoccupation with the 'scientificity' of sociology and Marxism where the object of inquiry, the problematic as it were, centered on 'society' and the disciplinary ways, past and present, of grasping it. Political economy (unavoidably) formed the third party here, but if Therborn was a Marxist first, his sociology came a very strong second. Whatever the vicissitudes of the discipline since the expansive days of the 1960s, he has in fact remained a devoted sociologist ever since. Curiously, however, he was not really involved in the most vibrant and contentious issue then within western Marxism and certainly Marxist sociology, namely, 'the capitalist state'. When he did move into this terrain towards the end of the 1970s, it was typically (and engagingly) at the level of institutional practices, answering, against the twin backdrop of modernity and capitalism, the formative question of sociology, 'how do things work in the social world and why?'

It should be noted, meanwhile, that those Marxist arguments about the state, and the capitalist state in particular, did not feature much exploration of the international or systemic effects. The State, whatever it happened to be, was ultimately *a product of the inside*. The classics of sociology offered not much more here than the classics of Marxism (Engels' informed writings on military affairs notwithstanding). Sociology did not provide much of an account of the state in an international context (the anomalous figure of Raymond Aron certainly did, but he was not always or chiefly a sociologist). The explanation, of course, is that 'society' is primary for both of Therborn's traditions: state and war are secondary results of the social. This was to be so – ultimately – even in Perry Anderson's bravura combo account in the early 1970s of the historical emergence of the state as the political condensation of the social structure and class relations: what kind of social class does it take, let us say, to make war the central feature of what the state does?[4]

Once the preeminence of 'society' (in the Marxist case, featuring political economy, contradiction and class) is established, the lay of the land invites *comparison*. There is an elective affinity between 'society' and the method of comparison. Along with a good deal of sociology, Therborn was and is essentially a comparativist. His explanations may not always be found in comparison itself, but the basic ingredients of what is being dealt with tend to be instances of something in comparison with something else, even when the object under scrutiny is a single social structure or practice. An obvious difficulty with comparison is that the entities may not be sufficiently distinct, demarcated and isolated; and hence, the explanatory yield is limited. This is why Michael Mann, in his celebrated first volume of *The Sources of Social Power* (1986), rejected it along with 'society' in favour of a matrix of overlapping networks (only to resurrect it in the following volume). From a Marxist standpoint, the issue of comparison is secondary, *a pragmatic question*: is it useful? Still, Marxism does presuppose a comparative, transhistorical concept, namely, 'mode of production', the premise of which is that, whatever the differences over time and space, human beings have to generate the wherewithal to survive and so enter into social relationships of a determinate kind that can then be compared with other such formations. Those 'kinds', in short, can be systematized, featuring contradiction, classes, exploitation and so on. Historical direction and development can then be read (or misread) against that foundational, comparative identity – above all, giving rise to the genre of 'typical routes to capitalism and modernity'.

4. Perry Andersons duo of classics here are of course *Passages from Antiquity to Feudalism* and *Lineages of the Absolutist State* which both appeared in 1974.

Just as Therborn has never given up on the scientific prominence of sociology and the social, so he has never given up on the comparative Marxist frame. In a way, he is of course right not to do so: comparison between, say, the effects of family policies in France and Japan or investigation of class inequalities in the US as opposed to Sweden over time (I am inventing things) are indispensable for the articulation of any critical and oppositional politics. Thus, when not writing about the ways in which society generally works (how 'ideology' operates, what the 'ruling' in the ruling class actually means and so forth), Therborn the Sociologist has typically pursued concrete, specific aspects of the social, and all for the best. I note, however, that this sociological sensibility, if I may call it that, along with the comparative way of thinking, has not been conducive to any sustained consideration on the place of geopolitics in the generation of the modern state, nor indeed on the very nature of geopolitics or international politics itself.

One must then go on too to say that Therborn's own discipline – belatedly but nonetheless – has provided some of the most interesting accounts we have on the topic, more interesting certainly than much of the US-dominated subfield of political science known as International Relations (as distinct, symptomatically, from 'comparative'). Several major figures in historical sociology, from the 1980s onwards, have explored in different ways and with different emphasis war, state, class, economy and indeed geopolitics in a way that goes beyond the several orthodoxies: Anthony Giddens, Michael Mann, Charles Tilly among them, and, in a different vein, Immanuel Wallerstein, though geopolitics was an after-thought to his epochal, market-orientated concept of a 'world system' (1974).[5] Two central and related problems are at stake in this regard: first

---

5. Relatedly, there was also William H. McNeill's *The Pursuit of Power* (1982). McNeill's kind of 'world history' had overlapping concerns with historical sociology. Wallerstein's interest in 'geopolitics' appeared not in his original formulation of notion of a 'world system' (1974) but in a series of essays in the 1980s collected in *Geopolitics and Geoculture* (1992). I realize that some of these figures, Giddens in particular, are more interested in the sociology of war in relation to the state than in geopolitics as such, though the distinction is not always easy to make.

and more specifically, the importance of war for the generation of the state as state, and second, the importance of what becomes the 'international system' (as opposed to, say, Roman or Christian notions of world empire) for the place and character of that state and by extension also 'society' (I ignore whether it is singular or a set of overlapping networks transcending the boundaries). While Tilly attacked the 'internalist' view of state formation and foregrounded the interactive importance of war, his conceptualization gave proper weight to the capacity of state and class to extract resources and capital for the purpose of that bellicist endeavour (Tilly 1990). Taking his cue in part from Otto Hintze, Mann pointed out meanwhile that, until the case of Britain in the late 19th century, military expenditure always represented the preponderance of state budgets. In his power matrix, indeed, the military domain is added to the classical Marxist triptych (economy, politics, ideology).[6]

The ins and outs of this whole problematic are beyond my scope here and, in any case, it is not incumbent on Therborn to deal with it. He is not a historical sociologist. He can write delightful historical vignettes, especially about cities, and he may well have made an excellent historian; but insofar as he has written 'histories', they belong rather to the genre of intellectual history – the history of sociology and the history of Marxism. Still, his concrete and exceedingly diverse work has centered on the 20th-century (especially the postwar era and the quarter century that follows, in effect his own lifetime): two epochs of continuous war and mass killings but not chiefly in the advanced, industrial world where, in a remarkable shift, there was almost no war and certainly nothing like the conflagrations of the first part of the century. Civilian aspects of the state dominate.

The genesis of the state system and its character, then, has not entered Therborn's proceedings. *And yet*, as a public intellectual of the

---

6. See Mann's exceedingly suggestive essays of the 1980s (where he develops, for instance, the notion of 'geopolitical privacy'), which appeared as *States, War, Capitalism* (1988). The difference between his first and second volume on *The Sources of Social Power* (where 'empire' oddly drops out and European comparison drops in) is striking (cf. Mann 1986 and 1993).

left, he has been called upon to pronounce on it and has indeed done so. On occasion, when not making stimulating, spatiocultural forays into the place of cities ('place' being his chief interest in space), he has indeed discussed 'geopolitics', usually in giving a tour d'horizon of what might be called 'trends in the world'. He never really theorizes it, however, turning it instead typically into a site for a series of discrete, often informative, accounts of particular powers or regions and their ups and downs. While eschewing considerations of military and geostrategic aspects proper – almost as though they were distasteful – he would condemn for example US militarism ('Occidental Despotism') in the most scathing *concrete* terms.[7] It is perhaps from that angle that one ask what happened to the line he drew from Petrograd to Saigon and how he wrestled with the aftermath.

The 1970s could still certainly be grasped at the time as intensified capitalist crisis: oil shortages, stagflation, dollar crisis, widespread working class resistance, the defeats in Indochina, the progressive movements in sub-Saharan Africa, the revolution in Portugal, continued legitimacy crisis in Washington (when Nixon resigned in 1974, he was only popular in Moscow and Beijing). With some difficulties, then, Therborn's projection remained in tact. The following decade, spearheaded by Margaret Thatcher and Ronald Reagan and featuring neo-liberalism and neo-cons along with radical transformation of capital, put it severely into question; and the 1990s terminated it peremptorily. The combined implosion of the Soviet Union and the rapid integration of the People's Republic of China into the now thoroughly financialized world of capital eliminated socialism briskly and emphatically from the historical agenda. As the centenary of Petrograd is approaching, we may well wonder if it will be remembered in anything but gaudy, Putin-orchestrated celebrations of the Great Russian present.

The chief 'event' for Therborn here is not the advent of neoliberalism and the world of derivatives but the implosion of the Soviet Union – the line from Petrograd ends, one might say, when Lenin-

---

7. See, inter alia, Therborn (2002a, 2006a, 2006b, 2002b, 2012). For a great example of Therborn's nuanced historical sensibility, see his travelling reflections in 'Transcacausian triptych' (2007).

grad becomes St Petersburg. Whatever it was, he says (and I agree), the Soviet Union was still 'a major pole of orientation of the left-of-centre world' and of course the only significant counterpoint to the massive power of the United States. The disappearance of the Soviet Union, then, ironically extinguished to his regret the remnants of that very 'bi-polarity' from which the progressive world had presumably been liberated according to his manifesto of 1968. In a different register, as the Soviet Union evaporated and capitalism, recharged and retooled, expanded vigorously, the old contradiction between the forces and relations of production, had also come to a halt: 'the Grand Dialectic' as he calls. Whether it is suspended or actually terminated remains for him nonetheless an open question. Meanwhile, 'the Little Dialectic (the class struggle) is still operative; but class will never fill the central role it did in western modernity during the 19th and 20th century.[8]

The account, empirically, is plausible enough, but how, in a deeper sense, could the transhistorical logic of the Grand Dialectic just stop? How could the 'truth' of most of the 20th century, its very historical direction along dialectical lines, the 'societalization' of the productive forces, be reversed in the capitalist world at the same time as the huge Eurasian area where it had actually been removed saw a return to capitalism? Therborn's explanation, a series of features and factors, seems ad hoc. What was true, empirically, up to about 1980 no longer holds true. In the absence of sustained exposition, we are left with an open-ended set of pragmatically articulated phenomena, the analysis of which may well be 'concrete' and right but not anchored in any theoretical standpoint. It reminds me rather of the response, an honourable one, from a veteran leader of the CGIL, the communist-led union confederation in Italy, when I asked her in the 1980s what was to be done when the certainties were gone:

8. Indicative, successive references here are Therborn 1984 (where he is still seeing societalization and some progress under the rubric of 'welfare state capitalism'); 1989; 1992; 2012 (wherein the elaboration of Grand and Little Dialectics appears); 2014. An alternative way of thinking this is Wallerstein's world system (there can be only one), but Giovanni Arrighi's concept of cyclical regimes of accumulation of ever-deepening historical reach is to me more suggestive because of the importance he accords to financialization.

'When you don't know what to do, you defend the people'. This is how I sense the spirit of Therborn's lifetime commitment to the left, to the analysis of the social and, above all, to what he has invoked, with every reason, as 'the core values of socialist culture – universal equality and solidarity' (Therborn 1992: 18).[9]

References

Altvater, Elmar and Hoffman, Jürgen (1990) 'The West German state deriva-tion debate: The relation between economy and politics as a problem of Marxist state theory', *Social Text*, 24, 134–155.

Anderson, Perry (1974a) *Passages from Antiquity to Feudalism.* London: NLB.

Anderson, Perry (1974b) *Lineages of the Absolutist State.* London: NLB.

Lenin, V.I. (1964) *Collected Works*, 22. Moscow: Progress.

Mann, Michael (1986) *The Sources of Social Power, Vol 1, A History of power from the beginning to A.D. 1760.* Cambridge: CUP.

Mann, Michael (1988) *States, War, Capitalism: Studies in Political Sociology.* Oxford: Blackwell.

Mann, Michael (1993) *The Sources of Social Power, Vol 2: the Rise of Classes and Nation Stes, 1760–1914.* Cambridge: CUP.

McNeill, William H. (1982) *The Pursuit of Power: Technology, Armed Force, and Society since A.D. 1000.* Chicago: Chicago University Press.

Molander, Anders (1977) 'Monopol och socialism i Lenins imperialismanalys', *Tekla*, March.

Neusüss, Christel (1972) *Imperialismus und Weltmarktbewegung des Kapitals.* Erlangen: Politladen.

Poulantzas, Nicos (1974 [1970]) *Fascism and Dictatorship: The Third Interna-tional and the Problem of Fascism.* London: NLB.

Rabehl, Bernd (1973) *Marx und Lenin: Widersprüche einer ideologischen Kon-struktion des 'Marxismus-Leninismus'.* Berlin: Verlag für das Studium der Arbeiterbewegung.

Stephanson, Anders (1983/84) 'On Soviet foreign policy', *Social Text*, 8, 25–39.

Stephanson, Anders (2005) 'The Cold War considered as a US project', in Pons, Silvio and Romero, Federico (eds.) *Reinterpreting the End of the Cold War: Essays, Interpretations, Periodizations.* London: Frank Cass.

---

9. The CGIL leader quoted is Giovanna Ricoveri, whom I interviewed together with Daniela Salvioni in 1985; but unable to find the actual reference, I am quoting from memory. Her response, ostensibly so simple, made a deep impression on me (and 'people' here I took to mean what Italians understand as 'the popular classes').

Therborn, Göran (1968) 'From Petrograd to Saigon', *New Left Review* 48, 3–11 (also in Swedish, in *Zenit* no. 4 1968).

Therborn, Göran (1984) 'The prospects of Labour and the transformation of advanced capitalism', *New Left Review* 145, 5–38.

Therborn, Göran (1989) 'New times: Vorsprung durch rethink', *Marxism Today*, February.

Therborn, Göran (1992) 'The life and times of socialism', *New Left Review* 194, 17–32.

Therborn, Göran (2002a) 'Monumental Europe: The national years. On the iconography of European capital cities', *Housing, Theory and Society*, 19, 1, 26–47.

Therborn, Göran (2002b) 'Asia and Europe in the world: Locations in the global dynamics', *Inter-Asia Cultural Studies*, 3, 2, 287–307.

Therborn, Göran (2006a) 'Eastern drama. Capitals of Eastern Europe, 1830s–2006: An introductory overview', *International Review of Sociology*, 16, 2, 209–245.

Therborn, Göran (2006b) 'The pole and the triangle: US power and the triangle of the Americas, Asia and Europe', in Hadiz, Vedi (ed.) *Empire and Neoliberalism*. New York: Routledge.

Therborn, Göran (2007) 'Transcacausian triptych', *New Left Review* 46, 68–88.

Therborn, Göran (2012) 'Class in the 21st century', *New Left Review* 78, 5–29.

Therborn, Göran (2014) 'New masses? Social bases of resistance', *New Left Review* 85, 7–16.

Tilly, Charles (1990) *Coercion, Coercion, Capital and European States, AD 990–1992*. Oxford: Blackwell.

Wallerstein, Immanuel (1974) *The Modern World-system. 1, Capitalist Agriculture and the Origins of the European World-economy in the Sixteenth Century*. New York: Academic P., Cop.

Wallerstein, Immanuel (1992) *Geopolitics and Geoculture: Essays on the Changing World System*. Cambridge: CUP.

RISTO ALAPURO

Finnish Demonstrations
as Confrontations

Hypotheses

The demonstrations are a form of confrontation. Charles Tilly has portrayed them as a variety of collective action in which 'some group displays its strength and determination in the presence of the public, of the agents of the state, and perhaps of its enemies as well', and which has taken, in this century, three basic forms: the massed march, the assembly with speechmaking, and the temporary occupation of premises (Tilly 1978: 177). For John Berger, to take another example, 'a mass demonstration can be interpreted as the symbolic capturing of a city'. He maintains that the demonstrators transform the open places intended for very different purposes 'into a temporary stage on which they dramatize the power they still lack' (Berger 1968: 755).

In these characterizations both a predominantly physical and predominantly symbolic confrontation are imminent. On the one hand, the demonstrators are in the presence of a possibly hostile public and maybe of their enemies – something that makes a physical confrontation or a face-to-face encounter feasible and the presence of the police easy to understand. The contestation is also manifest in the takeover of a space – especially in the occupations because they usually confront the demonstrators with the owners of the premises (the workers with the employers in the occupation of the factories, for example). On the other hand, the participants put forth demands, a definition of situation, or even a whole symbolic universe that confront or are at variance with the others' definition of situation – be they spectators or enemies.

The physico-spatial and the symbolic elements of confrontation are of course intertwined in the actual demonstrations. The demonstrators *personify* a contentious demand, or an alternative definition of situation or reality. It is (re)presented through them, or it is played by them to the public, as implied in Berger's image of a stage or of a symbolic capturing of a city. Therefore it is understandable that traditional forms of popular contention linked to the festival and the spectacle can become effective in modern demonstrations (see below). Seen from another angle, what the demonstrators do in personally presenting or displaying the alternative definition of situation, is to expose themselves to the others and their judgment – which recalls us that besides being a confrontation the demonstration is also a form of contact. It is a kind of *figuration* in which groups of individuals are (physically) involved at the same time as allies and as opponents.[1]

The Finnish demonstrations seem, from a comparative point of view, remarkably peaceful and disciplined. On that point many observers are in agreement (see especially Suppola 1973: 55–58; Taipale 1970: 10–14, 22–24; Hentilä 1970: 25–26). Also, quantitative comparisons of political violence and 'civil strife' point to the same direction: they have brought about a conclusion that the 'class struggle' in the post-World War II Finland has been 'uncommonly peaceful and organized' (Alestalo 1986: 113).[2]

In this paper it is argued that the Finnish demonstrations are indeed comparatively peaceful and law-abiding by character. It seems that the avoidance of open confrontations is valued both in a positive and in a negative sense. Positively in the sense that the maintenance of order in the demonstrations is considered a point of honor by their organizers, and negatively in the sense that very easily the disorder is felt to be lurking around the corner. It is as if the order and the discipline were highly charged, perhaps to an exceptional degree, with their opposite, the disorder and the chaos. It is as if the Finnish repertoire of demonstrations were poor for 'play-

---

1. On the concept of 'figuration', see Elias (1978: 13–312).
2. Alestalo's conclusion is based, among other studies, in Gurr 1969 (see esp. pp. 613–614, 630) and Feierabend et al. 1969 (esp. pp. 650–652).

ing' open confrontations: these are either not tolerated or, if gotten under way, readily seen as a sudden release of dark forces.

The character of the Finnish demonstrations and a few factors arguably accounting for it will be set forth by reviewing the main traditions of demonstration in the country, created principally by the workers and the students and, to a lesser extent, by the peasants.

Worker demonstrations

The May Day movement and the institutionalization of the worker demonstrations

The history of the workers' demonstrations in the modern Finland goes back to the 1890s, when the Finnish workers initiated the May Days evolved in 1890 in the core countries of the labor movement. Originally the first of May consisted of a single simultaneous one-day strike and demonstration for eight-hour day. It resulted from a deliberate political decision, made by the Second International, to give political and cultural unity to the working class in different countries (Hobsbawm 1983b: 283; Perrot 1984a: 143–145). In France, to take up one case, the first May Day was a mixture of a political demonstration, a public holiday, and a strike, which sparked off 'a wave of unexpected strikes' and thereby 'escaped from the control of its initiators'. The 'Great Day' displayed 'a vision of rapid change', provoked fear in the bourgeoisie, and revealed 'the comparative isolation of the working classes in French society'. As other labor demonstrations, it was expressed 'in the ritual form of popular festivities' (Perrot 1984a: 157, 162–165; 1986: 88).

In contrast to this varied confrontation and display – which had its counterparts in other big countries (Hobsbawm 1983b: 283–287) – in Finland the May Day was initiated and for several years continued in a very moderate form, by one group of skilled workers, the printers in Helsinki. On May 1, 1890 they organized an 'outing which had the character of a demonstration' to an island (!) in front of Helsinki, as a deliberate response to the Second International. Characteristic of the overall conciliatory line of this demonstration was not only the absence of any opponent in the physico-spatial sense but also the fact that in the subsequent years it was held only on the first Sunday of May (in 1890, May 1 happened to be Sunday) (Soikkanen 1961: 41; 1975: 69).

Nationally the First of May gathered momentum in 1898, accelerated by the so-called strike for temperance. It aimed both at prohibition and equal and universal suffrage, and it played a part in the foundation of the national worker party the following year. Mass meetings and marches gathered from 8 000 to 15 000 people in the largest towns, and thereby demonstrations gained a new visibility as a mass phenomenon (Soikkanen 1975: 68; Sulkunen 1986: 222, 225, 230, 235). In other words, in becoming nationally important, the May Day did not definitely confront the workers with other social groups. It rather joined them with other popular efforts to increase political and cultural freedom. In line with this orientation, the marches to the headquarters of the authority or to the seats of power apparently played a more modest and less regular role than in France, for example. There the urban demonstrators marched, as a customary practice, to 'the town-halls, prefectures or subprefectures' (see Stenius 1977: 83–87; Perrot 1984a: 157).

Then, from 1899 to 1905 a period followed that has been called the first period of demonstrations in Finland (Suppola 1973: 5–6). The demonstrations and other expressions of resistance multiplied after the Russian emperor, from 1899 onwards, initiated an integration of the Grand Duchy of Finland into the Russian administrative system. Particularly 1902 and in early 1905, masses of people and agents of the state were against one another in a few demonstrations in Helsinki, or in Helsinki and some other towns. But significantly, the main dividing line between the demonstrators and the troops was national, not social. The former were Finns (not only from popular groups), and the latter were mainly Russians (or other non-Finns of the Empire) (Jussila 1979: 42–46, 58–61, 63–64). Therefore this period did not consolidate the demonstration as an open and direct confrontation between social classes within Finland, or at least the importance of a common national front confounded or retarded the rise of demonstrations as a form of working-class challenge against the upper classes. Besides, and importantly enough, these demonstrations remained moderate in the sense that they never resulted in killings or other serious casualties. The picture is not radically altered even by the General Strike that broke out in the fall of 1905, as a consequence of the first Russian revolution. It began as an enormous national demonstration against the Russians, with the bourgeois groups and the socialists acting together (see Jussila 1979: 74–75).

However, in this period, especially from 1904 on, also a specific working-class campaign of demonstrations began to evolve. It aimed at replacing the antiquated four-curia diet of corporate representation by a unicameral assembly based on universal suffrage, and was directed mainly against the domestic powerholders (Soikkanen 1961). But even this opposition did not lead to major confrontations, not to speak of violent encounters – apparently because, first, the political conjuncture in 1905–06 really made the universal suffrage to materialize rapidly and easily, and second, this great mobilization period was also great organization period. In the first general elections in 1907 the Social Democrats gained 80 seats of the total of 200 and became the overwhelmingly largest party in Parliament. The immense growth of the party took place in a remarkably organized manner. A movement took shape that effectively eliminated all extraparliamentary ways of exerting political pressure and soon institutionalized the massed marches as a disciplined activity down to the level of the local associations. 'It has remained a permanent and deep-rooted aspiration of the organized working-class movement to eliminate the *spontaneous* resistance and contestation, be it collective or individual. Only the organized resistance (and power) has appeared as a legitimate activity to the [Finnish] working-class movement' (Parikka 1987: 133, emphasis added).

The rapid expansion of electoral politics

What the early stages of the worker mobilization clearly suggest is the importance of the transformation of the political system for the comparatively peaceful and orderly rise of the demonstrations in Finland. Indeed, 'the forms, frequencies and personnel of collective action depended intimately on the existing structure of government and politics', as Charles Tilly expresses the main conditions for demonstrations (1978: 170). In most Western countries in the late nineteenth and early twentieth centuries, political rights were gradually won through hard and often protracted struggles in which the workers slowly learned to organize, mobilize, and act collectively against state machineries, first in strikes and then, after gaining some rights, in elections fought with their own parties (see Abendroth 1965, esp. pp. 51–86; Tilly 1978: 113). This process took, as a rule, at least several decades. Demonstrations as a distinct form of collective action evolved from this process (Tilly 1981: 22).

The expansion of electoral politics legitimated and rewarded forms of collective action which had previously been little known, dangerous, unproductive, or all three. Under a regime of elections, special-purpose associations, statements of programs, displays of strength, solicitations of popular support, and threats to withdraw support all acquired a legitimacy and effectiveness they had lacked under most eighteenth-century conditions. They compounded into the actions in the new nineteenth-century repertoire: the protest meeting, the demonstration, the rally, and the strike. Important enough, the picture of slow and protracted struggles in which the popular groups learned this repertoire, does not hold in Finland. It is striking how rapidly and easily the estate-based diet was replaced by a unicameral assembly in 1905–06, thanks to the defeat of Russia in the war with Japan, and the ensuing power vacuum in the Empire.

Consequently, so it seems, a varied repertoire of popular contention, and regular confrontations with the state machinery never had chance to really evolve. The easy and complete victory in the political sphere encouraged the early movement to focus almost solely on the electoral politics, and to stay strictly within the bounds of legality.

Class structure, local society, and nineteenth-century forms of collective action

But not only was the political breakthrough easy. Also the period preceding the expansion of electoral politics was marked by a distinctly moderate popular organization and collective action. In his book on Russia's western borderlands Edward C. Thaden points out that, among all western minority regions of the Empire, only in Finland the social tranquillity prevailed uninterrupted during the nineteenth century. Everywhere else – in the Baltic Provinces, in Poland, in Ukraine – rebellious groups challenged, at one time or another, the authority of the autocracy or of the local landlords (Thaden 1984: 135–140, 155–161, 177–178, 183–186, 206, 234).

In Finland, instead, the organization of the masses was successfully initiated by the dominant groups, as shown above by the importance of the temperance movement among the workers. The authority of the upper classes was newer seriously questioned in the nineteenth century. The minor role of the active resistance to the dominant classes in this period, or, from another perspective, their considerable responsiveness to certain popular demands apparently played a part in checking the growth of contentious demonstrations into 'a way of doing public business' (Tilly 1978: 169).

Reasons may be sought in the Finnish social structure and the statemaking. The dominant groups seem to have had comparatively strong incentives to establish a sense of obligation among the popular groups. The position of the upper classes was based much more on a central role in the administration than on landownership, and they were managers of a vulnerable polity, dependent on the Russian autocracy. In this perspective it seems clear that the dominant class in Finland had no strong incentives to attempt the subordination of the peasants or of the workers with repressive political methods, but rather had good reason to promote the attachment of the popular groups – notably the freeholding peasantry that was the principal landowning class – to the emerging Finnish state (see, in more detail, Alapuro 1988, ch. 5).

But the character of the pre-industrial and early industrial local society undoubtedly played a part as well. It apparently affected above all the aspects of the festival and the takeover of a space – or their weakness – in the Finnish demonstrations.

Those forms of the pre-industrial popular culture and collective action that could have served as a potential reservoir for the modern culture of demonstrations were weakly developed in Finland. According to Charles Tilly, the most dramatic recurrent forms of the collective action in eighteenth-century Western Europe were twofold.

There were, first, 'the food riot, concerted resistance to conscription, organized invasions of fields and forests, and rebellion against tax-collectors' (Tilly 1981: 20). Most of these modes of collective action, even the food riots, were little utilized in Finland, with only few local exceptions.[3] Much longer than Western European fellows, the Finns were able to reduce the scope of open conflicts with the state or with the landlords by retreating to distant uninhabited areas.

The same holds for those forms that were less openly contentious and less visible but 'in some ways more influential', namely 'established public festivals and rituals during which ordinary people voiced demands or complaints, and stated assemblies of corporate groups – communities, gilds, religious congregations, and the like' (Tilly 1981: 20). They too remained little utilized, again with one partial exception – religious congregations (Ylikangas 1979).

This is certainly not surprising, given the long winters and the sparse population. The Finnish rural 'sociability' was austere in comparison to the Central European one – to use this originally French term that means the aptitude for living within the group and consolidating the group by forming associations based on the structures of the everyday life (see Agulhon 1984: 38; and Perrot 1986: 87). In Western Finland where the villages were more densely built than in the east, the social control seems to have been very severe in the nineteenth century, with even nightly curfews as a way of controlling the unruly behavior of the youth (Kallio 1982: 232–284, 256–265). As to the urban sociability, its forms seem considerably less varied than in the more southern parts of Europe. 'The institutions that had fostered a spirit of camaraderie and union in the West European cities, guilds and fraternities, cafés, celebrations, carnivals, were totally absent in Finland' (Kirby 1988: 69).

The character of the pre-industrial and early industrial society helps to understand why the aspect of festival and display of specta-

---

3. It is above all the province of Ostrobothnia in western Finland that has a tradition of rural collective action, with a self-conscious provincial spirit. In different epochs the Ostrobothnians have reacted vehemently to the intrusions of the state. Also village fights proliferated there (see e.g. Ylikangas 1976 and Haavio-Mannila 1958).

cle and confrontation as a form of contact, have remained marginal in the Finnish mass demonstrations. The contrast is sharp with the French tradition, referred to above, there in rural demonstrations 'la politique fournit l'occasion et le but de l'expression, et le folklore [charivari (shivaree), for example] son moyen', as Maurice Agulhon puts the significance of the rural sociability in his book about politics and culture in the Midi during the first half of the nineteenth century (Agulhon 1979: 266). And for the early (urban) strikers the demonstrations were consubstantial with the festivals, tells Michelle Perrot. The strikes were 'the great holidays of the proletarian'.

They meant, above all, a complete break with the everyday routine of the factory. 'Bien des manifestations de rue ne sont que de joyeux défilés, au son de l'orphéon, l'occasion de chanter, de se dégourdir, de prendre de l'air.' 'Le 1er Mai 1890, premiere fête du travail et, si l'on veut, premiere greve générale, a porté au plus haut point cette ambiance de joie populaire' (Perrot 1984b: 160).

On the sociability was also based the importance of the space, of the capturing of the street in France – again an element that was weakly developed in Finland. The nineteenth-century French workers 'had definite views concerning urban space: the right to cross the city freely, to use the commons [the old peasant term is purposely use here] …, to be at the heart of the city …' These aspirations were well rooted in the setting of everyday life – shops, taverns, dance halls, vacant lots. Workers 'demanded a right to the city and to the street'. The strike was not only an instrument for exercising pressure but also 'a means of expression in which the working class and the people within which it encased, meet again in the street they have reclaimed' (Perrot 1986: 87, 88, 106).

All in all, then, in Finland the combination of the festival and the contention was never learnt in the same way as in large parts of Western Europe. 'People *learn* how to strike, to invade fields, to burn in effigy, just as they fail to learn a great many other forms of action'; 'the analogy of actors choosing among the limited number of performances with which they are familiar, and of audiences prepared to jeer, cheer, and understand the actors' interpretations, nicely captures the learning and circumscribed choice involved in all real-life collective action' (Tilly 1981: 19). The repertoire the Finnish popular groups learnt was more uniform, more disciplined, less spectacular and apparently less contentious than in large parts of Western Europe.

Political crises

This picture is accentuated by the enormous significance certain political crises have had on the image of the demonstrations in Finland. The most contentious and violent of these occurred, first, in 1917, or just before the Civil War, and second, in the years following World War II. During these critical periods massed marches and public meetings were occasionally transformed into violent confrontations with the agents of the state. In 1917 the mass demonstrations in cities grew more intense than ever before or after, due to the absence of a domestic army and even a police force in Finland. On some occasions food was confiscated and political organs led by the bourgeois were harassed. At this time, i.e., after the February revolution, the uncertainties of Finland's position vis-à-vis Russia greatly exacerbated the disquietude the demonstrations would have provoked in any case. Later they were taken, moreover, as a prelude to the Civil War, which broke out in January 1918, almost immediately after the Finnish declaration of independence. In the bourgeois imagery the demonstrations in 1917 became crystallized as a sudden release of dark forces. The Russian word *svoboda*, meaning freedom, became a symbol of chaos, and linked the Finnish 'hooligans' with the undisciplined Russian soldiers stationed in the country in 1917.

In 1945–49 the Communists and left-wing socialists were allowed, according to the stipulations of the armistice with Soviet Union, to enter the political scene after a period of effective repression for fifteen years. They gained a significant role in the Finnish worker movement and politics, and launched a number of demonstrations challenging the country's political orientation and supporting strikes. In 1949 the demonstrations culminated in an encounter in which the police killed two people. This is unique in the Finnish history of demonstrations.

Obviously important for the consolidation of demonstrations as something to fear or to abhor, is the fact that both in 1917 and in 1945–49 the confrontations were linked to a crisis with Russia (or the Soviet Union). In both periods an internal threat to the prevailing relations of power and authority seemed to fuse with an external threat, which among the bourgeois groups forcefully added to the fear of chaos. It was felt that the chaotic elements in the internal, working-class challenge were inspired by an external, Russian, infection.

It is not surprising, then, that these periods provoked horror among the bourgeois groups. But it is significant that the spontaneity and 'actionism' were largely rejected in the labor movement as well. In 1917 the Social Democrats dissociated themselves from the spontaneous demonstrations, and actually the fear of disorder figured among the principal motives for founding specific workers' militias that year.[4] And after World War II even the leadership of the Communist party took pains to restrain the contentious forms of the workers' collective action (Parikka 1988a: 10–11; 1988b: 24–27).

The events in 1917 and 1918 apparently affected the image of demonstrations in another sense, too. The only moment that possibly could have made a somewhat richer repertoire of demonstrations to evolve or at least a distinctly positive attitude towards them to arise was perhaps missed just in those years. As stated, the Great Strike of 1905 and the concomitant transformation of the political system began as an enormous national demonstration against the Russians, with the bourgeois groups and the socialists acting together. Although they soon went in different directions, the fact remains that this wave of collective action was a most powerful catalyst in the nationalization of the political life, a largely shared experience of national liberation. It had a good chance to become the founding act of the modern collective action in Finland, 'a warehouse of ritual, symbolism and moral exhortation', to paraphrase E.J. Hobsbawm (1983a: 6), with demonstrations as an important element of the evolving matrice. But the terrible shock of the Civil

---

4. Salkola 1985: 207–208, 229–232, 238; '... especially in the summer months in 1917 organized workers founded militias to maintain order' (ibid.: 232).

War, linked to the Russian revolution, was to powerfully affect its image only one decade later. The shadow of the abortive revolution was to fall dark across the Great Strike, making it appear a prelude to the Civil War and consolidating a sharp twofold division between order and disorder.

The Peasants' March in 1930

Above it was suggested that the most important recurrent forms of collective action familiar in the eighteenth-century Western European countryside were virtually unknown or poorly developed in Finland. The austere Finnish rural sociability was not conducive to demonstrations modeled after food riots or public festivals and rituals. Still in one instance just this sociability seems to have served as the cultural frame for a major demonstration. In a paradoxical way it confirms and perhaps deepens the image of the Finnish demonstration as an organized and disciplined event.

During its heyday, in July 1930, the Finnish variant of fascism carried out a display of determination in Helsinki. About 12 000 people, mainly farmers, marched on the capital calling for the extermination of every form of 'Marxism' in Finland. At the main demonstration were present the most central political figures in the country. The Peasants' March, as it was called, was a disciplined manifestation of the religious and patriotic virtues of the stout Finnish peasant as a contrast to the alleged reign of decadence and the denial of God which were again plunging the country into the disorder prevalent in 1917. The march became a spectacular symbolic counter-display to the 'Red' forces of 'chaos', rooted in the traditional values of the peasant society. It recalled the Whites' victory parade in Helsinki after the Civil War.[5] In the collective memory of the Finns this event arguably plays (or at least played, perhaps up to the 1960s) a more central role than any other massed march in this century.

---

5. On the march, see Siltala (1985: 120–123).

Students' demonstrations in the nineteenth and early twentieth centuries

Besides the workers, it is especially the university students who in Finland have a history of demonstrations of their own. This tradition goes from the early nineteenth century up to the post-World War II period and seems to confirm, with one notable qualification, the above image of the Finnish demonstrations. As a rule, the student demonstrations have been disciplined and law-abiding; open confrontations have been restrained or forestalled. Striking is the recurrent call for self-discipline on the part of the students themselves, that is, an apparently thorough internalization of the restraints.

Self-control vis-à-vis Russia

In the nineteenth and early twentieth centuries reasons for self-imposed restraints were built in the structure of the political position of Finland. Finland's status as a separate political entity, a Grand Duchy in the Russian Empire, ultimately rested on a tenuous political balance; the Finnish bureaucratic leaders were well aware that the limitations of the Russian influence were imposed by Russian considerations of broader policy over which Finns had no effective control. Hence the basic problem of the Finnish political elite: first, what is the Russians' (real) stand, and second, how should the Finns define their own line of action in relation to the Russian one? Both aspects were important. The need for a continuing assessment of the Russians' stand implied that the Finns continuously *anticipated* their possible reactions in critical situations or, more precisely, anticipated what were the situations the Russians would consider critical or unacceptable in their relations with the Finns. This was seen important to maintain or enhance Finland's margin of manoeuvering.

In the case of demonstrations this position meant that, first, the Finnish elite aimed at minimizing *in advance* all instances of collective action that might have been understood as contestations by the Russians and, second, it attempted to do this without publicity and without an open confrontation even with the would-be demonstrators. That is, it tried to persuade them to give up the envisaged contentious action, through negotiations, if possible. The situation resulted in a voluntary restraint of demonstrations on the basis of an assessment of the possible or probable Russian reaction. It was bound to develop a strong element of self-imposed control that included not only the dominant group but also the demonstrators; these were made internalize, to a large extent, the risks of their planned display.

All this concerned, in the nineteenth century, above all the academic community, both as a whole, i.e., in its relations to the political-bureaucratic leadership of the country and, more specifically, the students vis-à-vis the professors and the leadership of the university. The academic aspect in the displays of strength and determination was accentuated because in the nineteenth-century Finland the bourgeoisie was weak and the towns weakly developed. The university in Helsinki, the capital, provided virtually the only forum of public discussion in the whole country well beyond the mid-century, and therefore the political control was brought to bear on it, and especially on the students (see Klinge 1967a and 1967b). Also, the problems the Imperial authorities had with the Russian universities, certainly sensitized them to any expression of liberal or separatist contention among the Finnish educated class. And finally, the heir to the throne was the chancellor of the university – which undoubtedly added to the visibility to the autocracy of all unrest among the students.

Consequently it is perhaps no wonder that the history of the Finnish student demonstrations from the 1810s to the turn of this century is a series of seemingly minor and innocent incidents which nevertheless are highly charged and whose significance seems to greatly exceed the actual events. The demonstrations grew in the course of the century along with the spring festivals which mostly remained a non-contentious (and on some occasions a decidedly loyalist) form of student sociability. One gesture or one unguarded expression or more or less unpolitical fights were reported to the Emperor and easily got strong political overtones. Incidents which in a European perspective were modest, could have grave consequences, notably the dissolution of the students' own organization in the 1850s.[6] The self-discipline lectured by the leadership of the university was in most cases adopted by the students. Usually they were highly aware that 'to use demonstrations was to play for very high stakes', as the historian of the students' organization process, Matti Klinge, puts it (1967a: 213). Even the nationalist demonstrations in the beginning of this century do not much alter the picture.[7]

Graphically the small scale and late evolvement of demonstrations is seen in the students' reaction to the revolutionary activity of 1848 in Europe and in their reaction to a delay in the Imperial authorities' decision to summon the Finnish estates in 1861.

In the former case – which has been considered the first political mass demonstration in Finland[8] – the reaction came only the following year, and then mainly in the form of a shivaree of about 150 students against a professor whose appointment had become a symbol of the conservative orientation in the university policy. All in all the students' demonstrations were 'very modest'. The echo of the demonstration went immediately to St Petersburg, and made the administration of the university to tighten the control of the students (Klinge 1967a: 168–171; Stenius 1980: 200, for the quotation).

The latter provoked no confrontation because it was not considered a challenge (even if it was somewhat suspect vis-à-vis the Russians), but an expression of sympathy to the Finnish political-administrative elite; and this elite had not gotten into any real conflict with the Russian autocracy. The demonstration of 1861 was nevertheless significant as 'the only "Parisian" demonstration of the century' in Finland. It was an event that undoubtedly influenced the participants themselves. What was new was, first, that this massed march gathered people from different social classes (not only students but especially artisans as well) and even more than one thousand people taken all together, and second, that the demonstrators expressed themselves in

---

6. See Klinge (1967a: 18–21, 28–29, 31, 36, 45, 50, 74, 135, 152–159, 206–209; 1967b: 129–133, 139, 231–240).

7. See Klinge (1968a: 208, 214–219, 232–236, 239–242, 246–250, 262–282).

8. This is implied in Matti Klinge's presentation of the demonstration (Klinge 1967a: 169).

favor of constitutional principles (Klinge 1967a: 169; 1967b: 131–134; Stenius, 1980: 200, again for the quotation).

Confrontations in the interwar period

It is not inconsistent with the earlier developments that students' demonstrations grew contentious at the same time as Finland broke away from Russia. In the newly independent Finland of the 1920s and the 1930s the educated class displayed an unprecedented hostility to Russia (transformed into a soviet state), and the student demonstrations as a whole became more violent and more aggressive than ever before. This was true not only in relation to Russia but also in relation to the domestic powerholders – which fits in well with the earlier double restraint: a self-control vis-à-vis the Russians had implied a self-control vis-à-vis the domestic (university) authorities.

The dominant student organization of the epoch, the Academic Karelia Society, campaigned against the Swedish-speaking and bilingual upper class (including parts of the university elite), and against Soviet Union (attacking monuments and other symbols from the preceding 'Russian period'). Besides militarily organized massed marches to the monument of the national hero J.W. Snellman and demonstrations in front of the Soviet legation, the AKS repertoire included the burning of flag, the shivaree, the burning in effigy, and the non-attendance of lectures or interference with them. Students even interfered with fights between Finnish-speaking and Swedish-speaking high-school students in the streets of Helsinki.[9]

The hypothesis of the importance of the Russian connection for the self-imposed discipline seems to find support from the student demonstrations of the late 1940s. Then again minor incidents became highly charged because of their alleged or real anti-Soviet overtones, and led rapidly to the tightening of both the outside control and the students' self-control (Klinge 1968b: 232–234, 251).

---

9. See Klinge (1968b: 99–103, 126–128, 135–136, 139–140, 147–148, 151, 154, 170, 173–174, 177–178, 182–183).

The student demonstrations of the 1960s

The most intense period of student demonstrations after World War II was seen in the 1960s. The displays were parallel to those organized by large-scale student movements elsewhere, but at the same time they were a distinctively Finnish phenomenon.

In 1964 the Committee of the Hundred, a student-dominated peace organization that took inspiration mainly from the contemporaneous English peace movement, organized its first demonstration. From the modest beginning in 1964 the demonstrations in Helsinki and other cities were gradually regularized in the subsequent years. Numerically they culminated in 1968. Then, from the early 1970s, they began to decline as contentious events. After the demonstrations protesting against the visit of the Persian Shah in Finland in 1970, they became partly fused with the institutionalized demonstrations of the worker movement, and partly dwindled away.[10]

Of the 184 demonstrations in a period from 1964 to 1970, identified in a study, the overwhelming majority took the form of the massed march or an assembly with speechmaking or a combination of both. In most cases the demonstrators expressed their opinions about international or related issues; above all they demonstrated against the Americans' warfare in Vietnam or expressed their solidarity with the peoples of the Third World. The period culminated in 1968, at which time the Soviet occupation of Czechoslovakia was added to the issues. The subjects as well as the character of the main organizing agents well shows the central role of the students and the close relation of their efforts to those of their fellows in other countries (Suppola 1973: 22–36).

The demonstrations were carried out inspired in part by foreign models; they displayed forms that were new in Finland, e.g. the shouting of slogans, the sitting down on the street, and the running in keeping time (Hentilä 1970: 28). There were tendencies to transgress the bounds of legalized collective action, in a way reminiscent of the contemporaneous demonstrations in France or some other countries,

---

10. See von Bonsdorff (1986: 87–88, 95–97, 176–212, 302–309; Suppola 1973: 22–29, 36–39).

with the burning of military passports, for example (on this incident, see von Bonsdorff 1986: 207–208; Lahtela 1967: 87).

Still the result was recognizably Finnish, with an emphasis on the order and discipline and the avoidance of open confrontations. Characteristic of the limited role of the street demonstrations for the peace activists is the fact that the group stressing their importance as a primary way of exerting pressure only painfully distinguished itself from the dominant group of these activists. The majority preferred research and rational argumentation and viewed the demonstrations from the perspective of furnishing (rational) information about issues that the dominant mass communication neglected: the demonstrations 'are a rational way to influence the decision-makers in the society' (von Bonsdorff 1986: 98–99; Mäkelä 1967: 89, for quotation). The demonstrators were proposed to learn and to practise '*non-violent* direct action' that required self-discipline; non-violence was to be made an overriding principle and the inviolability of persons was to be respected (Suomela 1968: 140, emphasis added; see also von Bonsdorff 1986: 207). No wonder then that legality or at least a deliberate avoidance of confrontations with the police was emphasized (Björklund 1968: 142; Suomela 1968: 140; Pirinen 1968: 134). The freedom to demonstrate was seen a constitutional right which had to be activated (Taipale 1970: 7), 'a democratic way to exert influence' (Hannula 1968: 135), and it had to be utilized in an organized manner. Even an idea of drawing up a demonstration guide was laid out. It was to be prepared at the initiative of the Ministry of the Interior ... (Mäkelä 1967: 89).

The importance of this attitude exceeds the Committee of the Hundred, because a few of its demonstration specialists remained main figures during the entire period, up to the beginning of the 1970s. One of them wrote in 1970:

> Generally speaking the demonstrations in Finland have been publicly organized and non-violent by character; [the demonstrators] have been ready to negotiate with the police, and at the same time they have tried to inform, through different channels, the public about the objectives of the demonstrations. These have been linked to more extensive campaigns, to the raising of consciousness. (Taipale 1970: 22–23.)

This view is confirmed by the study cited above. It concluded that in the 1960s 'relatively few violent demonstrations have occurred in our country'. Making resistance to police remained a rare phenomenon (Suppola 1973: 55, italics deleted). Actually only once in these years did a violent confrontation take place. In 1970, the culmination point already passed, demonstrations against the visit of the Shah led to open encounters between the police and the demonstrators (Suppola 1973: 44, 55; von Bonsdorff 1986: 307–308).[11]

Graphically the Finnish abhorrence to open confrontation was shown by the visit of K.D. Wolff, one of the principal leaders of the German student movement, in Helsinki in the summer 1968. When he broke through the police cordon in front of the commercial agency of Western Germany in order to seize the flag of the Federal Republic, nobody followed him. Wolff was 'infuriated'; he could not understand the 'caution' of his Finnish fellow students (von Bonsdorff 1986: 192, 211–212).

Another contrast is provided by May 68 in Paris. There the confrontation with the police was not only accepted but, after a certain point, actively sought for. There was an action-reaction process on an increasing scale, an escalation of confrontations from the early occupations in Nanterre and in Sorbonne and the expulsion of the students from the Sorbonne by the police, up to the street battle between the students and the police in the night of May 13. For the Finnish activists the immediate lesson of May 68 lay in the political backlash, i.e., in the result of the subsequent elections. For them the victory of the Right proved that the French students had been wrong in choosing a line of direct – and violent – confrontation with the authorities and in failing to give 'any real information' to the public.[12]

Also, the festival and the spectacle obviously constituted a much more central aspect in France than in Finland. In France they – as the movement as a whole – were a combination of 'la grève et la fête,

---

11. See also the collection of articles on the anti-Shah demonstrations: *Mielenosoitukset ja poliisi 22-26.6.1970* (1970).

12. Hamon and Rotman (1987: 427–433, 441–446, 449–456, 460–468, 470–489); 'Ranskan opetukset' (1968: 107, quotation).

les meetings dansés, les murs éloquents, l'ordre du désir' (Hamon and Rotman 1987: 529). 'Militer et s'amuser' were the two sides of the coin for Daniel Cohn-Bendit (ibid.: 432), who himself incarnated the continuing efforts to transgress the limits of the everyday life, to maintain the festival. Also the sense of spectacle apparently heightened during the escalation process. Many people were highly conscious of appearing on the (national) scene, a situation that at one level was expressed in the occupation of the Odéon theatre: 'Une scene, il leur faut une scène!' (ibid.: 511).

But despite the overall orderly and disciplined conduct that was well in line with the Finnish tradition, neither the organizers nor the public saw the demonstrations as something familiar. For the organizers they were a new and living form of collective action, a potentially effective way of communication that should retain its unpredictability and avoid an ossification into a ritual, as had happened with the traditional demonstrations (Mäkelä 1967: 89; Taipale 1970: 7).

In the attitude of the public most evident was a discernible hostility. It was evident in various reactions from denigrating and insulting remarks on the street to the opinions in the press. Largely the demonstrations were seen as a release of disorder and/or inspired by the Communists.[13] Also, in the established student organizations certain hostility existed. 'It is not in the Finnish student's tradition to go to the streets', said the Chairman of the National Union of Students in 1968 (cited in von Bonsdorff 1986: 205).

Even among the workers the reaction was negative or at best they were indifferent. This probably resulted from the fact that 'in the Finnish labor movement the tradition of demonstrations is very serious by spirit', as a commentator engaged in the student demonstrations put it (Hentilä 1970: 28).

It is not far-fetched to suggest that in these reactions the above-sketched double attitude manifested itself. In the Finnish tradition the maintenance of order was not only valued as such but also forcefully accentuated by sensitivity to the disorder and chaos. It was in

---

13. See *Mielenosoitukset ja poliisi 22-26.6.1970* (1970), and von Bonsdorff (1986, passim).

these conditions that the students' new repertoire even if it did not dissociate itself much from the tradition, and even if it remained little contentious by international standards, provoked antipathy and irritation among different social groups.

An interesting aspect is the self-conscious emphasis on demonstrations as a way of communication, as a way to *inform* the public. In transmitting the message great care was taken to avoid irritating or offending the public.[14] But still minor novelties in gesture and display became highly charged, and their significance easily grew in overpowering proportions. For an outstanding activist 'making a display' was a grave error: it gave arms to the opponents of demonstrations (Taipale 1970: 14). It is as if minor confrontations in the physico-spatial sense had implied major confrontations in the symbolic sense.

The relationship between the two aspects is clearly discernible in the demonstration in which the Finnish student movement climaxed and which in the subsequent years has acquired a quasi-mythical character. On November 25, 1968, one day before the centenary celebration of the Union of the Students of the University of Helsinki was to take place in the students' own club house (an imposing building in the heart of Helsinki), students occupied this house. The official celebration, with a number of established guests, including the President of the Republic, had to be moved elsewhere (see especially von Bonsdorff 1986: 9–41).

On the one hand, the contentious aspect of this takeover of a space seems comparatively limited. Significantly, the Finnish movement culminated in the occupation of the students' *own house*. Therefore the demonstration did not confront the students directly with an adversary. They were within a physically isolated space owned by their own union, between themselves. In France, instead, to take another case, both the occupation of the meeting room of the direction of the university in Nanterre (one important step in the escalation of the May 68 movement) and the occupation of the university of Sorbonne, directly confronted the students with the

14. See the above-cited articles of Taipale (1970), Björklund (1968), Suomela (1968), Mäkelä (1967), Hannula (1968), and Pirinen (1968).

university authorities and, in the latter case, with the agents of the state as well. The first occupation of Sorbonne was put down by the police (see Hamon and Rotman 1987: 427–429, 450–456).

Moreover, in Finland the culmination point implied the absence of a distinct adversary not only physically but also symbolically. The act of occupation did not include an open challenge to the authorities or to other groups distinct from the students themselves. True, the occupation was a protest but its target was only vaguely defined. It was the 'bureaucratized' or 'elitist' direction of their own organization and the 'establishment' more generally. It is characteristic of the protest that the occupants sent a greeting to the 'comrade President' who as a guest of the centenary celebration could feel offended along with the other celebrants (see von Bonsdorff 1986: 10–20, 28 for the quotation, 29–41).

Interestingly, the high point of the Finnish student activism was so much inward-oriented that it only with difficulty may be considered a demonstration if Charles Tilly's qualification of 'the *presence* of the public, of the agents of the state, and perhaps of the enemies as well' is accepted. In the occupation of the student house in Helsinki practically no public and no agents of the state were present – in the concrete, physical sense of the word. (It is perhaps not only an accident that the presence of the police or of opponents fails to figure in the definition of demonstrations utilized in the Finnish study cited above (Suppola 1973: 1, 19).)

On the other hand, however, the event had an enormous echo in the press, the TV, and the public opinion in general, as a challenge to the accepted order, and it functioned as a catalyst in crystallizing the ideological confrontation of the student movement with the Right and the Social Democrats. In other words, although in the narrow physical sense it was hardly a confrontation, symbolically the occupation was highly charged. In Finland a nationally significant demonstration effect arose without spectacular encounters or confrontations. This apparently implies that the resolution of conflicts or the facing of antagonisms (and by the same token, the avoidance and acceptance of contacts) is differently placed in Finland than, say, in France: the public space and its control, and by implication also the demonstrations, seem to play different roles in the conflict resolution in the two cultures.

Finnish demonstrations in comparative perspective: problems

The Finnish demonstrations as confrontations may be related to demonstrations elsewhere at least in two (partly overlapping) respects which seem illuminating for the Finnish case. One can study the adoption of elements from other demonstration cultures and their possible modification in Finland; and one can compare parallel forms of demonstrations in Finland and other countries.

Above the forms of demonstration were presented as a repertoire which is learnt, in the same way as the actors choose among a number of performances and of audiences that understand the actors' interpretations. This metaphor suggests that the mutual understanding between the demonstrators and their milieu essentially rises from a common culture and a common (national) history. For example, the French repertoire of the 1960s was solidly embedded in a domestic tradition from which innovation and new symbols could evolve. Besides being a festival with a dramaturgy of its own, the demonstrations were linked to a long political tradition of making politics in the streets ('Le pouvoir est dans la rue!') from the French Revolution to the Commune of Paris and beyond.[15]

What happens when parts of a repertoire evolved in another society are utilized in Finland? Obviously new elements are understood and adopted in a way conditioned by the Finnish culture, i.e., reshaped to correspond to the cultural context to which they are linked in Finland. For example, the novel forms of collective action adopted in the 1960s – the shouting of slogans, the running in keeping time etc. – were apparently trapped, at least partly, by the highly charged Finnish opposition between order and chaos. These forms were felt much more contentious than in the countries in which they were invented.

15. E.g. Perrot (1984b: 156); Perrot (1986: 85–88, 90–91, 106); Ozouf (1976: 17–18); Hamon and Rotman (1987: 467, quotation).

Another example is provided by the role of the Committee of the Hundred. It drew inspiration, including its title, from the British peace movement and from the marches for the peace in various European countries. But unlike elsewhere, it proved absolutely central for the mobilization of the student youth in the 1960s just in Finland, and it has retained its vigor much longer than in other countries. Arguably one reason for its importance in Finland lies in its non-violent strategy. The nonviolence matched extra-ordinarily well the Finnish tradition of demonstrations, which abhors openly contentious collective action. Perhaps for this reason the Committee of the Hundred was singularly well adapted to channel the aspirations of the 1960s, and especially in the opening stages.

As to comparisons in the proper sense of the word, a few hypotheses have been suggested above. At least the May Day movement and the student demonstrations of the 1960s could provide starting points for comparisons.

Another interesting but difficult comparative problem is the relationship between the physico-spatial and symbolic elements of confrontation. Above it was suggested that in the history of the Finnish student demonstrations a modest repertoire of physical confrontation has been accompanied by a great symbolic weight addressed to it. Could comparisons throw light at this relationship? Would they suggest, for example, the importance of a close 'correspondence' between the word and the deed in Finland, a kind of transparence between them, or even a 'subjection' of the former to the latter – something that is arguably present in some other spheres of the Finnish intellectual culture?

And finally, the relationship of the demonstrations to the state seems an intriguing problem in the Finnish case. Demonstrations may clarify the alleged state orientation of various social and political movements in Finland: on the one hand the alleged Finnish tendency to formulate popular demands systematically in relation to the state, and on the other hand the allegedly easy penetration of the mass movements into the state or, looked at from the opposite angle, the state's phenomenal capacity to incorporate them (see, e.g. contributions in Alapuro et al. 1987). Various aspects of worker demonstrations (the early common action with other groups against tsarism, the systematic emphasis on the organized and peaceful ways of exerting pressure on the authorities, the Communist leaders' attitude in the late 1940s, etc.) and of student demonstrations (the willingness to find common rules with the police, the idea of preparing a demonstration guide, etc.) test to a kind of state orientation but its possible role in shaping confrontations should be assessed comparatively. What does it mean, for example, that the state has been apparently responsive to popular demands but at the same time its authority remains virtually unquestioned in the demonstrations?

References

Abendroth, Wolfgang (1965) *Sozialgeschichte der europäischen Arbeiterbewegung*. Frankfurt am Main: Suhrkamp.

Agulhon, Maurice (1979) *La Républiaue au village*. Paris: Seuil.

Agulhon, Maurice (1984) 'Working class and sociability in France before 1848', in Thane, Pat, Crossick, Geoffrey and Floud, Roderick (eds.) *The Power of the Past: Essays for Eric Hobsbawm*. Cambridge: Cambridge University Press.

Alapuro, Risto (1988) *State and Revolution in Finland*. Berkeley and Los Angeles: University of California Press.

Alapuro, Risto et al. (eds.) (1987) *Kansa liikkeessä*. Helsinki: Kirjayhtymä.

Alestalo, Matti (1986) *Structural Change. Classes and the State: Finland in an Historical and Comparative Perspective*. Research Group for Comparative Sociology, University of Helsinki, Research Reports, no. 33.

Berger, John (1968) 'The nature of mass demonstrations', *New Society*, 23 May.

Björklund, Ilkka-Christian (1968) 'Pari sanaa suomalaisesta poliisista', *Ydin* 2.

von Bonsdorff, Johan (1986) *Kun Vanha vallattiin*. Helsinki: Tammi.

Elias, Norbert (1978) *What Is Sociology?* London: Hutchinson.

Feierabend, Ivo K., Feierabend, Rosalind L. and Nesvold, Betty A. (1969) 'Social change and political violence: Cross-national patterns', in Graham, Hugh Davis and Gurr, Ted Robert (eds.) *The History of Violence in America*. New York: Bantam Books.

Gurr, Ted Robert (1969) 'A comparative study of civil strife', in Graham, Hugh Davis and Gurr, Ted Robert (eds.) *The History of Violence in America*. New York: Bantam Books.

Haavio-Mannila, Elina (1958) *Kylätappelut*. Porvoo and Helsinki: WSOY.

Hamon, Hervé and Rotman, Patrick (1987) *Generation. 1. Les années de réve*. Paris: Seuil.

Hannula, Risto (1968) 'Väkivaltainen pasifismi?', *Ydin* 2.

Hentilä, Jorma A. (1970) 'Tavoitteet ja toteutus', in *Mielenosoitukset ja poliisi 22-26.6.1970*. Helsinki: Otava.

Hobsbawm, Eric (1983a) 'Introduction', in Hobsbawm, Eric and Ranger, Terence (eds.) *The Invention of Tradition*. Cambridge: Cambridge University Press.

Hobsbawm, Eric (1983b) 'Mass-producing traditions: Europe, 1870–1914', in Hobsbawm, Eric and Ranger, Terence (eds.) *The Invention of Tradition*. Cambridge: Cambridge University Press.

Jussila, Osmo (1979) *Nationalismi ia vallankumous venäläis-suomalai-sissa suhteissa 1899–1914*, Historiallisia tutkimuksia 110. Helsinki: Suomen Historiallinen Seura.

Kallio, Reino (1982) *Pohjanmaan suomenkielisten kylien oltermanni-hallinto*. Jyväskylä: Studia Historica Jyväskyläensia 23.

Kirby, David (1988) 'Folket och föreningarna' (a book review), *Historisk Tidskrift för Finland* 73.

Klinge, Matti (1967a) *Ylioppilaskunnan historia*, vol. 1. Porvoo and Helsinki: WSOY.

Klinge, Matti (1967b) *Ylioppilaskunnan historia*, vol. 2. Porvoo and Helsinki: WSOY.

Klinge, Matti (1968a) *Ylioppilaskunnan historia*, vol. 3. Porvoo and Helsinki: WSOY.

Klinge, Matti (1968b) *Ylioppilaskunnan historia*, vol. 4. Porvoo and Helsinki: WSOY.

Lahtela, Markku (1967) 'Täten eroan puolustus-laitoksesta', *Ydin* 1.

Mäkelä, Klaus (1967) 'Hyödyllinen väkivalta?', *Ydin* 1.

Mielenosoitukset ja poliisi 22-26.6.1970 (1970) Helsinki: Otava.

Ozouf, Mona (1976) *La fête révolutionnaire, 1789–1799*. Paris: Gallimard.

Parikka, Raimo (1987) 'Paikallinen työläisyhteisö, työväenkulttuuri ja työväenliike', in Hyrkkänen, Markku et al. (eds.) *Väki voimakas 3: Näkökulmia työväen ammatilliseen ja paikalliseen historiaan*. Tampere: Työväen historian ja perinteen tutkimuksen seura.

Parikka, Raimo (1988a) 'Työväenliikkeen vallan strategioista', *Kommunisti* 44, no. 8–9.

Parikka, Raimo (1988b) 'Työväenliikkeen suhde valtioon', *Kommunisti* 44, no. 10.

Perrot, Michelle (1984a) 'The First of May 1890 in France: The birth of a working-class ritual', in Thane, Pat, Crossick, Geoffrey and Floud, Roderick (eds.) *The Power of the Past: Essays for Eric Hobsbawm*. Cambridge: Cambridge University Press.

Perrot, Michelle (1984b) *Jeunesse de la grève*. Paris: Seuil.

Perrot, Michelle (1986) 'On the formation of the French working class', in Katznelson, Ira and Zolberg, Aristide R. (eds.) *Working-Class Formation: Nineteenth-Century Patterns in Western Europe and the United States*. Princeton, NJ: Princeton University Press.

Pirinen, Esko (1968) 'Johdatusta mielenosoituksen teoriaan', *Ydin* 2.

'Ranskan opetukset' (1968) *Ydin* 2.

Salkola, Marja-Leena (1985) *Työväenkaartien synty ja kehitys punakaartiksi*, vol. 1. Helsinki: Valtioneuvoston kirjapaino.

Siltala, Juha (1985) *Lapuan liike ja kyyditykset 1930*. Helsinki: Otava.

Soikkanen, Hannu (1961) *Sosialismin tulo Suomeen. Ensimmäisiin yksi-kamarisen eduskunnan vaaleihin asti*. Porvoo and Helsinki: WSOY.

Soikkanen, Hannu (1975) *Kohti kansanvaltaa*, vol. 1. Vaasa: Suomen Sosialidemokraattinen Puolue.

Stenius, Henrik (1977) 'Järjestö-Suomen kehityspiirteitä', in Kuusi, Matti, Alapuro, Risto and Klinge, Matti (eds.) *Maailmankuvan muutos tutkimuskohteena*. Helsinki: Otava.

Stenius, Henrik (1980) 'The breakthrough of the principle of mass organization in Finland', *Scandinavian Journal of History* 5.

Sulkunen, Irma (1986) *Raittius kansalaisuskontona. Raittiusliike ia järjestäytyminen 1870-luvulta suurlakon jälkeisiin vuosiin*. Helsinki: Suomen Historiallinen Seura, Historiallisia tutkimuksia 134.

Suomela, Kalevi (1968) 'Milloin mellakointi on oikeutettua?', *Ydin* 2.

Suppola, Salme (1973) *Suomalainen mielenosoitus*. Helsinki: Oikeusministeriön lainsäädäntöosaston julkaisuja 10.

Taipale, Ilkka (1970) 'Hiljaa – kun osoitatte mieltä', in *Mielenosoitukset ja poliisi 22-26.6.1970*. Helsinki: Otava.

Thaden, Edward C. (1984) *Russia's Western Borderlands, 1710–1870*. Princeton, NJ: Princeton University Press.

Tilly, Charles (1978) *From Mobilization to Revolution*. Reading: Addison-Wesley.

Tilly, Charles (1981) 'Introduction', in Tilly, Louise A. and Tilly, Charles (eds.) *Class Conflict and Collective Action*. Beverly Hills and London: Sage.

Ylikangas, Heikki (1976) *Puukkojunkkareitten esiinmarssi*. Helsinki: Otava.

Ylikangas, Heikki (1979) *Körttiläiset tuomiolla*. Helsinki: Otava.

PER H. JENSEN

Origins of Danish Flexicurity

Introduction

In the 1980s, a central theme in the work of Göran Therborn was how processes, institutions and actors affect the construction and the development direction of the welfare state, which he defined as 'a state in which welfare activities dominate everyday state routine' (Therborn 1984a: 32) and where welfare expenditures are 'the predominant kind of state spending' (Therborn 1984b: 17). He analyzed the trajectories of welfare states using comparative statistical records and praised empirical scholarship. He was very skeptical, however, towards a number of empirical analyses, which he accused of replacing a historically based explanatory logic with a pure correlation logic (Therborn et al. 1979: 3), just as he doubted the claims made in these analyses about how Social Democratic governments have had crucial significance for the development of the welfare state (Therborn et al. 1979: 2). By applying historical time series, he pointed out that the parliamentary hypothesis was an oversimplification of the social realities and that writing history in this manner was akin to 'ideologization'. He insisted that the growth of the welfare state was a highly complex process, which could not be reduced 'to a Social Democratic or, for that matter, any other easy political explanation' (Therborn 1984b: 15).

Therborn's main claim was that the welfare state has deep historical roots and can only be understood in a historical, socio-economic context. While this also means that the cause of an effect can be rather different in different social settings, he argued that, for example, full employment may be an outcome of the success of a politically dominant labor movement but might just as well be an outcome of a conservative concern with order and stability (Therborn 1986: 23f). Nonetheless, Therborn identified class-based collective action as a major determinant of welfare state forms (Therborn 1984a: 17). He emphasized, however, that collective actors do not act in any uniform or predetermined manner; not all labor movements in industrial societies have the same aspirations and worldviews. Rather, the forms, practices and ideology of a given labor movement are developed in a dialectic relationship between class formation and capitalist politics (Therborn 1983). As labor movements differ from one country to another, it is therefore no easy task to assess how much a labor movement in a given country has actually contributed in the making of contemporary welfare states. According to Therborn, such an assessment requires an answer to the questions: 'What did the workers and the workers' movement think and do about the "workers' question?" And what did they demand and fight for?' (Therborn 1984a: 20).

Based on these ideas, this paper seeks to identify the historical origins of the Danish flexicurity model, the main message being that this model is deeply rooted in Danish trade unionism. Analyzing the Danish flexicurity model relates to another central theme nurtured by Therborn in the 1980s: his ambition to explain divergences in the unemployment rates of different countries (Therborn 1986: 16). Thus, the Danish flexicurity model is often associated with the Danish 'employment miracle' in the 1990s (e.g. Madsen 2006), and the question thus becomes: does the Danish flexicurity model represent a (new) strong political and institutional commitment to the goal of full employment (cf. Therborn 1986: 1)?

The paper is divided into four sections. It starts by showing how the Danish flexicurity model has become a Europe-wide point of orientation, especially in EU discourses and the European Employment Strategy. Next, the paper provides a very brief, overall description of the Danish flexicurity model. I then move on to analyze – theoretically and empirically – the historical preconditions for the Danish version of flexicurity. Finally, the paper is rounded off with a summary and discussion.

Danish flexicurity in the European context

As an idea, discourse and concept, the notion of flexicurity emerged in the scientific and political debate in the early/mid-1990s. In the face of Reaganomics and trends toward deregulation, the flexicurity concept holds the claim that social policy can be seen as a 'productive factor' facilitating economic growth (Schmid and Reissert 1991; Auer 2000; Ganssmann 2000; Tros and Wilthagen 2013). As social protection is not an obstacle but rather a means to enhance the flexibility of labor markets, promises are that flexicurity may serve to combine social justice and economic efficiency.

The idea that high levels of social protection and inclusion are compatible with a competitive capitalist market economy ties in with EU policies and strategies, especially the conception of the European Social Model, which is often portrayed as the antidote of the US liberal market economy. Not surprisingly, then, the European Commission adopted flexicurity as a key concept within the European Employment strategy as of 2006–2007 (European Commission 2006, 2007; Keune 2008; Rogowski 2008). It has subsequently been argued that flexicurity has become an 'overreaching vision' and 'flagship policy' in relation to EU reform initiatives (e.g. Bredgaard 2013; Tros and Wilthagen 2013), and flexicurity is even mentioned in the EU 2020 strategy.

From the outset, Denmark (and the Netherlands) functioned as a showcase for flexicurity and its potentials. In the late 1990s, Denmark demonstrated how a generous welfare state and high levels of social cohesion were compatible with strong economic performance, and Denmark became the most prominent example of flexicurity in the EU discourse (e.g. European Commission 2006: 78). Flexicurity, however, has never been easy to define or measure. There is no universal or commonly agreed definition of the phenomenon, just as it blurs the picture that flexicurity – as a multidimensional concept – can assume different forms and variations in outcomes (cf. Wilthagen and Tros 2004).

In 2006, however, the European Council stressed the need to develop common principles on flexicurity as a precondition for a

Europe-wide understanding of flexicurity, the idea behind it and the challenges it is supposed to meet. In effect, the European Commission (2007) defined flexicurity as follows: 'Flexicurity can be defined as an integrated strategy to enhance, at the same time, flexibility and security in the labour market.' This rather broad conceptualization of flexicurity supposedly could be achieved by employing four mutually supportive policy components: (1) flexible and reliable contractual agreements; (2) comprehensive, lifelong learning, (3) effective labor market policies, and (4) modern social security systems. Member states, however, were not expected to copy the full package of flexicurity policies. The European Commission and European Expert Group on Flexicurity (2007) emphasized that there is no single pathway to flexicurity. The four flexicurity components propagated by the EU were supposed to function as a source of inspiration – a type of toolbox – rather than a one-size-fits-all, copy-ready format. Thus, it was left to the member states to adapt and implement flexicurity in accordance with specific national conditions and constrains.

Although member states can choose different pathways and decide for themselves which solutions are most urgent for them, it goes without saying that the Danish flexicurity model from the very start has been looming in the background of the flexicurity discourse. Bredgaard et al. (2008) even argue that EU flexicurity policies are to some degree an imitation of the Danish version of flexicurity.

The Danish flexicurity model

The Danish flexicurity model is founded on a configuration of institutions, often referred to as the 'magic formula' (Sarfati 2003) or the 'golden triangle' (e.g. Madsen 2004; Bredgaard et al. 2008), characterized by (1) very low levels of employment protection, (2) generous unemployment benefits, and (3) active labor market policies. The internal 'logic' of the model is supposedly the following:

– Low levels of employment protection allow employers to hire and fire employees at their discretion, which is expected to foster a flexible labor market, primarily in the form of numerical flexibility, and enhance macroeconomic performance. OECD data substantiates that employment protection in Denmark is rather low (Venn 2009), while EU data (cf. DTI 2008) shows that, among EU countries, Denmark has the highest job mobility levels (after the UK) and the shortest average tenure (after Lithuania, Estonia and Latvia).

– Generous unemployment benefits imply that the social risks of becoming unemployed are marginal. Therefore, workers do not fear or resist getting fired to the same degree, meaning that generous unemployment benefits support the willingness of workers to become subject to various forms of mobility. This has a spillover effect in the sense that generous unemployment benefits support the inclination of trade unions to adapt to changing labor markets and technologies in an offensive rather defensive manner (cf. Schmid and Reissert 1991: 101). Data from 2010, however, shows that unemployment insurance gross replacement rates in Denmark are not particularly generous compared to other EU countries (Esser et al. 2013).

– Unemployed people (whether first-time job seekers or those subject to redundancy) are offered new opportunities and life-prospects in the form of active labor market policies, where the instruments employed are geographical mobility and human capital investments (e.g. training, skill upgrading, LLL). Active labor market policies thus help the unemployed to regain employment, usually with a different company. In effect, the perception of 'employment security' or employability among Danish employees is very high (OECD 2004), which probably owes to the fact that Denmark – without comparison – is the country that spends the most on active labor market policies among all OECD countries (OECD 2013).

The outcome of the combined effect of the three institutional pillars of the 'golden triangle' is supposed to be high degrees of labor market flexibility, income security, employment security and economic growth.

Where did the model come from?

It is commonly agreed that the Danish flexicurity model is preconditioned by corporatist structures, a social dialogue and mutual trust among the social partners, and that the Danish economy has been dominated by small- and medium-sized enterprises, which is not compatible with extensive employment protection regulations (Madsen 2008; Bredgaard 2013). That said, however, there is some measure of disagreement as to the point in time when flexicurity floated to the surface. Some have argued that the origins of flexicurity as a premeditated choice was introduced by the Danish Social Democratic government in 1993 (e.g. Viebrock and Clasen 2009), while others claim that flexicurity is the outcome of a lengthy historical development and that it was established without any preconceived, overall plan (Berg 2008; Madsen 2008); that is, that the different pillars or building blocks were established at different points in time.

This 'gradual development' hypothesis is supported by the fact that high quality unemployment benefits were established in the late 1960s (Klindt and Rasmussen 2015: 129), active labor market policies consolidated in the 1960s and 1970s (Jørgensen 2006: 28f), while low levels of employment protection were established as early as 1899 in connection with the so-called September Compromise. Here, Danish unions officially accepted an employer's right to freely hire and fire in exchange for the employers recognizing the unions' right to organize and accepted unions as a legitimate collective actor and counterpart in collective agreements about wages and work conditions.

Yet the question now becomes whether the finding of when different institutions were established can actually account for or explain the formation of the Danish flexicurity model. It explains

neither why the September Compromise was settled nor why generous unemployment benefits and active labor market policies were
institutionalized; even less so why social trust and dialogues among
social partners are a predominant feature of the Danish system of
industrial relations or that the system has gained legitimacy and loyalty among Danish employees.

It can largely be argued that the Danish flexicurity model is a 'mir-
ror image' of the Danish Social Democratic labor movement (e.g.
Anderson 1966: 34). Social Democracy is hostile neither to market
economies nor capitalism (Przeworski 1985). Under the banner of
parliamentary reformism, the belief is that living conditions can be
improved by improving the functioning of markets (e.g. Olofsson
1979). Thus, contrary to the argument put forward by Esping-
Andersen (1990), social democracy is not about anti-market policies.
Rather, Social Democracy is about 'politics along the market', an idea
that fits nicely into the flexicurity mechanism, which is both supportive to market dynamics and social security.

Historically, the social democratic worldview has hardly been
challenged by ideological rivalry or competing political wings of the
labor movement. The Danish social democratic labor movement has
performed as a unified whole, and there has been a strong degree
of coordination between the Social Democratic Party and the trade
union movement. The degree of unionization has been very high
(e.g. OECD 2004), and there has been a high degree of unity within
the trade union itself. Most importantly, the trade union movement
has historically been organized along craft principles, which are
highly supportive to flexicurity ideologies.

The morphology of Danish trade unions
– and how they are linked to flexicurity

A central theme in the industrial relations tradition has been to
examine the policy implications of the organizational structure of
unions. It has thus been hypothesized that there is a link between
the organizational properties of a trade union and the policies it will
adopt or sustain (Clegg 1970; Visser 1987). A distinction is usually
drawn between geographical, general, industrial and craft unionism

(Cole 1918; Turner 1962; Beyme 1980; Cella and Treu 1987). Although pure forms of unions are hard to find, the Danish trade union movement has historically resembled craft unionism very closely (Galenson 1955). It will therefore be discussed how (Danish) craft unionism relates to flexicurity in a totally different way than, for example, industrial unionism. Figure 1 shows how craft and industrial unionism ideal typically position themselves in the labor market, and it will be shown how the two types of organizations embody different types of solidarity and aspirations towards the regulatory order of labor markets.

Figure 1

Qualifications/wages

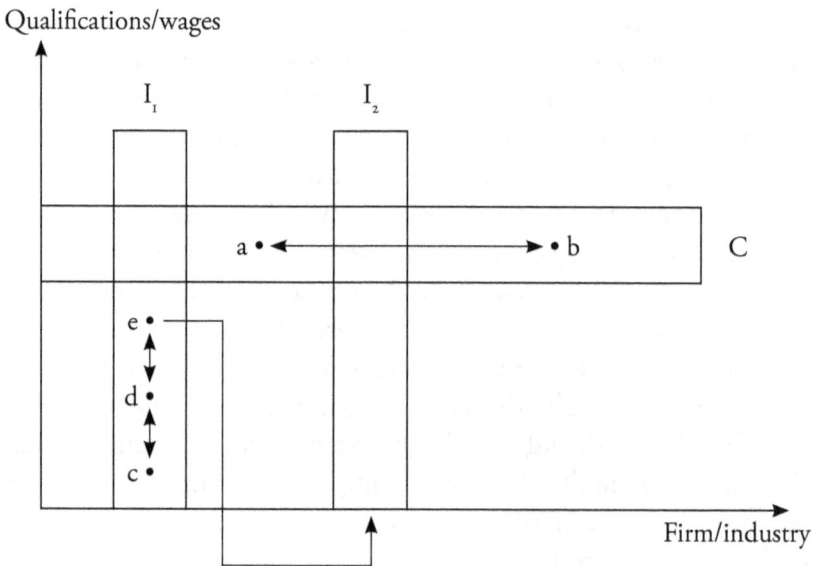

Firm/industry

Solidarity within craft unions is based on the common training of apprentices and distinct vocational qualifications, meaning that all workers with the same type of qualifications are organized in the same trade union. In effect, craft unions establish themselves across employers and industrial boundaries; that is, they are horizontal in nature. In Denmark, for instance, carpenters, bakers, painters etc. have historically been organized in different unions, while the lower, unskilled strata of the working class (at the bottom of the hierarchy) have had their own union for unskilled workers. As the craft market is horizontally organized (Figure 1: C), craft workers are horizontally mobile. An employer can discharge a person from a specific job but not from the market (Figure 1: a to b). The worker enjoys their employment security or employability (as in the flexicurity system), not from the individual employer but from his skill, the competitive supply of which is controlled by his union; and he is known as a carpenter and not as an employee of a certain company (Kerr 1954: 98).

Consequently, craft unions are only marginally preoccupied with any form of employment protection. As such, the first pillar in the golden triangle, that being low levels of employment protection, is fully compatible with craft unionism.

The so-called September Compromise was reached in 1899. It meant that the employers partly recognized the right of the workers to organize themselves in trade unions, partly recognized the trade unions as negotiation and agreement partners. In turn, the trade unions recognized the right of the employers to manage and distribute work. Compared to other countries, the Danish employers were among the first to accept trade unions and collective agreements (Therborn et al. 1979).

A special feature of craft unions is that they are extremely preoccupied with the relative status of their members in the qualification and wage structure rather than with the wage levels in general (Turner 1962: 250), and unemployment within a given craft may seriously pose a threat to this ambition. That is, insignificant unemployment is a precondition for craft unionism to retain the relative status of members in the wage structure. To this end, craft unions have tried to maintain or enhance their scarcity, and thus their reward power, by various institutional means (cf. Parkin 1971: 21). Historically, such institutions have been:

First, craft unions have tried to establish restrictions on entry into the occupation to which the union confines itself by limiting the intake of new apprentices. Danish unions have never fully succeeded in this endeavor. Nonetheless, as craft unionism is based on the apprenticeship system and since employment security derives from the skill of the individual worker, one might expect craft unions to be highly attentive to the skills of their members and maintaining their qualifications. One might therefore argue that craft unions are inclined to adapt or sustain active labor market policies in the form of training, skill upgrading and LLL, which may help keep workers (with outdated skills) within the occupation.

The Danish labor market education programs have roots that date all the way back to the mid-19th century, when municipal-based craft associations provided a supporting function for the crafts training programs by offering courses in reading, writing, arithmetic and drawing. A circular from the Ministry of the Interior from 1862 encouraged the creation of this type of educational activity, which developed into that which came to be known as technical schools. In the 1870s, these schools were included in the annual budget appropriations, and public oversight with the technical schools was introduced in the 1880s. The technical schools were further consolidated in the period 1930–57, where practical workshop instruction was introduced in many technical schools, resulting in an actual 'apprentice law' in 1956 with unconditional compulsory education for apprentices (cf. Rasmussen nd.). In the early 1930s, the technical schools were also opened up to unskilled laborers. The national confederation of unions for unskilled workers had a hand in this initiative, and this activity grew in scope, particularly in the course of the 1950s, which led to the creation of a commission in 1957 that was tasked with analyzing the need for education and continued education among unskilled workers. This led to legislation on vocational training for unskilled workers in 1960 (Pedersen et al. 2012). These education programs were aimed at unemployed and employed adult workers alike, and the vocational education programs were tailored to the specific needs of Danish companies; some of the larger companies had their own business schools. Passage of the law on vocational training in 1960 created a formal and economic framework for the formation of a national school structure for skilled and unskilled workers. The state assumed most of the financial responsibility, while the social partners played a key role in and took responsibility for the continued development and management of the content in the vocational education programs.

Second, craft markets are horizontally organized and there is an imperative among craft unions to develop highly sophisticated knowledge and insight into job opportunities within the given craft market, which in the event of frictional or structural unemployment may cause unions to stimulate horizontal mobility; that is, movements from areas of unemployment to areas where there is a shortage of skilled workers – a phenomenon that has often been institutionalized and implemented by means of union-run employment services. This also indicates that craft unions may be inclined to adapt or sustain active labor market policies in the form of geographical mobility.

Craft unions in Denmark started to establish craft-specific employment agencies in the beginning of the 1880s in order to obtain insight into job opportunities, control the labor supply, and reduce unemployment by stimulating geographical mobility. The trade unions for unskilled workers were not able to establish employment agencies, but a public employment agency was established in 1913, which primarily served unskilled workers. This meant that until 1968, there were two-tier employment services: a public system serving the unskilled workers and a private, craft union-based system serving skilled workers. In 1968, the state assumed responsibility for employment services in Denmark, meaning that the union-organized employment agencies were taken over by the state.

Third, if unemployment should occur on a larger scale, unemployment benefits are conceived by craft unions to 'help hold workers available for openings in the same craft' (Kerr 1954). Otherwise, these workers would risk being expelled from the labor market or function as sweaters. As such, unemployment benefits may function as a means for preserving members' status and qualifications during periods of unemployment and as a means of maintaining solidarity concerning the relative wage level. Not surprisingly, then, craft unions have been frontrunners in the formation of union-run unemployment funds, and craft unions have historically fought for state subsidies for union-run unemployment funds (i.e. the Ghent system) in order to improve benefit levels (Jensen 2007). Thus, it can hardly be questioned that craft unions are inclined to adapt or sustain generous unemployment benefits.

The first craft union-run unemployment funds in Denmark emerged in the 1880s. In 1905, union density was very high compared to other countries – about half of all employees were union members (cf. Therborn et al. 1979: 9), and about 32 per cent of all union members were covered by union-run unemployment funds in 1906 (Jensen 2007). To improve the coverage and quality of unemployment benefits, as off the mid-1890s unions started to fight for state subsidies to union-run unemployment funds. Here, the Social Democratic Party supported the unions, and the Ghent model was established in Denmark in 1907. The formation of the Danish Ghent system was preconditioned by that which Therborn (1984a: 11) calls the 'crucial constitutive movement'; that is, a point in time where a unified party had been established and trade-union organizations had the same territorial range as the state authority.

The evidence thus far points in the direction of a structural homology between craft unionism and flexicurity. All of the components in flexicurity are embedded in craft unionism. A structural homology, however, does not refer to there being identity between the two phenomena; rather, it refers to how craft unionism and Danish flexicurity are organized along the same principles. This will become clearer when craft unionism is confronted with the rationalities of industrial unionism.

Industrial unions seek to recruit all of the workers within the same plant, company or industry, irrespective of the degree of skill which they possess (Figure 1: I(1) and I(2)). Historically, industrial unionism has developed in countries with no formal apprenticeship system. Qualifications among employees have been acquired by means of on-the-job-training, internal training or re-training. In effect, workers are tied to the plant and movements within the internal plant market are vertical, implying that labor is recruited for each occupation vertically from a lower grade in the same company (Turner 1962: 244f) (Figure 1: c, d, e). Industrial unions are therefore attentive to (solidarity) principles according to which workers move up the job ladder, and they work to ensure that jobs are filled in accordance with seniority rights (Kerr 1954).

As the qualifications of employees are particular to a specific company or industry – and not transferable to other industries (Hughes 1967) – unemployment among workers who have climbed up the job ladder would be a catastrophe. Unemployment in vertical markets thus separates the man from the market (Kerr 1954), as they would have to start at the bottom of the job ladder in a different company (see Figure 1: I(1) to I(2)). Workers in industrial unions therefore agree on lay-offs or firings being regulated according to institutional rules for dismissals, such as the 'first in, last out' principle. This kind of employment protection may be supported by redundancy arrangements, as seniority-based redundancy payments penalize arbitrary dismissals. This type of employment protection tends to concentrate unemployment on new entrants, while most of the employees with seniority are secured employment by the specific employer. In some cases, however, employment protection rules have established that laid-off workers may be re-engaged in order of seniority (Turner 1962) if the company should recover its lost employment opportunities.

In most countries where industrial unionism prevails, employment protection is a major regulatory order of labor markets. In the Scandinavian countries, Norway has a lengthy historical tradition for industrial unionism and employment protection. In Sweden, the trade union movement began to orient itself towards employment protection regulations in the 1960s, first with collective bargaining in 1964 and later through legislation in 1974. The increased focus in Sweden on employment protection reflects a number of fundamental decisions about converting to industrial union principles (first decided at the confederation of trade union congress in 1906), which were basically realized in the 1960s/70s (Elvander 1980: 170; Nordin 1980: 42).

Industrial unions are only moderately attentive to the quality of unemployment benefits; partly because only a small fraction – and only the lower echelons – of members risk unemployment; and partly because there is a very weak, unclear link between unions and the 'outside' group of unemployed people. Unemployed people are potential job seekers in all industries or companies. It is first when they actually get a job (at the bottom of the job ladder in a given company) that it becomes clear to which industrial union they belong. In countries where industrial unions prevail, such as Germany, unemployed people have until recently been excluded from unions.

Conclusion

The Danish flexicurity model, combining dynamic labor markets and social security, has been singled out as a model worth emulating on a Europe-wide scale due to its excellent economic performance. Some scholars hold that the Danish flexicurity model is an outcome of new ideas and new insights implemented by a creative and insightful Social Democratic government as of 1993. However, such 'ideologization'-based explanations do not hold water. In practice, the Danish flexicurity model has deep historical roots. Danish flexicurity is embedded in specific forms of solidarity and can largely be attributed to specific properties of Danish labor organizations and the Danish system of industrial relations. Especially craft unionism, which has been predominant in Denmark, is closely associated with flexicurity. Within the framework of the three legs in the so-called golden triangle, one might thus argue that craft unions are (1) inattentive to employment protection, are (2) likely to adapt or sustain active labor market policies, and (3) are paying attention to the quality of unemployment benefits. The question then becomes whether flexicurity – as an export article – is attainable or adaptable in countries that are overwhelmingly marked by industrial unionism (with its strong focus on employment protection). That is, craft unionism is an institutional pre-condition for (the Danish version of) flexicurity.

Danish scholars studying flexicurity generally agree that all three of the institutional pillars of flexicurity fully matured in the 1960s, which casts doubt on the connection between flexicurity and

Danish macro-economic performance. Although the Danish flexicurity model was fully functioning as of the late 1960s, Denmark experienced a lengthy period of sustained unemployment from the mid-1970s until the mid-1990s. Thus, many other factors beyond the flexicurity system have possibly driven the employment miracle in the 1990s, where unemployment declined from more than 12 per cent to about 5 per cent between 1993 and 2001. Andersen (2011: 113), for instance, mentions that Danish exports were booming, stimulated by German unification, and that oil became an important factor in the Danish economy in the 1990s. As of around 2000, Denmark became the only net exporter of oil in the EU. As opposed to Norway, the Danish oil money was not accumulated in an oil fund, used instead for public spending; that is, a sort of Keynesian, demand-side policy. This coincides with Therborn's basic findings, who has argued that 'countries successful in the sphere of employment have all pursued expansive Keynesian-type policies' (Therborn 1986: 1).

References

Andersen, J.G. (2011) 'From the edge of the abyss to bonanza – and beyond: Danish economy and economic policies 1980–2011', *Comparative Social Research*, 28, pp. 89–165.

Anderson, P. (1966) 'Origins of the present crisis', in Anderson, P. and Blackburn, R. (eds.) *Towards Socialism*. Ithaca: Cornell University Press, pp. 11–52.

Auer, P. (2000) *Employment Revival in Europe: Labour Market Success in Austria, Denmark, Ireland and the Netherlands*. Geneva: ILO.

Berg, A. van den (2008) *Flexicurity: Theory, Practice or Rhetoric?* Paper presented at the 25th Anniversary Conference of the Centre for Labour Market Reseach (CARMA) at Aalborg University, 9–10 October.

Beyme, K.von (1980) *Challenge to Power: Trade Unions and Industrial Relations in Capitalist Countries*. London: Sage.

Bredgaard, T. (2013) 'Flexibility and security in employment regulation: Learning from Denmark', in Stone, K.V.W. and Arthurs, H. (eds.) *Rethinking Workplace Regulation: Beyond the Standard Contract of Employment*. New York: Russell Sage Foundation, pp. 213–233.

Bredgaard, T., Larsen, F. and Madsen, P.K. (2008) 'Flexicurity: In pursuit of a moving target', *European Journal of Social Security*, 10, 4, pp. 305–323.

Cella, G. and Treu, T. (1987) 'National trade union movements', in Blanpain, R. (ed.) *Comparative Labour Law and Industrial Relations*. Deventer: Kluwer, pp. 197–228.

Clegg, H.A. (1970) *The System of Industrial Relations in Great Britain*. Oxford: Blackwell.

Cole, G.D.H. (1918) *An Introduction to Trade Unionism*. London: George Allen and Unwin.

DTI (Danish Technological Institute) (2008) *Job Mobility in the European Union: Optimising Its Social and Economic Benefits*. The report was prepared under contract to the European Commission, Directorate General for Employment, Social Affairs and Equal Opportunities in response to tender no. VT/2006/043.

Elvander, N. (1980) *Skandinavisk arbetarrörelse*. Stockholm: LiberFörlag.

Esping-Andersen, G. (1990) *The Three Worlds of Welfare Capitalism*. Cambridge: Polity Press.

Esser, I., Ferrarini, T., Nelson, K., Palme, J. and Sjöberg, O. (2013) *Unemployment Benefits in EU Member States*. European Commission: Employment, Social Affairs & Inclusion.

European Commission (2006) *Employment in Europe 2006*. Luxembourg: Office for Official Publications of the European Communities.

European Commission (2007) *Towards Common Principles of Flexicurity: More and Better Jobs Through Flexibility and Security*. Luxembourg: Office for Official Publications of the European Communities.

European Expert Group on Flexicurity (2007) *Flexicurity Pathways: Turning Hurdles into Stepping Stones*. Brussels.

Galenson, W. (1955) *Arbejder og arbejdsgiver i Danmark*. Copenhagen: Det danske forlag.

Ganssmann, H. (2000) 'Labor market flexibility, social protection and unemployment', *European Societies*, 2, 3, pp. 243–269.

Hughes, J. (1967) *Trade Union Structure and Government. Part One: Structure and Development*. London: HMSO (Research Papers 5(1), Royal Commission on Trade Unions and employers' Associations).

Jensen, P.H. (2007) 'Grundlæggelse af det danske arbejdsløshedsforsikringssystem i komparativ belysning', in Pedersen, J.H. and Huulgaard, A. (eds.) *Arbejdsløshedsforsikringsloven: 1907–2007*. Copenhagen: Arbejdsdirektoratet.

Jørgensen, H. (2006) *Arbejdsmarkedspolitikken fornyelse – innovation eller trussel mod dansk 'Flexicurity'*. Copenhagen: LO & FTF.

Kerr, C. (1954) 'The Balkanization of labor markets', in Bakke, E.W., Hauser, P.M., Palmer, G.L., Myers, C.A., Yoder, D. and Kerr, C. (eds.) *Labor Mobility and Economic Opportunity*. New York: John Wiley & Sons, pp. 92–110.

Keune, M. (2008) 'Flexicurity: A contested concept at the core of the European labour market debate', *Intereconomics*, March–April, pp. 92–98.

Klindt, M.P. and Rasmussen, S. (2015) 'Indkomstsikkerhed', in Bredgaard, T. and Madsen, P.H. (eds.) *Dansk Flexicurity*. Copenhagen: Hans Reitzel Publishing, pp. 125–156.

Madsen, P.H. (2006) 'How can it possibly fly?: The paradox of a dynamic labour market in a Scandinavian state', in Campbell, J.A., Hall, J.A. and Pedersen, O.K. (ed.) *National Identity and the Varieties of Capitalism: The Danish Experience*. Montreal: McGill-Queen's University Press, pp. 321–355.

Madsen, P.K. (2004) 'The Danish model of "flexicurity": Experiences and lessons', *Transfer*, 10, 2, pp. 187–216.

Madsen, P.K. (2008) 'The Danish road to "flexicurity": Where are we compared to others? And how did we get there?', in Muffels, R. (ed.) *Flexibility and Employment Security in Europe: Labour Markets in Transition*. Cheltenham: Edward Elgar, pp. 341–362.

Nordin, R. (1980) *Den svenska arbetarrörelsen*. Stockholm: Tiden.

OECD (2004) *Economic Outlook*. Paris: OECD.

OECD (2013) *Public Expenditure on Active Labour Market Policies*. DOI: 10.1787/20752342-table9.

Olofsson, G. (1979) *Mellan klass och stat: Om arbetarrörelse, reformism och socialdemokrati*. Lund: Arkiv förlag.

Parkin, F. (1971) *Class Inequality and Political Order*. London: MacGibbon & Kee.

Pedersen, V.H., Andersen, S. and Lassen, M. (2012) *En fortælling om AMU*. Aalborg: Aalborg University Press.

Przeworski, A. (1985) *Capitalism and Social Democracy*. Cambridge: Cambridge University Press.

Rasmussen, W. (nd.) *De tekniske skolers historie*. Available at: http://www.uddannelseshistorie.dk/images/pdfer/a-1969-werner-rasmussen.pdf.

Rogowski, R. (2008) 'Governance of the European social model: The case of flexicurity', *Intereconomics*, March–April, pp. 82–91.

Sarfarti, H. (2003) 'Welfare and labour market reforms: A new framework for social dialogue and collective bargaining?', *European Journal of Industrial Relations*, 9, 3, pp. 265–282.

Schmid, G. and Reissert, B. (1991) 'On the institutional conditions of effective labour market policies', in Matzner, E. and Streeck, W. (eds.) *Beyond Keynesianism: The Socio-Economics of Production and Full Employment*. Aldershot: Edward Elgar, pp. 81–110.

Therborn, G. (1983) 'Why some classes are more successful than others', *New Left Review* 138.

Therborn, G. (1984a) 'Classes and states: Welfare state developments, 1881–1981', *Studies in Political Economy*, 14, pp. 7–41.

Therborn, G. (1984b) 'The prospects of labour and the transformation of advanced capitalism', *New Left Review* 145.

Therborn, G. (1986) *Why Some Peoples Are More Unemployed Than Others.* London: Verso.

Therborn, G., Kjellberg, A., Marklund, S. and Öhlund, U. (1979) 'Sverige före och efter socialdemokratin: en första översikt', *Arkiv för studier i arbetar-rörelsens historia*, 15–16, pp. 1–39.

Tros, F. and Wilthagen, T. (2013) 'Flexicurity – concepts, practices, and outcomes', in Greve, B. (ed.) *The Routledge Handbook of the Welfare State.* London: Routledge, pp. 125–135.

Turner, H.A. (1962) *Trade Union Growth, Structure and Policy.* London: George Allen & Unwin.

Venn, D. (2009) *Legislation, Collective Bargaining and Enforcement: Updating the OECD Employment Protection Indicators.* Paris: OECD Social, Employment and Migration Working Papers, no. 89.

Viebrock, E. and Clasen, J. (2009) *Flexicurity: A State-of-the-Art Review.* Recwowe, REC-WP 01/2009.

Visser, J. (1987) *In Search of Inclusive Unionism.* University of Amsterdam: Academisch Proefschrift.

Wilthagen, T. and Tros, F. (2004) 'The concept of "flexicurity": A new approach to regulating employment and labour markets', *Transfer*, 10, pp. 166–186.

ROBIN BLACKBURN

From Miliband to Corbyn

British Labour Struggles to Reinvent Itself

The Labour governments of Tony Blair and Gordon Brown promoted financial deregulation, bailed out the banks, and abetted US military aggression. Faced with global distempers they endorsed NATO and the IMF and ignored the crisis of the Ukanian state. The Conservatives endorsed these policies in opposition and government in the years after 2010. Approaches that seemed successful at first gradually unraveled, destroying trust in politicians and pushing party leaders to search for greater legitimacy. Labour Party members were all given an equal say in choosing the leader. After Labour's defeat in 2015 the new method of choosing its leader unexpectedly allowed a radical socialist, Jeremy Corbyn, to emerge victorious in the leadership contest which followed in September 2015.

Surprises for the Conservatives soon followed. In a move motivated by internal party management David Cameron, the Conservative leader, offered 'Euro-sceptic' Conservative Members of Parliament the promise of an 'in/out' referendum on British membership of the European Union. The Tory leader delayed at first but eventually made good on his referendum pledge in June 2016. The result was a historic defeat for his 'Remain' grouping. The Leave victory was narrow – 52 per cent to 48 per cent – but, as set up, enough to remove Britain from the European Union after four decades of membership. It did not take long to show just how disruptive this defeat was to the United Kingdom and its ruling class. Göran Therborn has always insisted that class interests are a poor guide to class behaviour and this is a spectacular case in point (Therborn 1978). What I aim to do in what follows is to re-examine the causes and consequences of these two unexpected outcomes – Labour's left turn and the UK's vote to break with the EU – focusing on Labour to begin with and then turning to the awesome train-wreck that is today's UK politics, its competing narratives and contradictory structures.

The Corbyn opportunity

Following Labour's general election defeat in May 2015 the membership of Britain's Labour Party elected as its Leader Jeremy Corbyn, a man branded a dangerous socialist and pacifist. The national press warned that Labour was now unelectable but was nevertheless panicked by the thought of Corbyn as Premier.

The new leader was certainly a break with the past. Previous Labour governments helped to found NATO and acted as cheerleaders for US foreign policy. In the era of Tony Blair 'New Labour' repudiated the welfare state and embraced the market. With election of Corbyn the party's members and supporters opted for a fresh start. For the first time the leader was elected by the OMOV principle – 'One Member One Vote' rather than fancy franchises which gave Members of Parliament and trade union bosses the determining say. The new system helped to produce a surge in membership, lending the result even greater significance. Labour became the country's largest party and Jeremy Corby emerged as the winner with more votes than his opponents put together. He was now the official Leader of Her Majesty's Opposition, with an office, staff, chauffeured limo and the right to question the Prime Minister every week that parliament is in session.

Corbyn, the new leader, was not a demagogue but a softly-spoken and quite charming individual who is thoughtful in utterance and studiously polite to opponents. His convincing victory – he won quarter of a million votes out of just over 400 000 – was a striking repudiation of Tony Blair and 'New Labour', with its foreign wars and 'Tory lite' domestic policies. The 66 year old Corbyn was faithful to the old time religion of Labourite socialism but also a contemporary figure who rides a bicycle, tends a garden allotment and insists that half of his Shadow Cabinet are women.

Corbyn ran a well-organized campaign that made adroit use of social media and came up with interesting new ideas once or twice a week. It was impressive to see how the Corbyn campaign withstood repeated attacks from the Labour 'grandees' and the mass media. There were scurrilous attempts to portray this tireless peace campaigner as a stooge of terrorists. Repeated broadsides from Blair and Lord Mandelson seemed only to convince Corbyn supporters that they were making the right choice.

To compare Corbyn with Donald Trump, as some have done, is egregiously wrong but his message and persona have certain undeniable parallels with Bernie Sanders, with the difference that he has been more sharply critical of Western military policy and that he eventually won the leadership of his party. Corbyn's support, like that of Sanders, came from popular hostility to the banks and austerity. Like Sanders, Corbyn is trying to reform an existing political apparatus rather than to set up a new political vehicle as Syriza has done in Greece or Podemos in Spain. Putting new wine in an old bottle is not recommended.

The next British general election is scheduled for 2020 and the new prime minister would find it difficult and risky to bring if forward. The electorate is still very unimpressed by the political class and will expect some progress on Brexit before another poll. Labour in opposition has the opportunity to remake itself – over years not weeks or months. Jeremy Corbyn needed time to reform his party, to elaborate a coherent develop a transformative programme or to reach out to potential allies. He had real legitimacy because of the size of his win and because it was owed in part to a massive influx of new party members and supporters, young and old, who crowded to his rallies and greeted hum with the cry 'Jez We Can!'

But any hope that the Labour party in parliament, the PLP, would welcome change was soon dispelled. From the outset the Blairite hard core of the PLP defied the new leader's mandate, some of them refusing to take posts in the Shadow Cabinet, others demanding a series of debilitating compromises on key issues of domestic, foreign and defence policy. Within less than a year Corbyn faced a leadership challenge. It was a sign of Corbyn's comparative success that his challengers chose not to focus criticism on his policies, instead claiming that he lacked the personal charisma needed to beat the Tories.

Britain's famously unwritten constitution gives little recognition to party organization outside parliament. In prior epochs the Labour Leader and Shadow Cabinet were chosen by the MPs alone, or by an electoral college in which the votes of party members were swamped by affiliated trade unions. The leader was ex officio chairman of the National Executive and was expected to have the final say in how the party's policies were to be presented in parliament. The party conference and its so-called 'Policy Forums' were still not selected by means of OMOV. But with Corbyn's election and an influx of about two hundred thousand new members, the PLP began to assert its autonomy and to frustrate Corbyn in every way it could.

Corbyn has been a dogged exponent of socialist politics within an unwelcoming party context so was well prepared – perhaps too well prepared – for factional trench warfare. I say possibly too well-prepared because some of his supporters were over-focused on tactical issues and lacked a long-term perspective. Given the outsider's unexpected victory some gaps were understandable. In his first months as leader Corbyn contented himself with compromises which he thought strengthened position and promoted party renewal. In the months from his election to the EU referendum in June 2016 Corbyn won some small-scale victories against the government and Labour did better than expected in the May 2016 local elections. In four bye elections caused by the death or resignation of MPs the Labour candidates increased the party's vote and showed a swing that, if repeated nationwide, would put Corbyn in Downing Street. In the Commons the Opposition leader put the prime minister on the defensive over steel plant closures and cuts to the pensions of the disabled. Nevertheless Corbyn's parliamentary enemies were a constant distraction, waiting for the opportunity to strike. That came in June 2016 following the shocking defeat of Remain in the referendum on EU membership. Half the members of the Shadow Cabinet resigned claiming that Corby's half-hearted support for Remain was responsible the Leave victory and he should resign too. Corbyn had spoken at over a hundred Remain meetings but refused to share a platform with Cameron and did not hide his criticisms of the EU Commission and of the ill-prepared consultation itself.

Surprisingly neither Cameron nor Corbyn addressed a structural flaw in the process, namely that the different components of the 'United Kingdom' might give different answers to the question – as they did. While England and Wales voted Remain, Scotland and Northern Ireland voted Leave. It also became clear that the government had failed to make contingency plans for a Leave win.

But before examining the crisis unleashed by the victory of Brexit, and the struggle between Corbyn and his opponents, I will sketch the run-up to Corbyn's victory and the help which he received from his predecessor, as Leader, Edward Miliband.

Labour in opposition in 2010–15

Labour's roller coaster began with the election of 2010, an even worse defeat – after twelve years in power – than 2015. On that occasion Gordon Brown, co-founder of 'New Labour', resigned as Leader leaving two brothers, David and Edward Miliband, to slug it out for the top spot. David Miliband was the chosen candidate of Tony Blair's wing of 'New Labour' while Edward Miliband, his younger brother, decided that the shift to a new generation needed to register the debacle of the Iraq war and of the Labour government's disastrous love affair with the financial sector, before, during and after the 2008 crash. Edward Miliband's critique was muted – he was himself a former close associate of, and adviser to, Gordon Brown, Blair's partner and successor.

Edward Miliband won the 2010 leadership contest by a wafer thin margin. The spectacle of two brothers battling it out for the top job was lent added piquancy by the fact that their father, Ralph Miliband, had been Britain's leading political scientist, a Marxist, and author of a highly critical study of the Labour Party, entitled *Parliamentary Socialism* (1961). Ralph died in 1994 but the political evolution of his two sons seems like the continuation of an argument in which mutual respect did not prevent deep differences. At all events Edward's decision to challenge his brother, with the pain that this was bound to entail, could only be justified if some major principle was at stake. The younger Miliband's claim was that Labour needed to distance itself from 'New Labour'. In his first years as leader Ed Miliband made some real headway but the attempt faltered and eventually failed.

The younger Miliband's successes and failures are still worth studying because Miliband at least began the work of furnishing Labour with a different narrative. He spoke about the ravages of 'predatory capitalism' and introduced a momentous new method of electing the party leader – one which at last empowered each member with an equal vote. These changes gave Corbyn and his supporters the opportunity they needed.

Ed Miliband's had some success in escaping the limits of Opposition and in formulating new lines of attack on the Conservative-led coalition government. Renewal began while he was leader, with a surge in party membership. Labour seemed competitive but it all went horribly wrong in the run up to the election. Nobody is more passé than a recently defeated politician, with close colleagues queuing up to disavow him. Miliband made many mistakes but he also strove to wrench his party away from the disastrous New Labour model, a daunting and difficult task. Miliband could not shake off the grip of rightwing leadership cabal, that was dedicated to Blair's foreign policy and Brown's subservience to the banks. By immediately resigning as Leader on the day of defeat Miliband plunged Labour into a contest held using the new, more democratic system, and at a time when the right had no convincing candidate to propose.

While Miliband was no doubt as surprised as anyone else by the scope of the Corbyn insurgency his own actions as leader helped to produce it, partly, to be sure, in reaction to his timidity and mistakes, but also in some more positive ways too, including a leadership contest that was awkward and unpredictable, as democracy often is. As well as acquiring an unexpected new leader Labour doubled its membership and registered supporters to make it Britain's largest political party. I will start with Ed Miliband's legacy, and the results of the election, before exploring the Corbyn phenomenon and the state of UK politics.

Miliband's early coups

Miliband and Corbyn, we should be aware, inherited a difficult role. The enmity of the tabloids is one thing but the hostility of their own colleagues was even more damaging. Miliband was far less radical than Corbyn but still had endless trouble with the PLP (Parliamentary Labour Party) which was still dominated by Blairites and Brownites who were alarmed when Miliband modestly challenged consensus politics.

Most of the time British Oppositions find themselves responding to the government, and to events. Miliband in his first two or three years sometimes managed to set an agenda which his opponents could not ignore. In 2011 he supported a back-bench attempt to rein in the Murdoch empire by reducing and separating its TV and press holdings. News International was mired in the phone-hacking scandal. By supporting this back-bench initiative Ed broke with the rotten New Labour tradition of toadying to Murdoch. Cameron was thereby also forced to drop his opposition to the measure or be exposed as a servile Murdoch minion. Miliband had not initiated the campaign but he had backed it at the critical moment. Such defeats for Murdoch are few and far between.

Ed Miliband scored a different sort of success when he used his leader's speech at the Labour Party's 2011 conference to attack the energy companies for exorbitant price rises. They aggravated what he called the 'cost of living crisis'. He urged the government to introduce an electricity price freeze. By now many millions were suffering from the government's swinging austerity programme, with average take-home pay lagging inflation down to the most recent times. Miliband's phrase established an effective and enduring concept and talking point. And for what it was worth the opinion polls registered a modest but steady Labour lead.

Ed Miliband also reached for a broader theme when he drew a sharp contrast between 'predatory capitalism' and 'productive' capitalism, with hedge funds in the former category, and responsible and regulated suppliers of needed products and services in the later. He called for taxes on the wealthy and the removal of the hedge funds' exemption from stamp duty. These measures would furnish timely resources for the NHS. *The Economist* later explained that it could not endorse Labour despite its valuable support for EU membership. The reason? 'Labour's leader wants to remake British capitalism in favour of a fairer society' (*The Economist*, 2 May 2015).

Ed Miliband's concept of 'predatory capitalism' was somewhat reminiscent of his father's notion of 'class war conservatism' (as outlined by Ralph Miliband in his book of that name, recently reissued by Verso: Miliband 2015 [1983]). The concepts are different but complementary. The former targets wasteful and unsustainable practices as well as economic exploitation. On the other hand the elder Miliband would warn that capitalism would find spaces – such as tax havens – hidden from the regulators. Nevertheless both approaches highlight the dangers of capitalism unleashed.

By 2013 there was a vociferous transatlantic campaign in favour of Western military intervention to overthrow Assad, the Syrian dictator. Ed Miliband was wary of a cause backed by so many of the authors of the Iraq War. Some back-bench Conservatives and Liberal Democrats were equally concerned. The Labour leader was prepared to listen to the government's case but, to the surprise of friend and foe alike, he eventually urged all his Ps to oppose a motion licensing military action. The government motion was defeated and this had immediate repercussions in Washington. The White House had been agitating for an invasion to oust Assad but now changed its tune, and declined to ask Congress for backing for such a move. The vote in the British parliament had helped the doves check the hawks. For a British opposition leader to have such an impact is rare indeed. In this case it allowed for diplomacy (concerted with Moscow) to destroy Syria's chemical weapons. According to an editorial in the *Financial Times* of 2 July 2015 David Cameron regarded this defeat as the worst moment of his premiership.

The Labour leader's string of coups led the Commons Press Lobby to award him the title of Parliamentarian of the Year in 2013. Coalition leaders were sore but it was fellow Labourites who were most alarmed. Former Labour Cabinet ministers began musing in public that Ed was disloyal to our allies and flirting with populism.

We may wonder whether veiled or coded Blairite threats in public, were supplemented by more brutal warnings in private.

Miliband appeases

Miliband knew how important it was to enter the election with a united party. He was determined to avoid the public divisions that had done so much damage to Labour in the eighties and the Conservatives in the nineties. Ed Miliband was anyway proud of the civility that he always strove to promote, notwithstanding the fact that the Shadow Cabinet was composed almost exclusively of former Blairites or Brownites. We will surely learn more when the memoirs are written, but the Labour leader did not startle with any new coups and he reached for more emollient language as the election hove into sight. The Labour Leader's stance on Syria was to prove quite exceptional. He had earlier backed Western airstrikes on Libya and the ouster of Gaddafi. Also endorsed were British engagement – and disengagement – in Afghanistan; in 2014 Miliband backed US and British airstrikes in Iraq which caused much mayhem without defeating ISIS. Nevertheless Cameron remained furious at his defeat over the Syria motion and continued to press lifting the ban, albeit that the enemy has changed – it was now ISIS, not Assad. Indeed Assad was now an ally.

Miliband's domestic options were sometimes equally compromising. Scottish Labour, a bastion of machine politics, was allowed a virtually free hand, after complaints that it was treated as a branch office. Such a belated move did nothing to ward off the verdict of the Scottish voters. The SNP urged the scrapping of the Trident nuclear submarine programme. The Lib Dems' stance signalled a willingness to negotiate when it mooted a reduction of the number of nuclear subs from four to three.

Ending the whole programme would release huge funds – £90 billion over ten years – to spend elsewhere. But Miliband was adamantly opposed. Labour's internal policy-police were content. Unilateral nuclear disarmament had long been a signature issue for the Labour Left. But the leader's stance against it was virtually uncontested. There were a few courageous mavericks in the PLP, like Jeremy Corbyn, but not a visible and vocal leftwing grass roots movement such as had animated Labour in the days of Nye Bevan, Michael Foot or Tony Benn. Without its leftwing Labour was a bird that could not fly. Absent the assertive presence of such a Left Miliband had little hope of taking on the rightwing majority of the PLP even if he had wished to do so. The party's policy director, Jon Cruddas, later complained that its policy-making process came to a shuddering halt, two years before the election was to take place.

We now know that Labour's membership was restless and growing, and would very probably have approved a more radical course. But back then, in what I now think of as BCE (Before the Corbyn Era), Miliband was still in awe of the 'New Labour' coterie and its threats.

The Blairites might, for the moment, hold their fire but the same was not true of the press which mercilessly seized on any unfortunate photo and minor stumble to ridicule and diminish the Labour leader. The poll lead narrowed a bit but it seemed that, at least in England, everything was still to play for.

In Scotland the prediction that the SNP would sweep the board led Scottish Labour to retreat into its Unionist bunker and to ignore the deep-seated crisis of the UK state. The Labour leadership concentrated its fire on the SNP and let off the Conservatives with warnings that they were alienating Scottish opinion. The Conservatives certainly fear that loss of Scotland would threaten to unravel the UK and diminish its claim to be a great power. But Conservatives, lacking support there for a generation, are not as alarmed as Labour by the threat of secession.

The Voters' complex verdict

On election night it was revealed that a late surge to the Tories had wiped out Labour's notional lead and given the Conservatives an absolute majority of seats. The Conservatives would be able to form a government by themselves. Since legitimacy is at stake the parties' share of the vote is also relevant. The Conservatives had attracted 37 per cent of the total vote, while Labour had only 30 per cent. Labour had lost in 48 constituencies it had previously held and retained only one MP in Scotland. The SNP had won 50 per cent of the vote in Scotland, and gained 56 out of 59 seats. The Liberal Democrats had been reduced from 57 to just 8 seats, with only one in Scotland, and a share of the total vote that fell from 22 per cent to 8 per cent. Meanwhile 1.1 million Green votes, 4.2 per cent of the total, earned them only one seat. An even more grotesquely disproportionate result for the UKIP saw it awarded one seat – though it had received 3.9 million votes.

Looked at as a verdict on the Coalition the results showed a retreat with Conservative gains being more than offset by larger Liberal Democrat losses. Contrary to the impression given by many commentators the Conservative share rose by only 0.8 per cent of the total vote, from 10.7 million votes in 2010 to 11.3 million in 2015. The Lib Dems had fallen from 6.7 million votes in 2010 to 2.4 million votes in 2015, losing 15.2 per cent of the total and with a net loss of 49 seats overall. Labour saw its vote rise from 8.7 million votes to 9.3 million. In England alone it attracted a million more votes than in 2010, and saw its share of the total vote rise by 3.6 per cent. Compared with its terrible result in 2010 Labour's recovery this year was too weak, leaving others – especially the SNP and UKIP – to harvest voter disaffection. UKIP, the rightwing populist party, received nearly 13 per cent of the total vote, boosting its share by 10.7 per cent of the total vote compared with 2010.

The complexity of this picture has not been sufficiently recognized. This was a terrible result for Labour because of Scotland and because, overall, it attracted 2 million fewer votes than the Conservatives and suffered a net loss of 26 seats. But the Lib Dem loss of more than 4 million votes and the UKIP gain of more than 3.5 million also weigh heavily in the overall result. In an awesome massacre of votes, millions of Lib Dem, Green and UKIP supporters laid down their ballots to enable the Conservatives to rule and Labour to survive. It would be wrong, of course, to conclude that over three million voters switched from the Lib Dems to UKIP. The constituency pattern suggests considerable 'churn' quite apart from the fact that over

five years those eligible to vote change. Exit polls enable some broad
shifts to be plotted, one of them being what seems to be the changing options of former Lib Dem voters. Much of Labour's increased
vote stemmed from this source, but there was also a significant shift
to the Conservatives.

The Conservative campaign on the ground focused its effort on
seizing Liberal Democrat seats with a ruthlessness towards yesterday's
allies that illustrates part of what Ralph Miliband meant by 'class war
Conservatism'. The relative success of this policy became apparent
when the Conservatives won 20 per cent of those who had voted
for the Lib Dems in 2010, compared with 24 per cent who opted for
Labour and 11 per cent who went to the Greens. Overall the Lib Dems
lost two thirds of their former share of the vote. Labour scored well
with those aged 18 to 34, especially young women, winning 43 per
cent of their votes. Unfortunately less than a half of younger voters
turned out to cast their ballot. The over-65s, by contrast, attained a
78 per cent turnout and only 25 per cent voted Labour. The Labour
share could have been raised a little if the party had paid more attention to addressing the escalating crisis of elder care.

The swelling of the UKIP vote meant that there had been a
major contraction of the middle ground in English politics. While
Thatcher's Conservatives never won more than 44 per cent of the
total vote the two rightwing parties have now won just under 49
per cent of all votes. However these parties are not a bloc, but rivals
and antagonists. They have been at one another's throats and are not
potential coalition partners. The Conservative party is par excellence
the party of respectable, English, bourgeois hegemony while UKIP
is a populist break-away, promising rejection of the EU and cuts to
welfare. Ralph Miliband argued in *Capitalist Democracy in Britain*
(1982) that 'first-past-the-post' promotes a concentration of power
in the hands of the potentially hegemonic bourgeois fraction. This is
well-illustrated by the Conservative victory and the unhappy fate of
UKIP, with its solitary MP and 3.9 million votes. The humiliation of
Nigel Farage, the UKIP leader, failing for the seventh time to win a
Westminster seat, provoked infighting and recriminations that further weaken the party. Following Leave's unexpected victory in the

Brexit poll Farage resigned as leader of UKIP, as already noted. This was not the first time that he had used a resignation to signal unhappiness but still reflected the party's ongoing malaise.

The overcrowded centre

Labour's dismal result was the cue for a chorus of senior Labourites to declare that the party had lurched to the Left and that, as Blair himself put it, British elections are won in the centre ground. Though widely echoed this verdict reflected an ostrich-like inability to see the wider pattern of UK politics which can no longer be read as a two horse race. Labour suffered historic rejection in Scotland because it had sacrificed the welfare state to the warfare state. In England the anti-centrist UKIP took support from Labour well as the Conservatives, portraying the centre parties' subordination to the EU as the source of all the country's woes. UKIP's support comes disproportionately from the swathes of England which have been left behind. UKIP is a party of the radical right, not the centre. Big business generally decline to back it – a few anti-EU City financiers take a different view, and help it pay its bills. The party caters to anti-immigrant feeling, with racial undertones. However, on other issues, it attacks several of the many undemocratic features of the EU and UK.

The Liberal Democrats are a genuinely centrist party and they tanked. Their collapse was many voters' withering response to that party's coalition with the Tories and backing for austerity. This fatal misstep reversed more than a decade during which the Lib Dems had built support by outflanking Labour on the Left, favouring a rise in income tax, opposing the Iraq war and urging electoral reform. If Labour had won most of those who deserted the Lib Dems it would have won the election. As it was, Labour only achieved this in London and elsewhere Lib Dem votes went to the SNP and UKIP, with only a trickle going to Labour and that some even went to the Conservatives on the principle that its better to engage the organ grinder than his monkey.

Labour in 2015 was haunted by a past that it refused to confront. Writing in 1983, Ralph Miliband had this to say about the then Labour leadership: 'The Labour Party is deeply embroiled in its own troubles. Its leaders are greatly handicapped by their own record in office, and by the fact that Conservative ministers, when challenged over their policies, are able to say "You did it first", to which it is not much of rejoinder to say "yes, but not so hard"' (Miliband 2015 [1983]: 284). If this hit home in the 1980s it was bang on target in 2010–15.

Labour's key failure

The key issue that sank Labour was, once again, its own record in office. Ed Miliband had been elected Leader because he took his distance from New Labour and its record but this was an unpopular theme with the Shadow Cabinet. The Brownites – and Gordon Brown himself – were utterly opposed to any serious criticism of the economic stewardship of the Blair/Brown governments, with its notorious claim to be 'relaxed' about galloping inequality and its empty boast to have ended the cycle of boom and bust. Since it was difficult to praise the measures that fostered the bubble economy the result was an awkward silence. Cameron and colleagues swooped on Labour's embarrassment to allege that the crisis was the result of the government's profligate public spending. In reality, of course, the mountainous debts which brought on the financial crisis stemmed from the private sector while the post-crisis spending was essential to prevent an even sharper downturn. Nevertheless Tory spokesmen got away with talking about 'Labour's recession' as if the melt-downs of Wall Street and the City were a mere side-show compared with the blunders of the British government.

Martin Wolf in the *Financial Times* and Paul Krugman in the *New York Times* wrote piece after piece arguing that it was the indebtedness and speculations of financial institutions that brought on the crisis and bailout. The UK national debt ran at around 37 per cent of GDP in 2006 and, by itself, was no cause for concern. But if all forms of debt are considered – including that of banks, companies and households – then the total ran to five times GDP and was very alarming. The bailout of the banks meant that net government debt doubled to reach 80 per cent of GDP in 2008. Wolfgang Streeck, the director of the Max Planck Institute for the Study of Societies, later confirmed that it was the private sector, not public spending, which set the scene for the financial crisis (see Streeck 2014).

Wolf and Krugman also insisted that austerity was making matters worse and weakening the recovery. Neither Ed Miliband nor Ed Balls, the Shadow Chancellor, took up the arguments laid out by these leading economists. Balls avoided any criticism whatever of the Blair/Brown governments (of which, of course, he had been a prominent member).

Labour bore much responsibility because it positively facilitated the orgy of financialization, which did so much damage to the UK and US economies. The notorious Private Finance Initiatives (PFI) concealed some debt off-balance-sheet. But this is a different proposition from claiming that state spending caused the crisis. Allowing this big lie to gain widespread credence was a decisive defeat for Labour before the campaign had even begun. For their part the Conservatives had also favoured de-regulation but, as Ralph had warned, Labour was not well-placed to point this out.

A signature stance of New Labour in the approach to the 1997 election had been a promise to adhere to the Conservatives' spending plans for the next two years. Ed Balls chose to repeat this assurance in 2012–15. Such a self-denying ordinance made nonsense of Labour's claim to offer voters an urgent alternative.

In Ed Miliband's case the failure to take up the cudgels may have reflected a wish not to lecture the voters and appear academic. Would the general voting public understand a grown-up discussion of economics? Would it be suicidal to attempt to explain the Keynesian argument? Miliband and Balls are not the only social democrats to decline the attempt. In contrast to this timidity Pablo Iglesias, the leader of Podemos in Spain, has gained credibility by bringing the voters into the real debate.

Ralph Miliband was no economist but he always respected the need for robust economic reasoning. When we formed the 'Independent Left Corresponding Society', an informal advisory group for Tony Benn, in the mid-1980s – Jeremy Corbyn was a member – Ralph suggested that we invite the Oxford economist Andrew Glyn to take part. Glyn was commissioned to set out what would be needed to reduce unemployment by a million jobs a year. Andrew had worked for the Treasury and his pamphlet made use of the Treasury model of the British economy. More generally Ralph was convinced that de-industrialisation and out-sourcing were reaching dangerous levels and endorsed the 'Bennite' Left's work on an 'Alternative Economic Strategy' (AES).

Much economic writing on Britain since the 1960s has emphasized relative decline, de-industrialisation, and growing inequality. The radical reconstruction of the Thatcher years and the hectic growth of the City financial complex in the mid and late nineties seemed temporarily to challenge the decline thesis. The dot-com bubble of 1999 and after, and the crisis of 2007–08 punctured the prevailing euphoria. Following the crisis nearly a decade of stagnant productivity give the relative decline thesis renewed currency. Shortly after the 2015 election the Bank of England reported that stationary productivity since 2007 meant the average household was 17 per cent – £5 000 a year – worse off in consequence. Stagnant productivity was accompanied by relatively low unemployment (at 5.5 per cent).

The weak recovery in 2014–15 was due to feeble consumer demand and a housing bubble. It created many new jobs but most of these were in low-income self-employment or in the unskilled service sector. Employers maximized their flexibility by offering 'zero hours' contracts, that is contracts that bound the employee to be ready and willing to work but gave them no guarantee of paid employment. Young people still found it difficult to find proper jobs. They were burdened with debt and even those who had paying jobs could not afford to buy a home of their own.

While London and the South East flourished, with a housing boom and buoyant stock market, the rest of the UK festered. The 17.4 million votes for 'Leave' in the 2016 EU referendum, against the 16.1 million who voted to 'Remain' was, among other things, a reflection of the 'Two Nations' divide. In the run-up to the referendum the UK was running a ballooning current account deficit and abysmal levels of investment. In the aftermath of the poll the value of the pound sunk by over 11 per cent in week, with £1 worth just $1.28, a historic low. The markets suddenly began to notice that despite the boasts of Cameron and Osborne the UK had a vulnerable house price bubble and high levels of debt.

With the benefit of hindsight the Alternative Economic Strategy (AES) was right both to oppose the dominance of finance capital and to focus on wealth-creation as well as redistribution. It is an error to suppose that only the private sector generates wealth and to ignore what Mariana Mazzucato calls, in the title of her recent book, *The Entrepreneurial State* (2013). The German economy's relative buoyancy reflects investment in R&D, using such institutions as the Frauenhofer Institute with its 18 000 researchers and budget of 1.8 billion euros. While the Keynesians have an important case to make concerning the weakness of demand, and the cheapness of capital, the voters' fear of public debt is not completely irrational. It is certainly wise to channel much public spending to investment – on infrastructure, higher education, new anti-biotics, green technology and other R&D – rather than to household consumption. Jeremy Corbyn placed his own economic proposals in the tradition of the AES, with the setting up of a National Investment Bank. John McDonnell, whom he chose as Shadow Chancellor, was involved in both the AES and the Left Corresponding Society meetings. (McDonnell explained the need for more effective corporate taxation and the role of a public Investment Bank in an Op Ed article in the *Guardian* on 15 August 2015.)

While drawing on economic expertise Ralph Miliband spoke of the need to make socialism the 'common sense of the age' and was well-aware that socialist 'experts' had something to learn from working people which would improve their plans. The popular belief that there can be no gain without pain may be too indiscriminate but any socializing plan will need to include an element of sacrifice – so long as it for a worthwhile objective. Investing in skills and in research offers the hope of raising productivity as well as supplying a demand-side boost.

It is claimed that the language of the Left is obsolete. As I noted above Edward Miliband found it impossible to drag the Labour Party to the Left because the party no longer had a vocal Leftwing which could articulate and support such a move. Yet a party appeared in this election that spoke incessantly about the need for a 'long term economic plan' and the need for a party that would reflect the interests of 'working people'. That party was, of course, none other than David Cameron's. Flouting Labour's caution Cameron used factory meetings to inform employees that they deserved higher pay and that this would strengthen the recovery. No-one on the Labour side responded to these provocations, beyond a lame claim that Labour had 'a better plan'.

The party that really did have elements of 'a better plan' was the Greens. Over recent years that the Greens have developed a radical, detailed and wide-ranging economic plan. The 90-page Green manifesto drew extensively on this making it a more substantial document than any offered by the major parties. However it is not always clear how its different parts work together. Natalie Bennett, the Green party leader often did a reasonable job of explaining her party's ideas but had the misfortune, on one critical occasion, to have a 'brain fade' when asked to explain an aspect of the party's monetary policy. The contest between party leaders in a British general election has a gladiatorial character which is merciless when it encounters human frailty. The Greens should have found a qualified economic spokesperson to present this aspect of their programme. Nevertheless their success in building support shows that voters are beginning to recognize the party and to appreciate that it really does have the makings of an alternative vision.

A visionary prospectus

Ralph Miliband had urged the Labour leadership of the mid-1980s that they lacked a connecting vision to bring coherence to the grab-bag of promises and improvements which they put forward at election time. Nowadays these are called 'retail offers' and they are tested out on focus groups and small scale polls, with little awareness that context and narrative are essential to coherence and effectiveness. Ralph urged that each measure should be conceived as part of a long term plan for a different society. To ask for such an approach today may seem like crying for the moon. Yet it was not long ago that an English film-maker, Danny Boyle, was commissioned to present a historical panorama to be performed on the opening night of the 2012 Olympic games. The resulting panorama of popular struggles for the vote, social justice, universal free health-care, access to education, technological progress and nuclear disarmament won widespread acclaim and showed that it is still possible to imagine the peoples of the British Isles as protagonists of their own fate rather than as consumers of pre-digested titbits of political pabulum.

Cameron's Cabinet was stuffed with millionaires and old Etonians. A former Cameron aide, Steve Hilton, warned that hedge funds and spread betting concerns were buying privilege. He warned: 'Democracy is in crisis. It seems to serve people no longer, but rather vested interests. Of all the bad that they do, perhaps their worst impact is the hold that they have on our governments. It seems today that political legitimacy stems not from votes but from money.'

The title of this appeal was 'Citizen's Arise!' and it was appeared in Murdoch's *Sunday Times* on the 17th of May. Obviously such rhetoric must be taken with more than a pinch of salt. But it is sad that Labour was no longer able to strike such a chord. (Hilton became a strategist for the Leave grouping in the 2016 EU Referendum.)

The Conservative side also produced Ferdinand Mount's, *The New Few: Or, a Very British Oligarchy* (2012). In this book Mount, a former adviser to Tory premiers, praised Ed Miliband for raising the need to tackle runaway inequality. But Ed's colleagues did not agree, as they made quite clear in their postelection recriminations. On the Labour side Owen Jones offered a valuable and informative critique in a best-selling book, *The Establishment* (2014), but the ammunition he offered was largely ignored by Labour.

The Scottish challenge and Charter 88

I have so far only briefly mentioned the Scottish dimension of the 2015 election, namely the virtually clean sweep made by the Scottish National Party, with its radical social democratic offer. In the months leading up to the poll the SNP had not just recovered from their defeat in the Independence referendum, but had more than doubled its membership to 80 000. Labour's immediate response to the revival and advance of the SNP was querulous and hostile. When Labour suffers from defeat at the hands of the Conservatives it is prone to an almost excessive self-criticism but the defeat in Scotland prompted little self-questioning.

Labour, Conservatives and Lib Dems had formed a common front against the SNP in the run-up to the referendum in 2014, offering more devolution on the eve of the poll, which they won by 55 to 45 per cent. Cameron's immediate reaction to the defeat was to blurt out that any further devolution to the Scottish parliament would need to be balanced by allowing only English MPs to vote on 'English questions' in the British parliament. This sparked controversy because it would exclude Scottish MPs from vital votes. Most government bills have budgetary implications so how could they be deemed 'English questions'? The Unionist parties concentrated their fire on issues where they disagreed, with muted criticism of one another's Scottish policies. Or so it seemed.

With only three or four days to go the Conservatives launched the political equivalent of a submarine attack on Labour and SNP. A barrage of messages on Facebook and Twitter warned that Labour would sign up to any SNP demand to get the keys to Downing Street. Miliband had explicitly rule out any 'deal' with the SNP in the BBC's *Question Time* debate the previous week. The Conservative message was that a vote for Labour was a vote for chaos and capitulation. The sneak attack occurred so late that Labour had no time for a proper response. Another win for 'Class War Conservativism', showing how a governing party can tap into a deep well of fear and *ressentiment*.

Labour did not have to be wrong-footed on Scotland. It is worth remembering that Labour and the SNP have not always been at war. There was a time, in the late 1980s and early 1990s, when Labour, under the leadership of John Smith, made common cause with the SNP. While this never became a formal pact, an informal multi-party alliance in Scotland helped to isolate the Conservatives and to elaborate a wide-ranging programme of democratization. Labour, the

Liberals and the SNP banded together to demand a Scottish Parliament and to confine the Conservatives to one Scottish constituency.

This highly effective axis of opposition was much more than a deal struck by party chiefs. It was carried forward by a popular movement for democratization that targeted the bureaucratic and remote 'ukanian' regime at Westminster, with its arcane rituals and its arbitrary first-past-the-post rules. Civil society bodies, the churches, artistic groups and campaigns for social justice came together at the Scottish Constitutional Convention of 1989. The Conservatives were beaten in Scotland in 1992 and ideas advance that paved the way to the Conservatives' massive UK-wide defeat in 1997.

The Scottish movement had reflected and promoted a diverse debate on Scotland's future from such writers as Tom Nairn, Neal Ascherson, Bob Purdy and Magnus Linklater. The Scottish movement also inspired a new spirit of democratic aspiration in England and Wales, with the Charter 88 manifesto being the most notable result. Charter 88 was an eclectic movement united by its commitment to the democratization the UK state. Though not party-political in character it challenged a Conservative regime that was visibly destroying all hope of social progress and respect for civil liberties. The Charter called for a written constitution, electoral reform, abolition of the House of Lords, a Human Rights Act, a Freedom of Information Act and a referendum on a Scottish parliament.

The Charter was the brain child of Stuart Weir, editor of the *New Statesman*, and Anthony Barnett, a former editor of *New Left Review*. and the first Director of Charter 88. Behind the scenes Liberal Democrats and Labourites anxious to see their parties form a common front played a role. The influence of Tom Nairn and Raymond Williams was easy to spot. Ralph Miliband endorsed the Charter, though with private reservations (should nuclear disarmament be added? What about social demands?).

These leading lights of the New Left converged in their critique of the UK state as a monstrous obstacle to a flourishing British democracy. The archaism and deference embodied in the monarchy and House of Lords, the arcane customs of the Commons, the distortions of first-past-the-post, and the overcentralization of political life and the civil service, all figured in this critique. Nairn's *The Break-up of Britain* (1977) and *The Enchanted Glass* (1988), Williams' recipe for reform in *Resources of Hope* (1989), and Miliband's *Capitalist Democracy in Britain* (1982) had quite different starting points but a common terminus on the terrain of the Charter. Edward Thompson's *Writing by Candlelight* (1980) shared several of these themes, though he seems never to have signed the Charter.

For obvious reasons Göran Therborn did not sign (he is Swedish) though his stress on democratic renewal is very similar in orientation and was set out in the lengthy concluding section to his book *What Does the Ruling Class Do When it Rules?* (1978), a work which also influenced the elder Miliband.

Tens of thousands of Britons – eventually hundreds of thousands – signed Charter 88, reflecting concern for the state of democracy in a country that had prided itself on being the 'mother of parliaments'. Magna Carta, the agitation of the Chartists, and Charter 77 in Czechoslovakia, were hailed as kindred movements. The Charter's aims remain largely unattained – on May 10th 2015 a delegation of MPs from the SNP, Greens and UKIP presented a petition of over 400 000 signatories supporting proportional representation. In some areas, notably those linked to the web and all aspects of electronic communication the Charter's policies need updating, but in the spirit of its original principles. The Brexit vote intensifies the crisis of the UK state and underscores the need for a new Charter.

When Tony Blair came to power in 1997 he did so on a manifesto that gestured towards both electoral reform and the Scottish parliament. The Scots got their referendum on the parliament but the latter-day English Chartists were denied proportional representation. Proportional representation invariably appears pointless to the parties which are flattered and favoured by first-past-the-post. Scottish MPs – whether Labour, Lib Dem or SNP – had the numbers to ensure that the Scottish parliament came into being, and that it was elected by a proportional system. But Scottish Labour lacked the foresight – and democratic instinct – to abandon first-past-the-post for the Westminster parliament too. They sowed the wind and reaped the whirlwind. In May 2015 Scottish Labour had just one MP despite winning over a third of Scottish votes.

The leader of the SNP, Nicola Sturgeon, is the First Minster of Scotland and not a member of the Westminster parliament. She lost no time in June 2016 in announcing that a referendum on Scottish independence was again on the table. Over 60 per cent of Scots had voted for Remain but they were about to lose EU membership because of the English vote. But when and how a second vote on Independence will be held is not clear, and will require the cooperation of the Westminster parliament. The SNP's critical positions on austerity, The PLP Trident an foreign policy will not immediately prevail they could help revivify a wearisome public discourse, so long confined by the narrow limits of what Tariq Ali calls *The Extreme Centre* (2015).

As the long-time leader of the 'Stop the War Coalition' Jeremy Corbyn's anti-imperialism and anti-militarism greatly appealed to many Labour members and supporters – and was the source of the bile shown against him by pundits and reporters. Throughout the campaign he was dogged by the accusation that at a meeting he had chaired in the House of Commons he had publicly greeted delegates from Hamas and Hezbollah as 'friends'. Corbyn did not apologize for this and pointed out that Tony Blair had met with Hamas leaders much more often than he had himself. The event Corbyn was chairing was an inter-parliamentary group. In the old days participants might have been addressed as 'comrades', or 'colleagues', or 'brothers and sisters'. The choice of 'friends' was perfectly in keeping with the 'people to people' diplomacy that Corbyn had practiced so long and that chimes in with the Quaker strand of British peace movements. The 'international community' is determined to monopolize the diplomatic space. It denigrates the efforts of peace campaigners and instead reposes its trust in the hands of such paragons of peacemaking as its long-time 'special envoy', Tony Blair.

In the course of the campaign Corbyn had been pressed whether he would agree to sending British troops to fight ISIS. He explained that he would not approve of such an action and that Western troops lacked the local legitimacy, knowledge and skills that would allow them to be effective.

'The lunatics are taking over the asylum!'

Ed Miliband's most important legacy may prove to be the changes he secured to the rules governing Labour leadership elections. The special voting rights given to MPs and the trade unions were abolished in favour of 'one member, one vote'. Moreover the party's supporters were invited to register as such, paying a £3 fee and receiving the right to vote in the leadership election. Members of affiliated unions had to be in good standing but did not need an extra payment. The party reported that 250 000 new members and supporters had signed up to mid August 2015, bringing the party's total in all categories to well over half a million.

The opening stages of the Labour leadership contest appeared very narrow with no leftwing contender (candidates needed the support of 35 MPs to qualify). Friendly commentators described all the initial contenders as 'Blairite'. However at the last moment Jeremy Corbyn announced that he had the necessary support to enter the contest. He had received the formal sponsorship of MPs who did not share his politics but believed that it would damage Labour to offer such a narrow choice. Ed Miliband's former aide Simon Fletcher was one of those who helped to organize support for Corbyn and run his campaign. Fletcher was previously chief of staff to the Ken Livingstone when he was London Mayor.

The contest was swiftly transformed as Corbyn garnered the most constituency sponsorships (161) and scored well in straw polls of potential voters. Corbyn was Tony Benn's right-hand-man in the 80s and 90s, and, from 2002 chair of the Stop the War Coalition. Even opponents concede that he is likeable and modest. During his three decades in parliament he has voted against the Labour whips' instructions 500 times. At the time of the MP's expenses scandal a few years back Corbyn's claims were the lowest of any member. As an MP he managed to combine the best of politics and anti-politics.

Party members and supporters found Corbyn a breath of fresh air compared with the bland New Labour jargon of the other candidates. At hustings he spoke his mind and urged a rise in higher rate income tax, levies on wealth, the end of student tuition fees, nationalization of the railways and opposition to military intervention in the Middle East. He spoke on these topics without the politician's usual evasiveness. Commentators explained the surge of support for Corbyn by observing that Labour – almost moribund in 2010 – had begun its radicalization and rejuvenation during the Miliband years. Ed Miliband should be given some credit for this but frustration at his excessive moderation was also a factor. Corbyn's opposition to Trident renewal expresses what Ralph Miliband called 'nuclear pacifism'. It frees up large sums for social expenditure and offers a bridge to the Greens, the SNP and even the Lib Dems.

The arrangements for the leadership contest had been approved by all when first introduced but as the polls began to point to an outright Corbyn win they were blamed for allowing alien 'entryists' and political enemies to infiltrate the party and sway the vote. But Corbyn's lead was so large – many tens of thousands of votes – that it was ridiculous to claim that tiny far left groups and hostile pranksters could have contrived it. The enrolment of new supporters and members was so large that at one point it overwhelmed the computers, but the insistence that applicants register with a valid bank card, and that voting slips were only sent to validated addresses, made fraudulent registration on any scale very unlikely. The real problem panicking the pundits was that the wrong candidate was winning and that this would destroy the Labour Party. Tony Blair, Alaistair Campbell, Peter Mandelson, Polly Toynbee, Phillip Stephens, and David Runciman had their differences but all were agreed on one point – Labour's most successful recruitment drive in its history was an utter disaster. The extreme centre had always decried Bennites as the 'loony Left'. They were thought to be an almost extinct species long before 2015. But now, they feared, they had returned en masse and the lunatics were taking over the asylum.

Parliamentary pretension and the dead souls

The central doctrine of historic Labour was to vest all authority in the parliamentary party and to see the party's membership as deferring to the PLP, because of the latter's greater wisdom, experience and proximity to government. The party leadership could always, or nearly always, rely on the trade union 'block vote' to come to the leader's aid whenever the constituencies declined an acquiescent role. The leaders of trade unions affiliated to Labour could claim votes equivalent to their entire membership and then vote them as a block when selecting candidates or policies. A few might go through the motions of consulting their members but the aggregation of the votes still meant that the votes of Conservative-voting union members were wielded by the trade union leaders. Tom Nairn memorably compared the trade union barons, casting a few million votes each, to the land developers in Gogol's *Dead Souls*. The later exploited a land grant system that allotted land in proportion to the number of serfs they could bring. The developers purchased the papers of dead serf and used these 'dead souls' to claim more land prior to registering the serf's death. The trade unions could inflate the size of their block vote simply paying subs for nominal members.

Ralph Miliband explained in the opening sentence of *Parliamentary Socialism* (1961): 'Of political parties claiming socialism to be their aim, the Labour Party has always been one of the most dogmatic – not about socialism, but about the parliamentary system.' Britain's parliamentary system is still embedded in pre-democratic institutions, notably the monarchy, Privy Council, and House of Lords, and non-democratic practices, such as first-past-the-post. Individual MPs are assimilated to the notional sovereignty of the 'Queen-in-Parliament' and swear allegiance to that and not to an extra-parliamentary entity, a party with members, who select leaders and policies. However the privileges of the PLP were clipped in the 1980s when, under Bennite pressure, an electoral college was set up for leadership elections with separate representation, roughly a third each, for MPs, trade unions and constituencies.

Under Blair the members had even less say, with the party's conference degenerating into a simple rally. The 'one member one vote' principle challenges all that. Corbyn was intent of giving real power to the constituencies and party conference. Whatever their failings, and they were many, the pre-'New Labour' party conferences still had life and debate. What is now needed is a veritable re-launch of the party, starting with a proper conference. Corbyn seems to realize this. But the party's impatient MPs decided in June 2016 that another leadership elections was needed because the first had picked the wrong candidate. But the protagonists of this new contest had no new ideas and no wider vision of a UK-wide progressive alliance against inequality, austerity, militarism and neo-liberalism. Their ostensible criticism of Corbyn was that he lacked the charisma to beat Theresa May, though their real yearning was for the lost world of Ukania, with its two party system, Atlantic alliance and Labour establishment niche.

The Brexit watershed

The unexpected triumph of the Leave side in the 2016 'in/out' referendum on EU membership provoked the immediate resignation of its architect, David Cameron. He explained that he was not the man to carry out a policy he had opposed. More to the point, he had fallen into an elephant trap of his own devising. With a long history of pandering to xenophobia and the Euro-sceptics he was not a convincing champion of 'Remain'. As the scale of the threat to the UK's living standards and territorial integrity became clear, they supplied further reason for him to go as soon as a new leader could be found. The referendum had posed a false choice. When the Scots campaigned for independence they had a coherent set of institutions ready to implement independence. 'Leave' had little more than bland assurances that British business would soon find friendly partners as Britain withdrew to the EU. Hostility to Brussels and to immigrants served in place of practical alternatives.

In the immediate aftermath of the poll there was a spike in racist graffiti and physical attacks on those deemed to be foreigners. The other EU states made it clear that the Brits should expect no special favours, while the market conveyed its own belief in the declining value of British assets as sterling sagged.

The Leave camp had cunningly crafted slogans emphasizing the need to 'restore control' over borders and government, but little of substance concerning trade outlets, investment in infrastructure or the continued funding of research, much of which had been ensured by EU budgets. Remain had limp slogans and was too confident of winning – it failed to mobilize its potential support, especially among younger voters. The eventual result was a great shock to many Remain-leaning voters because it stripped from them their European identity, a taken-for-granted membership of a European 'imagined community'. Within a week of the result the 'I Love EU' movement mounted a demonstration of 30 000 young people, led by comedians and rock musicians protesting the rejection of the EU and the rise in racism. Only 36 per cent of voters aged 18–24 had voted, compared with 83 per cent of over-65s. Of the young people who did vote 73 per cent supported Remain while 27 per cent voted Leave, according to Lord Ashcroft's polling organization.

The Conservative government had failed to register that its pursuit of austerity had discredited its rhetoric of inclusion. Leave racked up majorities in areas where factories and pits had closed, and in seaside towns who had lost their fishing fleet and sold their EU quota, and were no longer visited by English holiday makers. Corbyn had tried to take a pro-EU-membership message to such places but it was an uphill struggle, as both main parties were responsible for their plight and the EU had failed them too.

Cameron's resignation was unavoidable because he could not head a Brexit government. He had called the referendum for the wrong reasons, and without adequate preparation, and the majority had defied him. More surprisingly, the two most prominent Tory Brexiteers – Boris Johnson and Michael Gove – fell out with one another and had to abandon their leadership bids. Instead the new Tory leader was Theresa May, who had supported Remain in a low-key manner and then successfully positioned herself to be the unity candidate. She appointed a three man ministerial team to negotiate Brexit. All were Leave supporters, giving them the task of implementing the policy they had advocated so vociferously.

In her first declarations as a Candidate and as prime minister she confirmed that 'Brexit means Brexit' and that her government would faithfully implement withdrawal. But she chose to devote most of her remarks to addressing the alienation of working people, to a takeover culture that ignored the interests of employees and to a culture of privilege which exclude the great majority of the sons and daughters of the working class from higher education. She promised measures to address such ills. For example there should be representatives of employees on the boards of large companies. Addressing the camera she declared that 'you' would be at the center of her governments plans and concerns. She was here addressing UKIP and Labour supporters rather than the Tory shires and suburbs. But all was not sweetness and light.

In her first days as party leader Theresa May declined to reassure migrants already in the UK that there was no question of expelling them. After an uproar in which even Farage of UKIP attacked her callous stance, May corrected herself, with her supporters explaining that her threat was just a 'negotiating' ploy designed to protect British expats resident in the Union.

The smooth Conservative transition reflected a traditional Tory instinct for power and contrasted with the PLP's treachery and confusion. But Britain's political class and its counsellors were well aware that Leave's victory handed them a series of conundrums. How could Britain retain access to the EU's Single Market without allowing the free movement of labour? Could the UK swiftly strike deals with the US and other major markets, when such negotiations are lengthy and require concessions? And now that Scotland had voted Remain by a larger margin than the UK had voted Leave, could the SNP be denied their second referendum on independence? These challenges had to be met in real time with an exposed economy. There were few foreign investors attracted by the chance to be part of the punt on Brexit. The Eurozone still has many difficulties – the debts of Italy's banks for example – but its governments know they must hang together if they are not to hang separately. The UK, on the other hand, faced fragmentation as Scotland goes its own way and as Northern Ireland and Wales consider their options. Scotland voted 62 per cent Remain, Northern Ireland 56 per cent Remain and Wales 47.5 per cent Remain. Both Brexit and – were it to happen – Scottish Independence, suggest a new settlement for Northern Ireland, clearing the way for the United Kingdom of England and Wales. (Some

Irish politicians have mused over the possibility of IONA, or Islands of the North Atlantic, a loose federation that would replace the UK and aim for membership in a democratized EU.)

While the Conservatives may once again face divisions over Europe, the referendum did greater immediate damage to the Labour Opposition than it did to the government, thanks to the PLP. The parliamentary challenge to Corbyn's leadership, prevented Labour from exploiting Tory divisions.

The 'extreme centre' rallied to support EU membership but so did many young people who were repelled by the xenophobia and racism that infected Leave's rhetoric, whether covertly or openly. The margin of victory – 52 per cent for Leave, 48 per cent for Remain – was awkward for all concerned. Asking for an immediate re-vote would flout the popular will. But if the results of Brexit are disappointing or dire then in a year or two the case for Remain or Rejoin could gain traction. This could even happen before negotiations on Brexit are concluded. A parliament with a considerable majority who support Remain will have to vote on how best to implement Leave. Even many Brexiteers believed it best to delay starting the formal process of withdrawal by invoking the EU's article 50. In fact there could be a succession of trip-wires preventing parliamentary approval of the negotiated withdrawal, supposing that to be achieved.

Beset by renewed crisis and with Britain gone the EU may develop more effective measures. However torrent of events will not abate to make life easier for English politicians. The Eurozone countries might take effective steps for greater integration and social protection. In recent years the leaders of the EU and the Eurozone turned away from the 'social Europe' of Jacques Delors and covered themselves in ignominy in their handling of the Greek crisis in 2014–15. The ugly spectacle of the EU bullying the Greek government in 2014 while enforcing counterproductive austerity – and 'odious debts' – reduced support for Remain.

Jeremy Corbyn offered critical support for the Remain Campaign leading to the incredible claim that he was responsible for Remain's defeat. The Ashcroft poll estimated that it was Conservatives who had given Leave its winning margin: 'A majority of those who backed the

Conservatives in 2015 voted to leave the EU (58 per cent) ... Nearly two thirds of Labour and SNP voters (63 per cent and 64 per cent), seven in ten Liberal Democrats and three quarters of Greens, voted to remain.' If the Conservative Remain campaign had been as effective as Labour's appeal to its voters, Brexit would have foundered.

But the emotional shock of defeat was such that Corbyn's opponents felt that the time had come to oust a leader whom they had always detested. Half the Shadow Cabinet resigned n the days after the vote. A letter of 'no confidence' in Corbyn was signed by 172 MPs, with 40 backing the embattled leader. Corbyn declared that he was ready to run for the leadership against anyone his opponents might nominate. In July 2016 the PLP considered candidates willing to stand as a challenger to Corbyn and chose Owen Smith. Smith began by promising that he would fight to stop Britain leaving the EU after all, or to rejoin if Brexit could not be stopped. But he was persuaded by supporters not to foreground this promise until some way was found to square it with respect for the popular will.

Corbyn's critical support to EU membership retained its value after the defeat of Remain since it pointed to areas where reform of the EU is urgently needed. While the EU often intervenes in a reactionary manner to enforce a type of free market capitalism it declines to intervene in many ways that would be justified and necessary to address climate change, to attack inequality or to challenge corporate power. Voters of varying political allegiance will be repulsed the reactionary record of today's EU – the obsession with austerity, the imposition of fiscal despotism, the bullying of weaker members, the notorious 'democratic deficit' and so forth. Many supporters of Jeremy Corbyn could be attracted to a critical stance towards the EU but will shun many of the former Brexit leaders, with their tolerance for xenophobic and racist 'dog whistles'.

In the Scottish referendum the 'Radical Independence' grouping ran their own campaign and had considerable impact. The British referendum saw no such grouping. The Greens, the trade unions and the supporters of Jeremy Corbyn failed to coalesce into a coherent entity capable of taking on Cameron and UKIP. On the basis of its existing positions the Green Party might have been critical of the EU since it regards most existing EU institutions as 'fundamentally flawed'. But in effect, like Labour, it supported Remain without being able to raise its own issues and proposals. The victory of Leave gives these political currents another opportunity to find European allies and to challenge the reactionary workings of the latter-day EU.

Disarray in the UK

Teresa May has to defuse the time bombs bequeathed to her by her predecessor. The Conservatives have staved off a split in their own party by re-awakening the threat to the United Kingdom. The details of Brexit will remain a concern and source of renewed strife in and between the parties. There are also other issues.

Cameron also offered a further response of devolution which was at once too modest for the SNP while being considerable enough to unsettle the UK's arcane and famously unwritten constitution and to threaten to create two classes of MP at Westminster, with the Scottish members being excluded from votes on English legislation. The distinction here is a very difficult one to make since most laws have knock-on effects, for example because they have budgetary implications. Some urge the need for a Constitutional Convention to address the consequences of devolution for other parts of the UK. If the break up of Britain gathers momentum then there will be an opportunity for the various opposition parties to advance their own programmes of democratization and reform. On July 14 2016 the Constitutional Reform Group, an alliance with members from all parties called for, as the *New Statesman* put it, a 'bold restructuring … replacing the existing Union with a system of fully devolved government in the four nations of the UK, with each given sovereignty over its affairs' ('Can Theresa May save the UK?', *New Statesman*, 14 July 2016).

The Corbyn movement will improve is chances of defeating he Conservatives if it reaches out to other oppositional social and political movements and organizations. Politically the UK opposition is highly fragmented. The support these fragments attracts underlined the narrowness of the recovery clamed by the Conservative government and the declining ability of the political elite to contain the estrangement this has generated.

Prior to the referendum Northern Ireland had long been consigned to an anomalous backwater where the English parties don't even run candidates. The July poll saw Northern Ireland vote for Remain. In recent years the border between the Republic of Ireland and Northern Ireland has been of little consequence, but that will change when Brexit is implemented. Anything which enhances this border will worry the Nationalist population and encourage Unionists. It could even threaten the Good Friday agreement. If Scotland moves to independence the Ukanian structures which define Northern Ireland will become increasingly untenable.

On the mainland Conservative hegemony must reckon with what Ralph Miliband termed 'de-subordination' and political alienation and whose more recent manifestations of civic unrest have been described as the appearance of 'new masses' by Göran Therborn (2014). In one way or another those who voted SNP, Green, Plaid Cymru and Sinn Féin were all voting against Cameron's Great Britain. These parties are already natural allies. In their different ways Labour and UKIP voters also express popular disaffection, with both engaged in a struggle for party survival.

Corbyn's election as leader was a sign that the party was again in contention and not the Zombie bequeathed by New Labour. The post-Brexit campaign to oust Corbyn was the work of parliamentarians not the party's grass roots. Those who demanded Corbyn's resignation argued that the MPs had been chosen by the electorate while Corbyn was simply the choice of the members. This argument overlooks the fact that the MPs had won because they stood for Labour and without that party endorsement they would not have been elected. The MPs who moved against Corbyn were attempting to make the party leader responsible to the PLP once again. If Corbyn is defeated in the election in late September 2016 this will be a bitter blow that will hand the initiative back to the PLP.

Corbyn's victory and its vicissitudes signal the emergence of a new Labour Left. While less experienced than past Lefts, it faces a disoriented and discredited parliamentary rump whose strength at

Westminster is at variance with it support in the country. The PLP began by constraining and weakening Corbyn but ended – inadvertinently – by doing quite the opposite. As the attacks multiplied Corbyn became calm but forceful in defiance.

When picking his Shadow Cabinet team Corbyn had only found it possible to appoint two or three close allies, notably John McDonnell as Shadow Chancellor, giving him some grip on economic policy. (McDonnell is a former financial director to the Greater London Council. His entry for 'Hobbies' in *Who's Who* lists, not entirely in jest, 'plotting the overthrow of capitalism'.) Corbyn could have been bolder in his original choice of Shadow Foreign Secretary, choosing Diane Abbott, someone much closer to his foreign policy stance, rather than Hilary Benn, the moderate son of Tony Benn. But over time Corby improved this body until it blossomed into a veritable latter-day Committee of Public Safety.

Following the mass killings in Paris in November 2015 by avowed supporters of ISIS the British press once again pressed for a lifting of the ban on British air attacks on targets in Syria. David Cameron decided that the time had come to return the issue on which he had been defeated by Edward Miliband in 2013. Aware of the volatile state of public opinion he promised that he was only requesting permission to bomb Syria from the air and that there would be no British 'boots on the ground'. The press reported that Corbyn was in a minority inside his own Shadow Cabinet and that if he tried to impose party discipline he would invite humiliation. Corbyn did allow a 'free vote' but the results were not as expected. Sixteen members of the Shadow Cabinet – a two-thirds majority – voted against the government resolution. Altogether 66 out of 210 Labour MPs voted for the government or abstained. Cameron won the vote without any need for Labour support. The Conservative side were demonstrably delighted by a rhetorically powerful speech from Hilary Benn in which Labour's Shadow Foreign Secretary praised the Government's action and went so far s to compare it with the valiant anti-fascist efforts of the International Brigade in Spain in the 1930s. However the *Financial Times* registered 'disappointment' with the debate since no one had explained how British aerial bombardment of ISIS in Syria formed part of a viable strategy for defeating the terrorist group. US and French airpower was more than adequate and had run out of useful targets. The option for massive air assaults without sufficient ground support maximized 'collateral damage', with towns like Kobane, Falluja and Ramadi being 'saved' by being razed to the ground. For some reason the Arab League offer of a 40 000 strong 'Arab Intervention force' at its Cairo meeting in March 2015 was declined.

Corbyn is a veteran of Labour trench warfare and may have reckoned his first eight months a success. His aim was to survive, to inflict some tactical defeats on the government and to re-shuffle his shadow ministerial team. He seemed to be making some headway but the EU referendum result led to a full-dress coup attempt which allowed Corbyn to completely overhaul his Shadow Cabinet with fellow spirits whom he should have appointed in the first place.

Corbyn has a small but coherent leadership team built around former members of the Campaign group of MPs and former members of the London municipal administration. The leftwing *Guardian* columnist Seumas Milne became his press secretary. The Campaign group had only ten members prior to the leadership election, though its numbers seem to be growing. The Syria vote showed that Corbyn could, on a good day, receive the support of two thirds of the PLP on a key issue, less than might have been hoped but considerably more than might have been feared. The fact that this was a 'free vote' makes it all the more significant as an expression of support. The new leadership and the new membership together could make Labour once again a force in English politics but only if recognizes that the political landscape has changed and Labour will have to adjust to that fact.

In different ways the Greens, the SNP, Plaid Cymru (Welsh nationalists), and Sinn Féin (Irish republicans) have carved out their own territory and will not be going away. Ed Miliband failed because he allowed the Blairites to blackmail and threaten him and because he failed to register the crisis of the UK state. Corbyn has the chance to do much better. To give him his due Edward Miliband did situate current woes within a crisis of capitalism and that remains an achievement. The new Shadow Chancellor is, like Corbyn himself, well to the Left of anyone who has previously occupied this post.

The Greens remain serious rivals but also potential partners. The Greens' economic programme does not use the word 'socialist' but has a progressive and transitional character. They also avoid the word 'capitalism', which is a mistake since they thereby fail to identify the systemic forces at work in the economy. Green parties elsewhere in Europe have a very mixed record, with the 'realos' serving as stooges of the extreme centre. The English Greens have these discouraging examples to learn from. They also have a good opportunity to join forces with the trade-union left, and the new Labour leadership, on Trident, austerity and infrastructure investment.

Corbyn's campaign set him several key tests. He has opposed the government's support for a new project of Western intervention and will continue making the case against Trident in England. One of Cameron's last acts was to secure a Commons motion backing a new submarine programme. Corbyn's opponents lent their support. But other aspects of the programme will be supplied by the US, the weapon's complex equipment is officially and implausibly claimed to be 'independent'. Possession of Trident did not prevented Putin's encroachments, nor the activities of ISIS. The weapon appeals to the macho instincts of some British politicians and its scrapping is long overdue. But Hilary Benn, the former Shadow Foreign Secretary, is a supporter of Trident, as is Tom Watson, the deputy leader, and a number of the trade unions, who worry at the loss of jobs that might be entailed (though Corbyn offers public contracts that would ease the problem). An encouraging sign on the latter issue was a vote to reject Trident at the Scottish Labour conference in late October. Scottish Labour is a bastion of moderation on most issues but on this they respond to Scottish public opinion. It is likely that the new membership in England will expect to have their say on the vital issue and will not allow it to be buried in the 'conference arrangements committee'.

Corbyn will also have to show again that he can rally resistance to cuts to welfare, education and health. October also witnessed growing opposition to the government in this area. A key measure in George Osborne's budget was a plan to reduce sharply the tax credits paid to late low income workers. As noted above Corbyn voted against this measure when it was first presented to the Commons. His opponents voted in favour or abstained, to show how responsible they were. Subsequently Corbyn repeatedly targeted this measure, bring it up at Prime Minister's Question Time. Conservative back-benchers were quoted as warning Cameron at an internal party meeting that penalizing the low paid was dangerous and made a mockery of the party's promises to hard-working families.

On 26th October 2015 the House of Lords voted down the measure and the government admitted that its details would have to be reconsidered. This rebuff for Cameron and his Chancellor could scarcely have been on a more significant issue. (There is also poetic justice in the Lords' defeat because Cameron and Osborne have long promised reform of the upper chamber without ever delivering it.)

One of the most distinctive Corbyn/McDonnell proposals has been to advocate a programme of 'peoples-QE' (quantitative easing) whereby the Treasury would print money to finance a public investment bank to fund badly-needed infrastructure investment. This would not fund welfare spending and would be carefully calibrated to have a counter-cyclical impact. But threats of a new recession, and low interest rates, make this a very timely proposition.

John McDonnell pledges that, as Chancellor, he would introduce new taxes on wealth and financial transactions. A useful funding source could be Ed Miliband's pre-election promise to take away the privileged exemption from stamp duty enjoyed by hedge funds and spread-betting outfits. Tory support for this privilege is muted because these unpopular financial concerns are major donors to the Conservative party. A radicalized Labour opposition should be able to reach out to a broader common front against austerity, against the UK state's democratic deficit at home, and against military action abroad.

One of Corbyn's central planks was a call for the re-nationalization of the railways, an idea that is endorsed by many commuters because of the relentless price gauging of the franchise operators, coupled with a poor record of investing in infrastructure. Polls show

70 per cent back a return to public ownership. In August the BBC aired a TV programme on the British railways by Ian Hislop, editor of the *Private Eye*, a satirical journal. Hislop's account of the malaise of a national institution under commercial ownership dwelt on rail's importance to sustaining communities and its salience in English literature and history. Corbyn had expressed a readiness to re-open rail lines that have been closed.

Corbyn's Labour should be prepared to seek alliances with the Greens and SNP rather than treat them as rivals or enemies. They should also be prepared for a wider, democratic overhaul of the United Kingdom and support the idea of a Constitutional Convention to address electoral reform, further measures of devolution and the future shape of the British Isles. Jeremy Corbyn has a long history of campaigning for a diversity of progressive causes and is one of the least 'tribal' of Labour politicians. The appearance of a new Labour Left should signal an era in which Labour re-learns how to fly (but reason to fear that it is still tethered to parliamentarism will be noted below).

One of Ed Miliband's worst mistakes was to rule out in as advance any agreement with the SNP. Corbyn's support for cancellation of Trident, and his willingness to negotiate with the SNP over further democratization and to resistance to austerity, mean that his election as Labour Leader would represent a radical challenge to the UK state. Blair and Brown understand this but it was already too late when they woke up to the threat. The moderate mass of Labour MPs will complain but, with the new members breathing down their necks, are not yet in the mood to split. The trade unions which help to finance the party and individual MPs will urge loyalty to the new leader.

Ralph Miliband used to warn against the disabling effects of an excess of realism. He did not like Vico's slogan 'Pessimism of the Intelligence, Optimism of the Will', because it gave pessimism too much importance and neglected the ability of politics to identify and, as it were, 'bring into existence' latent social forces. No clearer example of this could be given than the sudden emergence of the Corbyn insurgency out of a blue sky. The Labour Party membership should certainly avoid euphoria and attend to the real condition of the United Kingdom, but they should not aim too low or paralyze themselves with structural pessimism concerning what they can achieve as the old order crumbles before our eyes.

The potential threat to democracy does not only, or even mainly, come from the Conservatives since Britain's whole political class feels menaced by the Corbyn insurgency, hence the panicky tone of centre left and centre right spokesmen and columnists. On August 31st Paul Collier, an Oxford political scientist, explained that a Corbyn win was intolerable in an article in the *Financial Times* entitled 'The Labour Party is too big to fail – just like banks'. Labour was a 'systemically important party', which had been put at risk when the Labour MPs had failed to perform their allotted task as censors with the power to exclude dangerous candidates before the voting takes place. Given this failure, he argued, another check would have to be found. In his view the solution was to open the franchise for party leader even wider: 'The only realistic option is for the selection of the leaders of systemically important parties to be opened to the entire electorate.' We may suppose that the very partial mass media and vociferous interest groups would continue their tireless reporting and commentating.

References

Ali, Tariq (2015) *The Extreme Centre: A Warning*. London: Verso.

Jones, Owen (2014) *The Establishment and How They Get Away With It*. London: Allen Lane.

Mazzucato, Mariana (2013) *The Entrepreneurial State: Debunking Public vs. Private Sector Myths*. London: Anthem Press.

Miliband, Ralph (1961) *Parliamentary Socialism*. London: Allen & Unwin.

Miliband, Ralph (1982) *Capitalist Democracy in Britain*. Oxford: Oxford UP.

Miliband, Ralph (2015 [1983]) *Class War Conservatism*. London: Verso.

Mount, Ferdinand (2012) *The New Few: Or, a Very British Oligarchy*. London: Simon & Schuster.

Nairn, Tom (1977) *The Break-up of Britain: Crisis and Neo-nationalism*. London: NLB.

Nairn, Tom (1988) *The Enchanted Glass: Britain and its Monarchy*. London: Radius.

Streeck, Wolfgang (2014) *Buying Time: The Delayed Crisis of Democratic Capitalism*. London: Verso.

Therborn, Göran (1978) *What Does the Ruling Class Do When it Rules?* London: Verso.

Therborn, Göran (2014) 'New masses? Social bases of resistance', *New Left Review* 85.

Thompson, Edward Palmer (1980) *Writing by Candlelight*. London: Merlin.

Williams, Raymond (1989) *Resources of Hope: Culture, Democracy, Socialism*. London: Verso.

ALIAKSEI LASTOUSKI, NIKOLAY ZAKHAROV
& SVEN HORT

Belarus – Another 'Iceberg Society'?

Class, Memory, Nation-building and State-formation in European Modernity

> One might say that post-Communist Europe was bound to become pro-American and right-wing, but in fact, the political process there after 1989 turned out to be much more complex.
>
> *From Marxism to Post-Marxism?*, Therborn 2008: 48.

Introduction: a society in the making?
Belarus – prototype of modern society?

What kind of society, or social figuration, is Belarus? Surrounded by Latvia, Lithuania, Poland, Russia and Ukraine the soil of White Russia has a long ante-human record, part of a larger, almost Arctic territory where the underground is always winter, and where later migrating survivors have cultivated not only the land but also a frozenology as a figure of thought. In the contemporary phase of the civilizing process, as a modern survival unit – a social formation beyond kinship – it has a fairly new and rather fragile demographic and institutional set-up with a distinct tsarist-Soviet history. Among current European societies its 'forgotten heart' – in 2008 by international authorities Polonsk was singled out as the continent's geographical centre – has few if any equals.

Is the legacy of the 'Iceberg Society' haunting Belarus' present inhabitants and rulers? Why did this country avoid the recommended shock therapy and why did its leadership choose another road than the 'usual one' into the present era? Why did strong nationalist movements and parties never appear, as they did in most other East European countries at, or immediately after, the end of the Soviet era? Was it just because the incumbent president managed to control the electoral system, rewrite the constitution accordingly and create a loyal electorate and state apparatus that has continued to support his manoeuvres? Reasoning along such lines produces a purely instrumental view on state-citizen/subject relationships and reproduces common sense thinking. To avoid such a trap, we will look at these and similar questions through an analysis of nation-building practices, its relationship to the social structure (social categories, classes and administrative strata) and its role in societal development during the post-Soviet era. Did the existing social structure and its extremely gradual transformation open up a space for a different type of transition closer to the global mainstream?

Here, an attempt is made to overcome the analytical division between the long-range, institutional approach and actor-centered explanations through the insistence on a social class nexus (cf. Kivinen 2006 and Rokkan 1999). By necessity it is still rather tentative and in need of further in-depth analysis of the changing 21st century class dynamics. The contextual dynamics are briefly spelled out: an outline of the historical trajectory of Belarus is followed by the ensuing interstate conflicts and civil society-state interpenetration during the post-Soviet era of state-formation, nation-building and memory-transformations. The making and consolidation of a fragile survival unit in our 'European' time is in forefront.

Belarus during the Soviet era: a society of peasants, workers – and cadres

Historically, present-day Belarus belongs to a wider territory on the borders between Baltic Lands, Poland, Prussia, Russia and Ukraine (cf. Petronis 2007). Also known as the territory of a medieval kingdom or commonwealth (of Lithuania-Poland), the famous Pale of Jewish settlement of 1791 comprised most of what today constitute the Belarus state. Eastern Galicia was not far away; the Habsburgs of

Austria-Hungary another historical and imperial neighbour at the time of Absolutist sundown (cf. Reynolds 2011; Wcieslo 2011; also Clark 2007). The transition from tsarist Russia to the Soviet Union in the lands of Western Russia was rather straightforward if in no sense without its peculiarities. With the collapse of the Russian Empire and the start of the 1917 revolutions, opportunities increased for the cultural and political forces that had previously been marginalized (cf. Nimtz 2014). This also was the case for the urban Belarusian national leaders with minimal support from a politically passive peasantry. In the midst of political chaos, with Bolshevik troops retreating from Minsk and the German army onslaught, the Belarusian People's Republic (BPR) was declared in March 1918, which was the first attempt to create a modern Belarusian state but lasted only a few months. The BPR was stillborn: Russian, Polish, Ukrainian, and Lithuanian territorial claims as well as aspirations to take Belarus under their custody; in addition, the German occupying power's interests – as well as the convictions by Jewish nationalists and by committed socialists – ran counter to the Belarusian Rada (Council) striving for national independence (Lindner 2005: 41).

With the 1918 treaty of Brest-Litovsk German troupes withdrew from Russian territory, but after the armistice the areas of modern Belarus were on and off involved in the civil war as well as war with Poland. Nevertheless, in 1919 the Byelorussian Soviet Socialist Republic with Minsk as its capital formally separated from the Russian SSR. BSSR was soon united with Lithuania to make a joint buffer state ('LitBel'), which existed from February 1919 to July 1920. Vilnius was the capital of LitBel rather than of the Belarusian republic. About half of the Belarusian ethnic lands were ceded to Poland after the Riga Peace Treaty of 1921. In 1922 Belarus became a founding constituent member of the USSR, although its territory was rather paltry compared to Russia, Transcaucasia and Ukraine. The Belarusian Soviet state became a result of compromise between the left wing of the Belarusian national movement and the Soviet government of the RSFSR. This alliance came into being because, first, of the non-recognition of the Belarusian statehood by Western powers and the failure of the national republic's diplomatic missions; second Poland's refusal to grant self-determination to Belarusians and its openly colonial politics during the inter-war period; third the consonance with the socialist ideology of the Belarusian revival underlying myth of social liberation of the village; and finally Moscow's approval of the Belarusian state in the federal union with other 'fraternal republics' (Babkou 2005). Revolutions and ensuing wars including War Communism meant the end to absolutist tyranny in the Pale and the start of a new short century (cf. Slezkine 2004; also Wilmers 2009).

Belarusization, the rapid development of the Belarusian culture in the BSSR during the 1920s, took place as part of the overall Soviet *korenizatsiya* policy to promote local languages and national elites. Federalism in the Soviet Union was encouraged only in the sphere of culture, while the rigidly centralized state dominated political and economic policies (cf. Fitzpatrick 2015). Both the promotion of local national languages as administration languages and the promotion of local elites were intended to increase the local perception of the Soviet government as congenial and friendly, in contrast to the previous, enforced Russian imperial authority. National identity was actively implemented and approved in different forms and through a variety of institutions – folk costume, museum, theater, opera, literature, historical narrative. The key objective was to depoliticize non-Russian peoples and their national identities through the accentuated cultural respect for them (Miller 2008: 211). Unity in one country under the dictatorship of the proletariat was the new music.

In the 1930s, the indigenization policy faded away, and the Belarusian Soviet identity was adapted via the language reform in 1933 and by repressing the Belarusian national intelligentsia who could resist the new policy to the all-Union 'Soviet' identity, which was focused on the leading role that the Russian people, proletariat, culture and nationhood were to play for all the peoples of the USSR. In other words, in the 1930s those who populated the region continued to be Belarusians – but they lived already a more Soviet culture and identity (Bogdan 2009: 106; cf. also Gronow 2004). Despite its small-size and minor signs of resistance Belarus nonetheless became an exemplary member of the Union of Soviet republics with cadres and party members, two classes – peasants, the majority in the republic, and workers – and one 'layer' (the intelligentsia), an administration under the vanguard party, a Komsomol, a women's congress and, of course, a security apparatus. Add to this a virtue of modern republican-secular society: know-how and knowledge – and the difference to tsarist society are apparent (cf. Derluguian 2005).

The present borders of Belarus date back to the 1939 division of Poland when the Red Army invaded what is now the westernmost part of the republic, Brest and Grodno *oblast*. During World War II, Belarus became a theatre of war occupied by the Nazis, a source of outmost importance for the latest Literary Nobel Laureate (2015); in recent decades Svetlana Aleksijevitj has made more than anyone to gender its memory and living history. A forth of Belarus' population was killed, male more than females. The Nazis destroyed Minsk and other cities and devastated the rural countryside. With the end of the war, the build-up of the republic started, and already in 1945 the BSSR became a founding member of the United Nations along with the Soviet Union and the Ukrainian SSR. From 1945 on, Belarus was the fourth largest of the 15th republics following Russia, Kazakhstan and Ukraine. After the Second World War, the country was preoccupied restoring the economy, which took the form of extensive industrialization and concomitant urbanization. Agriculture had to be restarted after World War II. Soon kolkhozes and sovkhozes of 'the kingdom of potatoes' became important providers of meat and vegetables to the entire Soviet Union. The post-war Stalinist rebuilding both industrialized and urbanized Belarus from scratch; its tractor industry reached international recognition. Belarusian peasants moved *en masse* to the cities and a new Soviet class society of workers, office-workers (from intelligentsia to nomenclature) and still some peasants – the rural proletariat – resolutely took form. If before the war Jews, Russians and Poles predominantly populated the Belarusian cities, in the post-war period urban demographics became predominantly Belarusian in its ethnic composition (cf. Haavio-Manila 2010; also Fahey 2010). If before the war the BSSR was one of the most rural republics of the Soviet Union (according to the 1939 census, only 20 per cent of the population lived in urban areas), after the war the rate of urbanization significantly increased due to the many large factories constructed in the cities. Throughout the post-war years and up to the moment when the country acquired its independence, the urban population increased by 4.3 times, and its specific share rose to 67 per cent; the Belarusian class structure entirely Soviet *sosloviia* (Kivinen 2006: 249 following Fitzpatrick). Minsk of the Khrushchev era became one of the most modern cities in the entire Union (Klinau 2011; Bohn 2008). At the end of this period, Belarus was the most industrialized and one of the richest Soviet republics, possessed an economic elite of its own, part of the *nomenclatura*, if not a politicized socio-cultural avant-garde.

In the 1960s and 1970s, a unique sociolinguistic situation appeared in the BSSR, whereby Russian and Belarusian languages acquired special social statuses. Belarusian language in its pre-literary form remained a living language spoken mainly in the countryside, while its literary form became a marker of 'the chosen', or a narrow group within the intelligentsia. In contrast, Russian language became a symbol of social achievement in cities, increasingly leading both to the loss of prestige of the vernacular and to the dwindling scope of Belarusian language education. However, the majority of the population of the BSSR continued to be bilingual and bicultural, whereas Belarussian and Russian cultures merged in a regional Soviet synthesis. The early 1980s witnessed, however, the rise of youth movements – predominantly sons and daughters of the provincial elite – that actively used Belarusian language, 'revived' the ethnic culture, and fought for the preservation of architectural heritage. In fact, these sub-cultural movements meant a break with previously generally accepted conventions. Traditionally, 'Belarusian' bore an ethno-cultural coloring and delimitation, and had a clear localization in the urban environment, being pegged to academic research and folklore festivals. For the young urban Belarusian intelligentsia, the traditional culture was already identifiable as a living and immediate source of symbols (Gapova 2008: 46–47; also Gapova 2012). *Glasnost* meant that young students began to raise their voices, less so an older generation of non-communists and other non-believers. However, no signs of religious revival were visible, Belarus thoroughly secularized. The second half of the 1980s was marked by demands to reconsider the Stalinist past as repressive and, in particular, protests against the silencing of the 1986 Chernobyl disaster's scale. Under the influence of the ongoing processes in the neighboring Soviet republics a Belarusian Popular Front (BPF) was established and – in the spirit of perestroika – seen as a social and political progressive movement for the democratic transformation of society and a revival of the Belarusian nation. The BPF's program radicalized quite rapidly, and while at its very beginning in 1989, it was intended for supporting democratization processes in the Soviet Union in a year and a half it adopted the 'real sovereignty' and 'independence' slogans. BPF became the only nationalist party in Belarus that invariably introduced symbols of the nation – and thus it became a central cultural location for the production of a nationalist ideology (Abdelal 2002: 472). As a class movement, however, it was limited by generation – and gender – by size and space. As a party in the post-1991 system in reach-out it was not different from all other political parties that in vain have tried but failed to gain a popular echo.

Throughout the post-war Soviet period, the local enterprise-government system was partly clannish based on the common partisan past of Communist party leaders in the BSSR (Urban 1989). The leaders of the republic were mostly loyal juniors in the inner circles of the Kremlin, even when they reached the politburo level. It was a subordinated and subjugated *nomenklatura* that ruled this rather well-functioning republic where dissent was not heard of – apart from a few language nationalists in the universities, at the Academy of Science, or in the Writer's Union. In contrast to Leningrad and Moscow, no significant oppositional intelligentsia came to the fore in Minsk or other larger cities; neither dissidents nor gerontocrats dominated these scenes. In retrospect, the Belarusian years up to 1991 were rather unglamorous (cf. Mailer 1995). The republic was a modest showcase – the most Soviet of all Soviet republics without any remarkable local characteristics or iconography apart from a few recently erected post-war monuments (cf. Johnsson 2011; Zadvornyj 1981; McDowell 1979). Despite the cultural ambitions of the USSR, Minsk had more of Chekhovian provinciality than bucolic urbanity with a thriving dissident culture.

ALIAKSEI LASTOUSKI, NIKOLAY ZAKHAROV & SVEN HORT

State-formation in Belarus after 1991: kibbutz-capitalism from below?

However, for a brief moment the pressure that BPF exerted on the communist system at the time of its collapse, Riga and Vilnius never far away, forced the BSSR Communist party leadership to intercept the rhetoric of independence. On 27 July 1990, the BSSR Supreme Council adopted the Declaration of State Sovereignty of the Byelorussian Soviet Socialist Republic. After the failed coup in Moscow in August 1991, the BSSR was renamed into 'Republic of Belarus', and after signing the Belovezhskije (Belaya Vezha) agreements in December 1991, the Soviet Union ceased to exist and Belarus gained full independence. Both events happened equally unexpected for the local power elite – such as CP chieftains and cadres of major industrial enterprises – and for the country's population at large. The former were latecomers to the party, and the latter could enjoy the ensuing social stability after a brief interregnum. The social structure was extraordinary slow to register change as a kind of low-profile 'Prague 68-spring' arrived in and around Minsk.

Belarus declared independence. Its future president until today claims that he was the only deputy to vote against secession (Ioffe 2014;[1] cf. Wilson 2011: 153 for a different version). In Minsk and other cities there was no singing revolution behind the break-up of the Soviet Union, no strong longing for an independent nation-state. The first new republican government was a caretaker regime of former Soviet *apparatchiki* which only cautiously took on the task to initiate a transformation of union organs of party-state dual command into a coherent traditional national public administration only slowly to come through (cf. Cohen 2009). This was only a beginning; still a process is in its infancy though more than twenty-five years have passed. For instance, within a few years courts' nominal position at arm-length from the executive was strengthened but

---

1. Sven Hort would like to thank Paavo Bergman who early on made him acquainted with the scholarship of Grigori Ioffe, a Huntington-inspired rural geographer born and raised in Moscow, with grandparents in Minsk and since roughly 25 years teaching at a US university.

not fundamentally altered. More important for the survival of the new-old regime the fiscal system proved robust and capable of generating the highest levels of revenue in any CIS – Commonwealth of Independent States – country. Income from export and import of gaz, oil and by refineries secured a less than rapid transition of the domestic economy (Balmaceda 2014). Tax money from companies and farms ran rather smoothly into the central administrative state coffer, and was not cut up by managers turned entrepreneurial robber barons, corruption at a low (Verena 2005: 220; cf. Bötker 2007 for a different post-Soviet case).

Whether urban or rural, the basic enterprise model or common pool resource (CPR) institutions that people had accustomed to only gradually was re-formatted towards what Ivan Szelényi (2016), following Weber, aptly has characterized as 'prebendalism'. Public administration as well businesses have been assigned to well-educated but loyal meritocratic servants prepared to listen, learn and mediate. The industrial proletariat initially mobilized on a large scale against austerity and privatization, agricultural conglomerates soon upgraded through major state subsidies. The Red Army was redesigned into the Armed Forces of Belarus with a downsized and reorganized officer corps at arms-length from politics leading brigades instead of divisions, and the number of conscript soldiers considerably reduced while contracted soldiers have increased over the years. How much the sale of former Soviet arms have yielded the state coffer is harder to estimate but this branch of the export industry was for a while singled out as a possible avenue for a Belarusian 'oligarchic turn'. In a similar vein the KGB went through a major restructuring cutting (at least formally) ties with Moscow. But neither the military nor the secret police was demobilized though the latter formally came under civilian Belarusian control. The new constitution, however, was soon changed in particular after a referendum 2004 which made life-time presidency a possibility – without any spectacular popular resistance. The tranquillity of the social structure stood out; minor social dislocations compared to its big neighbour, and the previous class structure basically remained intact; limited change of previously established government institutions followed in its wake.

The year of 1994 proved to become fatal for independent Belarus despite the appearance of the non-state European Humanities University (EHU) with ties to a resurrected Orthodox Church. The country's first presidential elections were won neither by the government representative Prime Minister Viachaslau Kiebich nor by leaders of the national-democratic opposition but by a mere people's deputy of the Supreme Council from Mogilev, the eastern, second-largest city: Aliaksandr Lukashenka (cf. Ioffe 2014). His populist speeches invoking the struggle against corruption and proposing cancellation of the emergent 'nationalization' (implying 'nationalistic revival') policy unexpectedly received support from the broad strata of the population. With his coming to power, a new stage begins in the history of the country that lasts until today. Using referenda (1995–96) the recently elected head of State achieved several radical transformations: the official status of Russian language has been restored, the ceremonial state symbols have been converted in favor of slightly modified BSSR symbols, the powers of the President have been significantly expanded, and the Parliament's powers have been minimized accordingly. Persistent attempts to create a union state with Russia become another major feature of the early presidential policy.

It was a remodelled authoritarian state prepared for a Union with Moscow that initially came out of this process: a Union with Russia was formalized in 1999; to no effect after the stabilization of the Putin presidency (cf. Keukeleire and Petrova 2014). At a time of great disorder in Great Russia, however, its little brother could present itself as a stable unionist partner able to instigate respectable incremental institutional reform, no major oligarchs on display. Domestic politics was otherwise much more complicated to redesign, the old two-party system of one in power and the other in prison hard to adapt global demands if there had been any, Belarus of minor interest for ravenous internationals. The first election after the dissolution of the USSR did not produce any distinct parties different from the old regime though a multitude was on display; the oppositional BPF too weak to have a major impact. During the first decade of the new millennium no serious alternatives were on the table able to challenge the incumbent leader and the peculiar 'post-Spring' system that has evolved over time. The CP was soon a shadow of it former strength, but nothing new that resembles the Western type of governance has appeared (cf. Oblene 2009). Formally independent MPs without joining parliamentary groups or parties became the representative norm.

With the apparatus in his hands, the head of State did not need a parallel line of order. The old political *kommissars* were dismissed, instead gradually appeared a unity of government and bureaucracy with a plurality of sub-apparatuses resembling many presidential systems worldwide — with the presidential chief-of staff as second in command; the PM more of a figure-head. New local government mechanisms have so far not challenged the centre, early on 'complete liquidation' in the words of an outspoken critic of the president (Babkou 1998: 109). National politics beyond the communist party era still has a long way to go to anything resembling the party system of advanced parliamentary states. A nation-state with several serious 'French' alternatives, right-centre-left and their in-betweens and mix-ups, has to this hour not seen daylight. Electoral welfare politics — policy pledges competing for the consumer votes — has not yet entered the national arena apart from at presidential election sessions. In the eyes of the international community, the transition from a planned economy to a less planned one did not bring the expected transformation of neither the representative nor the welfare system. But the latter was sustainable within the nation-building project.

Nation-building in Lukashenka's Belarus: class, nation and power

Without social popular mass movements, political parties or similar nationwide associations, how to, and who could, carry the national project further? What about the space, time and cyberspace of nation-building in Belarus after the end to the Soviet man and woman? Although the BSSR parliament had declared the sovereignty of Belarus in July 1990, the first years of independence was characterized by national ambiguities; in March 1991 over 80 per cent of the population wanted the Soviet Union to survive. At the time, and still so, almost ten million people were residing on a territory of roughly the size of England and Scotland – of which most lived in the major cities. Belarusians were first of all Soviets, and for the overwhelming majority of the *nomenklatura* only with caution turned into a new national elite (or middle class) without oligarchs, a return to the old master was considered a matter of time or at least a realistic option. There was no need for a special 'nationhood' in the words of Benedict Anderson (2006; cf. also Nairn 1997), or to remind you of what Göran Therborn wrote before Lukashenka was in office: 'Belorussia is, perhaps, an extreme case, of serenity, basically moved by external contingencies, little affected by internal challenge' (1995: 327). Even in the *Handbook of European Societies* edited by Therborn with Immerfall, Belarus is not yet included among 48 country codes at the start of this volume though this initially forgotten entity appears in a few individual chapters (2010: xiii; cf. see for instance Cipriani below; also Barberet and Joutsen; and Rucht in that volume).

Following Soviet-era ethnic registration demographically well over 80 per cent were considered Belarusians, while Russians accounted for roughly ten per cent, the rest being Poles, Ukrainians or Jews. In terms of religious faith, though, there is more of diversity with Jews and Muslims as extreme minorities in a secular society within a predominantly orthodox community (Cipriani 2010). Language-wise, however, more than 70 per cent of the Belarusians consider themselves as Russian-speakers while the proponents of the native language form a clear minority among Belarusians. Since the mid-1990s both languages are official languages. Thus, the struggle for recognition never caught the imagination of the great majority whether it is the population or the intelligentsia that were in focus. A social order composed of workers, office-workers and a rural proletariat centred on the enterprise/kolzhos CPR-institution has only gradually moved in the direction of a capitalist economy and society, Belarus still a kind of Histradut kibbutz with an emerging managerial and political 'ruling class' (Ioffe 2014: 118). On and off a politician such as the incumbent has used the language issue as a rallying cry but abandon it as soon as it was deemed necessary and other alternatives such as welfare became more winning (Hort and Zahkarov forthc.). Thus, internal challenges have taken precedence over external contingencies, which more than twenty years after the first election in 1994 of the serving head of State have put its marks on both the state and the social formation including the class character of the new republic.

Added to the domestic road to a new nation the plights of and relations to its neighbouring countries under transformation must also be taken into account. Here state diplomacy and leadership was of crucial importance (Ioffe 2014: 156–184 drawing on the sociological works of Anatoly Lysyuk and Pitirim Sorokin). Today, the magic of charisma is alien to established routines of the photo-shopped international community. In contrast, leadership style came to the fore as a new nation-state slowly emerged and deviant Belarus became one of the epitomes of the society of the (global) spectacle. Its exoticism has been highlighted by the post-modern conditions of a spectacle of a higher order, capable of dissolving the boundaries between the private and the public. In Belarus as well as in Russia the personalized style of the ruler is firm on the border of toughness; instead of silent diplomacy and backroom negotiations the chilly magnetism of steel and stone. From Ivan IV to Stalin, the brutal imposition of order has been more often admired than feared; personal charisma coalesces with conquering and palatial (Anderson 2005). In the early 1990s, the presidential candidate was looked upon as a champion against corruption; at the time a minor problem in Belarus while of a different order in Moscow (cf. Rothstein 2003). Gradually the winner took all and became *bat'ka*, the Good, or God, Father of the New Nation taking care of its children. Moreover, the Belarusian commander-in-chief never sent the sons of the country to deathly war (remember Chechnya; cf. Wood 2007) and the new republic was never under external management; its daughters not, like their Moldovan sisters, going en masse to Amsterdam or Berlin for the meat market (cf. Johansson 2011). For a decade, moreover, foreign-sponsored – EU and Swedish money – EHU was open to the children of the *nomenclatura* turned the new economical and political ruling or upper middle class. From 2005 EHU was closed but Belarusian students and their professors have without major obstacles continued to make a three-hours commute to its re-opened Vilnius campus (during its last semester in Minsk one of us taught 'European modernity and beyond' there, later also in the capital of Lithuania when the late Per Unckel was in charge of the Nordic donor constellation). Adding pride to nation-building Belarus became a sovereign state – achieved statehood – when Russia was still under IMF tutelage, and many other post-Soviet republics and territories were plagued by chaos, disorder and war.

In Grigori Ioffe's (2014) remarkably balanced yet highly critical portrait both friends and foes of the robust Dynamo ice-hockey player president stood firm when the international community rather unanimously began to raise its voice against the sovereign's rule of domestic law (cf. also Keukeleire and Petrova 2013). In Moscow things also changed with the arrival of Putin; in showing a combination of determination and deterrence Lukashenko was several years ahead of his later Russian counterpart. It is probably fair to say that the charisma had already been vested in the Belarusian head of State at the time of Putin's inauguration. Though the former may not have the cultural qualities of the latter he had served in office well in advance of Yeltsin's successor and it took some time before Putin had reduced the lead and was on par with, later ahead of, his neighbour colleague. Only with the arrival in late 2010 of mass protests on the streets of Minsk did the Belarusian president's star begun to fall and charisma slowly if in no sense fully to fade away. Nevertheless, despite a luck-lustre recent performance of the economy, in 2011 its currency collapsed but few seem willing to take part in oppositional political civil society activities. The price is considered too high; civilizing the public sphere has yet a long way to go (cf. Papakostas 2012), and an economic recovery has since arrived.

In spite of numerous accusations of presidential 'denationalization' of the state, this policy represents a specific version of nation-building. Indeed, unlike in the other newly formed East European states, the Belarusian state politically marginalizes such ethnic referents as national language, while bringing to the fore the collectivist repertoire, borrowed from the Soviet era of social unity (cf. Hroch 2015). Hence, the collective fantasy in Belarus is based on national mobilization overcoming social cleavages and class distinctions, and relies on fundamental principles of national sovereignty. National ideology is ethnically and socially inclusive, where 'Belarusians' are determined not by blood but by shared values, the so-called 'national character' (Leshshenko 2008). The Belarusian authorities promote the image of homogeneity, social cohesion, and total unity of the people, implying the absence of disagreements, disputes, and different opinions 'inside' of the people. This is a kind of auto-training in national unity, when the need for unity is inculcated primarily via creating an unfavorable image of what would happen if the people of Belarus were not uniform, supplemented with the 'unity, stability, confidence in the future' formula (Denis 2010: 83–84). The internal class enemy is inside but outside, a 'fifth column'. For many years, the country's leadership declared as its main strategy the improvement of the living standards and the population's welfare, leading to a partial rehabilitation of wealth as a desired ideal (during fifteen years of continuous economic growth) – but only to the extent that it is not speculative but 'earned'. This ideology of minimal but stable consumption has become a new public faith that has infused the entire public life according to a domestic social researcher (Gornykh 2008: 180). Allegedly, a defining feature and a basic characteristic of the Belarusian people is their loyalty to the authorities. It may not last forever. The criterion for the exclusion from the collective body of the people is oppositional manifestations and any malevolent desire to go contrary to the collective aim (Lastouski 2011). The Soviet class enemy has returned by the back door, he is no longer a former communist turned fascist – i.e. Trotskyist etc. – but a mere anti-patriotic Quisling.

In fact, the Belarusian project creates a 'soft class-nation' identity, whereby self-awareness by a Belarusian is cultivated based on his or her belonging to the political body. It is difficult to call this body a political community, as it does not involve the activity of citizens and horizontal linkages. A Belarusian scholar, Lyudmila Naumenko, draws attention to the low representation in Belarusians' auto-stereotypes of any ethno-differentiating characteristics and, especially, ideas of their own ethnic and cultural distinctiveness (Naumenko 2012: 156). This blurring of ethnic identifications is popular – according to the results of censuses (1989, 1999 and 2009), the number of Russians and Poles (the two major ethnic minorities in the country) tends to be significantly reduced over time in the absence of migration – essentially a process of acculturation without appropriating the culture. A modern Belarusian rather speaks Russian and is brought up in Soviet-Russian culture, but his or her identification is usually based on the criteria of residence in Belarus.

Formally, this concept of the nation is close to nationhood or political nationalism, implying the entire population as a nation, regardless of their origin, religion or culture, a unity of the social categories. However, a fundamental difference is in the emphasis still placed on public authorities which represent the nation rather than on 'civil society'. This concept is culturally engaged by stressing the political and cultural – if not the ideological-communist – continuity with the Soviet period, which is perceived as a source of useful experience and the beginning of statehood. The existence of the Belarusian national culture is not denied, but it is perceived as an ethnographic, 'folk' etc. phenomenon, and thus its social space is circumscribed by corresponding areas (history, literature etc.). Here we observe some obvious resemblance to the practices of the late Soviet period (Kazakevich 2011). The nationalist version of history has not disappeared entirely, even though it has been displaced from its privileged position in public discourse. A 'nativist' project is isolated from society, but its followers comprise a tight-knit community united by their conscious choice of Belarusian language and their joint fight against Russian colonialism. Assessing the scope of the support of the informal memory is currently a vexed question, but Kazakevich (2012: 251), upon considering some sociological data, comes to a rough estimate of 20–30 per cent of the entire population. Supporters of alternative versions of nation-building in Belarus can be estimated as constituting roughly the same portion of the population.

Alternative nation-building projects such as 'civil society and human rights' are thus pushed to the periphery of the public sphere, where they mainly engage in various cultural initiatives. What once seemed as a united and pro-European democratic civil society camp now crumbles into a succession of divergent projects, where you can meet glossy liberalism alongside pagan traditionalism, Russian-language Belarusian nationalism, etc. We deal with a living archive, where the Belarusian authorities can borrow some currently attractive ideas. The process of nation-building bypasses any marginalized 'eccentrics'. The president has become the 'general institution' linking Belarusians by accumulating and expressing the resources, views and values of the predominant social-conservative part of Belarusian society, while ignoring and marginalizing the values and limiting the life chances of its smaller, but more dynamic part located in the new 'sophisticated' middle class (Manajew and Drakokhrust 2012: 44). The rapid disappearance of the propertied class after 1917 did not after 1991 in Belarus produce a similar abrupt appearance. The two and a half decades following independence for the *nomenclatura* turned prebendal class has been a soft version of 'living dangerously in Soviet politics'.

Geschichtspolitik and collective representations of the past: Sovietization without communism

After the creation of an independent state in 1991 there was an acute need for a new historical narrative that would explain the past of the Belarusian state on the assumption of its erstwhile independence and not as a history of the Soviet republic. This time witnessed a sharp rise in the national historiography inspired by the romantic national 'rebirth'. The new historical narrative draw its inspiring imagery from the past but was interrupted by Stalin's repressions; the late 19th century teleology that had aspired to implement the idea of Belarusian statehood as rooted in the early Middle Ages, its 'Golden Age' proclaimed to be the period of the Grand Duchy of Lithuania, which was followed by a long period of the loss of statehood and by foreign domination — first Polish, then (even more repressive) Russian, smoothly replaced by the Soviet oppression up until the 'national revival'.

However, the configuration of power and knowledge again changed drastically after 1994. Lukashenka's victory took place under the slogan of restoring the positive experience of the Soviet past as well as returning to allied relations with Russia. Naturally, the system of historical knowledge should be brought into line with the new political currents. The colonial legacy is so strong in Belarus that all attempts by the national historiography to create a mythological past have failed. In contrast to its rapid disappearance in most post-communist countries, historiography returned to its pan-Slavic, Russophile, and Soviet roots (Kuzio 2002). In 1995, the state system of historical knowledge was reformed: first by rewriting history textbooks, introducing ideology as a special curriculum subject, and later through tightening control over academic scholarship. In fact, there has been a resuscitation of history, newly restored, retouched, and adapted to the realities of the day.

The following basic principles have gained a new life and have since become the basis for the official Belarusian narrative stories: first, the axiomatic recognition of the East Slavic character of the Belarusian people (from its belonging to the Russian Orthodox culture and civilization ensues the positive nature of the historical ties of the Belarusian and Russian peoples); second a positive image of the secular Soviet past, which formed the basis for modern Belarusian statehood; and third the fundamental myth of the Victory in the Great Patriotic War – the Soviet interpretation of the Second World War – as a key event in the Belarusian history and the foundation of the legitimacy of the Republic of Belarus.

The last component of the Belarusian historical policy must be considered here in some detail. The victory belongs to Soviet mythology, but its employment has acquired an even more grandiose scale in post-Soviet Belarus. The new reading of the war has its own specifics. First, it highlights a huge number of victims among the Belarusian people, who acquire the status of not only a people-hero but also a people-martyr, who paid a tragic price for the victory in the war. This is facilitated by the constant re-creation of a 'one in four' rhetorical figure, of Belarusians who lost their lives during the war (in fact, this figure recently rose to 'one in three'). This is the discourse Aleksijevitj has gendered and transcended. Secondly, the new reading highlights the exceptional role of the Belarusian people in the victory over fascism, where a special role is played by another, so-called 'Guerrilla myth', which began to be formed by the Soviets, already during the war. According to the head of State, referring to certain 'reputable foreign sources', Belarusian partisans and underground fighters caused more damage to the Nazis than the allied forces in Europe. Gradually, the image of the Soviet people as conquerors of fascism fades, and the Belarusian people takes pride of place. In contrast to the Soviet period, what is commonly referred to as the Great Patriotic War is now used not as an example of international brotherhood in the fight against the ruthless invaders but as an event that has featured the Belarusians (Marples and Padhol 2008: 92). The extraordinary emotional potential to be found here is used to create a negative image of political opponents, who are equated with the enemy – the fifth column – during the Great Patriotic War (Goujon 2010: 12). The solemn affirmation of the Belarusian people's role in the victory over fascism strengthens the legitimacy of the state in terms of its claim to political and cultural autonomy. The country's leadership is the main agent of commemoration and presents its actions as a constant concern for the preservation of national memory, successfully collecting the symbolic bonuses that are associated with this stance.

In the 2010s history textbooks are being rewritten again – this time based on a moderate synthesis, by integrating the Soviet and the national versions of Belarusian history. This synthesis takes place by removing such points of extremum as the communist ideology as removed from the Soviet version and radical nationalist and anti-Russian claims – from the national version. There is a marked trend of nationalization of the official narrative of Belarusian history – even though it takes place slower than in the neighboring countries and hence can be metaphorically referred to as 'creeping nationalization', but the trend is doubtless. Since 2010, conflicts between the leadership of Belarus and Russia reached a new status of periodic information and trade wars. This necessarily affected the public interpretation by the Belarusian authorities of historical relations between the two countries. The accentuation of the common past has been continued with and affixed in presidential addresses, but the relationship with the past is now to be built not in the geneal-ogy of continuation where past brotherhood serves as the natural basis for the present-day brotherhood but in the amended frame of 'falsification'. In the latter case, the historic unity of the Belarusian and Russian peoples is understood as a 'historical truth', protected by a conscious agent – the Belarusian authorities, while the Russian leadership is represented as a deliberate forger and therefore as an anti-national institution.

In the center of the whole complex of historical memory, there is an unshakable monument – the Victory of the Belarusian people in the Great Patriotic War, the emphatic and expressive cult of which out-shadows all other events of the Soviet past. It is no wonder that the victory causes pride among Belarusians and tops the list of events in the history of the country, according to a survey conducted by the Institute of Sociology in 2008 (Lastouski 2009). What is most surprising in these results is an amazing void of historical memory. All significant events that have hit the top of the ranking refer to the recent past. Although respondents were asked about history, they mostly reported on some recent achievements of the present-day Belarusian state. In fact, only the victory myth provides the necessary significance for historical memory. Another survey, conducted by the Independent Institute of Socio-Economic and Political Studies in March 2012,[2] also features the Victory in the Great Patriotic War as the most significant base of Belarusian's historical memory: 80 per cent of respondents believe it to be the most significant event in the history of the twentieth century and something of exceptional pride for Belarusians. Both supporters and opponents of the Belarusian authorities are uniform in this assessment. It is a cementing factor for the common understanding of the past as well as for overcom-ing political division including a possibility to accommodate to the international recognition of Aleksijevitj's successful re-writing of wartime events and experiences.

Thus it is also difficult to speak of a full-scale Soviet renaissance, such as the revival of the cult of Soviet leaders – Belarusians nega-

---

2. IISEPS, http://iiseps.org/old/03-12-08.html.

tively assess both Lenin and Stalin. Even Stalin's leadership of the country during the victory – the highest feat in the collective history of Belarusians – does not improve his present-day perception. For both the country's leadership and for the people, the Soviet period remains a bright and nostalgic era and a time of material prosperity. However, there is no desire to return to all-out Communist mobilization. 'Soviet' refers to the increasingly distant, and increasingly secure and unproblematic past. The distant past is a diffuse area of ancient legends, where you can borrow some characters to build tourist attractions. In terms of their collective identity and memory, Belarusians remain to be 'soft'. Their neighbors (especially Poles) sometimes reproach Belarusians in their failure to become a nation and to retain historical memory. But this softness and flexibility provides them with a tangible advantage of adaptability to changing conditions. Choosing between East and West, between Europe and Russia, a Belarusian would choose both. Ioffe (2014: 101) writes that 'It is little wonder that many in Belarus came to understand that for the West, moving Belarus away from Russia *is* an end in itself, the true idée fixe; whereas democracy promotion is a smokescreen.' This is not to say that post-Soviet Belarus was not able to live on its own is any unique, since it resembles the early 17th century pre-semi-peripheral Sweden, when in Oxenstierna's dictum 'all our neighbours [were] our enemies' (cf. Backhaus, Jönsson and Ottosson 1999). With age, also the lands of White Russia may cease to be a rudimentary dynastic 'prebendal society'.

Still an iceberg society?

In the 21st century, Belarus is first and foremost a political 'nationhood project', a new state in a rather lawless interstate system where global force and weapon's of mass deception rule the day (cf. Stephanson 2015; Therborn 2014a). Nevertheless, there are other, predominantly internal, dimensions to the new nation and its peoples as emphasized from the beginning of this article. Recently Tony Wood has argued that given the depth of ignorance about what lies beneath Russia's unchanging political surface it might be described as an 'iceberg society' (Wood 2012; cf. also Kravchenko 2012; Furman 2011). Is something similar applicable to forgotten Belarus?

In contemporary social and historical research the 'Belarusian project' is often formulated in negative terms, either treating the country as a 'denationalised nation' (Marples 1999) or emphasising its anachronistic 'sovietisation' (Leshchenko 2004). The official discourse in Belarus distinguishes the country from its former centre by reaffirming the Soviet ideals that have been abandoned by Russia, e.g. the patriotic 'partisan' narrative, yet it at once undermines this reaffirmation by appealing to the 'Slavic trinity' of Russia, Ukraine, and Belarus. Equally, hostility to globalised modernity accompanies modernist re-assertions of Soviet values. These contradictions match the unofficial Belarusian revivalism, whereby anti-Russian-ness coexists with Slavic pride, where Catholicism and Orthodoxy collide, and where European liberalism competes with critiques of Western 'political correctness' (Miazhevich 2012). If in the beginning of Aliaksandr Lukashenka's rule history was re-written in a way to support the ideological unity with Russia as part of its Slavic civilisation, in more recent years the official and alternative, revivalist, projects of historic memory have moved closer to each other. The topics of rapprochement include the significance of ancient duchies that existed on Belarusian lands and the Great Duchy of Lithuania, for the statehood and nation formation in Belarus. For instance, textbooks on history refer to the Medieval Age as the cradle of Belarusian statehood; at the same time, elements of medieval culture are promoted in the media – festivals of knights etc. – and memorials. At the same time, the historical significance of the Russian Empire that presumably liberated Belarusians from the serfdom imposed by Polish or Lithuanian masters is not accepted (Smok 2015: 30).

Whatever the validity of such contradictions and simplifications, as a complement the long arm of tsarist-Soviet history – in particular its post-Stalinist civilizing process – has been invoked in this article. In contrast to its neighbours, from 1991 the after a chaotic while the rather prosperous survival unit of Belarus allowed itself a state-formation process where external economic forces did not take the command in nation-building, no domestic oligarchs entering the scene. This is the land where no Soviet Cold War defeat has occurred while its power ideology became extinct. Politics – soft prebendalism – retained its primacy over economics in the making of a new post-communist consumer society still in its infancy. Caught between the global forces, for the Belarusians it has not been an easy road towards equality, justice and liberty. In the intersection of external contingencies and internal challenges a new system of social mobility and stratification gradually has taken form, akin but different from the previous one. Its (post-)Soviet class structure – contradictory class locations and bonds, cleavages and ties beyond kinship sister- and brotherhood – has remained a stabilizing element in a social transformation that has gone against the grain of academic-cum-geopowerpolitical transitology. Neither 'capitalism from outside' (EU Central and Eastern plus Baltic Europe), nor 'capitalism from above' (Russia, later Ukraine et al.), Belarus comes closer to a homespun version of the initial Chinese 'capitalism from below'. Business economics and growing social disparities aside, class and memory has forged an emerging imagined community or social landscape on its way towards another republican-secular order than the contemporary statehood. Obviously, at lot more needs to be done and said about the class nexus than we have been able to do so far (cf. Therborn 2014b and 2012). Whether Belarus will become paradigmatic for post-communist capitalisms pregnant with forces that point to a drift from the general liberal model is of course an entirely different question.

References

Abdelal, R. (2002) 'Memories of nations and states: Institutional history and national identity in post-Soviet Eurasia', *Nationalities Papers*, 30, 3, pp. 459–484.

Anderson, B. (2006) *Imagined Communities*. London: Verso (3rd ed.).

Anderson, P. (2007) 'Russia's managed democracy', *London Review of Books*, 25 January.

Babkou, I. (1998) 'Belarus: Dual modernity', in Junefelt, K., Peterson, M. and Wallenius, L.-L. (eds.) *Cultural Encounters in East Central Europe*. Stockholm: Forskningsrådsnämnden, pp. 105–109.

Babkou, I. (2005) 'Henealogija bielaruskaj idei' ['Geneology of the Belarusian idea'], *ARCHE*, 37, 3, pp. 136–165.

Backhaus, H., Jönsson, A. and Ottosson, P.-G. (eds.) (1999–2007) *The Works and Correspondence of Axel Oxenstierna*. I:01/02. Stockholm: The Royal Swedish Academy of Letters, History and Antiquities in cooperation with the Swedish National Archive.

Balmaceda, M.M. (2014) *Living the High Life in Minsk: Russian Energy Rents, Domestic Populism and Belarus' Impending Crisis*. Budapest. Central European University Press.

Barberet, R. and Joutsen, M. (2010) 'Crime and justice', in Immerfall, S. and Therborn, G. (eds.) *Handbook of European Societies*. New York: Springer.

Bogdan, S. (2009) 'BSSR i belorusskiy natsionalizm' ['BSSR and Belarusian nationalism'], *Perekrestki*, 1–2, pp. 101–133.

Bohn, T. (2008) *Minsk – Musterstadt des Sozialismus Stadtplanung und Urbanisierung in der Sowjetunion nach 1945*. Köln: Böhlau Verlag.

Bötker, P. (2007) *Leviatan i arkepelagen: Staten, förvaltningen och samhället – fallet Estland* ['Leviathan in the Archipelago: The state, the administration and the society – the case of Estonia']. Huddinge: Södertörn UP.

Cipriani, R. (2010) 'Religion and churches', in Immerfall, S. and Therborn, G. (eds.) *Handbook of European Societies*. New York: Springer.

Cohen, S. (2009) *Soviet Fates and Lost Alternatives: From Stalinism to the New Cold War*. New York: Columbia UP.

Clark, C. (2007) *Iron Kingdom: The Rise and Downfall of Prussia*. Cambridge, Ma: Belknap Press.

Denis, S. (2010) 'Strategicheskaya "smes" dlya natsii: analiz novogodnikh obrashcheniy A. Lukashenko (2003–2009)' ['Strategic "mixture" for the nation: Analysis of New Year's addresses by A. Lukashenka (2003–2009)'], *Palitychnaya sfera*, 14, pp. 80–89.

Derluguian, G. (2005) *Bourdieu's Secret Admirers in the Caucasus*. Chicago: The University of Chicago Press.

Fahey, T. (2010) 'Population', in Immerfall, S. and Therborn, G. (eds.) *Handbook of European Societies*. New York: Springer.

Fitzpatrick, S. (2015) *On Stalin's Team: On Living Dangerously in Soviet Times*. Princeton: PUP.

Furman, D. (2011) *Dvishenie po spirali: Politicheskaia sistema Rossii v riadu drugikh politicheskikh system*. Moscow: Ves'Mir.

Gapova, E. (2008) 'O politicheskoy ekonomii "natsional'nogo yazyka" v Belarusi' ['On the political economy of the "national language" in Belarus'], in Usmanova, A. (ed.) *Belorusskiy format: nevidimaya real'nost'* ['Belarusian Format: Invisible Reality']. Vilnius: EHU, pp. 30–70.

Gapova, E. (2012) *Feminism in Post-Soviet Belarus*. Warsaw: Heinrich Böll Stiftung.

Gornykh, A. (2008) 'Vechnoye vozvrashcheniye po-belorusski' ['The eternal return in Belarusian style'], in Usmanova, A. (ed.) *Belorusskiy format: nevidimaya real'nost'* ['Belarusian Format: Invisible Reality']. Vilnius: EHU, pp. 166–186.

Goujon, A. (2010) 'Memorial narratives of WWII partisans and genocide in Belarus', *East European Politics and Societies*, 24, 1, pp. 6–25.

Gronow, J. (2004) *Caviar with Champagne: Common Luxury and the Ideals of Good Life in Stalin's Russia*. New York: Berg.

Haavio-Mannila, E. (2010) 'Sexuality and family formation', in Immerfall, S. and Therborn, G. (eds.) *Handbook of European Societies*. New York: Springer.

Hort, S.E.O. and Zakharov, N. (forthc.) 'Social welfare in present-day Belarus?'

Hroch, M. (2015) *European Nations: Explaining their Formation*. London: Verso.

Immerfall, S. and Therborn, G. (eds.) (2010) *Handbook of European Societies*. New York: Springer.

Ioffe, G. (2014) *Reassessing Lukashenka: Belarus in Cultural and Geopolitical Context*. Basingstoke: Palgrave Macmillan.

Johansson, A. (2011) *Dissenting Democrats: Nation and Democracy in the Republic of Moldova*. Stockholm: Stockholm University.

Johnsson, P. (2011) 'Minsk. Kurapaty. Khatyn.', *Baltic Worlds*, vol. IV, no. 1.

Kazakevich, A. (2004) 'Bielaruskaja sistema: marfalohija, fizijalohija, hieniealohija' ['The Belarusian system: morphology, physiology, genealogy'], *ARCHE*, 4, pp. 51–84.

Kazakevich, A. (2011) 'Concepts (ideas) of the Belarusian nation since gaining independence (1990–2009)', *Belarusian Political Science Review*, 1, pp. 47–68.

Kazakevich, A. (2012) 'Współczesna białoruska tożsamość historyczna', in Radzik, R. (ed.) *Tożsamości zbiorowe białorusinów*. Lublin: UCMS, pp. 245–266.

Keukeleire, S. and Petrova, I. (2014) 'The European Union, the Eastern Neigbourhood and Russia: Competing regionalisms', in Telò, M. (ed.) *European Union and New Regionalism*. Farnham: Ashgate.

Kivinen, M. (2006) 'Classes in the making? The Russian social structure in transition', in Therborn, G. (ed.) *Inequalities of the World*. London: Verso.

Klinau, A. (2011) *Minsk, drömmarnas solstad*. Stockholm: Erzatz.

Kravchenko, Z. (2012) 'Class as crucible: Remarks on Tony Wood's analysis of social differentiation in Russia', *Baltic Worlds*, vol. 5, no. 3–4, pp. 69–70.

Kuzio, T. (2002) 'History, memory and nation building in the post-Soviet colonial space', *Nationalities Papers*, 30, 2, pp. 241–264.

Lastouski, A. (2009) 'Spetsifika istoricheskoy pamyati v Belarusi: mezhdu sovetskim proshlym i natsional'noy perspektivoy' ['Specificity of historical memory in Belarus: Between the Soviet past and national prospects'], *Vestnik obshchestvennogo mneniya: Dannyye. Analiz. Diskussii.*, 4, pp. 88–99.

Lastouski, A. (2011) 'Vobrazy ŭlady, narodu i "čužych" u publičnych vystupach vyšejšych dziaržaŭnych asobaŭ Bielarusi pieryjadu "libieralizacyi" (2008–2010 hady)' ['Images of power, the people and the "others" in public statements by senior government officials of Belarus in the "liberalization" period (2008–2010)'], *Palitychnaja sfera*, 16–17, pp. 5–72.

Leshchenko, N. (2004) 'A fine instrument: Two nation-building strategies in post-Soviet Belarus', *Nations and Nationalism*, 10, 3, pp. 333–352.

Leshchenko, N. (2008) 'The national ideology and the basis of the Lukashenka regime in Belarus', *Europe-Asia Studies*, 60, 8, pp. 1419–1433.

Lindner, R. (2005) *Historyki i ŭlada. Nacyjatvorčy praces i histaryčnaja palityka ŭ Bielarusi XIX–XX stst* ['Historians and Power. Nation-building Process and the Historical Policy of XIX–XX Centuries in Belarus']. Minsk: Nieuski prasciah.

Mailer, N. (1995) *Oswald's Tale: An American Mystery*. New York: Random House.

Manajew, O. and Drakokhrust, J. (2012) 'Właściwości współczesnej tożsamości białoruskiej', in Radzik, R. (ed.) *Tożsamości zbiorowe białorusinów*. Lublin: UCMS, pp. 11–54.

Marples, D. (1999) *Belarus: A Denationalized Nation*. Singapore: Harwood Academic Publishers.

Marples, D. and Padgol, U. (2008) 'Palityka novaj pamiaci ŭ druhoj rasiejskamoŭnaj dziaržavie' ['New memory politics in the another Russian-speaking state'], *ARCHE*, 11, pp. 91–100.

McDowell, M. (1979) *Resa genom Ryssland*. Malmö: Liber (translation; originally *Journey Across Russia*, 1977).

Miazhevich, G. (2012) 'Religious affiliation and the politics of post-Soviet identity in Belarus', in Kelly, C. and Bassin, M. (eds.) *National Identity*. Cambridge: Cambridge University Press, pp. 341–361.

Miller, A. (2008) *Imperiya Romanovykh i natsionalizm* ['Empire of Romanovs and Nationalism']. Moscow: NLO.

Nairn, T. (1997) *Faces of Nationalism: Janus Revisited*. London: Verso.

Naumenko, L. (2012) *Belorusskaya identichnost'. Soderzhaniye. Dinamika. Sotsial'no-demograficheskaya i regional'naya spetsifika* ['Belarusian Identity. Content. Dynamics. Socio-demographic and Regional Specificity']. Minsk: Belaruskaya navuka.

Nimitz, A. (2014) *Lenin's Electoral Strategy from 1907 to the October Revolution of 1917: The Ballots, the streets – or both*. London: Palgrave/Macmillan.

Obelene, V. (2009) *Discontinuity in Elite Formation: Former Komsomol Functionaries in the Period of Post-Communist Transition In Lithuania and Belarus*. Florence: European University Institute.

Petronis, V. (2007) *Constructing Lithuania: Ethnic Mapping in Tsarist Russia, ca 1800–1914*. Huddinge: Södertörn UP.

Reynolds, M. (2011) *Shattering Empires: The clash and collapse of the Ottoman and Russian Empires 1908–1918*. Cambridge: Cambridge UP.

Rothstein, B. (2003) *Sociala fällor och tillitens problem*. Stockholm: SNS.

Rucht, D. (2010) 'Collective action', in Immerfall, S. and Therborn, G. (eds.) *Handbook of European Societies*. New York: Springer.

Slezkine, J. (2004) *The Jewish Century*. Berkeley: University of California Press.

Smok, V. (2015) 'How cultural NGOs struggle for the right to be Belarusian', in Bulhakau, V. and Lastouski, A. (eds.) *Civil Society in Belarus, 2000–2015*. Warsaw: EEDC, pp. 27–46.

Stephanson, A. (2015) 'Summary and introduction', in *Diplomatic History*, 39, 2.

Szelényi, I. (2015) 'Post-communist capitalisms', *New Left Review* 90.

Therborn, G. (1995) *European Modernity and Beyond: The Trajectory of European Societies, 1945–2000*. London: Sage.

Therborn, G. (2008) *From Marxism to Post-Marxism?* London: Verso.

Therborn, G. (2012) 'Class in the 21st century', *New Left Review* 78.

Therborn, G. (2014a) 'Europe: Trading power, American hunting dog, or the world's Scandinavia?', in Telò, M. (ed.) *European Union and New Regionalism*. Farnham: Ashgate.

Therborn, G. (2014b) 'New masses? Social bases of resistance', *New Left Review* 85.

Urban, M. (1989) *An Algebra of Soviet Power: Elite Circulation in the Belorussian Republic 1966–86*. Cambridge: Cambridge University Press.

Verena, F. (2005) *State-building: A Comparative study of Ukraine, Lithuania, Belarus and Russia*. Budapest: CEU Press.

Wcislo, F. (2011) *Tales of Imperial Russia: The Life and Times of Sergei Witte*. Oxford: Oxford University Press.

Wilmers, M.-K. (2009) *The Eitingons: A Twentieth-century Story*. London: Faber and Faber.

Wilson, A. (2011) *Belarus: The Last Dictatorship in Europe*. New Haven and London: Yale University Press.

Wood, T. (2011) 'The Iceberg society', *New Left Review* 74.

Wood, T. (2007) *Chechnya: The Case for Independence*. London Verso.

Zadvornyj, L. (1981) *I bil genom Sovjetunionen*. Stockholm: W&W (translation; originally *Na avtomobile po Sovetskomu Sojuzu*).

ELISABETH ÖZDALGA

Islam-Oriented Trajectories and Turkey's Fluctuating Encounters with European Modernity

'Modernity' is primarily associated with transformations that result in more complex and rationally organized economic and political configurations in the form of the market and the nation-state. Less obvious, but equally fundamental, is the formation of national communities – an elusive and thorny element in the same process. In this chapter, I draw on a couple of works in Göran Therborn's extensive oeuvre and reflect upon this complex aspect of modernity as it applies to Turkey, a Muslim-majority country closely linked to Europe geographically, economically, politically and culturally. In no other country in the Muslim Middle East has secularism penetrated so far into the judicial, educational and religious institutions as in Kemal Atatürk's modern republic. And in no other country has the dismantling of the rule of law and political liberties been as bewildering and disappointing.

The chapter starts with an overview of how Turkey's postwar relationship with Europe was strengthened, despite many ups and downs. Secondly, it focuses on the complications arising from this rapprochement on the development of the country's collective identities, especially after Islamic values became more powerfully articulated in public life. The development of two Islam-influenced nationalist discourses – 'Turkish Islam' and 'Milli Görüş' – will be elaborated: over the years these have played distinct roles in shaping Turkish national identities. Third, by following up on the mounting politicization of Islam throughout the wider region, I discuss the upsurge of radical Islamism and/or jihadism and the recent challenges to territorial boundaries in the form of military confrontations and civil war, and their effect on Turkey's ideological landscape. The chapter ends with tentative reflections on the effect of these developments on European modernity. In the present global order, eruptions in one part of the world can hardly pass unnoticed or be ignored elsewhere, and especially in the case of Europe and the Near/Middle East, two regions with long historical ties.

Turkey and European modernity after the Second World War

In *European Modernity and Beyond: The Trajectory of European Societies, 1945–2000* (1995) Göran Therborn provides a panoramic survey and analysis of Europe after the Second World War. This was a period marked by relative political stability, uncontested national boundaries and a strong determination among leading actors to deepen economic and political cooperation among previously hostile nation-states. In a 1996 conference paper touching on related topics that was later published as 'Beyond civil society: Democratic experience and their relevance to the "Middle East"' (1997), Therborn critically analyses the 'mainly normative' notion of civil society and its relationship to the theoretically more stringent and elaborated concept of political democracy. The article, which can be read as an addendum to the book, extends the analysis beyond Europe to the former colonial world, including the Middle East, but is limited to the post-Soviet period. The focus of the book, by contrast, remains within Europe's borders, but involves a longer time perspective. It is the book that constitutes the basis for the following deliberations.

The postwar period was the 'golden age' of the modern welfare state. Not only Sweden, which luckily had been spared the devastation of the war, but also states directly involved such as Great Britain, France, Germany, Holland, Denmark and Norway initiated social and economic reforms on an unprecedented scale. In this optimistic atmosphere, which formed the foundation of the whole European Economic Community (EEC) (and later European Community and European Union) project, territorial boundaries faded in significance. Money and labour could move more freely and there were also initiatives to fashion a common diplomacy and joint action in the international arena. The 'beyond' in European modernity tended towards national borders of lesser moment, a vision that also permeates Therborn's approach.

The seamy side of the story is of course the Iron Curtain, which until 1989 divided the continent, thereby exacerbating existing cultural and developmental differences between Eastern and Western Europe. However, the author, writing in the mid-1990s, and taking due note of the Soviet Union's dissolution, displays a more holistic perspective on the region. This allows him to bring to bear more unconventional transnational perspectives on the structuring of European societies. So, for example, alternative approaches to describing and classifying the economic and cultural landscapes (Chapter 10: 'The European Economic Space' and Chapter 11: 'Europe's Cultural Space') point towards a federalist system safely removed from the political convulsions caused by the nervous arrogance and hostility associated with narrow nationalist interests.

As part of the optimism prevailing after the war, partner states in the newly formed EEC were also sought on the fringes of the continent. Turkey is a case in point. By becoming a member of the Council of Europe (1949), signing the European Convention of Human Rights (1953), joining the European Court of Human Rights (1959), and by becoming a member of NATO (1952) and introducing multiparty parliamentarianism with free elections in 1950, this Muslim-majority country had clearly declared its attachment to Europe and the West and was a viable potential EEC candidate.

In July 1959, about two years after the Treaty of Rome had been signed, Greece applied for associate membership in the EEC. This set off heated reactions in Ankara and was followed, two weeks later, by a similar application from Turkey. Greece's application was approved in 1961, but Turkey had to wait a further two years before the 'Ankara Agreement' was signed (1963). The delay was partly due to the military coup of May 27, 1960. Less than a decade later, in July 1970, Turkey and, since 1965, the European Community (EC), signed an agreement foreseeing eventual full membership for Turkey. This was followed up in 1978–79, when the EC invited Turkey to apply for full membership along with Greece. However, then Prime Minister Bülent Ecevit declined the invitation on the grounds that it would lead to too much economic intervention from abroad, with supposedly negative consequences for the already vulnerable Turkish economy.

The next initiative was mounted by Turkey during the prime ministership of neo-liberal Turgut Özal. In April 1987, an application for full membership was submitted, which, however, and much to the disappointment of Özal and others, was refused. These efforts were followed up in 1996, when Turkey, in the hope of eventually achieving candidate status, entered the EU customs union. This was an important step in opening up Turkey to imports of industrial goods from other EU member states. A further application for candidate status in 1997 was yet again turned down. Finally, at the EU summit in Helsinki in December 1999, candidate status was approved. Thereafter reforms were undertaken to improve Turkey's human rights standing and reduce the military's undue political influence, a process of democratization that was accelerated under the leadership of the Islam-oriented, conservative Justice and Development Party (AKP), which came to power with a majority in the election of November 2002.

During its first two terms (2002–07 and 2007–11), AKP implemented many economic, social, judicial and political reforms, which had widespread positive repercussions for the overall quality of life, not least of the poor and the lower middle class. After these 'good years', however, developments went into sharp reverse: the country came under the one-man rule of President Recep Tayyip Erdoğan, resulting in a kind of authoritarianism that is increasing the prospect of civil war between the Turkish state and the Kurdish guerrillas in the PKK (Kurdistan Workers' Party). This illegal organization has over the years built up considerable grassroots support among the Kurds, not least due to the mismanagement of the Kurdish question by the AKP leadership in 2013–15.[1]

---

1. The Kurdish population amounts to about 20 per cent or 15 million of a total population of 78 million. About half the Kurds still live in the eastern parts of the country, while the remainders have migrated westwards to big cities like Istanbul, Izmir, Ankara, Antalya and Mersin.

Ambiguous national identities

In the context of European modernity, Turkey's current position raises serious questions: is Turkey drifting away from its European legacy towards the kind of dictatorships that have, with few exceptions, dominated politics in the modern Middle East; or, is Turkey passing through a phase of European modernity that most Europeans prefer to pass over in silence? Put differently: is Turkey being drawn into the orbit of its Middle Eastern neighbours, or is it preserving its place in the European sphere, even as it goes into a kind of totalitarian eclipse? Even though these questions cannot yet be authoritatively answered, they hint at the ambiguous character of Turkish identities. That Turkey is culturally and geographically situated at the frontier between Europe/West and Asia/East is a commonplace. What I want to address relates to a somewhat different problematic of identity formation – namely what happens when Islam is drawn into the process of modern nation formation? Therborn speaks of the many trajectories to and through modernity. One of the features that have given the Turkish venture into modernity a distinct character is the way in which Turkish and Islamic identities have fed one another. This fusion has developed in waves and with different ideological leanings, but has resulted overall in an increased role for Islam as the popular masses have been drawn into politics.

Turkish Islam

The politicization of Islam was already evident during the last decades of the Ottoman Empire, when almost all political actors, including Sultan Abdulhamid II (r. 1876–1909) and the Young Turks – the leading opposition group – drew on religion to strengthen their respective positions. The sultan supported Pan-Islamism in order to shore up the unity of his weakening empire, and the Young Turks used Islam as a tool to stir up the Muslim masses against the sultan, to undermine his legitimacy from an Islamic point of view and to summon the people against European imperialism (Hanioğlu 2001: 306). After the revolution of 1908, the Young Turks assumed responsibility for 'national' unity. To that end, they appealed now to

Turkism, now to Pan-Islamism and Ottomanism in an effort to pro-
pitiate the disparate ethnic and religious elements still constituting
the empire (Hanioğlu 2001: 298). It was in this mixture of ideologies
that Turkish nationalism first took root. What appeared to be rallying calls for the royal house (Ottomanism) or a summoning around
religion (Pan-Islamism) were in fact expressions of Turkish proto-
nationalism. In particular Pan-Islamism, which has been regarded
as purely based on religious sentiments, was in fact an ideology that
was closer to nationalism and anti-colonialism than religion (Khalid
2005: 201–202).

After 1923, the leaders of the modern Turkish republic put a firm
lid on the use of Islam for political purposes. Although the War of
Independence (1919–22) was draped in jihadist (holy war) language,
Islamic rhetoric was toned down dramatically once the new republican regime was established. The banning of Islam as a unifying element within official nationalist ideology was sharp and radical, since
religion was regarded the most important culprit for the country's
backwardness. Islam was regarded as the religion of the Arabs, meaning that it was inherently alien to the Turkish people.[2] The elimination of important religious institutions such as the *medreses* (religious
schools of higher learning), the *ulema* (the religious learned), the *vakıfs*
(the pious foundations); prohibition of the Sufi orders and Koranic
schools; and abolition of the Arabic alphabet (the alphabet of the
Koran) drastically diminished the space allowed to Islam in Turkish
society. The reforms did not leave the common people untouched,
but since there were no formal channels for voicing discontent, the
common people remained mute.

During the era of the one-party regime (1923–46), leading Kemal-
ists launched a kind of secular (or secularist) nationalism, which
emphasized the Central Asian Turkic origin of the Turkish people
and ignored the legacy of both the Ottomans and the Islamic past.
This was an ideology that paradoxically looked towards the future,

2. Mustafa Kemal Atatürk was regarded a freethinker and has been quoted
as saying: 'I have no religion, and at times I wish all religions [were] at the
bottom of the sea. He is a weak ruler who needs religion to uphold his government; it is as if he would catch his people in a trap.' From Grace Ellison's
Turkey Today (London: Hutchinson 1928, p. 24), quoted in Mango 2004: 463.

wanted to settle accounts with the recent past, *and* looked for its historical roots in an even more remote, pre-Islamic, but essentially invented past.[3]

The official Central Asian-inspired Turkic nationalism did not go unchallenged, however, not even during the heyday of Kemalism. While the authorized version of nationalism emphasized the cultural aspects of Turkism (especially language), another group that grew up around the historian, novelist and activist Hüseyin Nihal Atsız (1905–75) developed a more racist version of Turkism. According to his interpretation, Turks were defined by blood relationships and ought to gather under the umbrella of Pan-Turkism. All non-Turkish elements were to be avoided, since whenever Turks had mixed with other peoples in the past, degeneration and disaster had resulted. Not only were other ethnic or racial groups such as the Arabs and Persians disapproved of, but so too was Islam, which was seen as a religion foreign to pure Turkishness. For example, *devşirme*, the practice of bringing up Christian boys to serve the sultan in the civil service or the army was viewed as a major factor in the decline of the empire, since it diluted the racial purity of the elite. Instead, Atsız and his followers regretted that Ottoman rulers had not created a genuine Turkish aristocracy. Lamenting the 'impurity' of the elite, they idealized the Anatolian peasantry as the purest representatives of the Turkish race. People living in the urban areas were too mixed. Atatürk was seen as no exception, since he originated in cosmopolitan Thessalonica, at that time a city with a large Jewish population.

Atatürk's death in 1938 meant more freedom for the racist-oriented nationalists. However, the revelation of Nazi atrocities after the war made this kind of ideology impossible to defend. The transition to multiparty politics in 1950 also tended to mute this kind of radicalism, since political actors and movements now had to look for support among the masses. During the Cold War, activism was

---

3. The official claims made about the history of the Turks were embarrassingly fictitious. According to the Turkish History Thesis, pronounced and defended by historians such as Afet İnan (one of Atatürk's adopted daughters) at the First Turkish History Congress in Ankara in 1932, many great civilizations, including the Chinese, the Sumerian and the Egyptian originated with the Turks.

instead channelled into the struggle against Communism and Soviet power.

A different, but equally notable, right-wing nationalist intellectual from the inter-war period was Necip Fazıl Kısakürek (1904–83). Despite being a poet and playwright of repute, he involved himself in an ideological cause and used his pen to fiercely defend Islam. As long as Atatürk was alive, he kept a low profile, especially as regards his Islamic leanings, but he found a willing audience after Atatürk's death. During the 1950s and 1960s, Kısakürek also became a devoted supporter of the Association for the Struggle against Communism (Komünizmle Mücadele Dernekleri) (Özdalga 1994).

After the war, both Turkist and Islam-oriented right-wing nationalists mixed and competed with one another (Göksu-Özdoğan 2001: 278). After the 1960 military coup, several political parties emerged out of these activist circles, the most important being the Nationalist Action Party (Milliyetçi Hareket Partisi) led by Alparslan Türkeş, one of the perpetrators of the coup. There were right-wing civil society associations as well, such as Aydınlar Ocağı (Hearth of Intellectuals), which became the most articulate advocate of Türk-Islam Sentezi, an ideology based on Turkism *and* Islam.[4]

The basic message of Aydınlar Ocağı was that being both nationalistic and religious involves no contradiction. What made this stance rather daring, even bold, was the previous renunciation of religion in both the official Kemalist (positivistic) and the ultra-nationalistic Turkist versions of nationalism.[5] By the late 1960s, more tempered expressions had replaced the interwar radicalism of Kemalist nationalism and the racist school. However, in proposing startling interpretations of history, Türk-Islam Sentezi did not lag far behind its forerunners. Thus, for example, Türk-Islam Sentezi was said to be a synthesis born a millennium earlier: 'Türk-İslam Sentezi is not just a theory [ideal, ideology], it is a fact, which has emanated from and is proved by a great history', Süleyman Yalçın, leader of Aydınlar

---

4. The following section is based on an earlier article of the author (Özdalga 2006).

5. 'It is as if a human being cannot be both "religious," "nationalistic," and "modern" [*medeniyetçi*]. By making these values parts of opposite programs, they are, for no reason at all, turned into "struggling forces"' (Arvasi 1979: 9).

Ocağı, pronounced at a congress in Istanbul in 1987 (Yalçın 1988; Özdalga 2006: 556 and 568). A few years earlier, another supporter had expressed the perfect harmony of Turkish and Islamic tradition in almost lyrical terms: 'It was as if the Turks had been searching for Islam for centuries' (Arvasi 1979: 238; Özdalga 2006: 568). This was an appeal to Sufi (Islamic mysticism) symbolism, whereby the reed flute (*ney*) is said to voice longing for the root from which it has been separated. According to this interpretation, the Turkish people and Islam are seen as being been meant for one another from the beginning of time. So strong was the union between Turkish people and Islam, that 'those who did not convert to Islam, but remained Shamanist, Manichean, Jewish or Christian also totally lost their Turkish identity' (Yalçın 1988).

According to Türk-Islam Sentezi discourse, Turks converted *en masse* as soon as they became acquainted with Islam and without any kind of external pressure. This assertion allegedly 'proved' the inseparability of Islam and the Turkish people (Şeker 1985: 65). Conversion was based on rational choice in the sense that Turks had for centuries encountered many other religions, such as Judaism, Christianity and Zoroastrianism before encountering Islam, but none of the former had spoken to their hearts. With Islam, the experience was fundamentally different. In a short time, Turks had adopted this religion and become its leading political protectors as rulers of the Seljuk states and eventually the Ottoman Empire.

Through this synthesis, Turks had, so it was thought, been strengthened morally, socially and politically, while Islam as a civilization had been rescued from looming disaster. Under Turkish leadership, Islam achieved new triumphs. 'The efforts made by Turks for the Turkification and Islamization of Anatolia were so great that history will never really be able to tell the whole story' (Şeker 1985: 151, 160). This divine fusion was based in equal measure on Turkish and Islamic culture. However, needless to say, the discourse was built on an oversimplification past recognition of the complex and intricate universe of Islam. The Aydınlar Ocağı intellectuals were not trained in the Islamic sciences, and their superficiality was also reflected in what they selected from the Islamic heritage as especially identifiable with the Turks. This particular Turkish legacy can be summarized thus: a will to conquer new areas for Islam; an ambition to reconstruct these areas according to Islamic traditions; an urge to be in the service of Islam; relying on Sufi orders (*tarikats*) for spreading the Islamic faith; an activism not content with seclusion in lodges for pure contemplation, but always prepared to stand up for the faith with sword in hand; and, lastly, a religion loyal to state power. Concerning the conquest of new areas for Islam, Turks were said to have been especially heroic. In this respect, the concept of jihad or holy war was a key attribute. 'The Turkish army is "God's army," the Turkish flag with its holy crescent and star is the symbol of Islam; its red colour the symbol of the blood shed by those who sacrificed their lives for Allah' (Arvasi 1979: 238).

In terms of its membership, Aydınlar Ocağı was too academic to spawn a great following. However, leading members saw an opportunity to increase their influence over state affairs when the military took power in 1980. The military leadership, especially the commander in chief, Kenan Evren, was not totally insensitive to Islamic trends. In that he can be compared to his contemporary in Pakistan, General Ziya ül-Hak. So, under the circumstances, a close relationship developed between Aydınlar Ocağı and the military leadership, which continued after Evren was elected president in 1982 until the end of his term in 1989. However, Aydınlar Ocağı's close links to the military leadership undermined its standing in the eyes of other intellectual and political networks. It was therefore in a somewhat different guise that the notion of Turkish Islam found its way into Turkish nationalist discourse in the 1980s and 1990s, namely through the popular revivalist movement that grew up around the charismatic leader Fethullah Gülen.

Gülen, who had made a name for himself as a popular sermonizer in and around Izmir in the 1960s and 1970s, set in motion a network of activists that over the decades developed into one of the strongest Islamic movements in Turkey. Especially since the 1980s, the Gülen community has grown continuously and now is at the heart of an extensive global network of educational institutions (high-schools and universities), business organizations, financial institutions and, of paramount importance, extensive and potent media outlets (Balcı

2002; Özdalga 2000; Turam 2004a, 2004b; Yavuz 1999). True, there are striking similarities between the Gülen community and Aydınlar Ocağı regarding their interpretations of Turkish Islam. Gülen activists describe their particular form of Islam as based on tolerance; piety inspired by Sufism; the ambition to be in the service of others (*hizmet*); the inclination to embrace all humanity with love (humanism); flexibility and openness to change; secularism; and loyalty to existing political power (Aras and Çaha 2000). However, despite these discursive overlaps, their respective forms of organization differed a great deal. The Gülen movement was and is in all respects a grassroots phenomenon, while Aydınlar Ocağı was limited to academic and official circles. Another important difference concerned their leadership. The Gülen movement gained much of its strength from the charismatic appeal of Fethullah Gülen (b. 1938), who was famous for his deep religious knowledge and didactic sermons. There was no corresponding personality or leader among the Aydınlar Ocağı intellectuals. It is therefore through the Gülen community that Turkish Islam as an identity discourse has found wider circulation and a large following. Both movements emphasized the allegedly peaceful and tolerant aspects of Turkish Islam, but this message was much more evident among Gülen's sympathizers. Because the Gülen movement is much broader and more global, it has also had greater exposure to the challenges of radical Islam. One of its key missions has been to draw a clear distinction between its softer and more tolerant Turkish form of Islam and that of other nations, where fundamentalism, fanaticism, and/or jihadism have found fertile ground. In this way, the Gülen movement has been active in sharply differentiating Turkey form other Muslim countries in the Arab world, Iran and Pakistan. Islam practised the Turkish way was thought to contain a kind of guarantee (or immunity) against all kinds of extremist manifestation.

Milli Görüş – the national vision

Aydınlar Ocağı and the Gülen movement were not the only activist groups embracing Islamic values as an expression of national identities. From the late 1960s, Turkey also saw the emergence of political parties with an Islamic agenda. The first was the National Order Party (Milli Nizam Partisi, MNP), set up at the very end of 1969. However, overly vigilant oversight by the military led to continuous setbacks, in that Islamic parties were closed down every time the military interfered in the country's political affairs. Consequently, MNP, closed during the 1971 military intervention, re-emerged the year after under the name of National Salvation Party (Milli Selamet Partisi, MSP). This party, which, relative to its electoral support (of between 8 and 12 per cent), was able to play an undeservedly prominent role during the 1970s, was shut down shortly after the military coup of September 1980. In 1984, it appeared again as Welfare Party (Refah Partisi, RP), which held on until the 'soft coup' of 1997. From the rubble of this party emerged within a couple of years the Justice and Development Party (Adalet ve Kalkınma Partisi, AKP), which, by rejuvenating its programme and leading cadres, succeeded in gaining a majority in the 2002 elections. AKP, under the leadership of Recep Tayyip Erdoğan, has remained in power ever since.

This branch of Turkish Islamic revivalism developed an ideology that differed in part from the 'Turkish Islam' discourse. The Turkish element was pushed into the background, which did not mean that these Islamists were less concerned about the formation of the Turkish nation. The interest in a well-integrated and stable nation that was courageously assertive in relation to others was instead captured in the catch phrase *milli görüş* (lit. national vision). National strength was dependent on both internal cohesion *and* vigour in relation to other nations in the international arena. The *milli görüş* movement was based on the idea that something significant had gone awry in Turkey, both with respect to internal cohesion and external power. The social fabric of the Turkish nation was being threatened by the fact that it was turning its back on religion. Therefore, the nation needed both moral and economic development.

Moral improvement (*manevi kalkınma*, i.e., raising the moral values of the nation) thus became a very basic objective of MNP, and later also of MSP and RP. Moral improvement, along with scientific, technological, and economic development, constituted the very essence of their philosophy. Moral improvement meant making greater efforts to improve the knowledge and consciousness of religious values. This programme had its roots in the long controversy in Turkish society over religious education and the role of the Koran and other sacred sources of learning in public school curricula. Building more Imam-Hatip schools (prayer leader and preachers' seminars), facilitating the establishment of Koran-courses, striving for more religious education in normal schools were high on the agenda.

National strength and self-confidence was also regarded as closely associated with economic development, especially within industry. For a nation to become fully independent, it must be able to set up its own heavy industry, and, what is more, be able to produce machine-generating machinery so as to maintain the country's national independence. All this was in tune with an anti-colonial, Third World discourse. In addition, a more equal distribution of wealth was thought to be closely related to the mission of creating an alternative social (read: Islamic) order based on justice. This included taking special responsibility for those parts of the country, especially inner Anatolia, whose development lagged behind the rest of country's, since they were ignored by the owners of big capital, who preferred to invest in the metropolitan areas. Enviously watching the expansive economies of Southeast Asia, successful Anatolian companies became known as 'Anatolian Tigers'. Such ventures became a special source of pride among the *milli görüş* parties. Finally, almsgiving, one of the five pillars of Islam, also constituted an important component in the *milli görüş* supporters' concept of the exercise of power. Official welfare measures or reforms were seen as an extension of this Islamic duty.

To sum up, after several decades of officially sanctioned secular nationalism built on ethnic and cultural identities, Islam gradually found its way into Turkish nationhood. Initially, Islam appeared as an addendum to ethnic/linguistic Turkishness. Out of this combination grew the Turkish-Islamic synthesis, mainly defended by two groups. The first was Aydınlar Ocagı, an association of academicians and intellectuals, which developed a discourse with somewhat militaristic overtones, in which emphasis was placed on the glorious conquests of Seljuk and Ottoman Turks, historical victories attributed to the moral strength granted by Islam. This belligerence meant these intellectuals enjoyed a special affinity with the military, with whom they collaborated during the decade following the military coup of 1980. The second group was the Gülen community, which had a more ambiguous relationship with the military. Adherents were full of admiration for the Turkish soldier, who sacrifices his life for his country, and were loyal to the military structures, but were at the same time despised by the military on account of the sectarian character of the their community and their romantic religiosity, which allegedly challenged the secularist beliefs of the military establishment. Apart from that, the Gülen network differed from Aydınlar Ocagı by being more oriented towards civil society. Thanks to its stronger grassroots appeal, it was through the Gülen movement that the Turkish Islam discourse reached a wider audience.

The *milli görüs* movement was different. First, it was linked to party politics and had the ultimate aim of achieving power political power and control of the state apparatus. Second, in terms of identity politics, Turkishness was moved backstage. Instead, the favoured word was '*milli*' or national, which in Turkey, a country with a large Kurdish minority, opened the way for a more flexible and inclusive discourse. The meaning of the term '*milli*' could shift according to context. In the eastern Kurdish areas, it could refer to all Muslims, Kurds and Turks, while in the western parts or central Anatolia it could refer to 'national' in a more exclusive, ethnic Turkish sense. In either case, however, it had clear religious connotations. References to Ottoman society were useful in this respect, since the related word *millet* was at that time used to designate various religious groups, for instance Muslims on one hand, non-Muslims on the other.

This Ottoman/*millet*/Muslim twist also widened the identity frame to include brothers in faith in neighbouring post-Ottoman Muslim countries. Solidarity was especially extended to Sunni Muslims in Palestine, Egypt, Syria and Jordan, including such groups as Hamas and the Muslim Brotherhood. This identification with Sunni Muslims also blended with Third World solidarity (ideology). Necmettin Erbakan (1926–2011), the long-time leader of the MNP,

MSP, RP movement, initiated the so-called D8 initiative during his short prime-ministership (1996–97) as an alternative form of international cooperation among Muslim countries to the G7. Erbakan's venture failed, but the ambition to play a more active role as a leading nation in the Muslim and post-Ottoman world was resumed about a decade later, after Turkey, following several years of far-reaching political, juridical and economic reform had raised its international standing. That national pride turned into expansionism, even hubris, and in just a few years tipped over into a kind of fascist dictatorship under the leadership of AKP and Erdogan, including heavy military suppression of the Kurdish minority, constitutes the latest act in Turkey's drama involving Islam and nationalism.

Expansionist visions built on Sunni loyalties

The establishment of the AKP in 2001 meant dissociation from much of the ideological heritage of the *milli görüş* ideology. Gone was the narrow understanding of national interests, including scepticism towards the EU and other engagements on the global market. Gone also was much of the Islamist rhetoric, such as the flirtation with jihad and sharia law. Consequently, AKP despised any reference to Islamic/Islamist or even Muslim terms and described itself as a 'conservative democratic party'. However, as the years passed and the party firmly entrenched its power, there was resurgence in Islamist tropes, especially in the rhetoric of the leader Recep Tayyip Erdoğan. This time, however, it was in the service of an authoritarian ideology, which, step by step, dismantled democracy.

When AKP came to power with a full majority in 2002.[6] Turkey had ten years of unstable coalition governments behind it. The 1990s

---

6. AKP got 34.3 per cent of the votes, which gave the party 363 of 550 seats in parliament. This high representation was due to the election threshold of 10 per cent. Four parties, with approximately 9, 8, 7, and 6 per cent of the vote respectively, were discounted. Only AKP and CHP (Republican People's Party) achieved representation, plus nine independent candidates. Thus, in total, 45 per cent of the electorate lacked representation in parliament from 2002 to 2007.

Table 1: GNI per capita in US$ and the inflation rate 1996/2000–2012/2014

Year	GNI per capita US$	Inflation per cent
1996	2 920	–
1997	3 190	–
1998	3 410	–
1999	3 530	–
2000	4 190	54.9
2001	3 470	54.4
2002	3 470	45.0
2003	3 800	25.3
2004	5 060	10.6
2005	6 510	10.1
2006	7 510	9.6
2007	8 500	8.8
2008	9 340	10.4
2009	9 130	6.3
2010	9 950	8.6
2011	10 490	6.5
2012	10 800	8.9
2013	10 970	–
2014	10 840	–

Source: World Bank.

was a 'lost decade' for both the economy and politics, including the sensitive Kurdish issue. Lack of capable leadership led to a deep economic crisis in 2000, which was overcome with IMF loans in combination with stringent reforms of the banking system and the budget process. Maintenance of these monetary and budgetary reforms laid the foundation for AKP's economic success during the following decade. As seen in Table 1, inflation dwindled from almost 55 per cent in 2000 to 9 per cent in 2012, while GNI per capita increased

Table 2: Percentage of the population below the national poverty line, 2006–12

Year	Percentage of population below the national poverty line
2006	13.3
2007	8.4
2008	6.8
2009	4.4
2010	3.7
2011	2.8
2012	2.3

Source: World Bank.

from approximately US$3 400 when AKP took power in 2002 to over US$10 400 in 2011. That this economic growth also benefitted the lower income groups is illustrated in Table 2, which shows how the percentage of the population below the national poverty line decreased from 13 per cent in 2006 to 2 per cent in 2012. After 2011, however, the reform programme more or less stalled, as reflected in the clear stagnation of GNI per capita after that date. This change in economic performance is related to the fact that politics took a more authoritarian, and later even dictatorial, turn.

In three successive elections, AKP steadily increased its vote from 34.3 per cent (2002) to 46.6 per cent (2007) and 49.9 per cent (2011). By the end of the first decade, AKP had firmly consolidated its power, not least through a referendum on constitutional amendment in 2010. Crucial changes included making it more difficult to outlaw political parties. In addition, many cases had been before the courts since 2007 against alleged efforts in 2003 to topple the AKP government. In short, the military was not as fearsome as it used to be.

In 2011, at the time of the Arab Spring, Turkey was a rising star among its Arab neighbours. Here was a Muslim country with a pro-Islamic government, a fast growing economy and a functioning parliamentary democracy. This lent Turkey, and especially the ruling party and its leaders, significant international prestige. Seemingly, however, this widespread interest in Turkey's 'success story', especially among countries in the neighbouring region, spurred new and more daring ambitions among AKP leaders for not only their own country, but also in the region.

The ambitions to play a role in political developments in the wider Middle East have been especially noticeable in relation to the Syrian conflict. The underlying assumption in the AKP vision for Syria was that Bashar al-Assad must be ousted. This would open the way to free elections. In Egypt, the Muslim Brotherhood gained ground after the democratic protests in Tahrir Square and Hosni Mubarak's deposition. Free elections in Syria would also, it was assumed, lead to similar successes for the Syrian 'Brothers'. Activists within the Muslim Brotherhood were not only sympathetic towards AKP, they admired its leaders, especially Erdoğan. Egypt and Syria under the leadership of the Muslim Brotherhood would presumably open their doors to wider regional cooperation based on deeper shared values and loyalty among activist Sunni Muslims.

This vision was never realized. Instead, in Syria the conflict has descended into bloody civil war, with militant jihadists gaining the upper hand and eventually declaring an Islamic State in June 2014. These developments did not affect the underlying policy of the Turkish government, which did not abandon regime change in Syria, even if this meant support for militant al-Qaida groups, including the Islamic State.

Not only regionally, but also at home the AKP leadership has drifted towards more Islamist and authoritarian leanings. If not earlier, these changes in leadership attitudes were clearly revealed to the general public during the Gezi protests in May–June 2013. These events, which started as a peaceful occupation by environmental activists of Gezi Park behind Taksim Square in central Istanbul, turned within a couple of weeks into violent confrontations between demonstrators and police, spreading to almost every provincial centre in the country. The violent turn of events was largely due to the heavy-handedness of the government: first, in the aggressive rhetoric adopted by Prime Minister Erdogan; second, in the increasingly harsh measures adopted by the police, which resulted in several deaths, severe injuries and much material damage.

The Gezi protests proved to be a wake-up call. Had the leaders wanted to resolve the controversy about rebuilding Gezi Park and Taksin Square in a peaceful way, they could have sought to do so by democratic means, using dialogue and compromise. The violent repression spoke a different language. It now became more obvious that AKP and its leaders were acting in terms of a different, and so far unknown, agenda. Gone was the relatively open and liberal tone of AKP's previous two terms. *La belle epoque* was over. Ahead lay harsher and more polarized political relationships.

The next step on the road to dictatorial rule came with a criminal investigation made public in December 2013, which unmasked extensive bribery, corruption, money laundering, fraud and gold smuggling involving several ministers, their sons and close family members of the prime minister. The reaction of the AKP government was severe – and panic-stricken. To sweep all corruption allegations under the carpet and avoid any judicial inquiry, many 'reforms' were enacted to bring strategic parts of the legal system under direct government control. The whole police force was also reshuffled in a re-organization that affected hundreds of thousands of police officers. With the help of government-controlled media, a totally distorted picture of the corruption allegations was broadcast. Media reports accused another branch of the Islamic movement in Turkey, the Gülen movement, of in fact staging a coup against the government through the criminal investigations. Having previously been on good terms with the movement, AKP now declared it to be the party's and government's principal enemy. A witch-hunt was launched against Fethullah Gülen and his followers. The result of these developments is that democratic rights and the rule of law have been totally undermined.

An intimidating face has also been presented to the Kurdish minority. At the end of 2012, a 'Peace Process' was initiated involving the PKK and the government. Weapons were to be surrendered in exchange for democratic reforms. These initiatives were generally greeted with optimism, since they promised a peaceful resolution to an armed conflict that had been going on for more than 30 years. However, the increasingly polarized political situation (Gezi-protests, corruption scandals, civil war in Syria) also undermined the Kurdish peace process. From the fall of 2014, Syrian Kurds[7] began making military gains against the Islamic State in northern Syria, advances that thwarted Turkey's efforts to support the anti-Assad opposition across the border, including militant jihadists. These developments, together with gains by the Kurdish Peoples' Democratic Party (HDP) in the Turkish parliamentary elections of June 2015, led the AKP leadership to interrupt the peace process. A campaign was launched against PKK using police and military forces. The confrontations occurred in well-known cities in the Kurdish areas, such as the provincial centre Diyarbakir (Sur district) and smaller cities and towns like Cizre, Nusaybin and Silopi, where the security forces also encountered resistance from the civil population. Through its confrontational policies against the Turkish and Syrian Kurds, its support for the anti-Assad jihadist opposition, and its alliances with Saudi Arabia and Qatar, the Turkish government has become deeply involved in the deteriorating situation in the wider Middle East.

Islamism and nationalism as overlapping ideologies

Turkey's efforts to play a more active role in Middle Eastern politics have backfired. The promising vision of promoting 'zero conflict' with neighbours, launched during AKP's first terms of office, has come to nothing. Instead, Turkey has become an increasingly isolated, less reliable and unpredictable regional actor. Regional expansionism, including efforts to bring about regime change in neighbouring Syria through outright interference, along with domestic violations of the rule of law and freedom of expression have harmed Turkey's prospects of EU membership in the foreseeable future. In an ever more unstable region, Turkey's increasingly warped foreign relations may in coming years have fatal consequences for the coun-

---

7. The Syrian Kurds are organized into the Democratic Union Party (PYD) and its armed division, the People's Protection Units (YPG), organizations with close connections to the PKK in Turkey.

try's capacity to maintain its territorial borders, especially in the Kurdish areas.

The Middle East is over-burdened with chaotic and vehement conflicts and dramatic changes. Not only Iraq and Syria, whose territorial borders are already seriously disputed, but a seemingly stable NATO country such as Turkey may be imminently afflicted by social and political convulsion. Many of the evolving conflicts are carried out in the name of Islamic/Islamist ideologies, be they Sunni Islam, Shi'a Islam, Salafism, Wahhabism. However, behind this religious rhetoric stand fierce nationalistic interests, such as Iran versus Saudi-Arabia; Saudi-Arabia versus Yemen, Syria and Iraq; Turkey versus Iran, General Abdel Fattah al-Sisi's Egypt and Bashar al-Assad's Syria. And, in the middle of all this, are the efforts by al-Qaida-associated groups to form a new caliphate, the Islamic State. The emphasis on Islamic values and traditions should not hide the fact that the underlying conflicts are about reshaping existing national borders. Allegedly Islamic polities such as Saudi-Arabia, Iran and the Islamic State are not primarily 'theocracies', but evolving, modern nation-states. Of the Islamic Republic of Iran, Sami Zubaida has written: 'The indications ... are that the Islamic elements of the republic fit in very well with the nation-state model both in terms of state organization and of the structure of the political field and its discourses' (Zubaida 1993 [1989]: 179). The late Fred Halliday expressed a similar point in the following words:

Nowhere is the import of the political, and with it the instrumental use of religion, more evident than in the case of Iran. The Iranian revolution appears to reject nationalism as a secular, alien, limiting ideology. Yet if one looks at what Khomeini has said and done before coming to power and afterwards a familiar nationalist political programme emerges. The main language he drew upon was populist: he referred to the struggle between ... the oppressed ... and ... the oppressor; the main enemy was imperialism ...; his Iranian foes were corrupt traitors and agents ... All this is familiar third world nationalist rhetoric. ... Khomeini's revolution was framed and worked out through the imperatives of the nation-state: now it is increasingly being recognized that Iran is adopting an ideology that can be termed 'national-Islamism', but this was ever so. (Halliday 2000: 49.)

Islam does not offer a blueprint for a polity, but provides the cultural values around which a national community can be – or is – formed. In a post-revolutionary European nation-state context, political legitimacy was rendered by ruling in the name of the people, what Elie Kedourie called 'politics in a new style' (Kedourie 1985 [1960]: 9).[8] The same is true of today's political systems in the Middle East. Even if political ideologies draw their colour more from Islam than from ethnic/linguistic identities, Islam still functions as a marker for social and national solidarity. The historian Frederick F. Anscombe, who has elaborated at length on the relationship between Islam and nationalism, especially in Ottoman and post-Ottoman contexts, writes:

> All religions focus primarily on the relationship between the believer and God [but, it] is the social aspects of religion, which over centuries have shaped populations' senses of morality and ethics ... that are of primary interest here ... [S]uch social power has made political authorities perennially interested in establishing strong relations with ... religion ... It thus joins nationalism as an ideology that has had great influence in legitimating ... state power across the region studied [i.e., post-Ottoman lands]. (Anscombe 2014: 6–7.)

In European history, the 19th century is regarded *the* century of nationalism. Among others, France, Greece, Italy, Germany were consolidated as nation-states during that century. However, nationalism was no less influential during the 20th century, even if in different – totalitarian as well as democratic – forms. The 21st century is also apt to be dominated by nation-state formation, however, with the epicentre in regions outside Europe. The forces at work in the Middle East are primarily related to nation-state formation. Religion adds to the fierceness of the emotions involved, but the driving force is the urge for a state and a closely united people/nation. Looked upon in this way, these developments may not appear as alien or 'other' to the European public mind as they would if viewed through Islam-tinted glasses.

---

8. For a more historically oriented discussion of the relationship between Islamism and nationalism, see Özdalga (2009).

The conflicts over state and nationhood in the Middle East will certainly have considerable and grievous repercussions for Europe as well. The migration crisis that descended on Europe in the late summer and fall of 2015 had direct effects on the visa-free Schengen system. Other, even more serious, challenges may appear as a result of changes in the party political landscape. Under such circumstances, the whole EU-project will come under heavy pressure. Ahead of the 'beyond' European modernity looms another beyond, which may lead to a backlash against the federalist projects in favour of a renaissance for more guarded national borders and new forms of nationalism.

Such a prospect is, however, entirely in accord with the laws of dialectics.

References

Anscombe, Frederick F. (2014) *State, Faith, and Nation in Ottoman and Post-Ottoman Lands.* Cambridge: Cambridge UP.

Aras, Bülent and Çaha, Ömer (2000) 'Fethullah Gülen and his liberal "Turkish Islam" movement', *Middle East Review of International Affairs*, 4, 4, pp. 30–31.

Arvasi, Seyyid Ahmet (1979) *Türk-İslam Ülküsü*, vol. 1. Istanbul: Türk Kültür Yayını.

Balcı, Bayram (2002) 'Fethullah Gülen's missionary schools', *ISIM Newsletter*, January.

Göksu-Özdoğan, Günay (2001) *Turan'dan Bozkurt'a. Tek Parti Döneminde Türkçülük (1931–1946).* Istanbul: Iletişim.

Halliday, Fred (2000) *Nation and Religion in the Middle East.* London: Saqi Books.

Hanioğlu, Şükrü (2001) *Preparation for a Revolution. The Young Turks, 1902–1908.* Oxford: Oxford University Press.

Kedourie, Elie (1985 [1960]) *Nationalism.* London: Hutchinson.

Khalid, Adeeb (2005) 'Pan-Islamism in practice. The rhetoric of Muslim unity and its uses', in Özdalga, Elisabeth (ed.) *Late Ottoman Society: The Intellectual Legacy.* London: RoutledgeCurzon.

Mango, Andrew (2004) *The Turks Today.* New York: The Overlook Press.

Özdalga, Elisabeth (1994) 'Necip Fazıl Kısakürek: Heroic nationalist in the garden of mysticism', *Meddelanden* no. 19, Swedish Research Institute in Istanbul, Stockholm.

Özdalga, Elisabeth (2000) 'Worldly asceticism in Islamic casting: Fethullah Gülen's inspired piety and activism', *Critique* no. 17, pp. 83–104.

Özdalga, Elisabeth (2006) 'The hidden Arab. A critical reading of the notion of Turkish Islam', *Middle Eastern Studies*, 42, 4, pp. 551–70.

Özdalga, Elisabeth (2009) 'Islamism and nationalism as sister ideologies: Reflections on the politicization of Islam in a Longue Durée perspective', *Middle Eastern Studies*, 45, 3, pp. 407–423.

Şeker, Mehmet (1985) *Fetihlerle Anadolu'nun Türkleşmesi ve İslâmlaşması*. Ankara: DIB Yayınları.

Therborn, Göran (1995) *European Modernity and Beyond: The Trajectory of European Societies, 1945–2000*. London: Sage.

Therborn, Göran (1997) 'Beyond civil society: Democratic experience and their relevance to the "Middle East"', in Özdalga, Elisabeth and Persson, Sune (eds.) *Civil Society, Democracy and the Muslim World*. London: Curzon, Swedish Research Institute in Istanbul, Transactions no. 7.

Turam, Berna (2004a) 'A bargain between the secular state and Turkish Islam: Politics of ethnicity in Central Asia', *Nations and Nationalism*, 10, 3, pp. 353–374.

Turam, Berna (2004b) 'The politics of engagement between Islam and the secular state: Ambivalences of "civil society"', *British Journal of Sociology*, 55, 2, pp. 259–281.

Yalçın, Soner (1988) 'Aydınlar Ocağı ve Türk İslam Sentezi', *Tercüman*, 1–6 February.

Yavuz, Hakan (1999) 'Towards an Islamic liberalism? The Nurcu Movement and Fethullah Gülen', *The Middle East Journal*, 53, 4, pp. 584–605.

Zubaida, Sami (1993 [1989]) *Islam, the People and the State*. London: I.B. Tauris.

ÅSA CRISTINA LAURELL

Structural Adjustment, Social Exclusion and Violence

The Mexican Case

An outstanding aspect of Göran Therborn's research is his reflections on the World. He certainly is very knowledgeable on the subject and an engaged and inquisitive globetrotter. He has systematically visited Latin America for decades and is a well-known and much read scholar in the region. He has provided empirical methodology to Latin American critical social sciences that frequently used to be quite theoretical before they were invaded by all kinds of metrics and there was a U-turn to the US mainstream model for reporting and presenting research results.

The issues of inequality are of course outstanding in Latin America, the most unequal region in the world. They have been studied long before the subject became an emerging concern in the western developed world and lately even for the International Monetary Fund (IMF). Therborn's *The Killing Fields of Inequality* provides an enlightening view of what is the state of affairs in a comparative and analytical approach that defines the fields and mechanism to be considered among which he includes exclusion. This global view necessarily depends on the use of existing indicators that are problematic. On the one hand there are difficulties in their correct measurements and, on the other and even more important, what they measure and how they are constructed.

This could be illustrated by the Human Development Index (HDI) that contested effectively the World Bank's fixation on poverty and not on human well-being. However a closer look at the HDI reveals both measurement and conceptual problems. Life expectancy at birth depends on a correct measure of infant mortality that is usually underestimated. Mean years of education and expected years of education tells nothing about educational quality and per person income adjusted to purchasing power in US dollars does not reveal distribution of income.

The scenario that these indicators convey is important but does not capture the complexity of specific country or regional processes. It is for instance difficult to analyse Latin America as a region since at least two diverging processes are taking place: those of the countries that follow a strict neoliberal path and those with progressive governments that have challenged the prescription of the 'Washington Consensus' embarking on a 'post-neoliberal' road. A different methodological approach, that is not easily applicable to the World, is to study history in movement with its interrelated economic, social and political processes. I will do so concentrating on Mexico, a typical neoliberal case but also deeply influenced by its vicinity to the USA, with the aim of discovering new scenarios that involve three fields studied by Therborn, namely inequality, globalization and democracy.

Thirty years of neoliberal structural adjustment

In 1983 the Mexican government adhered to the 'Washington Consensus' and made a sever fiscal adjustment cutting mainly social spending to pay the external debt that had rocketed as the result of a six time increase of the interest rate (Borja 2012). Since then the country has gone through repeated cycles of structural adjustment-financial crisis.

The next financial crisis followed in 1985–88 due to speculation with government bonds. In 1989 the privatization of state companies at very low prices was initiated but did not attract new productive investment since it mainly consisted of selling government assets not conditioned to new investments. The Constitution was also reformed to permit privatization of state or collectively owed land (*ejido* and communal land). The cherry of the pie of liberalization was the signing of the North American Free Trade Agreement (NAFTA) in late 1993.

A new financial crisis broke out in late 1994 due to speculation with government bonds and against the peso, and to massive capital flight. In order to save the banking system the government absorbed the debts of the banks, mainly those corresponding to big companies. However, many small and medium businesses as well as indebted families could not pay their debts and most of them were ruined. This situation together with the consequences of the NAFTA led to the destruction of Mexico's agricultural and industrial productive structure and to the transformation of the economy into an export led economy, mainly based on cheep labour.

The rescue of Mexico by the Treasury of the US and IMF in 1995 was also conditioned to a set of structural social policy reforms. The most important was a reform of the public social security institute for private sector workers (IMSS) that was pushed trough Congress despite massive mobilizations. Its main purpose was to put pension funds under private management with a scheme of individual accounts, which put huge monetary assets under the control of the mostly foreign private financial sector.[1] It also aimed at privatizing medical care with the introduction of private health fund administrators and providers. However the health reform failed for various reasons. One was the institutional strength of IMSS that provided health services to about 60 per cent of the population (121 million in toto 2015). This fact together with the resistance of workers and the middle and high IMSS bureaucracy made it very risky to dismantle the institution since it could have caused a health service collapse.

During the following period (2000–12) privatizations, liberalization and deregulation of the financial system were accelerated and a third of the national territory was given as concessions to national and international mining companies. The last assault on the national economy was the privatization of oil and electricity in 2013/14 that deprives the state of its main source of income. It is also a hard blow to national identity and sovereignty.

Despite the promise that economy would grow as a result of the structural reforms this has not been the case. Since the shift to the neoliberal export led model the Mexican economy has grown on an

---

1. These pension funds equalled 14 per cent of GNP in 2014 (OCDE 2015).

average less than 1 per cent annually. Some economists even sustain that the economy could not grow faster since the dependency on imported intermediate and consumer goods would trigger a growing commercial deficit with higher growth rates. Nor has the export led economy created national integrated production chains but is basically an assembly process of imported parts taking advantage of low wages.

One can also suppose that the criminal economy[2] boomed as a result of the destruction of agriculture and the lack of jobs both in the countryside and in poor urban areas. There are also reasons to believe that economic criminality such as money laundry through the private and deregulated financial system increased considerably and turned into a vital part of Mexico's balance of payments.

It is obviously difficult to have reliable data on the amount of money managed by cartels and in illegal transactions. However the US Congress estimates that 19 000 to 29 000 million dollars from illegal activities pour into Mexico annually and the Mexican Ministry of Finance registers a 10 000 million dollars surplus in the financial system. On the other hand, some estimates suggest that 78 per cent of economic sectors are infiltrated by cartels in Mexico.

Economic and social exclusion

The slow economic growth and the destruction of the productive structure have been deleterious for employment with a rising lack of formal and decent jobs. An estimated 1 200 000 new jobs are needed to employ those entering the labour market each year but at best 800 000 jobs are created. The deficit of jobs has pushed people into the informal sector, i.e. into activities with very low incomes and without social benefits or into criminal activities. By 2015 51.4 per cent of the economically active population belongs to this sec-

---

2. The concept 'criminal economy' is quite vague but includes; illegal drug production; trafficking with drugs, arms and humans, including migrants; extortion; professional hit man (*sicario*) murder; kidnapping; prostitution; etc. (Shirk 2011). Buscaglia (2015) argues that frauds and corruption are essential parts of this economy.

tor nationwide, but it is 75–80 per cent in the poorest states. The economic model has thus created a vast precariat. There are no unemployment insurance or specific social assistance programs for the unemployed so people have to invent ways to make a living. Therefore Mexican employment statistics are not comparable, for instance, to European statistics.

The government has encouraged emigration and from 2001 to 2005 an estimated half a million Mexicans crossed the border yearly and their remittances became vital to balance government accounts. However, emigration has gradually been shut down particularly with the 'Great Recession'. Border crossing is today a risky venture with ever-higher walls and armed border patrols, legal or illegal. Lately, however, more Mexicans are returning home than those that emigrate risking their lives.

Like in the rest of the world youth is the hardest hit and Mexico has an estimated seven million NEET[3]. Although the concept has been questioned the fact remains that millions of young Mexicans do not have access to decent jobs or to education. Unemployment is also high among individuals with a university degree so education is no longer a means of social mobility as is usually assumed.

The Mexican pattern is the same as in the rest of the world (Bauman 2005) with a combination of destruction of family based rural production causing a rapid expulsion to urban centres, a growing failure of the economy to absorb productively the labour force, and emigration. The concentration of the population in urban slums is not new in Latina America but the new conditions of the labour market are causing permanent structural social exclusion. So it is not a problem of poverty as such but speaks to the impossibility of the liberalized economy to create jobs and to regressive labour reforms causing increasingly precarious employment.

Given this process particularly the NEET might be a source of manpower for illegal activities in the context of an ideology that values individuals for their power, money and consumption. It is for instance estimated that drug cartels employ around a million young people (Sánchez-Castañeda 2014).

---

3. Not in Employment, Education or Training or *NiNi* in Spanish.

Wages and incomes are very low given the employment situation and the immense precariat. Since the first adjustment program in 1983 the minimum wage has dropped about 41 per cent and is now around 5 US dollars a day. Even worse, the purchasing power of the minimum wage dropped 78 per cent from 1987 to 2015 and the cost of the food basket for a family, considered the absolute poverty line, corresponds to 2.87 minimum wages (Centro de Análisis Multidisciplinario 2015). A large majority of Mexicans then has an income below the poverty line and only 6.7 per cent earns more than five minimum wages (OCDE 2015) or 9 200 US dollars a year.

The concentration of income is also extreme (Esquivel 2015: 12–20). According to OECD, using data from national income surveys, the Gini coefficient went from 0.45 in 1983 (1st fiscal adjustment) to 0.52 in 1996 (2nd fiscal adjustment) and then dropped to a minimum of 0.46 in 2010 but started to increase again in 2012. However adjusting national income survey data with national accounts a contrary tendency appears. Using this methodology the percentage of income that corresponds to the highest decile is around 60 per cent versus an unadjusted participation of close to 45 per cent. The adjusted data also show a 7.7 per cent increase of the income participation of the highest decile between 1992 and 2012 while the unadjusted data suggest a decrease of 7.3 per cent. Using a similar methodology it is estimated that the top one per cent concentrates 21 per cent of total income in Mexico, which is one of the highest in the world.

Not unexpectedly the concentration of wealth is also higher than in most other countries. The top Mexican multibillionaires, significantly enough, made their fortunes as a result of the privatization of state assets and of mining concessions. This is, for instance, the case of the emblematic Carlos Slim that competes with Bill Gates for the first position on the Forbes list of the wealthiest in the world. Incidentally the Mexican *capo*, Joaquín 'El Chapo' Guzman, has been listed twice on the same list.

These data show that neoliberal/neoclassic economic policy has not had a 'trickle down effect'. Instead the governments have carried out their 'war on poverty' with specific programs based on conditional cash transfers that currently cover about 20 per cent of all families. These programs have had a very modest impact on poverty and extreme poverty or indigence. Extreme poverty (an income below the cost of necessary food) went from 21.4 to 19.7 per cent between 1992 and 2012, with a maximum of 37.4 per cent in 1996 and a minimum of 14.0 per cent in 2004. Poverty (an income lower than the cost of food, clothing, housing, health, education, and transport) went from 53.1 to 52.3 per cent between 1992 and 2012, with a maximum of 69.0 per cent in 1996 and a minimum of 42.9 per cent in 2004. The variations illustrate the country's susceptibility to external shocks, which is a direct effect of liberalization and dependence on the US economy.

Capture of political power and a dysfunctional representative democracy

One could wonder how it has been possible to impose such regressive policies on the Mexican people. During the dark years of Latin American dictatorships, Mexico was one of the few countries of the region that never suffered a *coup d'etat* and that upheld formal democratic institutions. This was mainly possible due to the existence of the state party,[4] PRI, originated in the aftermath of the Mexican Revolution (1910–17). The Revolution culminated with Lázaro Cárdenas (1934–40) who carried out a profound land reform, expropriated oil and established socialist education, supported by organized armed peasants, workers and rural teachers. The PRI preserved for decades its legitimacy and most politics were made inside the party that harboured right, centre and left forces.

However, popular movements increasingly questioned the state party during the 1960s, particularly the student-popular movement in 1968. The governments also used widespread and deceitful repression against popular movements and the opposition. Several democratizing reforms were implemented to ease political discontent but

4. The legend has it that the creation of a party to resolve conflicts between the revolutionary fractions was proposed by the Soviet ambassador to Mexico 1925–26, Alexandra Kollontai.

the imposition of Carlos Salinas, a neoliberal technocrat, as PRI's presidential candidate in 1987 split the party and the son of Cárdenas was postulated by a large left-centre coalition. He won the 1988 presidential election but a large-scale fraud was instrumented which is now widely recognized.

Salinas was the architect of the complete neoliberal transformation of Mexico that provoked a profound political crisis. The Zapatist armed rebellion in 1994 was a forceful expression of popular resistance against neoliberal reform and the NAFTA. It was supported by millions of Mexicans all over the country but the massive claim for change and justice was also for peace and against state violence, a position that the Zapatists have honoured. Violent conflicts also shook the ruling political elite with the assassinations of the PRI presidential candidate and its congressional leader, two political crimes that were never satisfactory clarified.

The next PRI president, Zedillo, paved the way for the right party (PAN). What was initially considered a democratic transition in 2000 became just an alternation of parties in government after 70 years of PRI rule (Ackerman 2015). The electoral platform of the new president, Fox, had been to implement democratic reforms since he basically shared the neoliberal economic policy. However these reforms that should lead to the separation of powers, fair elections, governmental transparency, free press, an end to corruption and impunity were never implemented. The new government soon started to copy all the illegal practices of the PRI but with less ability to disguise them. So, Fox expanded high paid government positions, influence trafficking skyrocketed, fraud after fraud was discovered but never punished, and corruption was widespread. Furthermore Fox gave up the traditional independent Mexican diplomacy with respect to the US that had balanced politically the deep economic dependence.

Fox's government contributed much to the discredit of politics and politicians and so did the political parties and the high level bureaucrats that secured indecent privileges for themselves. For instance, senators and congressmen bestowed on themselves incomes corresponding to around 100 minimum wages and so did supreme court judges and top bureaucrats of autonomous institutions created to grant fair elections and transparency. The popular belief is that this has been possible trough secret negotiations and concessions to those that hold real power in Mexico, a small oligarchy of extremely rich groups forged in the neoliberal economic model. The capture of political power has then weakened whatever there was of democratic representative politics.

There were however some notable exceptions. One was the Mexico City governor, López Obrador, who also came into government in 2000. His priority was a broad territorialized social policy that included education, youth, a universal old-age pension, health care, housing, wage increases, support for small companies, etc. In order to finance these policies he introduced 'Republican Austerity' that implied lowering the salaries and ending the many privileges of high government officials as well as confronting corruption. This made a striking difference with the federal government and showed that it is possible to instrument a progressive social policy through redistribution even if the local government is not in control of economic policy or taxation. New forms of accountability were also introduced through assemblies at the 4th level of government, the Territorial Units, where the objectives of the social program were presented with numerical local targets so people could discuss them and check that they were actually met.

The popularity of López Obrador who showed that peaceful change might be possible in Mexico turned him into the enemy number one of the ruling oligarchy that set out to impede him from gaining the presidential election in 2006. The process that culminated with the 'fixed' victory of the PAN candidate, Calderón, with a 0.58 per cent margin, is a compendium of the nuts and bolts of electoral fraud (Giordani 2006), that included a collusion to impede López Obrador's participation in the election, a dirty media campaign, large amounts of illegal monetary support, and a sophisticated cybernetic manipulation of the data (López 2006). Later even Calderón admitted that he had lost but that nevertheless he had 'legally' been declared president.

Hundreds of thousand of Mexicans resisted the fraud for months without any concrete result. The fact that two massive electoral frauds have been committed against left-centre forces in less than two decades should be understood as soft *coup d'états*.

Calderón took office in extreme conditions of illegitimacy. To gain public recognition he decided to launch a Drug War without a clear strategy or an informed understanding of how criminal economy and criminal syndicates operate. The consequences have been catastrophic for Mexico with the escalation of violence that caused the loss of around 50 000 lives and 23 000 forced disappearances between 2007 and 2012. During this period the armed forces and a new federal police implanted fear and terror in the population because there was a *de facto* suspension of human and citizen rights as a way of maintaining the 'democratic order' (Sánchez 2005). This has by now been recognized by three UN reports.

The undeclared domestic war also led Calderón to establish a new relation with the US that allows its security forces to operate in Mexico. Part of the deal was to give Mexico a central role in protecting the US from migrants in what Ashby (2014) calls 'NAFTA-land Security' that has cost thousands of lives and forced disappearances. A special report from the Council on Foreign Relations (Shirk 2011), an organization based in New York, analyses the complex interrelations between violence, drug cartels, money laundry, arm trafficking and undocumented migration. It coincides with most observers or scholars that the US-Mexican joint actions have been inconsequential for the cartels since money laundry, arm trafficking, corruption and the extended use of illegal drugs in the US (the world's largest drug market) have not been seriously addressed.

Such was the discontent among Mexicans with the twelve years of PAN governments that the PRI managed to win the presidential elections in 2012 trough massive purchasing of votes and large scale media support to its candidate Peña Nieto. PRI changed the public profile of the government striking a pact between the three main parties – PRI, PAN and PRD – to continue structural reforms 'needed to grant economic growth', i.e. to conclude the neoliberal transformation. Simultaneously reports on violence were deescalated in mass media. Also the *capo* of the most important cartel, *El Chapo* Guzman, was captured. However the public endorsement of the new government was not long-lived (Ackerman 2015) and its approval rating tumbled to 35 per cent at the midterm of its mandate.

Economic stagnation persisted and the public debt grew rapidly and so did unemployment, low wages and social exclusion. The new anti-trust law did not affect government allies but only those who were critical of the government's handling of the economy. The partiality in the appointment of the members of the Supreme Court was blatant and so was the choice of cabinet members with obvious conflicts of interest. The independent press documented several corruption cases involving the president and cabinet members but their impunity was total while the reporters were fired after secrete negotiations between the owners of their medium and the government. Also the struggle against organized crime was deeply questioned with the escape of *El Chapo* from a high security prison after the refusal to extradite him to the US to be tried on drug trafficking and murder charges.

Mass movements persistently resisted the privatization of oil and the educational reform and the government turned to old style PRI authoritarianism and repression to control them. For instance, in some states teachers were forced to present evaluation tests at military installations under the 'protection' of thousands of soldiers.

The longstanding fear and acceptance of state violence on part of the population came to an abrupt end with the forced disappearance of 43 rural trainee teachers in September 2014, a couple of days after Peña received the World Statesman Award. The event spurred a huge nationwide civic movement against state violence and terror. It also drew international attention to the lack of democratic functioning of public institutions in Mexico that led to reports with recommendations to the Mexican government from supranational institutions.

Political illegitimacy and violence

Although Mexico in some respects is a unique case like all other countries it shows some basic tendencies, distinctive of neoliberal globalization. Let's first have a look at the most terrible effect of violence and its tolls in human lives that today amounts to about

70 000 deaths, 25 000 disappeared and a calculated 265 000 displaced. As argued above criminal economy and economic criminality are closely related which means that shared interests leads to corruption of the state and an escalation of violence against the population, both criminal and public.

In Mexico this violence is so intense that life expectancy dropped in some states mainly because of violent deaths among young people. The victims are both men and women between 15 and 49 years and the percentage increase is high for both sexes. Nevertheless the ratio of homicide between men and women shows that it is from 7 to 10 times higher for men.

Table 1: Homicide increase for men and women in numbers and percentage between 2006 and 2013 in México

Age group	Number		Ratio men to women	Percentage	
	Men	Women		Men	Women
15–19	860	118	7.3	124	77
20–24	1 748	219	8.0	149	156
25–29	1 723	179	9.6	136	129
30–34	1 469	192	7.7	111	152
35–39	1 365	167	8.2	124	156
40–44	1 064	106	10.0	123	102
45–49	763	75	10.2	117	104

Source: Instituto Nacional de Estadística y Geografía.

While female deaths are socially accepted as femicides, i.e. rooted in gender discrimination, male deaths are considered a security problem that should be treated as criminal transgressions and, if necessary, fought with legitimate state violence. This was the case of the Drug War in Mexico that has caused an unstoppable spiral of violence (Espinosa and Rubin 2015) involving the state's repressive forces, drug cartels and even political authorities.

From 2007 the federal government increasingly used the military or a new federal police to fight drug cartels. It put the armed forces train to kill on the streets and in rural areas, which led to generalized abuse against the population. When proven that civilians not involved with the drug gangs were killed it was considered 'collateral damage'. A *de facto* suspension of civil and human rights prevails and the federal forces are protected against legal prosecution. Human rights violations such as extrajudicial executions, excessive lethal force, torture and forced disappearances became frequent and still are as have been widely documented by independent observers, among others the UN Human Rights Council and the Inter-American Commission of Human Rights. In the obscure zones of violence, where it is unclear who is acting – state repressive forces, local authorities, paramilitaries, criminal gangs or all together – migrants, human right activists, journalists, social leaders and activists have been frequent victims. This situation has led to what could be characterized as state terrorism.

During this violent spiral agreements between cartels and the federal government broke down although some cartels continued to have political protection. The decentralization and multiplication of government institutions (Ríos-Contreras 2013) also spurred violence, corruption and complicity between local political authorities and cartels. The pacts were also broken between cartels that set out to gain new territorial strongholds and trafficking routs. Additionally the arrest or assassination of important *capos* provoked the emergence of new, usually smaller, and uncontrolled cartels that prompted murderous and cruel infighting. Most experts agree the cartels also diversified its criminal activities with extortion, kidnapping, 'protection', and hit man assassinations, among others. Killing and torture became a mechanism to create cohesion and complicity in the gangs. On the other hand it became clear that impunity is very elevated and the probability to get killed is higher than to go to jail.

The changing boundaries between state repressive forces and cartels can be exemplified with the cartel 'Los Zetas'. It has its origin in elite troops that deserted and became the armed branch of the Gulf Cartel and later formed its own cartel that recruited 'Kaibiles', ex soldiers of the Guatemalan Special Forces renowned for their extreme cruelty against civilians during the civil war.

The extensive use of illegal power by both official armed forces and cartels against the population has led in some states to the formation of armed self-defence civic groups. They justify their action with the lack of state protection against criminal groups breaking thereby the government's legal monopoly of repression.

In the context of generalized violence a toxic ideology has developed. It mixes 'machismo' values, violence and death with the neoliberal values of individualism, power, money and consumerism (Abad-Domínguez 2015). This ideology and its concrete expressions has been analysed by Valencia-Triana (2012) using the concept of 'Gore capitalism' in reference to the Gore video culture. It is important to understand that violence needs an ideological justification and cannot rest only on brute force. In that sense it should be noticed that a core element of this ideology is precisely the neoliberal one.

Globalization, democracy and social exclusion

Reflecting on the Mexican historical process during the last decades raises some questions that could apply to more general developments during neoliberal globalization. First, it seems more useful to focus on social exclusion as a structural phenomenon than on inequality. Social exclusion is not limited to peripheral countries under neoliberal globalization but also occur in core capitalist countries as can be seen for instance in the European Union and the US. On the one hand increasing inequality is a manifestation of the failure of economy to create sufficient decent jobs that causes structural social exclusion. On the other jobs are degraded as the result of regressive labour reforms supposedly done to increase competitiveness.

In order to enact this economic model or pattern of accumulation national representative democracy has been subordinated to supranational institutions, be they the IMF, the World Trade Organization, the World Bank or the *Troika*, that represent the interests of global corporations. They can and have imposed their prescriptions against the determination of democratically elected governments, despite knowledgeable opinions regarding their ineffectiveness. An alternative road has been to negotiate in secrecy free trade agreements, such as the NAFTA, the Trans-Pacific Partnership or the Trade in Services Agreement. Once negotiated they are submitted to parliaments general using the 'fast track' mechanism that means that their approval or rejection without any changes.

These undemocratic procedures and the unchecked influence of power groups on many occasions explain illegal operations such as corruption, conflict of interests, tax evasion, money laundry, and lack of transparency.

However the question of legitimacy becomes a central problem when social or political movements oppose government actions or policies. There are many expedients to counteract these processes. One is to discredit politics and politicians to provoke the rejection of collective organized action and to strengthen individualism. Another is to manufacture social consent trough non-electoral processes of disperse social participation and intensive use of mass media.

When this is not enough the allegation of external threats or obscure internal enemies are methods to restrict civil and political rights and to create wide spread fear among citizens. Klein (2007) masterly describes this phenomenon in her *Shock Doctrine* that also includes the fear of social exclusion. The US Patriot Act is the most infamous example that with some changes remains in force under the name of the US Freedom Act. In the specific case of Mexico the Drug War was the expedient to re-establish government legitimacy after electoral fraud and provoke wide spread fear in the population. With time it had the opposite effect and seriously weakened not only the government but also the state. It took the Ayotzinapa forced disappearances to break generalized fear.

Massive migration has become a central issue when local communities wither and whole countries have their productive structures destroyed by free trade and liberalization or by annihilating wars to get access to valued natural resources like oil with the excuse of external threats or to impose western brands of democracy. The Mexican-US boarder is an enduring example of the frequently violent methods used to control undocumented and unwanted migration. Whilst the fall of the Berlin wall is celebrated over and over again, new walls are erected to keep people out from the rich countries. Migration is also presented as a new threat and a source of fear.

To many observers the Mexican case might seem too extreme to provide elements for the understanding of the changes that are occurring in the world with neoliberal globalization. It should be admitted that the spiral of violence is obsessing Mexicans but one could make the case that extreme violence is also suffered by the citizens of war stricken countries that are innocent victims of power politics related to globalization and deep changes in the meaning and content of democracy.

References

Abad-Domínguez, F. (2015) 'Reinos culturales del crimen organizado', *Voces del Fenix* 42.

Ackerman, J. (2015) *El mito de transición democrática*. México DF: Planeta.

Ashby, P. (2014) 'How Canada and Mexico have become part of the U.S. policing regime', *NACLA Report on the Americas*, 12 January. Available at: www.globalresearch.ca/nafta-land-security-howcanada-and-mexico-have-become-part-of-the-u-s-policing-regime/5417940, consulted 20 December 2015.

Bauman, Z. (2004) *Vidas desperdiciadas*. México DF: Paidos.

Borja, R. (2012) *Enciclopedia de la Política*. México DF: Fondo de Cultura Económica.

Buscaglia, E. (2015) *Lavado de dinero y corrupción política*. México DF: Penguin Random House Grupo Editorial.

Centro de Análisis Multidisciplinario (2015) *Reporte de Investigación 120. México: Esclavitud moderna*. UNAM. Available at: http://cam.economia.unam.mx/reporte-de-investigacion-120-mexico-esclavitud-moderna-cae-78-71-el-poder-adquisitivo/, consulted 9 December 2015.

Espinosa, V. and Rubin, D. (2015) 'Did the military interventions in the Mexican drug war increase violence?', *The American Statistician*, 69, 1, 17–27.

Esquivel, G. (2015) *Desigualdad Extrema en México. Concentración del poder económico y político*. México DF: OXFAM.

Giordani, A. (2006) 'Mexico's presidential swindle', *New Left Review* 41.

Ibarra, C. (2011) 'Maquila, currency misalignment and export-led growth in Mexico', *CEPAL Review* 104.

Klein, N. (2007) *The Shock Doctrine*. New York: Knopf.

López, J.A. (2006) *Data Manipulation in the Mexican Election?* Available at: http://www.stat.columbia.edu/~gelman/stuff_for_blog/Data%20Manipulation%20in%20Mexican%20Elections.pdf, consulted 17 December 2015.

OECD (2015) *Review of Pension Systems. Mexico.* Paris: OECD.

Ríos-Contreras, V. (2013) *How Government Structure Encourages Criminal Violence: The Causes of Mexico's Drug War.* Cambridge: Harvard University.

Sánchez-Castañeda, A. (2014) 'Los jóvenes frente al empleo y el desempleo', *Revista Latinoamericana de Derecho Social* 19, 133–162.

Sánchez, M. (2005) 'El ciclo "perverso" de violencia e inseguridad como relación de poder en América Latina', in Atencio Bello, H.E. (ed.) *Violencia, Criminalidad y Terrorismo.* Caracas: Editorial Fundacion Venezuela Positiva.

Shirk, D.A. (2011) *The Drug War in Mexico: Confronting a Shared Threat.* New York: Council on Foreign Relations.

Valencia-Triana, S. (2012) 'Capitalismo Gore y necropolítica en México contemporáneo', *Relaciones Internacionales* 19.

LENA LAVINAS

The Untold Battlefields Against Inequality in Latin America

In the introduction to his most recent book, Göran Therborn lays out his intellectual and existential commitment to make knowledge a means for mobilizing hearts and minds in the arduous but urgent task of successfully facing the *killing fields of inequality* (2013). First, he says, it must be understood as a global and multidimensional phenomenon of lethal potency. Yes, 'inequality kills' is the opener to the first chapter, setting the tone for a work that the author labels 'civic intervention sustained by empirical evidence' (*The Killing Fields of Inequality*, p. 35). In fact, the book is a quasi-manifesto interrogating us from start to finish, demanding that we take an unambiguous, definitive stance as we cross the many battlefields against inequality.

He starts by asking: 'if you don't agree with the current state of inequality, what institutions have to be changed first of all? What social forces can you hope for, and join if you should want?' (p. 5). The reader's perplexity must be as profound as the author's line of questioning is uncommon. How to respond, if this is a matter of rather absorbing Therborn's uncomfortable, incisive, and consistent revelations, laid out in a vast and diverse array of information where indignation and rigor are interwoven in the use of data and its interpretation?

The book must not be misunderstood: what this book is not is a pure exercise of enlightenment, though it wields a whetted saber against our profound ignorance of contemporaneous processes and moments at which equality prevailed or was subjugated.

The tacit objective of Therborn's book, meticulously plotted over nearly 200 pages, is to buffet the apathy that consumes us, seeking to feed our aversion to inequality and sweep us towards a commitment to equalization (p. 4). To that end, he also indicates a few paths forward. Unquestionably the work's greatest achievement, however, lies in its disentangling of the different mechanisms that fuel inequality, be it vital, existential or resource-based. Therborn does this with such didactic accuracy that we feel at home with his concepts and categories.

His definition of inequality is drawn from Amartya Sen, but recontextualized and enlarged. 'Inequalities are violations of human rights preventing people from full human development' (p. 41). This is, no doubt, a very powerful and straightforward statement of meaning, one that is easy to take up. Bit by bit, doubts fade and there comes a growing understanding of the gravity, urgency, and relevance of the problem Therborn is setting before us; moreover, we find ourselves increasingly inclined to respond to his call.

Now, those who have followed his trajectory and learned with him are intimately familiar with the many facets of his intellectual fingerprint: he is an internationalist at heart, able to wield comparative approaches that combine conceptual refinement with genuine empirical experience; a masterful craftsman in dealing with intersectionalities, the hierarchies of which are not rigid and thus challenge the deconstruction of inequalities; an intellectual dedicated to tackling the minefield of misleading commonplaces on the topic, formulating impeccable, markedly unconventional theoretical frameworks that recast worn-out themes sapped of their ability to mobilize the 'fellow citizens of the world'; an astute activist for whom 'strength and struggle' (p. 142) are unavoidable ingredients in attempts to overthrow inequalities. As he puts it: 'The deconstruction of inequalities will ultimately depend on the strength and the skills of the forces of equality' (p. 159).

At times of austere orthodox models, the simplicity and efficacy that Therborn presents speak to his joviality, the unmistakable mark of a nonconformist. Another characteristic of his, and which calls for a brief but heartfelt homage, is his recognition of the centrality of feminist thought and struggle in the construction of a more egalitarian world, especially in the last third of the 20th century. In this, Therborn set himself apart from many of his contemporaries in academia, for whom recognition did not necessarily mean incorporation. He chose to do so, and has done so with generosity and precision.

After recalling that 'inequalities are produced and sustained socially by systemic arrangements and processes, and by distributive action, either individual as well as collective' (p. 55), Therborn identifies four major mechanisms – also cumulative in their mode of operation – that produce and reproduce inequalities: distanciation, exploitation, exclusion, and hierarchization. By the same token, he acknowledges that for each of them there is an antidote which may counteract and rectify their pernicious consequences. To distanciation corresponds approximation; to exploitation, redistribution and/or rehabilitation; for exclusion, the equality mechanism is inclusion; and for hierarchization, de-hierarchization.

He also acknowledges that 'inclusion is perhaps the most widespread of equality mechanisms. It is intrinsic to the modern nation-state, which entitles its citizens, and normally also its permanent residents, to certain rights and public services' (p. 64–65). Inclusion consists of enforcing membership for those previously excluded, democratizing access, and combating stigmatization, a marker of exclusion.

In his view, these four equalization mechanisms were largely behind the dismantling of existential inequality, a major human advance in the recent past. Income (resource) inequality and vital inequality, in contrast, have not made similar strides worldwide (p. 145).

Therborn highlights Latin America as one of the regions to achieve significant progress in the recent past, especially in terms of the existential equalization 'of indigenous peoples, of women, and of Afro-descendants, above all' (Therborn 2015: 25). Despite the fact that 'the Latin American hour' (ibid.: 14) seems bound to fade as a result of the commodities downswing, Therborn's organizing categories may help us reflect upon the dynamics of inclusion set in motion in Latin America as of late. If inequality is about excluding people from the possibilities produced by human development, then it seems fair to say that the Latin American outlook is still quite bleak.

Mechanisms of (in)equality in motion in Latin America: controversies

Not too long ago, Latin America was the flavor of the month. Against the global tide of deepening socioeconomic disparities, the continent – although still topping the rankings of inequality – harbored hopes of becoming a role model on many fronts, particularly, but not exclusively, regarding existential equalization. Resource inequality was another field in which Latin America stood for the promise of inclusive economic growth, breaking with a long tradition of the marginalization of the working classes and minorities in terms of progress and well-being.

In the Andes, countries like Ecuador (2008) and Bolivia (2009) redefined themselves as plurinational entities, shedding the homogeneous nation-state as inherited from European notions of modernity. Their Constitutions not only recognize the plurality of political nations that comprise the state, but also adopt Indigenous concepts of Sumak Kawsay (living well, or *buen vivir*), thus accounting for a diversity of ways of life. Ecuador's Constitution was a milestone in terms of environmental rights, the first in the world to recognize the rights of nature and the human right to water. Nature became a subject with rights, a move all the more significant in a place with a centuries-long tradition of extractivism as the key to an international insertion rooted in the commodification of nature and expropriation from Indigenous peoples. Extractivism's days seemed numbered.

On the other hand, extreme destitution was addressed through conditional cash transfer programs, which were put into place in nearly all the countries of the region with almost no exceptions. For the first time, the poor were recognized by the State and included on a large scale by public programs aimed at extinguishing monetary deficits and vulnerabilities. These programs' low cost and high impact, as they incorporated tens of millions of people into the consumer market who had previously been living largely on a subsistence basis, seemed to indicate that the domestic market would overcome its internal barriers, take on new scope and scale, and drive a new virtuous cycle of development. Thus would the worst-off escape from the segregation and stigmatization that had condemned them to second-class citizenship.

The return of economic growth, after a decade of stagnation followed by another of high volatility and uncertainty, revitalized the job market in the 2000s: informality dipped and opportunities swiftly multiplied, contributing significantly to a marked drop in poverty. Regulating mechanisms such as the minimum wage leveraged distribution in a good many countries, acting decisively to push down income inequality. The rise in formal employment and average income indicated that structural heterogeneity, a hallmark of the region, was on its way to being overcome, thus promoting greater social cohesion and more homogenous patterns of consumption. The *myth of economic development*, in the phrase coined by Furtado (2013 [1974]), now seemed a part of the past, with the present inaugurating a new model – that of Latin American exceptionality.

Novelties in terms of social protection – such as *renta dignidad* ('dignity income') in Bolivia or the return of public (PAYG) pensions in many countries where they had been replaced by fully funded individual accounts – suggested that the incompleteness and weakness of welfare systems would be remedied. Social spending gradually grew, bringing with it optimistic prospects for equalization via an increase in schooling and greater access to colleges. Healthcare systems and housing policies drew some public investment. It seemed only a matter of time before the ascendant curve on this sort of spending would take on new dimensions.

All this was taking place under democratically elected governments, demonstrably progressive and in line with a South-South perspective. Three women occupied their countries' highest posts in Brazil, Argentina, and Chile, signaling that the patriarchy – so deeply rooted in everyday gestures and social relations – might be definitively routed.

The balance, beyond being positive across the board, justified Therborn's question as to whether 'equalization efforts [would] keep their momentum' (2015: 26) in Latin America. This was not a sure bet, given the characteristics of the inclusion process along this decade of progress and a discreet attenuation of inequalities. These are structural traits that inequality measures do not always grasp. Similarly, we might ask what sort of 'economic inequality has gone down' in the region, since none of its tax reforms were effectively redistributive (Valdéz 2015).

Drawing on Therborn's method, I have gathered data to support my line of argument.

Should processes of inclusion, de-hierarchization and rehabilitation lead to criminalization?

Indigenous resistance criminalized

In a radical rupture with the colonial State, Andean countries refounded their constitutions and adopted plurinationality. Bolivia elected an Indigenous president; Ecuador's constitution has over 25 articles defining collective rights, including rights to self-determination and prior consultation for projects on Indigenous territories. In practice, however, governments have expanded concessions to extractive industries without Indigenous consent. Indigenous resistance to extractivism has resulted in violent criminalization, and even death.

The Observatory of Mining Conflicts in Latin America (OCMAL) estimates that there are 195 active conflicts due to large-scale mining. Peru and Chile have 34 and 33, respectively, with 28 in Mexico, 26 in Argentina, and 20 in Brazil. Mega-mining alone affects nearly 300 communities, many located on Indigenous territories. In Ecuador, over 200 people have been criminalized as of 2015, mostly Indigenous leaders defending water rights. In Peru an estimated 200 activists were killed between 2006 and 2011 for resisting extractivism (Zibechi 2013). Indigenous peoples constitute only 5 per cent of the world population, but they account for nearly half of environmental homicides globally. According to Global Witness, about two environmental activists were murdered per week in 2014; 40 per cent of them were Indigenous.

The challenge is that extractivism is – yet again – largely taking place on Indigenous land. For instance, the UN Permanent Forum on Indigenous Issues reported that Colombian mining concessions had been awarded in 80 per cent of the country's legally recognized Indigenous territories in 2010.

Yet conflicts against extractivism should not be dismissed as matters pertaining solely to Indigenous peoples. They reveal the continuous role of extractivism in Latin American politics and contest a development model based on the corporatization of natural resources. Patterns of intensive and unregulated exploitation of natural resources, far from overturning a historical trend, have accentuated dependency on extractivism, leading to the multiplication and worsening of conflicts over land and water use. The most immediate result of this, derived from decades-long concessions on Indigenous land granted to multinational mining companies (mostly based in China or Canada) has been the reproduction of the colonial model in treating such holdings as *terra nullis*, once again expropriating those recently included in the realm of civic rights, as well violent repression and the criminalizing of Indigenous resistance (Picq 2015).

In Brazil the picture is even bleaker. As we read in the 2014 CIMI report on *Violence Against Indigenous People in Brazil*, 'unfortunately, despite the surmounting of the military dictatorship, violence against those peoples was only updated and heightened. Genocide and ethnocide are still happening in Brazil, well into the 21st century' (CIMI 2014: 3). The report indicates a surge in human rights violations in general and suicide and murder cases in particular. In 2014, there were 135 suicides, most of them committed by young people. A look at records from between 2000 and 2014 in the State of Mato Grosso alone reveals the alarming number of 707 suicides. As for murders, in 2014, 138 were reported on the grounds of land conflicts. Most occurred as an attempt to curb Indigenous resistance. One emblematic case was the brutal homicide of young leader Marinalva Kaiowá. She lived in a tarp encampment on the fringes of a land that her community has been trying to get back for over 40 years. Marinalva was stabbed 35 times, two weeks after she had been to the Federal Supreme Court (STF) in Brasilia to protest a court ruling that annulled the process of demarcation of the Guyraroká Indigenous Lands.

Public power is equally remiss to the point of cruelty in terms of the provision of public services and the welfare of native populations, particularly on the score of healthcare. 'Official data point to the shocking number of at least 785 deaths of children aged 0–5. The most alarming situations took place in Xavante villages, with 116 deaths of children aged 0–5, and among the Yanomami, with 46 records of deaths of children aged 0–1. As for the Xavantes, child mortality reached over 141.4 for each thousand born and a similar ratio is on record in Altamira, in the state of Pará, where the child mortality ratio reached 141.84 deaths for each thousand' (CIMI 2014: 15–16). Meanwhile, the average infant mortality rate for Brazil dropped from 29.02 per 1 000 in 2000 to 14.40 in 2014 and was celebrated as a huge achievement by a 'left-wing' government.[1]

The State's omission and delays in land regulation have also led to growing and damaging conflicts over territorial rights and the protection of a balanced environment. Federal-led ratification of Indigenous lands has fallen steadily since the Cardoso administration, when 145 came through over the course of his two terms (1995–2002). Under Lula (2003–2010), this number was cut by almost half (79), only to drop to 11 during Dilma's first term (2011–2014) (CIMI 2014: 43). Demarcation of Indigenous lands has been shut down. Even previously demarcated territories are systematically invaded by agribusiness; the expansion of soy and cattle on Indigenous territories is feeding a devastating death toll. The Kaiowa-Guarani have a homicide rate nearly 500 times higher than the Brazilian average, exceeding that of countries at war.

Beatings, humiliation, racist practices and intimidation are commonplace, to say nothing of degrading living conditions either in confined areas or in temporary encampments. As I write, Brazil's Commission for Justice and Citizenship in the Chamber of Deputies, given over to the most conservative sectors of the country,[2] has just

---

1. See figures from Instituto Brasileiro de Geografia e Estatística: http://brasilemsintese.ibge.gov.br/populacao/taxas-de-mortalidade-infantil.html.
2. The three major caucuses in Brazil's Congress, or the 'Three Bs', are: *boi* (cattle, for the rural caucus), Bible (the evangelicals), and bullet (those who support unlimited access to firearms and harsher punishments for crimes).

passed a bill (PEC 215/00) that transfers the right to recognize Indigenous lands, conservation units, and *quilombola* descendent communities from the executive branch to the Congress. This would freeze 228 demarcations of Indigenous lands, and appears to be unconstitutional. In the words of Deputy Molon in his critique of the bill, pending Congressional approval, 'a bloodbath is to be expected'. This law is designed, in short, to pursue an even more aggressive expropriation of Indigenous lands.

Rights only exist if they are practiced, claim leaders of the Confederation of Kichwa Peoples in Ecuador (ECUARUNARI). Self-determination was established in international treaties such as ILO Convention no. 169 and the 2007 United Nations Declaration on the Rights of Indigenous Peoples, then adopted in national law, but in practice neither governments nor multinational corporations respect Indigenous rights. The extraction of metals like silver and gold since colonial times has now expanded to crude, monoculture (soy), and intensive agriculture (especially cattle).

The Latin American economy's return to a dependence on raw materials is visible in their outsize role in total exports. According to ECLAC's 2014 *Statistical Yearbook*, in 2013 they stood at: 66.9 per cent in the Argentine case; 63.6 per cent for Brazil; 96 per cent for Bolivia; 86.1 per cent in the case of Chile; 93.3 per cent for Ecuador; 75.6 per cent for Uruguay, and 97.6 per cent for Venezuela. In Peru, mineral exploration expenditures increased tenfold in a decade. In 2002, 7.5 million hectares had been granted to mining companies; by 2012 that figure had jumped to almost 26 million, or 20 per cent of the country's land. About 40 per cent of the land is licensed to or being solicited by multinational companies for mineral and crude mining projects (PBI 2011). According to OCMAL, 25 per cent of Chile's territory was under exploration or operation as of 2010. Mexico's government opened the state-controlled energy sector to foreign investment, changing legislation to allow private multinationals to tap the country's oil and natural gas resources for the first time since 1938.

What all this indicates is that – at least in Latin America – when it comes to the recognition and application of the letter of the law as a safeguard for Indigenous rights, mechanisms of existential equalization are far from promoting more 'autonomy, dignity, degrees of freedom, and of rights to respect and self-development' (p. 49). Existential inequalities continue to run deep, and have been neglected since the development model of late has fallen back on a commodity export-based basis for growth. Still worse, they severely aggravate vital inequality for minorities, who seemed to finally be benefiting from a more promising, reparative legal context. In practice, the violation of Indigenous humans rights remains the rule.

Existential equality still denied to women

Women have also been criminalized, despite their education levels being on the rise and superior to those of men, their marked participation in the job market, their role in generating household wealth and welfare, and despite constituting a considerable part of the so-called new middle class, whose tendencies and values ought to prioritize respect for individual liberties. None of this has brought broad and definitive recognition of their right to control their bodies in case of undesired pregnancy, through access to safe and free abortion.

According to the *Investigación sobre Aborto en América Latina y el Caribe*, the region has seen the highest estimated rate of unsafe abortions in the world (Ramos 2015: 20). Since abortions are generally clandestine, estimates say that a million women are hospitalized per year across the continent for complications resulting from high-risk abortions. In Brazil alone, for example, the public, universal-access Unified Health System (SUS) treats over 220 000 women every year for curettage-related complications post-abortion, whether the result of miscarriages or – as is the case with the majority – unsafe procedures.

Given the need for clandestinity, estimates of deaths resulting from unsafe abortions are difficult to measure.

The Latin American territories where the voluntary interruption of pregnancy is legal and guaranteed under adequate conditions are few and far between. They are Cuba; the provinces of Yucatán and the DF in Mexico; Guinea and Barbados, given their ties to the UK;

Puerto Rico, under the American flag; and Uruguay, since 2012. It should be noted that, in the latter country, women who try to procure abortions after the period established by law (12 weeks) remain subject to criminal proceedings. That is to say: Uruguay has legalized, but not completely decriminalized, abortion, preserving legal mechanisms that may be triggered and punish the interruption of an unwanted pregnancy with jail terms.

Across the other countries, abortion is an offense included in the penal code. In the vast majority of Latin American countries, it is tolerated in certain conditions, such as acephaly or malformation of the fetus, risk of death for the woman, rape, or incest.

Restrictions, however, vary from country to country. Ecuador, Peru, and Bolivia, for example, do not allow abortions in case of rape (Ramos 2015: 156). Once raped, women are debased and stripped of their dignity, punished for having been victims of sexual violence. The principles of justice are inverted. In Venezuela, Paraguay, and Guatemala, meanwhile, therapeutic abortion is only authorized if the woman's life is in danger. That is to say: patriarchal society continues to exert power over women's bodies and their right to life.

In Chile, El Salvador, Honduras, Nicaragua, and the Dominican Republic, abortion is a crime under any conditions. In addition to having the most repressive antiabortion legislation in the region, they have imprisoned significant numbers of women for the practice of illegal abortions. These imprisonments ultimately signal the cruelty and humiliation to which those who question the sex-gender system are subjected. The effect is that civil liberties remain only partially accessible to women, since they are unable to do with their bodies as they please. Chile's Bachelet administration is currently attempting to adopt the less prohibitive restrictions that have already become standard in the majority of Latin American countries.

The UN has already recommended the revision of legislation criminalizing abortion in nearly all the countries of Latin America, given its absolute incompatibility with women's rights to life, dignity, and security. Moreover, keeping abortion illegal and unsafe flouts the principles of the Convention on the Elimination of All Forms of Discrimination Against Women, dating back to 1979. The criminalization of the practice does not prevent it from being carried out, nor does it reduce the rates of usage, but it does keep cases from being duly registered and puts the health and lives of women (especially when poor) in jeopardy.

Illegal abortion has kept maternal mortality rates high across Latin America, an indicator on which many countries in the region (Ecuador and Brazil, to name two) have not seen satisfactory performance in the latest statistics from the Millennium Development Goals. One of the reasons for that is precisely the widespread practice of clandestine, illegal abortions.

By way of example, here we may look to official data from the government of Ecuador, which recognize a significant increase in maternal mortality in the nation over the 2000s, particularly so under the Correa administration. Indeed, such deaths had been declining since 2001 (56.63 per 100 000 live births), shrinking to a rate of 38.78 in 2006. This trend, however, would soon be reversed as the prevalence spiked at 70.44 deaths per 100 000 live births (INEC 2013: 505). This abysmal performance reveals the indifference of this and so many other countries to sexual and reproductive rights in general, ultimately victimizing women. There is no record of the role that abortion plays in these elevated maternal mortality rates, but in Brazil it is estimated to be the fourth most significant cause.

Equally grave is the fact that even where restricted, regulated access to abortion is available, public health systems do not provide adequate, safe care. On the contrary, we find discriminatory, punitive treatment born of the prejudices of attending staff. This is symptomatic of the deficient, biased, moralistic training of healthcare professionals in terms of reproductive rights.

Another extremely troubling aspect is the repeated refusal to adopt alternative, cheap, and accessible abortive techniques, such as Plan B and other prophylactics available on the market. Why turn down existing products that might prevent pain, harm, and death, preferring to impose suffering on women as a way of expiating their guilt?

Here, Brazil steps in to prove that even a state of affairs as devastating as this can always get worse. In October 2015, the Congress approved a bill that goes against existing law and further curtails the right to a legal abortion in case of rape. It provides that permission to interrupt a pregnancy would be subject to the physical verification of rape via a medical examination and a police report, making the woman's word on the matter worthless. Arguing that 'the legalization of abortion has been imposed across the world by international organizations [...] financed by American foundations tied to super-capitalist interests' seeking to promote 'population control', the bill seeks to jail those who induce, instigate, or aid a pregnant woman to get an abortion. The current version of the bill would imprison only those directly involved in the abortion – the pregnant woman, and the person performing the procedure. The discriminatory cherry on top is the bill's prohibition on the circulation of information about and the sale of other abortive methods, such as Plan B.

According to the World Health Organization, countries with restrictive legislation see 22 million abortions performed annually, leading to an estimated 47 000 women's deaths. In nations where the interruption of pregnancy is legal and safe, that mortality rate is closer to zero.

Restrictions on reproductive autonomy that stifle women's ability to participate fully in society are a threat to democracy. However, these checks go beyond the realm of sexual and reproductive rights. The curtailment of female autonomy in Latin America – down to women's ability to come and go as they please, threatened as they are by acts of extreme physical violence, mutilations, and rapes – reveals the vices of processes of existential equalization that fail to go beyond superficiality, merely extending the logic of the market without breaking with standing hierarchies and other forms of exploitation and domination.

A recent report on femicide (*Mapa da Violência. Homicídio de Mulheres no Brasil,* Waiselfisz 2015a) reveals that a murder rate of 4.8 women per 100 000 inhabitants (or 4 762 murders in 2013, as opposed to a thousand fewer in 2000) places Brazil in fifth place on the world ranking of this sort of crime, falling behind El Salvador, Colombia, Guatemala, and Russia. It should be noted that of the 10 countries with the highest rates of femicide, 7 are Latin American.

It is clear that patriarchy and misogyny remain predominant beyond Asia or Sub-Saharan Africa, nor has multiculturalism succeeded in guaranteeing recognition and respect to Indigenous communities in Latin America.

Racism and discrimination continue to claim thousands of lives and provoke mass incarceration

A final topic for reflection is the situation of people of African descent in many Latin American countries. Moreover, the contingent of juvenile delinquents is growing at alarming rates. Here, the Brazilian case threatens advances observed in the fields of education and socioeconomic inclusion.

Today, homicide is the main cause of death for youths ages 15–29 in Brazil, taking an especially large toll on Black youths living in peripheral communities and the metropolitan areas of urban centers. Data from the Ministry of Health's Mortality Information System reveal that over half of the 56.337 homicide victims in 2012 were young people (27 471 or 52.63 per cent), 77 per cent of whom were Black (*pretos* and *pardos*) and 93.30 per cent were male.[3] This considering that half of the Brazilian population is Black.

There is thus a clear imbalance in terms of the lethal impact of racism and discrimination, which can be seen mowing down lives. Between 2003 and 2012, 320 000 Black youths were killed with firearms, according to the 2015 *Mapa da Violência* (Waiselfisz 2015b). Over the same period, while the rate of homicides by firearm dipped from 14.5 to 11.8 per 100 000 Whites, for Blacks (*pretos* and *pardos*) it rose from 24.9 to 28.5 Thus, rates for Whites fell 18.7 per cent while they increased 14.1 per cent for the Black population.

The same document indicates that of the 13 most violent countries in the world, with elevated homicide rates per 100 000 inhabitants, Iraq is the only one outside the Americas. Venezuela held that tragic record in 2012, with 55.4 murders per 100 000 inhabitants; that number was 32.3 in Guatemala; 31 in Colombia; and 29 in Brazil (according to Anistia Internacional Brasil and Waiselfisz

---

3. At the global level, males account for 82 per cent of all homicide victims.

2015b). As for Venezuela, it should be noted that the homicide rate went from an average of 20 deaths per 100 000 from 1994–98 to over 55 per 100 000 in the second decade of the 21st century (Briceño-León 2012).

Violence has been a hallmark of Latin America, and self-proclaimed progressive, redistributive administrations over the pink decade (and they were not a few) did not manage to turn around a trend that has only deepened, as a few of the indicators mentioned here can attest. It is true that interpersonal violence is a universal challenge, 'making homicide a more frequent cause of death than all wars combined' since 2000 (*Global Status Report on Violence Prevention 2014*: 2). Nevertheless, comparative data show Latin America's appalling lead in the field: the annual homicide rate for middle- and low-income countries in the region is 28.5 deaths per 100 000 inhabitants, more than twice that registered in all African countries – the second-highest, at 10.9 per 100 000. The global average stood at 6.7 deaths in 2012, while high-income countries in all regions display a homicide rate of 3.8 per 100 000. While this rate fell quickly in high-income countries, the rest saw a near stagnation. According to the WHO, a homicide rate over 10 is considered epidemic.

As if these macabre trophies weren't enough, Latin America is also the region with the highest rate of homicides by firearm in the world (75 per cent, as opposed to an average of 48 per cent). That is, access to firearms is not duly regulated and repressed. Yet again, the Brazilian legislature is in the process of adopting a new law with a view to making it easier to carry firearms. The reform of the 'Disarmament Statute', to be voted on at some point in 2016, has already had a preliminary text approved by the relevant committee. It calls for the reduction of the minimum age for carrying a firearm from 25 to 21; authorization to carry firearms at home, at the workplace and on rural properties; an increase in the period of license renewal from 3 to 10 years; arms license availability for those charged or under investigation for crimes; and the ability for lawmakers to circulate with arms, even inside Congress. The chances of this bill's being approved are considerable, with this backsliding justified 'in name of the people's right to self-defense'. This deliberately ignores all the studies that indicate the preventive nature of policies for the repression and control of firearms in addressing youth homicides (Waiselfisz 2015b: 96).

In addition to making up the bulk of homicide statistics, youths (ages 18–29) also represent 54.8 per cent of the Brazilian incarcerated population, which lives in subhuman conditions in prisons falling far short of any humanitarian standards. Occupancy levels in Brazilian prisons reached 153.9 per cent in 2014, according to the World Prison Brief and the Institute for Criminal Policy Research. Degradation and brutality in prison conditions are, however, even more drastic in Bolivia (298.7 per cent), Venezuela (269.8 per cent) and Peru (231 per cent).

'Penal selectivity' – defined by color, age, and sex – puts Brazil at fourth place in global rankings of prison populations, as well as undisputed leader in South America. The prison population rate per 100 000 inhabitants has already reached 300 (Conectas 2015), putting the country ahead of Uruguay (282); Colombia (244); Chile (232); Peru (239); Venezuela (178), and Ecuador (162), to name a few (from World Prison Brief in 2015).

This becomes even more serious, however, when we see that each year brings more young people into the prison system. The *Mapa do Encarceramento – Os Jovens do Brasil* (2015) shows that the group of adolescents ages 12–21 has systematically increased its presence in juvenile prisons, where they are detained for a period of social/educational rehabilitation. Moreover, despite the existence of the Statute for Children and Adolescents (ECA),[4] these youths are subject to the same punitive measures in place in adult prisons (p. 12), often marked by abuses and cruelty.

In Brazil, over 42 per cent of detainees are in prison for non-violent crimes. In Bolivia, pre-trial detainees account for 83.2 per cent, a surprising and dramatically high figure, but one not so far off

---

4. According to the ECA (Estatuto da Criança e do Adolescente), which has been in place since 1990, adolescents found responsible for infractions are processed through different channels: they are sentenced to socio-educational rehabilitative measures, which may be administered at home or while detained, depending on the gravity of the act and/or recidivism.

from what we can see in Paraguay (75 per cent) or Venezuela (68.4 per cent).

In Latin America as a whole, the situation is equally worrisome. Correa (2015) recalls that, 'in a recent debate about human rights in Latin America, Emilio Alvarez, the executive secretary of the Inter-American Commission on Human Rights, made the point that despite the democratic consolidation of the past 30 years, the region is undergoing the worst incarceration crisis in its history. Never before have so many people been imprisoned on such precarious conditions, subject to brutal violations of human rights.' In Latin America, prison is used as the rule, not the exception, as proved by widespread arbitrary detention – a form of denying recognition.

By way of conclusion

The evidence above may inspire a certain doubt as to whether, as Therborn suggests, Latin America has seen existential equalization take a sustainable path (p. 143) or whether 'the dismantling of existential inequality in recent years is a major human advance' (p. 145) by any measure.

I would argue that criminalization of Indigenous communities who resist the violation of their rights, the mass incarceration of the formerly economically excluded and socially discriminated, and the savage repression of women for having claimed control over their bodies and sexuality are not a transient paradox in the process of development, but rather entrenched and long-lasting existential inequalities that have survived market incorporation in Latin America. This has been the great change of recent years, a sign of the transition to a mass consumer economy without a real transformation of inequality-reproducing structures, whatever they may be. Segregation, polarization and marginalization persist as crucial features of Latin American inequality and prevent the full realization of equalization attempts.

Young Blacks in Brazil, whose color seems to constitute an infraction; the populations of Latin America's peripheries, who rarely see the public investments that might even out access opportunities leave the drawing board; poor and not-so-poor women for whom the cost of a reasonably safe clandestine abortion is ultimately prohibitive; and the Indigenous communities savaged by the prioritizing of economic development and modernity appear in this essay as warnings of a covenant that, while widely celebrated in the most unequal region on the planet, was a failure: the covenant of growth with redistribution and equity. The time for its fulfillment has been postponed yet again, as it is unthinkable that we Latin Americans accept a mere veneer of change. This is not a matter of being radical, but rather demanding the healthy, prosperous combination of a democratic and truly egalitarian environment.

The most recent report from CEPAL (2015) demonstrates that poverty reduction has stagnated since 2012, while extreme poverty has resumed its upward trajectory. It also indicates that as of 2014, only 49 per cent of the region's population found themselves outside poverty, extreme poverty, and the zone of vulnerability that indicates a high risk of returning to severe levels of destitution. For half +1 per cent, existential and resource inequality continue to undercut and outright impede vital equality.

Though Latin America appears miles away from a real and unequivocal egalitarian move, Therborn's call for action echoes in our ears and drives us to the battlefields for the fight against inequality. As he prophetically says (p. 184): 'The battle is about to start. Nobody knows how it will end. Which side will you be on?'

References

Briceño-León, R. (2012) 'Three phases of homicidal violence in Venezuela', *Ciência & Saúde Coletiva*, 17, 12, 3233–3242.

CEPAL (2015) *Panorama Social de América Latina y Caribe 2014*. Santiago de Chile.

CIMI (2014) *Violence against Indigenous People in Brazil – 2014 Data*. Brasília.

Conectas Human Rights (2015) *Mapas das Prisões*. http://www.conectas.org/en/actions/justice/news/26571-map-of-prisons.

Correa, S. (2015) *Direito ao aborto legal e seguro como tema da democracia*, 7 August. At: http://sxpolitics.org/direito-ao-aborto-legal-e-seguro-como-tema-da democracia/13270.

ECLAC (2014) *Statistical Yearbook*.

Furtado, C. (2013 [1974]) 'O Mito do Desenvolvimento Econômico', in D'Aguiar, R.F. (ed.) *Essencial Celso Furtado*. São Paulo: Penguin/Companhia das Letras, pp. 167–175.

Global Status Report on Violence Prevention 2014 (2014) Geneva: WHO, UNDP & UNODC.

INEC (2013) *Anuário de Estadísticas Vitales: nacimientos y defunciones*. Quito.

Mapa do Encarceramento – Os Jovens do Brasil (2015) Brasília: Secretaria Geral da Presidência da República, Secretaria Nacional de Juventude – UNDP.

Picq, M.L. (2015) 'Extrativismo: a pedra no caminho do desenvolvimento', in Souza, P. de (ed.) *Brasil, sociedade em movimento*. Rio de Janeiro: Paz e Terra.

Ramos, S. (ed.) (2015) *Investigación sobre Aborto en América Latina y El Caribe: una agenda renovada para informar políticas públicas e incidência*. CEDES; Population Council; Promsex.

Therborn, G. (2013) *The Killing Fields of Inequality*. Cambridge: Polity Press.

Therborn, G. (2015) 'Moments of equality: Today's Latin America in a global historical context', in Fritz, B. and Lavinas, L. (eds.) *A Moment of Equality for Latin America? Challenges for Redistribution*. Farnham: Ashgate.

Valdés, M.F. (2015) 'Is tax policy becoming more pro-equity in the region? Five case studies of commodity-dependent economies', in Fritz, B. and Lavinas, L. (eds.) *A Moment of Equality for Latin America? Challenges for Redistribution*. Farnham: Ashgate.

Waiselfisz, J.J. (2015a) *Mapa da Violência. Homicídio de Mulheres no Brasil*. Brasília: FLACSO.

Waiselfisz, J.J. (2015b) *Mapa da Violência. Mortes Matadas por Armas de Fogo*. Brasília: Secretaria Geral da Presidência da República, Secretaria de Políticas de Promoção da Igualdade Racial.

Zibechi R. (2013) 'Latin America rejects the extractive model in the streets', *Americas Program*, 27 October. Available at: http://www.cipamericas.org/archives/10983 (accessed 29 January 2014).

CHANG KYUNG-SUP

Post-Socialist Class Politics with Chinese Characteristics

Partial Marketization, State-Mediated Inequalities, and Communist Liberalism

Introduction

In his recent essay in *New Left Review* on 'New masses?' (2014), Göran Therborn offers a cogent panoramic view of the 21st century conditions of social classes and masses across the world as the (potential) antithetical force to globalized capitalism. Broadly speaking, his observations are focused upon, on the one hand, the increasing complexities of class structures and relations in most nations and, on the other hand, the rapid ascendance of nations and masses in the Global South as a main axis of the new capitalist order. However, he would not yet present any definitive conclusions on the world's present social situation or clear prescriptions for critical reforms in national and global capitalism, perhaps mainly because humanity has just entered a new stage of globally integrated and financially manipulated capitalism with most of its full social, political, cultural, as well as economic impacts yet to be realized.

This cautious stance also reflects Therborn's careful and extensive consideration of the astounding, unpredicted, and unpredictable developments in China as a prime factor for the global community's sociopolitical and economic transformations in the new century – with its economic growth, urbanization/population movement, income growth, and inequalities all at historically and internation-

The author has benefitted from Yoon Jong-Seok's valuable suggestions for revision.

ally incomparable rates. In another, slightly earlier essay in *New Left Review* on 'Class in the 21st century' (2012), Therborn offered an account of China as a complicated or compressed social entity comprised by quite diverse social classes that roughly correspond to the above explained masses of the contemporary world. He elucidates on the sectoral composition and sociopolitical nature of China's contemporary (urban) masses:

> The industrial baton has been passed to China, the emerging centre of world manufacturing capacity. Its industrial workers are still largely immigrants in their own country, because of the lingering *hukou* system of urban and rural birthrights. Yet Chinese industrial growth is strengthening the hand of the workers, as Marx would have expected: strikes have become more frequent and wages are rising. A new round of social conflict over the distribution of wealth, now displaced from Europe to East Asia, is not to be excluded ... Manual workers are a force to be reckoned with in urban China, although their numbers are difficult to pin down. What seems to be the best estimate counts them as a third of the registered population. But migrants *without* residency permits make up more than a third of the total labour force in the cities, and the great majority of them are manual workers in manufacturing, construction and catering. Adding the two groups should make something between a good half and two-thirds of urban China's manual working class. The emergence of a powerful movement based on this proletariat would have a tremendous impact throughout the developing world, but we can hardly describe that as a likely prospect. (Therborn 2012: 20–21.)

Migrant workers without urban *hukou*, who are subjected to various segregative and discriminatory terms of work and living, are officially *nongmin* (farmers) with a familial right-cum-duty to cultivate an equally allocated farmland in their home villages. They and their village-remaining family members, kinsmen, and neighbors still maintain farming as the largest occupation in China, at least in formal statistics. The widespread poverty of farming families renders rural-urban inequalities one of the thorniest political concerns of the Communist leadership in Beijing. Therborn adds the issue of middle class to the already complex picture of Chinese society:

Chinese scholars now tend to idealize the middle class, drawing on US stereotypes while avoiding critical discussion of the concept ... Some perceptive commentators have noted, however, that it is the widening income gap which has laid the foundations of this new middle class: China is now Asia's most unequal country, its Gini coefficient having soared from 0.21 in the 60s to 0.46 at present. (Therborn 2012: 17.)

In Therborn's observation, post-Mao China is as much characterized by social complexities and disparities as by developmental achievements. In this respect, despite its enviable economic growth, the country has not been able to fully differentiate itself from most of late developing capitalist countries in the deprivation and alienation of masses.

Consequently, Therborn critically compares China with its capitalist neighbors in social inequality or cohesion:

After the Second World War, nationally cohesive capitalist development was the aim of the elected rulers of Japan and the military ones of Taiwan and South Korea alike, resulting in industrial societies that, in the capitalist world, were second only to European welfare states for their low levels of economic inequality. For the PRC's rulers, social cohesion remains a decisive criterion of political performance. The extraordinary inequality spawned by China over the past 35 years—so different from the egalitarian, rapid-growth trajectories of Japan, South Korea and Taiwan—renders its self-image as a 'harmonious society' untenable. This may also become the case in other parts of the South. (Therborn 2014: 13.)

Even at the official level, Communist China's capitalist developmental success and its various risks and costs are yet to be accommodated in a clearly formalized system of economic governance and politico-legal rule beyond the improvised pragmatist communitarian – and, by its origin, neo-Confucian – ideology of 'well-off society' (*xiao-kangshehui*, 小康社会). Therborn directly pinpoints China's (and Vietnam's) key dilemma:

In East Asia, in particular, industrial capitalism is delivering higher levels of consumption, in a way that slower-developing European economies took much longer to achieve. True, Communist Party rule in China and Vietnam means that an anti-capitalist turn is not inconceivable—and would be feasible, if attempted. Yet for this to happen would require both a halt to growth and effective working-class mobilization against the enormous inequality the system has generated, which threatens the 'harmony' or social cohesion of Communist capitalism. This is imaginable but highly improbable, at least in the medium term. (Therborn 2014: 9–10.)

That is, any serious attempt at fundamentally redressing China's current inequalities cannot but sociopolitically endanger the ruling Communist party because of its very success in promoting economic development with socially disequalizing tendencies.

In this essay, by drawing on and updating my earlier work, I wish to elaborate on Therborn's attention to China as a key clue to the new century's global social order. I will analyze the main structural dynamics of new class relations and inequalities in post-Mao China in terms of state-market-class interactions and appraising the theoretical-ideological quality of the thereby evolving political economy.[1] In China's market-oriented economic reform, state power has not been replaced by market rules but reinvigorated through strategic selection of the operational scope and direction of market rules. On the part of each social group, efforts are made to influence the intervention process of state power after reckoning whether adoption or exclusion of market rules is advantageous in its economic domain. In China, where a sort of *partial marketization* has been effected, class relations are centered on state-dependent adoption/exclusion of market rules. The social realities in post-Mao China invite a state-centered explanation of class relations which refuses to regard class relations as the competition and conflict among social classes separated from state power but instead emphasizes the *access to state power* of each social class as the crucial determinant of class order.

---

1. See Chang Kyung-Sup (2001a). The sections 'Historical and theoretical backgrounds' and 'Post-Mao reform' in the current article contain thoroughly rewritten, updated, and expanded contents from this earlier work where most references to works published before 2001 are available.

Historical and theoretical backgrounds: state power and class relations in post-revolutionary China

Mao Zedong argued that socialism in China had engendered contradictions of its own, which would require new stages of revolutionary political struggle. In his view, the supposedly classless society of post-revolutionary China was still subjected to inequality and class conflicts. His address in 1957 indicated two types of contradictions: between enemies and us (people) and among people themselves (Mao 1971: 432–479). The contradictions between enemies and people were supposedly evidenced by the resistance of reactionary groups to China's post-revolutionary socialist transformations as well as to the socialist revolution itself. The contradictions among people themselves denote the disharmony and conflict that arose among various social and political groups and elements even after the completion of the revolution and the basic socialist transformations. More specifically, the latter contradictions were revealed: among workers, among peasants, among intellectuals, between workers/peasants and intellectuals, between workers and national bourgeoisie, among national bourgeoisie, and between people and their government.[2] The contradictions between people and their government, in turn, were revealed: among the competing interests of the state, collectives, and individuals, between democracy and centralism, between leaders and the led, and between bureaucratic cadres and people. The contradictions among people themselves implied conflictual relations and inequalities among various groups and classes hinged on diverse occupational, political, administrative, and regional statuses and thus necessitated additional political efforts beyond the suggestions of Marx, Lenin and Stalin.

Mao's above analysis was no academic task on its own but served as a rationale for his subsequent political efforts at rectifying Chinese society. His observations and views were directly translated into fierce ideological campaigns and violent political struggles, in

2. The contradictions between people and their government were part of the contradictions among people themselves because the government belonged to people.

particular, during the Cultural Revolution. Then, party and government cadres, factory managers, and office directors with bureaucratic and/or authoritarian posture were demoted and purged; intellectuals, whether scientific or political, were ostracized; urban workers with improper attitude and job-waiting youth were sent to villages to 'learn from peasants'; technical, educational, or bureaucratic criteria for differentiating and discriminating among workers were abolished; and class enemies of *heiwuliu* (former landlords, reactionaries, etc.) were warned and threatened again.[3] These efforts and events, however, did not fundamentally alter the existing structures of class conflict and inequality although some aftermaths were left in terms of clientelistic relationship between cadres and masses, strengthened *pingjunzhuyi* (equalitarianism) among workers, and so on. In this social context, Deng Xiaoping's reform was launched immediately after Mao's death.

In post-revolutionary China, aside from Mao's analysis, the class positions and inter-relations of party and state cadres, intellectuals, workers of urban state and collective enterprises, peasants of rural collective farms, and former class enemies and their offspring were constructed as state-set or state-dependent properties in a political economic system comprehensively organized and tightly directed by the state (as opposed to what Max Weber conceptualized as market-based class properties in capitalist society). What matters here decisively was *access to state power*. While state power in the context of supposed proletarian dictatorship and state-command economy was overpowering, there was always fierce competition among different social and political groups to magnify their connection to and influence on it for advancing their respective class interests.[4]

---

3. An ironical development during the Cultural Revolution was that children of *heiwulei* families interpreted Mao's critique of socialist China as a pardon of their familial backgrounds and/or an encouragement of their counter-attack on the existing leadership in work units and political offices.

4. This line of theoretical interest is most closely related to Mancur Olson's thesis in his *The Logic of Collective Action* (1965). He argues that the competition among various social and political groups in a democratic society to induce favorable government policies concerning the use of public resources is usually won by the group of big business runners because their smaller

Access to state power had an essential theoretical property in class affairs of post-revolutionary China (and reform-era China), broadly comparable to ownership of the means of production in capitalist society. Each social group's access to state power was either formally institutionalized through the political and administrative framework for governance and economic management or informally pursued through individual relationships and/or collective political pressure.[5] The particular historical constellations of class relations in post-revolutionary China can be understood only when access to state power as materialized in various distinct ways is fully taken into account. Class relations were forged and transformed *through the state*.

The thesis on access to state power can be meaningfully compared with earlier literature – in particular, Vivienne Shue's thesis on the 'reach of the state' into society.[6] According to Shue (1988: 71),

---

number allows them to coordinate their interests tightly and carry out a most effective lobbying to government offices and parliamentary committees. However, the access to state power in post-Mao China appears to be affected more sensitively by the political group dynamics and ideology inherited from the Maoist era than by such immediate social ecological conditions for political actions as emphasized by Olson (i.e., group size, etc.).

5. Xueguang Zhou (1993) argues that a tight institutional structure has governed state-society relationship in China such that any collective action (against state power) based on 'organized interests' is extremely difficult. However, his argument does not preclude the possibility that this institutional structure can serve a mechanism through which various social groups seek state support in advancing their 'undefiant' group interests.

6. Peter Evans' thesis on the 'social embeddedness' of the (developmental) state also merits (comparative) theoretical attention. According to him, the ability of the state to penetrate social organizations and relations and manipulate them for effective policy implementation has been a key to national economic success in various cases of the so-called state-led capitalist development. When such efforts are made by the state, as implied from the current theoretical perspective, the streams of influence and pressure will form a two-way traffic in which social groups try to capitalize on the social penetration of the state to advance their own interests. This possibility will assume a constantly increasing significance in twenty-first century China as its key function in national economic management turns from institutional system reform to developmental industrial promotion.

'Chinese socialist state builders of the Mao era seem to have looked ... for ways "to domesticate" localist loyalties, to incorporate them into state socialist structures, and turn them, where possible, into a positive force for socialist development.' In an effort to build an effective force in social transformation and economic development, the Maoist state had to respect local social structures and relations but, whenever feasible, utilized them for a maximum mobilization of grassroots efforts. The social reach of the state become particularly crucial if the state – having emerged out of but become independent from society – repenetrates social structure and redirects social change to achieve its autonomous goals. In contrast, access to state power becomes essential if social and political groups, having been formed or allowed to form by the state, influence the state back to expedite their class interests. The social reach of the state, by extending the neo-Marxian debate on state autonomy and capacity, indicates that the state is not simply autonomous from class interests but persuades, reorganizes, and, where inevitable, compromises with them. Access to state power, by extending the Marxist critique of 'degenerated party-state dictatorship' over producer classes in socialist societies, denotes that various social and political groups not only recognize the monolithic authority of the state but also attempt to influence or collude with it to augment their class interests.

It should be emphasized that Chinese people's concern about access to state power was not historically unprecedented. According to Frederic Wakeman (1991: 255), in traditional China,

> first, that gentry status could be reduced to a common denominator – power-holding through office or access to power-holders – and, second, that people who spoke or thought in ways we now identify with the high culture of China were better able to protect their local interests than those who did not share this language and way of life with Chinese officialdom ... Corporate interest groups did, of course, exist, but they were usually outside the limits of acceptable political behavior.

Seeking the support or influence of the state in managing social relations is nothing to blame politically or morally in China's corporatist historical tradition.

In China's post-revolutionary era, competition and check in gaining, maintaining, and aggrandizing access to state power came to constitute a lively corporatist political society (rather than a totalitarian machine society), of which rich historical documentation is available. Cadres at various divisions and levels of the party-state apparatus were busy not only in capitalizing on their official authority for their own benefits (or against the interests of peasants and workers under their supervision) but also in establishing connections to cadres in higher offices; workers in urban industrial enterprises – vis-à-vis peasants in rural collective farms – were considered politically more threatening and thus endowed by the state leadership with larger influence on macro-economic policies of the state, making worker-peasant material disparities ever widening; managers and grassroots members in urban enterprises and rural collective farms competed hard to win the support of unit party leadership while party cadres themselves were always concerned about the competing goals of economic performance and political stability; a total denial of access to state power was made toward former class enemies and their offspring, who could not expect to join cadredom at any level or receive any preferential treatment in allocation of jobs and benefits in their work units. Ironically, most of these tendencies and policies were rather reinforced during the Cultural Revolution; a political project intended to eradicate the contradictions of class conflict and inequality in post-revolutionary *China*. The political motif of transforming the disappointingly bureaucratized socialist system into a democratic and organic one rather became responsible for the arbitrary use of state power by individual leaders whose primary concern was to bolster their political position in various state and party organizations. As a concomitant trend, social and political groups had to compete even harder to forge and strengthen particularistic ties with state power elite. The legacy of such state-shaped class structure and relations is still evident in post-Mao or reform-era China, despite the fact that now state power is usually expressed in terms of market economic outcomes.

Post-Mao reform: partial marketization and state-mediated class relations and inequalities

Partial marketization

Chinese reform, despite constant modifications in its direction and emphasis, has been centered on step-by-step changes in economic institutions and policies. In this regard, China is often contrasted with Russia and Eastern European countries where abrupt political transitions triggered no less radical economic changes. Broadly speaking, two main dimensions China's economic system transition can be identified as follows: privatization and/or rationalization of production organizations at the micro-level and institutionalization of market transactions of labor, consumer goods, capital goods, enterprise ownership rights, finance, as well as welfare services at the macro-level. The following two crucial points should be made to caution against any hasty generalization on the nature and outcome of post-Mao reform. First, the contents and courses of actual reform have never been fully planned in advance by the Chinese government. Reform has instead been a constant trial-error-revision sequence as shaped by the tense interplay between the pragmatist state leadership and various social and political groups in conjunction with individual and collective economic interests. Second, institutionalization of the market, while it certainly signals reduction of the plan, by no means necessitates replacement of the state in the macro-coordination of economic activities. The authority and functions of the state have been substantiated not only through the bureaucratic control of economic activities and resources but also through the (mal)functioning of market dynamics. These two tendencies have been jointly responsible for the emergence of a partially marketized economic system in which the degrees and/or directions of marketization of commodities, services, and labor critically affect the competing class interests of various groups and individuals.

This patched or partial marketization has had a macroeconomic rationale because the party-state leadership has tried to pursue reform without foregoing the economic and political utility of pre-reform economic institutions all at once.[7] More crucially, partial marketization has ramified a sort of favoritism by which the party-state preferentially protects the vested interests of state-dependent groups such as workers in state enterprises, cadres in party and state organizations, and entrepreneurs with political connections while the interests of grassroots groups in marketized sections are subjected to the uncertainty and instability of market conditions as well as the discriminatory allocation of public economic resources. Under particular circumstances, however, marketization works to promote new economic opportunities and windfall profits for certain groups at the expense of others under bureaucratic control.

It is far from difficult to detect abundant social symptoms of partial marketization in post-Mao China. A brief glance at the industrial and employment structures enables an immediate realization that full-scale market forces operate only in certain segments of the Chinese economy, for instance, in private and foreign enterprises, family farms, etc. Labor markets do exist but their effects are actualized only through complicated political and social contingencies. Numerous legal urban residents with tenured jobs have managed to remain in a sort of state-underwritten internal labor market, whereas rural-to-urban migrants, called *mingong* (peasant worker), have been subjected to all the adverse impacts of marketization. Besides, marketization of social services accruing to the demise or decline of *danwei* (socialist work units) has taken place quite unevenly – that is, most rural families and individuals have had to suddenly rely on paid services and goods from markets while many of their urban counterparts have been assured sustained or rearranged basic protection of their welfare needs. The *shuanggui* (dual track) price system has led administered low prices and market-set high prices for a significant number of consumer and producer goods. Similarly, banks have offered two types of loans according to market and administrative criteria correspondingly. A nearly inexhaustible list of related examples exists.

It is true that some of these symptoms are simply transitory phenomena and thus will disappear as time lapses or deregulation

7. In an informal discussion, Lin Justin Yifu and I came to agree on this aspect of Chinese reform.

proceeds. However, partial marketization in post-Mao China is far from a mere outcome of *gradual* or *gradualist* marketization. It has an economic as well as political logic of its own and will last for a considerable period of time. A crucial part of such logic is derived from the reality that pre-reform corporatist political society still prevails with a heavy influence on the contents and directions of reform policies. In a nutshell, the competition among different social and political groups to aggrandize their connection to and influence on state power is as fierce as in the pre-reform era and has serious ramifications in the scope and manner of marketization. After calculating what outcomes may arise when market parameters enter their respective economic domains, these groups will attempt to facilitate, obstruct, or deflect the scope and direction of marketization by staging political pressure on or nurturing favorable relationship with concerned political and administrative offices. Under China's partially marketized economic system, the contents and degrees of marketization decisively affect competing class interests. To the extent that the marketization process is a task of the state itself, class relations in reform-era China continue to be forged and transformed through the state.

In this respect, the prevailing debate on the political consequences of China's marketization – focusing on the changing relative primacy of state power and market (business) force – appears seriously flawed.[8] In post-Mao China, state power has been expanded through market-related domains and affairs and strengthened through thereby generated macroeconomic outcomes. This process meaningfully corresponds to the political developmental of the modern state in advanced democracies which has often been predicated upon the formation and activation of independent civil society as an essential milieu of competent state functions and activities. In addition, the developmental experiences of China's advanced neighbors (e.g., Japan, South Korea, Taiwan) insinuate that even its maturation in postsocialist system reform may not necessarily result in a laissez-faire market economy where the state simply regulates, or that

---

8. This debate was initiated with Victor Nee. See Goodman (2014: 149–153) for a succinct summary of the debate.

markets and industries are there to be strategically managed by the (developmental) state.

Peasants, workers and mingong: *dual dualism*

Post-Mao reform began by sequentially transforming China's eight hundred million rural population from collective agricultural laborers in People's Communes into family-based private farmers whose economic autonomy led to both sharply improved agricultural productivity and diversification of rural income sources. While the prime means of production (i.e., land) is still under formal collective ownership and leased to villagers for independent cultivation for a certain delimited period, their class status does not fundamentally differ from that of pre-revolutionary ancestors. As basically autonomous economic producers, Chinese peasants have been confronted with both new opportunities for wealth creation and structural uncertainties emanating from the market economy. Paradoxically, the institutional and social autonomy of Chinese peasants accruing to agricultural decollectivization has been most explosively expressed in their vibrant desire for quitting agriculture and/or leaving villages. Under a chronic shortage of farmland supply, Chinese rural families have frequently been confronted with difficulty in securing durable subsistence. When the party-state suddenly withdrew its long-held suppression of villagers' nonagricultural activities and allowed them short-term/short-distance migration to nearby towns and cities, nonagricultural employment and rural exodus expanded at quite dramatic rates. A majority of peasant-turned-workers have been employed in rural collective industries called *xiangzhenqiye* (village and township industry); whereas an ever increasing number of 'unprepared' rural masses, derogatively dubbed *mangliu* (blind flow), have entered large and distant cities, triggering various social and economic problems. In a situation where even an increasing number of regular urban residents (with the urban residence permit called *hukou*) have had to accept lay-offs, pay-cuts, and job delays amidst the prolonged stalemate in urban economic reform, these new, illegal, and unwelcome entrants from villages (called *mingong* or *nongmingong*) have not been comfortably accommodated in the urban economy. Nonetheless, urban areas immediately began to be restructured into a socioeconomic entity sustained materially by the cheap, abundant, and easily exploitable supply of migrant labor from villages.

With the managerial rationalization of state and collective enterprises being the most crucial task of urban economic reform, various experiments with new forms of management and ownership have inevitably affected the social and economic status of urban workers. The pressure on these socialist enterprises for profitability and financial independence has led to a rapid destabilization of workers' employment conditions, so that their differences from workers in capitalist economies – and from migrant workers from villages – have constantly been weakened. Those enterprises which have decided to accept foreign investment have concomitantly been exposed to capitalist labor relations as a condition for such investment, thereby causing local Chinese workers' deep anxiety (Chang 2001b). With all these marketizing tendencies, the living conditions and employment status of urban workers, whose potential for political disruption is unparalleled, have been given perhaps the most careful considerations by the successive leaderships in Beijing. While all grassroots citizens, whether in rural or urban areas, have undergone abrupt and fundamental changes in their socioeconomic status, urban resident workers have been provided by the state with various shock-absorbing mechanisms against such changes (Chang 2003). Relatedly, their income level and living standard have kept widening the already substantial leads over those of peasants even during a period when the rural economy frequently excelled the urban economy in performance and growth (Chang 2005). The party-state did not avoid risking a serious financial burden of covering the huge and chronic deficits of urban state enterprises in order to protect the employment status and welfare benefits of workers therein. In a sharp contrast, it kept refusing to approximate (i.e., adjust upward) its procurement prices for farm products to the actual market prices since the mid 1980s, thereby aggravating agriculture's profitability crisis. Even the price subsidies for urban residents' foodstuff and other basic consumer goods, which amounted close to the total national defense budget in the 1980s, were maintained into the 1990s.[9] Furthermore, marketization (or commodification) of social services and security benefits, resulting from the demise or reform of *danwei* (socialist production units), has been a fundamentally uneven, and unfair, process.[10] Regular residents in most cities continued to expect, not entirely in vain, that their basic welfare needs should be met mainly as employment-linked benefits, but the widespread deconstruction of the communal welfare mechanisms since agricultural decollectivization has necessitated villagers to increasingly turn to commodified services at their own expenses.

Broadly speaking, the state-mediated (or state-imposed) inequalities between urban and rural permanent residents have been systematically reproduced within urban areas in terms of the inequality between regular urban workers and village-originated migrant workers. Frustrated with the protracted stagnation in agricultural productivity and household income, an ever-increasing number of Chinese peasants have considered and eventually executed a new life path of quitting agriculture and/or leaving villages. Once they enter urban places, however, their migrant status (and illegal worker status) immediately results in various kinds of social and economic discrimination by those local city governments and urban enterprises that are either determined or obliged to protect the exclusionary employment and welfare entitlements of regular urban residents (Chang 2003). As pointed out above, even though labor market has been formally instituted as part of urban economic reform, its adverse social impacts have frequently been contained or diluted in respect to regular urban residents. The official effort at thoroughly marketizing labor relations within state and collective enterprises –

---

9. The Chinese government would not hide such spending even in its formal budget tabulation as published in the *Zhongguotongjinianjian* (Statistical Yearbook of China) series.

10. In pre-reform China, where nationally effective programs for social security were absent, socialist production units such as state enterprises and collective farms had also functioned as welfare provision units for their workers and peasants. Consequently, the recasting or demise of these production units in the reform era unavoidably threatens the welfare status of their workers.

namely, *laodonghetongzhi* (labor contract system) – has been only partially successful in actual implementation (Lee 2007). In the initial period of the labor contract system, i.e., the mid-to-late 1980s, few enterprise managers and local governments could overcome the staunch resistance of workers to annulment of their permanent job security (secularly called *tiefanwan*, meaning iron rice bowl); in later years, workers gradually began to accept the status of contract laborer, however, with the actual contents of their contract ensuring their *tiefanwan* in various disguises (Chang 2001b). By contrast, migrant workers have been demanded to endure all sorts of social and economic hardships germinated from the structurally *segmented* labor market even though such endurance rarely facilitates stable permanent employment. Besides, it is extremely difficult, if not permanently impossible, for migrant workers to gain stable access to adequate social services, even at their own expenses.[11]

In sum, there exists a dual inequality structure between rural and urban permanent population that has been created and buttressed by the party-state.[12] This *dual dualism* of the reformist state has manifested itself, on the one hand, in the class relations between peasants (and their *mingong* relatives) and urban workers and, on the other hand, in the class relations formed respectively by migrant workers and regular urban workers with their employers. Interestingly, the double dimensions of inequality used to be mutually reinforcing in the social attitude of peasant-turned urban workers. Despite their immediate and often lengthy status as urban worker, most of them used to identify themselves as members of rural/agricultural

---

11. In some areas, migrants have responded to this adverse situation by setting up their own communal networks and institutions for emergency relief, education, etc.

12. The bondage between migrant workers and their family members in villages is not only a moral and cultural phenomenon but also a crucial economic phenomenon in labor-intensive industrialization. On the one hand, the immediate motivation for migration is to relieve the economic burden of their family under land shortage and/or earn additional family income. On the other hand, when migrant workers have difficulty in attaining an adequately paying permanent job, village-remaining family members often support them with living and training expenses, foodstuffs, etc.

communities (*nongmin*) and thereby accept their everyday disadvantages as a natural outcome of being as such. This submissive attitude has recently been changed in a critical way, particularly among the so-called 'second-generation' migrant workers in South China industrial enclaves of transnational capital (Chan and Pun 2009; Pun and Lu 2010; Leung and So 2012). The rise of class consciousness and activism among foreign-capital employed migrant workers conversely indicates that globalized (or globally marketized) labor relations have helped to eradicate a quasi-fatalist attitude of migrant workers framed through the party-state's unique institutional segregation of socioeconomic citizenship between rural and urban on-paper residents.

Associated worker-entrepreneurs in xiangzhenqiye

Post-Mao reform gave birth to rural based, labor-intensive industries, called *xiangzhenqiye* (village and township enterprises) on such a massive scale that Chinese villagers suddenly came to find jobs therein in numbers nearly comparable to those of urban industrial workers. With all the economic difficulties generated from inefficient and deficit-making urban state enterprises and stagnant family farms, this rural industrial sector alone was almost exclusively responsible for China's economic overheating in the mid 1980s and the 1990s. This has been a family-propelled, quasi-Lewisian industrialization within rural areas. The entrepreneurial initiative, regional distribution, organizational structure, and internal class relations of these rural industries were quite distinct from those observed in other societies. In particular, if seen from the Lewisian perspective, there is a crucial missing link in this industrialization process – i.e., the initial absence of urban-originated capital and entrepreneurship (to be combined with rural surplus labor). Instead, the tripartite interactions among peasants, local collectives, and the pragmatist state leadership came to fill such economic vacuum and led to a rural-contained but autonomous industrialization. It engendered a unique process of market-oriented industrialization without typical capitalist social transformation. Thanks to agricultural productivity gains and (upward) price adjustments of farm products since agricultural decollectivization in the early to mid 1980s, Chinese peasants were equipped not only with abundant surplus labor to be utilized in non-agricultural sectors but also with desire *and* purchasing capacity for new consumer goods, cash surplus to be invested in nonagricultural ventures, farm-produced raw materials to be processed, and individual and collective entrepreneurial experiences. Villagers were linked to the new industries not just as passive labor sellers but also as main consumers, investors, raw-material providers, and entrepreneurs/ managers. Consequently, many rural enterprises were labor-managed firms, with which countries like former Yugoslavia had tried to build a new line of socialist economy.

These efforts and initiatives of peasants did not result in isolated and dispersed trials but came to drive a rebirth of rural economic collectivism across China. It was not so much because Chinese peasants were ideologically awakened as because local collective units (villagers' committees) and state organs (*xiang* governments) were actively engaged in organizing, managing, and financing the new industrial enterprises. On the part of village leaders and local cadres, running rural industries was no new experience since they had been in charge of many rural industries set up under Mao Zedong's initiative during the Great Leap Forward and the Cultural Revolution. Due to agricultural decollectivization, rural industries remained the only identifiable collective economic basis on which their positional benefits as well as the communal financial resources would be secured. On the other hand, marketization of the rural as well as the national economy opened up a wide array of economic opportunities for these new industries. Rural cadres and village leaders across China tried to prepare a favorable political and administrative environment for new industrial ventures, renovate or build factories, set up corporate organizations, mobilize villagers' economic resources, secure financial and/or technical cooperation from urban or foreign enterprises, and staff or appoint the management of rural industrial enterprises. Even a strong tendency of local industrial protectionism came to prevail across China (Wedeman 2003). On the part of the rural local governments and village collectives, rural industrialization constituted a socioeconomic platform for reinstating and sustaining the public basis of decollectivized rural communities in the increasingly marketized economic environment. This feature of *xiangzhenqiye* would not fundamentally subside even when their ownership and management structure gradually assimilate that of ordinary private enterprises.

Villages and townships were allowed and even encouraged to develop various nonagricultural industries and ventures within their own localities, however, without relying on other localities or the central state for financial and other resources. A sort of contained industrialization was sought for by the Beijing authority as under-employed and undernourished peasants were expected to be eco-nomically absorbed by nonagricultural enterprises within their own localities, or at least outside the already congested big cities. It was hoped that the massive rural labor surplus be released into nonagri-cultural sectors without forging a direct, hostile market relationship with urban workers who were then confronted with their own trou-bles of lay-offs, un(der)employment, and so on. This hope was not betrayed badly. However, the central state leadership at least indi-rectly pitted the interests of rural and urban industries – and inevita-bly those of rural and urban industrial workers – against each other. For it frequently intervened in the competition, in both administra-tive and market channels, of the two sectors for scarce capital, raw materials, energy, and skill, mostly to the advantage of the urban sector. More fundamentally, the long-term direction of national eco-nomic development, as purposely targeted by the party-state and/or circumstantially adjusted to domestic and global economic condi-tions, has ultimately downgraded the weight of rural industries.

Private entrepreneurs: political managerialism

While family farmers and workers in state and collective firms still account for a large majority of the Chinese labor force, those employed in various newly formed private economic units have rapidly been increasing in their size and proportion. The new eco-nomic units include: *getihu* (individual or family-based economic operations, sometimes with a few hired hands, engaged mostly in petty service trade); *siyingqiye* (privately run small enterprises with a certain limit to the size of hired workers); foreign-invested enterprises; Chinese-foreign joint venture enterprises, etc. As these units are able to operate without necessarily subscribing to the socialist rules and practices in ownership and management, the class characteristics of their workers, managers, and investors do not fundamentally differ from those of their counterparts in a capitalist system. In some cases where they enter joint management and/or investment with state or collective enterprises, workers, managers, and investors of such joint ventures take on extremely complicated class characteristics reflecting the systemic attributes of the combined enterprises. As such, Chinese society in the reform era has become one of the most complex class structures in human history.

Just as the ownership and managerial characteristics of newly formed enterprises in the reform era are extremely complicated, those entrepreneurs who own and/or manage such enterprises assume extremely complex class characteristics. Nevertheless, whether they belong to state/collective, private, or joint-ownership enterprises, most of the contemporary Chinese entrepreneurs may not be considered purely professional managers equipped with such economic rationality and managerial skills as are necessitated for improving corporate profitability in a genuine market economy. On the contrary, these entrepreneurs have to act frequently as a sort of political/administrative troubleshooter if their enterprises are to survive durably in China's partially marketized economic system. They should keep keenly analyzing the areas and manners in which the state intervenes in or combines with the market economy and then persuade or even bribe policymakers and local cadres in order to induce administrative decisions favorable to their own enterprises. Besides, they should handle the corporate sociopolitical climate (composed of workers, local residents, local government officials, enterprise-level party cadres, as well as themselves) in such direction as to minimize any political costs incurring complaints and resistances of these constituencies. Undertaking these functions efficiently requires even private entrepreneurs to attain the attribute of an able political/administrative coordinator who can skillfully secure access to local state power and take advantage of it whenever necessary. Consequently, any entrepreneur who has a past career as party or state cadre will enjoy a most useful leverage in corporate management because they can utilize their *guanxi* (connections) with currently incumbent officials in the local government and/or party. Political protection, if not outright political collusion, is a minimum condition for viable private business.

Successful private entrepreneurs in reform-era China, most of whom have shown distinct talent in strategic dependence on or skillful cooptation of state power, constitute as much a political as an economic class. This reality is reinforced by the complex manners of administrative intervention (or interference) in the allocation of economic resources and business opportunities. The Chinese economy has adopted: the *shuanggui* (dual track) system by which two prices, market-cleared (higher) and administratively set (lower) correspondingly, co-exist for many raw materials, producer goods, and consumer goods; the dual financial lending system by which loans are distributed at two different interest rates, market-cleared (higher) and administratively set (lower), depending on the sources and functions of funds; and the preferential taxation system by which various corporate taxes are reduced or exempt by the criteria set by the central and local governments. Those entrepreneurs who can mobilize state power in acquiring materials, machinery, and funds at the administratively-set preferential costs and/or avoid taxes lawfully may not be classified as the same social class as those who cannot – at least, not by the political criteria. An even more decisive effect of state power has been revealed in terms of certain entrepreneurs' exclusive entry into structurally lucrative sectors with monopoly profits. This type of strategic business entry has been most distinctly performed by the so-called *taizidang* (party of princes) entrepreneurs who have abused their politically powerful parents' authority in various monopolistic businesses. The intergenerational family relationship of many of China's top political elite has often functioned to arbitrarily harness state authority to private business interests. The rent-seeking alliance between the state and private entrepreneurs cannot but sacrifice the public interests of grassroots people by unjustifiable allocation of economic benefits and institutional distortion of the still fledgling market economic system.

Party-state cadres: class against itself

Chinese reform, as opposed to those politically driven reforms in Russia and Eastern European countries, has often been referred to as one focused on or confined to the economy. Nevertheless, although it has seldom been proclaimed loudly, there have been a series of political and administrative reform measures undertaken to enable a rational apportionment of state power and create an adequate institutional environment for market-based economic activities. Even if the Communist party has not given up its monopoly over political power, numerous measures have been taken to supervise and control the exercise of power by organizations and cadres at various levels of the party-state hierarchy. The kernel of Deng Xiaoping's strife for political and administrative reform consisted of, on the one hand, separation of the functions and authorities of the government and the Communist party and, on the other hand, substitution of cadres who are young and professionally qualified for those who are not.[13] The formation of a modern administrative class, by training and empowering professional civil servants with rational attitude, was considered an indispensable condition for the firm rooting and sustained development of the market economic system. These professional administrators were then expected to pursue their individual advancement by performing a good leadership function for economic development and social stability.

However, if cadres behave such that their formal status as state manager and their private status as exclusive interest seeker diverge rampantly, the institution of the state may easily degenerate from a civil mechanism for delivering public goods into a private tool for suppressing and exploiting grassroots citizens. This possibility, while commonplace in human history, has become a serious reality in post-Mao China. Innumerable former and current cadres at various levels and sections of the party-state apparatuses have not hesitated abusing their political influence and administrative authority over the rapidly restructuring (in particular, privatizing) national and local economies in order to receive illegal fees and kickbacks

13. The principal program in this regard was a new system of state civil service, i.e., *guojiagongwuyuan*.

from private entrepreneurs, initiate their own business in secrecy and/or preferentially support their family's and clique's business. These acts constitute what may be called *privatization of the privatization process*. In Russia, such distortion of the privatization process has often been called 'nomenklatura privatization' in that it has been dominated and abused by former nomenklatura members. In China, the continuing political power of the party-state and the sustained rapid economic growth have induced party and government cadres to adopt a double-track strategy of maintaining their official politico-administrative status and power and using such status and power to indirectly augment own material interests by preferentially and/or secretly backing their family, clique, and even moonlighting other selves for usurping public economic resources and exclusively accessing new business opportunities (Pei 2006).

Market-oriented reform in China has been accompanied by Beijing's strenuous effort to minimize the political and administrative intervention of the state in economic sectors and production units under the doctrine of managing the economy 'according to economic principles'. However, there is no empirical ground for believing that reform has structurally weakened the ruling class status of party and state cadres. To the contrary, reform has brooded on a situation in which state power is exercised in an increasingly expansive and complex manner – in particular, through politico-bureaucratic allocation of various private economic opportunities. Numerous state and party cadres have tried to convert their political power into economic wealth by usurping the limited opportunities for wealth accumulation themselves or assigning such opportunities to their family members, relatives, close friends, or political clients in secrecy, thereby constituting what Alvin So (2003; 2013) considers 'the cadre-capitalist class'.[14] The basic conditions for a stable and lasting political survival

---

14. Even in abrupt market transitions in East Central Europe, according to Eyal, Szelenyi, and Townsley (1997: 84), there is 'reproduction of the managerial elite', a phenomenon which 'runs directly counter to theoretical expectations that cadres would lose economic power in a transition to market economies'. They interpret this continuity on the basis of the 'cultural capital' or 'technical know-how' supposedly possessed by former cadres, professionals as

of the Communist regime have been undermined much more seriously by its agents at various ranks and sections than by dissident social groups like students and intellectuals.

Although the privatization of nationally owned production organizations and resources and the private-sector allocation of newly arising business opportunities may be regarded as an indispensable task for the market-oriented economic transition, the particular privatization process should be undertaken in such a rational and impartial manner as to facilitate national economic development and collective welfare improvement most effectively. This will enable the Communist political regime to reinforce its power basis through a sort of *instrumental legitimacy* for economic development, and individual cadres to maintain their class status as political and administrative leaders. Concrete realities in reform-era China, however, reveal that too many cadres have tried to realize their class interests not by fulfilling their political and administrative leadership role effectively, but by abusing the state power entrusted with them for accumulating personal wealth illicitly (Pei 2006). The party-state has often been taken hostage to the self-defeating class interests of its agents at various administrative and regional units. In this respect, Beijing's repeated anti-corruption campaigns are not merely a political scrubbing for public sentiment but an indispensable requisite for sanitizing the party-state's proper leadership status in national development and public welfare.

(New) middle class by human vs. sociopolitical capital

Middle class has recently been added as a new political term as well as a sociological concept for describing the current and prospective rise of a diverse set of materially stable and socioculturally advanced groups that are not immediately classifiable in terms of China's hitherto conventional class categories. Unlike most capitalist societies where the so-called old middle class of petty bourgeoisie in agrarian

---

well as dissident intellectuals. In China, where the Communist party-state has maintained its monopoly power, political office is still the most important basis for the superior economic status of current and former cadres although their human capital does help them in their social transformation into private entrepreneurs or professional managers.

and commercial sectors accounts for a major proportion of middle class, post-Mao China's middle class is mainly composed of various new middle strata in administrative, managerial, legal, financial, educational, cultural, medical, and technological sectors (Li 2010; Hu, Li and Li 2012).[15] (Of course, if a purely material criterion is adopted, many of self-employed entrepreneurs and private industrialists and urban workers in profitable industries may also belong to middle class.) The earlier explained politico-administrative reform in conjunction with institutionalization of markets has, on the one hand, helped professionalize (and depoliticize) ordinary public officials in purely technocratic divisions and service-oriented levels (So 2013), thereby inducing them to shed ruling-class attributes, and, on the other hand, urgently necessitated the formation and supply of independent but officially certified professionals in legal, financial, educational, cultural, medical, and technoscientific services. Besides, many of corporate employees with special managerial expertise and experience or technological skills and knowledge assume an equivalent socioeconomic status to that of the certified professionals.

The above class elements by and large correspond to the so-called new middle class in modern capitalist societies, and their growth does seem to indicate a certain degree of China's sound development in material and cultural terms – a desperate longing by the authoritarian developmentalist party-state at a time of rampant inequalities and inequities. However, any rigorous examination of these professions and occupations easily reveals that their professional principles and technoscientific criteria are chronically compromised or contaminated in conjunction with the complicated entanglements of economic, social, and political interests through nested human and organizational relationships. In a sense, the official certification of professionals and experts is an act of market segmentation for allowing the concerned social groups' exclusive practices, so their associational class solidarity is usually very strong. In reform-era China, however, many professions cannot thrive on the basis of associational class solidarity and individual expertise alone. What is demanded of

---

15. For a useful summary of local Chinese scholars' research on middle class, see Goodman (2014: 94–109).

lawyers and many other professionals in reform-era China does not stop with task-specific functions and services, but broad and/or deep sociopolitical capital for flexibly dealing with the state-embedded market economy and society (e.g. Scott 2008; Kwock, James and Tsui 2013). For instance, in Michelson's (2007: 352) incisive observation, 'Lawyers' dependence on state actors both inside and outside the judicial system preserves the value of political connections inside the very institutions that some sociologists have argued are responsible for obviating the need for such *guanxi*.' For this reason, many of those professionals whose certified expertise has been won in consideration of their previous cadre career in related administrative/ political divisions (Chang and Lee 2003) have led their occupational positions and activities rather confidently. There exists what may be considered the *cadre-professional class*, which corresponds to the cadre-capitalist class indicated by Alvin So (2003) in terms of the personified socioeconomic extension of government authority and political power in supposedly private and civil sectors.

The politics of communist liberalism

It seems Therborn's (above-introduced) judgments about the sociopolitical future of China and the world are significantly corroborated by the preceding analysis of post-Mao China's partial marketization as the socioeconomic basis of state-mediated class relations and inequalities. The party-state's complex engagement in post-Mao China's supposedly market economic system has engendered: (1) an unprecedentedly complicated class structure composed of workers and employers/managers in industrial enterprises of extremely diverse ownership types, precarious migrant workers at various urban sectors, self-employed petty entrepreneurs in urban and rural areas, private farmers cultivating collective land, moonlighting local cadres in disguised private business, party and government officials, as well as various professionals and experts of the new middle class; and (2) a sociopolitical atmosphere in which nearly all class inequalities are, not incorrectly, perceived by the masses as an outcome of government policies, party positions and/or cadres' influences. Under these conditions, it seems, sustained high economic growth and repeated anti-corruption campaigns seem to serve as the very basic political staples for the historically unplanned liberal rule by the Communist regime whoever is elected into the supreme leader position. On the other hand, class conflict and struggle in any sector or form cannot but be translated into a political quandary that is structurally difficult to solve unless the party-state readies itself for substantial or fundamental revisions on its power basis. If rapid economic growth and anti-corruption politics do not constitute a sufficient condition for preventing class conflict and struggle, further remedial measures are necessitated, including social welfare in particular. Likewise, Therborn argues, 'A more promising scenario may lie in connecting workplace struggles with community ones, over housing, health, education or civil rights' (Therborn 2014: 9–10). To Therborn (2012: 10), the welfare state was 'the most important achievement of 20th-century reformism' in the capitalist world and, in the 21st century, may serve as an essential buffer for post-socialist class inequalities in China, etc.

The market economy's association with alienation, inequality, and poverty has been universal, but its adverse effects have been variously contained, mitigated, complemented, amplified, or aggravated in conjunction with the wide historical diversity of political regimes and social forces that have espoused the market economy. The so-called socialist market economy of China is a new variant with a colossal significance to humanity as well as Chinese people themselves. Despite the sustained pace of rapid economic growth and remarkable improvement in grassroots living conditions, the market-oriented reform in post-Mao China has engendered widespread tendencies of alienation, discrimination, and inequality, for which Chinese people blame the Communist party-state much more strongly than the abstract market system or any clear class enemies therein. It has become part of ordinary Chinese citizens' casual street chatter to criticize and/or curse the Communist party – of course, not in the presence of cadres or security officers – for everyday socio-economic hardships and wrongs. Partial marketization, by which the party-state has generated and mediated various socioeconomic inequalities among an incomparably complex array of social classes, has been most crucially responsible for such political culture and popular attitude.

From the preceding analysis of state-interwoven class relations and inequalities, it is rather obvious why China's disadvantaged underclasses often regard the authoritarian party-state (or its local agents) as the main culprit for their chronic mishaps in an era of market economy. The alienating, discriminating, disequalizing, and impoverishing effects of the market economy are too often inter-twined with the decisions of state organs and the interests and acts of party-state cadres. In the mind of grassroots people, the sectoral bias, self-interest, and outright corruption of policy-makers and local cadres sway much more horrifying than any inherent tenden-cies of the market economy to cause inequality and alienation. In this milieu, as Ching Kwan Lee (2009: 216) observes, 'The market was widely accepted as an institution for allocating rewards but ordi-nary people also believed that undue advantages accrued to political elites, and that this seriously compromised the inherent fairness of the market.' A chilling implication hereby derived is that a serious rectification of the reform-era tendencies of discrimination, alien-ation, inequality, and poverty indispensably requires the party-state's self-sacrificial reform of the most essential element of its own power basis – namely, its political control of the market economy.

Against this background, most of grassroots people's grievances, resistances, and even riots have broken out against local cadres or government/party offices, rather than against any purely market-based *nouveau riche*. In many inland provinces, peasants have cease-lessly rioted against corrupt and extorting local cadres.[16] In many 'rustbelt' cities, unemployed and impoverished groups of people have staged routine rallies against variously responsible units of the local and central governments to speak out for their socioeconomic mishaps.[17] These grassroots acts had long before been prefigured

16. In particular, peasants in Sichuan Province have stages numerous revolts against local cadres in the 1990s.

17. For instance, I noticed through my visit in the 1990s that residents of Shenyang, a rapidly decaying heavy industrial metropolis, launch a monthly downtown demonstration to complain about their economic mishaps.

during the Tiananmen uprising in 1989 when many disenchanted workers, peddlers, and even small entrepreneurs sympathized with (and sometimes joined) students in the demand for political democratization (Levy 1995). Incidents of class struggle against ungenerous rich neighbors and harsh employers are not infrequent. Even in such cases, there often lies grievance against local cadres who have either implicitly or explicitly sided with the hated rich neighbors and merciless employers in everyday social and economic affairs.

Even if grassroots Chinese citizens may not have such refined consciousness about their democratic political right as students and intellectuals have, many of them nonetheless seem to feel that democratization of state power will enhance economic justice in an era of state-embedded market economy. At the least, close supervision and strict punishment of corrupt, biased, and despotic cadres at their localities, work units, and economic sectors are eagerly asked for. Such grassroots political sentiment may not have been articulated in a coherent class ideology or organization, but the sheer number of similarly critical populace alone – a factor, according to Xueguang Zhou (1993), that leads to collective action through the 'large numbers' effect – poses a formidable political threat to the Communist liberal dictatorship. This is why the supreme party-state leaders of the post-Mao period, including the current leader Xi Jinping, have successively launched anti-corruption campaigns with all possible intensity. Even when they may not be successful in thoroughly controlling corruption, it can be the most appealing political act of a supreme leader to the eyes of most grassroots citizens. The anti-corruption campaigns are thus a disguised form of class politics catering to an emotional desire, if not always a material necessity, of various groups of grassroots masses in market-era China.[18]

Back in history, socialist revolution was a radical way of uprooting market-associated socioeconomic problems, in particular, by mobilizing underclass grievance and struggle; whereas the welfare

---

18. Another aspect of the anti-corruption campaigns, often pointed out in foreign news media, is that each supreme leader's political rivals and their followers have been pursued and punished in these campaigns. This high-level political infighting, however, is not incompatible with the class politics for grassroots persons.

state has been a conciliatory method of lessening the same problems through redistributive social policies and programs. China had already experimented with the former option under Mao's initiative, and the Deng leadership reached a conclusion that it was not practical, especially at the current level of national development. Thus, as far as known models of reformism are concerned, (partially) marketized China is left only with the latter option. Policy directions and developmental goals as announced since the 1990s do attest to the party-state's recognition of such position.[19]

The option of redistributive state intervention, however, has an inherent contradiction with the grassroots as well as the intellectual demand for democratization within China and with the Western historical experience of democratization. First, in the West, the welfare state emerged as a series of grassroots political demands and resistances concerning (substantive) socioeconomic justice led to the social enfranchising of alienated and impoverished social classes by the democratic polity (Marshall 1964). Thus, social citizenship (or the welfare state) is often considered a symbol of full-fledged democracy. In China, however, the newly emerging welfarism is consciously dissociated from any political content of democratization and hoped to remain a material and, for that matter, technical issue. Second and relatedly, even grassroots people, let alone intellectuals, would not agree with the Chinese political leadership on such depoliticization of the material justice issue. They tend to perceive the increasing inequality and alienation as fundamentally rooted in the tyrannically self-serving interests and postures of party-state offices and officials. To the eyes of a constantly increasing number of ordinary Chinese citizens, inequality is usually inequity (Lee 2009). Perhaps the Western historical experience of democratization is a scholarly and intellectual issue with a limited political significance for ordinary Chinese people, but their disagreement, though not openly expressed, with the Communist leadership about the main cause of alienation and inequality presents a formidable obstacle to the sustainability of market socialist – or Communist liberal – dictatorship.

19. See Zhonghuarenmingongheguo Guojiajingjitizhigaigeweiyuanhui (People's Republic of China, State Economic System Reform Committee) 1995.

References

Chan, Chris King-Chi and Pun Ngai (2009) 'The making of a new working class? A study of collective actions of migrant workers in South China', *China Quarterly* 198, 287–303.

Chang, Kyung-Sup (2001a) 'The politics of partial marketization: The state and class relations in post-Mao China', *Asian Perspective*, 25, 4, 239–268.

Chang, Kyung-Sup (2001b) 'Junggugui "yeognodongjahwa": Jeongchaek-jedojeok hwangyeonggwa sanding nodongjaui gyeongheom' ['"Reverse proletarianization" in China: Policy and institutional environments and Shandong workers' experiences'], *Journal of International and Area Studies*, 10, 4, 23–56.

Chang, Kyung-Sup (2003) 'Market socialism and *ruralist* welfare reform in post-Mao China', *Development and Society*, 32, 2, 147–171.

Chang, Kyung-Sup (2005) '*Ruralism* in China: Reinterpretation of post-collective development', *International Journal of Asian Studies*, 2, 2, 291–307.

Chang, Kyung-Sup and Lee Dong-Jin (2003) 'Junggugui sijangsahoejuui beopjilseo: Beopchiwa inchi maegaejaroseoui jungguk byeonhosa' ['China's market socialist legal order: Chinese lawyer as mediator between the rule of law and the rule by person'], *Sunggoknonchong*, 34, 2, 235–283.

Eyal, Gil, Szelenyi, Ivan and Townsley, Eleanor (1997) 'The theory of post-communist managerialism', *New Left Review* 22, 60–92.

Goodman, David S.G. (2014) *Class in Contemporary China*. Cambridge: Polity Press.

Kwock, Berry, James, Mark X. and Tsui, Anthony Shu Chuen (2013) 'Doing business in China: What is the use of having a contract? The rule of law and Guanxi when doing business in China', *Journal of Business Studies Quarterly*, 4, 4, 56–67.

Lee, Chang Kwan (2007) *Against the Law: Labor Protests in China's Rustbelt and Sunbelt*. Berkeley: University of California Press.

Lee, Ching Kwan (2009) 'From inequality to inequity: Popular conceptions of social (in)justice in Beijing', in Davis, Deborah and Wang Feng (eds.) *Creating Wealth and Poverty in Postsocialist China*. Stanford: Stanford University Press, pp. 213–231.

Leung, Parry and So, Alvin Y. (2012) 'The making and remaking of the working class in South China', in Carrillo, Beatriz and Goodman, David S.G. (eds.) *China's Peasants and Workers: Changing Class Identities*. Cheltenham: Edward Elgar, pp. 62–78.

Levy, Richard (1995) 'Corruption, economic crime and social transformation since the reforms: The debate in China', *Australian Journal of Chinese Affairs*, 33, 1–25.

Li, Chunling (2010) 'Characterizing China's middle class: Heterogeneous composition and multiple identities', in Li, Cheng (ed.) *China's Emerging Middle Class*. Washington: Brookings Institution Press, pp. 135–156.

Mao Zedong (Mao Tsetung) (1971) *Selected Readings from the Works of Mao Tsetung*. Beijing: Foreign Languages Press.

Marshall, T.H. (1964) *Class, Citizenship, and Social Development*. Garden City: Doubleday.

Michelson, Ethan (2007) 'Lawyers, political embeddedness, and institutional continuity in China's transition from socialism', *American Journal of Sociology*, 113, 2, 352–414.

Olson, Mancur (1965) *The Logic of Collective Action*. Cambridge: Harvard UP.

Pei, Minxin (2006) *China's Trapped Transition: The Limits of Developmental Autocracy*. Cambridge: Harvard UP.

Pun Ngai and Lu, Huilin (2010) 'Unfinished proletarianization: Self, anger, and class action among the second-generation of peasant-workers in present-day China', *Modern China*, 36, 5, 493–519.

Scott, Wilson (2008) 'Law *Guanxi*: MNCs, state actors, and legal reform in China', *Journal of Contemporary China*, 17, 54, 25–51.

Shue, Vivienne (1988) *The Reach of the State: Sketches of the Chinese Body Politic*. Stanford: Stanford UP.

So, Alvin Y. (2003) 'The making of the cadre-capitalist class in China', in Cheng, Joseph (ed.) *China's Challenges in the Twenty-First Century*. Hong Kong: CUHK Press, pp. 73–87.

So, Alvin Y. (2013) *Class and Class Conflict in Post-Socialist China*. Singapore: World Scientific Publishing.

Therborn, Göran (2012) 'Class in the 21st century', *New Left Review* 78.

Therborn, Göran (2014) 'New masses? Social bases of resistance', *New Left Review* 85.

Wakeman, Frederic Jr. (1991) 'Mr. Wang vs. Mr. Chen: A high Ch'ing parable', in Dernberger, Robert F. et al. (eds.) *The Chinese: Adapting the Past, Facing the Future*. Ann Arbor: Center for Chinese Studies, University of Michigan, pp. 253–256.

Wedeman, Andrew (2003) *From Mao to Market: Rent Seeking, Local Protectionism, and Marketization in China*. Cambridge: Cambridge UP.

Zhonghuarenmingongheguo Guojiajingjitizhigaigeweiyuanhui [People's Republic of China, State Economic System Reform Committee] (ed.) (1995) *Shehuibaozhangtizhigaige* ['Social Security System Reform']. Beijing: Gaigechubanshe.

Zhou, Xueguang (1993) 'Unorganized interests and collective action in communist China', *American Sociological Review*, 58, 1, 54–73.

SECTION II
Sex, Gender and Power

ANITA GÖRANSSON & KARIN WIDERBERG
Göran between Sex and Power

Göran Therborn laid the foundation for his academic and political reputation already in the 1960s and 1970s when he published important books on contemporary Marxist discussions, but also and more lastingly by synthesizing and analyzing the development and composition of the Swedish class society and particularly the ruling class and its exertion of power. More recently he turned his interest to studying global inequalities and has shown his strength in studies of the effects of globalization and in comparative analyses.

When *Between Sex and Power* was published in 2004 it met with great expectations and excitement among gender scholars: Would he use his encyclopedic knowledge and comparison skills to analyze gender relations in a global perspective and put our research subject in focus for scholars in other fields once and for all? As a gender scholar you are not used to the attention from the academic establishment that Göran's books usually gets from his colleagues. This was a chance to turn academic attention to the importance of gender in an economic, political and social context at a global scale. By analyzing commonalities and differences this synthesizing book could result in important new knowledge about the mechanisms in gender relations and how they evolve and according to what they change.

But we had missed the subtitle: *Family in the World, 1900–2000*.

GT's approach is a global analysis of institutional change of family systems. The words 'in the world' are not so much a reference to how aspects of the world affect the family, as they are a reference to how the family unit per se is constructed in different regions. Or more precisely, how it handles sexuality and procreation. Who (in the family) has the power over these fundamental categories of life?

Approach and findings

The theme of the book is accordingly the family as a social institution in a global perspective and the focus is on change during the last century. What are the social forces behind the changes of internal relations, structure and functions of the family? And then what are the consequences for society? GT states that the family – here defined as a set of norms defining the members' rights and duties to one another and also in relation to non-members – is our oldest and most widespread social institution. As an institution it regulates sexuality (and reproduction) and power between its members but also their relation to society. GT states that 'it makes good analytical sense to view an institution in terms of an equilibrium ...' (*Between Sex and Power*, p. 1–2) regarding rights and duties, since this 'balance or equilibrium is what explains the resilience of an institutional form ... once established' (p. 2). Even though he exemplifies this balance with inequality – that those privileged have the resources of control and sanction to match their rights, while those who have fewer power resources have more duties than rights (p. 2) – we find this standpoint both strange and troublesome.

GT's reason seems to be a wish to be able to focus the attention on the external events and processes that upset this balance (p. 2). That is, once again what is happening within the four walls is made unworthy of attention. Yet, it is precisely this focus on how family and family-life are done that have been explicated by feminist researchers so as to question the importance in everyday life of prevalent family normative or mainstream understandings of the relations, structure and functions of the family. That is, research that challenges the very definition of and focus on the family in trying to understand the social role of intimate relations locally and globally. By using the normative perspective and definition of the family, GT reproduces society's own image of itself, while making other understandings of the family invisible. We can understand and accept other reasons for the choice of a normative standpoint, for example that having a global perspective limits the available data – an issue we will come back to below – but not an un-problematized starting point.

The focus on external events and the historical specific forces that can explicate family changes globally, is on the other hand most welcomed by us all, gender or non-gender researchers. And here GT works like a detective, following one clue after another, making it a thrill to read. He is guided by a global and empirically comparative perspective where variations also regarding explanations are focused. As such it is a major pioneer work, with implications not only for understanding the family and families but also for our understanding of the structure and functioning of society and societies.

GT makes use of three entrances to describe change in the family institution: patriarchy, marriage and fertility, each a separate part of the book covering several chapters.

Patriarchy is defined by GT as the internal male-dominated relations within the family unit, using the traditional anthropological definition of the father's rule over his wife and children of both sexes, as opposed to the nowadays more commonly used definition of patriarchy as men's rule over women generally, which in turn he chooses to call *phallocracy* and does not include in his overview. This definition narrows the theme considerably. A limitation of the subject is of course a necessity as his ambition is to achieve a global comparison. His interest is to compare the conditions and developments of human reproduction and its organization in the family form in different regions of the world. From this follows his narrow definition of patriarchy as concerning gender and generational relations within the family (p. 13). Patriarchy in this sense is 'a major force in the world' (p. 130) since only 30 per cent of the world's societies can be defined as post-patriarchal, according to GT. We would argue that the historical development could be described in other words as a change from a clan (or status) society to a contract society (Maine cited in Weiner 2013), and so GT's conclusion follows logically from his definition of patriarchy.

The first part of the book covers *patriarchy* in this sense. He distinguishes five major family types in his huge data material: the African (Sub-Saharan), the European (including the New World settlements), the East Asian, the South Asian, and the West Asian (including the North African) family systems. Furthermore, he includes the 'interstitial family systems' of Southeast Asia and Creole America. All these are obviously territorial, geocultural regions even if they are also tempered by religious divisions (p. 11–12).

GT uses a cluster of variables in order to make variations and change empirically visible. This is also done in synthesizing figures and tables throughout the book, which gives the reader an exemplary and very clear overview. He uses primarily previous traditional family research and very little of the extensive gender research from the latest 40 years. The dominance of public statistics and other available historical materials among his sources seems to contribute to his strong emphasis of the formal, institutional level, although ideological differences are also seen as important. But by taking the public statistics as 'facts', there is a risk that one will reproduce the image that society has of itself. And the more patriarchal a society is, the more invisible other relations and values can be expected to be.

Around 1900 when he typically starts his story, male dominance in the family was general in all regions, albeit with important differences.

In Europe there had been a gradual individualization of women from the (economic) household and later from the (reproductive) family, where they had been more or less subordinated. During the first part of the 20th century they acquired citizen rights in one field after another – political, economic, juridical and social rights. The old subsistence system of the household (including the family) was dissolving. In other parts of the world such as West Asia, Africa and South Asia the harsh subordination under the father and husband continued and continues even today. The most extreme subordination today seems to exist in India as well as in the Arab countries, as opposed to what GT calls 'post-patriarchal Euro-America'. These regions – we might note – are the ones where the clan society is still strong.

In sum however, GT concludes that patriarchy in his sense has lost out and gender and generational equality has gained during the past 100 years. This he attributes mainly to the waves of emancipation after the two world wars and to the youth protests in the 1970s. He points especially to the role of Communist revolutions, which seems a bit odd to a present-day feminist. It is true that formal equality was introduced under Communism, and that women would carry out heavy work in the labor market, as well as study science and technology which were/are usually male-dominated fields in Western countries. Daycare for children was introduced in order to free women's labor. But it is also true that women had very few power positions (or even supervisory jobs) in Communist countries, and that they alone were responsible for all housework as well as for the children even though they usually worked full-time. This was the empirical fact behind the feminist movement's conclusion that women's oppression had nothing to do with private property or capitalism as such. (This and the fact that men's superordination predates capitalism historically.) The horizontal gender division of work was relaxed (if only in one direction, as men did absolutely no female-coded jobs), but the hierarchical gender division was very strict and remains so after the fall of Communism: The strict division of labor within the family is an expression of internal power relations.

But even if we were to accept GT's definition of patriarchy and use it as a starting-point, we would still question the time-period chosen. It is not theoretically motivated and makes change and variation over a longer time period invisible. We can understand the practical motivation, but again we would have expected that the picture hereby given was discussed in relation to possible historical variations. Gender research has for instance found that the North-west European pre-modern family model is unique in being based on the married couple instead of the joint family household that characterized the rest of Europe (Solheim 2012). This we believe is important to take into account in trying to understand the relatively smooth development to gender equality and family change that take place in this region during the time period studied by GT. This is however but one example of how internal relations may go hand in hand or counteract upcoming external events and processes. As such the balance or equilibrium of the family accordingly needs to be investigated and taken into account, also historically, so as to understand the chances for change of the family institution.

In spite of these comments we find that there is a lot to learn and applaud when reading about the de-patriarchalization process that takes place throughout the world during the past century. GT illustrates how the reasons may differ between continents and how historically specific events, such as for instance war, in combination with economic development and social movements creates cracks in the patriarchal armor. That a change in the family institution in the Scandinavian context is a result of industrialization and economic development is for example a truth here deconstructed. Instead he points to secularized liberalism as a broad socio-cultural movement that opened up the doors to socialism and feminism and the development that we are the proud inheritors of today. In spite of the retreat of patriarchy and the dismantling of men's power and authority, due to dramatic socio-economic, political and cultural changes, it is still the variation as to when and how it occurs that to GT is the most important characteristic for the 20th century.

In the second part of his book GT discusses *marriage and the organization of sexual relations* in different parts of the world. Here he points to the well-known division between Western and Eastern Europe when it comes to marriage and the constitution of families (for instance Hajnal 1965 and 1982). In a global context Western Europe stands out as historically different from the rest of the world, with many people who remain unmarried, late marriages in general, and married couples moving out from their parents' house and establishing their own households. This contributes to the autonomy of the new family. GT argues that in the rest of the world marriage is universal, couples married/still marry early and often stay in (the husband's) parents' house. This of course will keep the new couple under the thumb of the patriarch and prop up traditional patriarchy. However, in Creole America as well as in Western Europe many couples would live together and/or have sexual relations without being married. This resulted in many so-called illegitimate children, especially in the big cities. (GT does not mention that one important reason behind this phenomenon at least in Sweden (the so-called 'Stockholm marriages') was probably a female strategy of survival: if she married, the woman would be formally subordinated under her husband who could then control her work and her wages. This was at a time when drinking was a big social problem, particularly among men. Women's subsistence rights were discussed during the 19th century both in literature, in media and in parliament, as were married women's (conditional) property rights and their limited access to the means of subsistence. The woman question was a subsistence question. (For instance Almqvist 1990 [1839], Matović 1984, Göransson 1988.)

Other forms of marriage such as polygamy or polyandry are only mentioned in passing in the book.

Around 1900 marriage was universal in Asia, Africa, in Russia and most of Eastern Europe. A century later not much has changed; in Asia and Sub-Saharan Africa marriage is still universal, and in Sub-Saharan Africa polygamy is still common. In Scandinavia, especially Sweden, but also in the rest of Western Europe cohabitation (without involving the church or state) has become quite common after 1970. Only a minority in countries like the UK, France and Germany marry before they move in together. In the US however marriage still precedes the first birth. But at the same time there is a high rate of teenage births there. The two different behaviors are found in different parts of the American population, and GT calls it a 'dualist system'.

Divorce is nowadays formally allowed in most countries, but in some regions still hard to achieve in practice. In for instance the US and in Russia, however, half of the marriages break up, but people remarry. So GT concludes that overall marriage has been a stable institution during the 1900s, but there is the exception of Western European cohabitation. Whether this is a sign of instability is however debatable in our view. People still live together, form families and raise their children. In Scandinavia new legislation has even been introduced to ensure that the cohabitants' rights are regulated.

In the third and last part of the book GT discusses *fertility and the regulation of childbirth*. And this becomes really interesting since here he identifies current and future power shifts at a global level due to fertility shifts and ageing generations. He mentions the historical so-called demographic transition from big families and many deaths to fewer children and longer lives in general, traditionally ascribed to long-term peace, better nourishment, and better medical treatments, an explanation that – as he mentions – has more recently been questioned by demographers who would rather ascribe it to industrialization, the better living conditions that followed and a more systematic use of family planning. This development may be seen all over the world at different points in history. In the second half of the 20th century the access to the pill facilitated women's control of their bodies and probably gave them a better sex life.

GT distinguishes two waves of reduced fertility (not counting institutionally induced birth control), one between 1880 and 1930 and one after World War II. He attributes these waves to two general attitude changes among people, 'a sense of personal mastery' and 'a sense of benefit from having fewer children' (p. 241). These key variables are in turn shaped by three determinants: cultural, structural and familial (p. 241).

This emphasis on general discursive factors may be related to the fact that he is restricted by his source material, public statistics, to the macro-level. We would suggest that it might also be interesting to study the changing composition and prevalence of different means of subsistence and of different social strata's access to them.

For it is well known that the number of children has historically been class-specific as different social strata have different interests in having children. The number of children may be directly connected to the household's means to support itself. Socioeconomic differences affect the number of children.

Another important reason behind the decline in birth rates is women's improved access to education. This is an important and nowadays well-known connection and therefore even a recommended United Nations policy that GT does not mention (for instance Boserup 2007 [1970]). He discusses the connection between literacy and fertility; but education for women, especially higher education, as a successful strategy for reducing the number of children is not mentioned.

GT's important conclusion concerning fertility and the future is that it develops differently in different regions. While Euramerica has fewer children, Asia and Africa still have many. This means that population growth continues in other parts of the world, while

Europe and the Americas have an ageing and shrinking population. Migration could be discussed in this context but it is not.

Concepts and options

GT's focus on biological reproduction and sexuality makes him choose the family as his unit of analysis. His point of departure is the powerful force of sexuality in history – and generational survival. But there is another powerful force – even more life-determining – hunger – and daily survival! And the problem in this context is that hunger and access to means of subsistence are not an optional theme; they have a crucial influence also on the family and its pro-creation decisions.

Another strategy would have been to study the *household*, that is, the economic unit of subsistence that included not only a married couple and their children (usually) but also other unmarried or widowed relatives, servants, apprentices, and other employees – people who supplied their labor but did not own any means of subsistence and so had to join someone who did and who needed their labor. The problem with studying only the (reproductive) family is that this will hide important determinants; the composition of the whole household as well as the character and volume of its means of production will affect precisely the factors that GT does study, such as fertility. Access to labor and to any means of subsistence at all was and is crucial for families and individuals. People were not stupid. A farming household that lived off the land would have more children in order to replace the hired help as they grew up (Winberg 1977, Fridlizius 1979).

The composition of the household will fluctuate over time and it will differ between regions that are characterized by different ways of making a living. An individual who has no access to land or other means of production will have to work for someone who does. But this will not automatically make it possible for him or her to marry and form a household of their own. The factory workers in 19th century Swedish industrial towns usually married women older than themselves. That way they did not have so many children, and also the wife would have a nest egg having earned wages for quite some time. The factory owners in contrast would wait until their thirties when they had an established position, and then married teenage girls (often the daughters of their mentor or other colleagues) and had large families. This could be seen as two different marriage strategies, adapted of course to the material interests of the men. Marriage was an economic and social strategy, no matter what social stratum you belonged to (Göransson 1988). It still is in some regions. Where labor is needed men may still marry several women, for instance in Sub-Saharan Africa. Where women are an asset, the husband-to-be has to pay her parents for her. Where women are only breeders to be kept secluded, their parents will have to pay in order to get rid of them (Boserup 2007 [1970]).

GT has chosen to study the family as such, and explicitly says that external factors will not be discussed. Fortunately he does mention some such factors after all. But the way he has drawn up the boundaries around his subject still makes it difficult for him to explain or analyze the development deeper. His family types are regionally defined, not theoretically based.

Conclusions – GT's and ours

At the very end of the book GT concludes what he finds most important theoretically and politically in his findings. That changes of the family institution neither follow an evolutionary nor a uni-linear pattern is his first point. The development of individual autonomy might for example go hand in hand with family dependency, a fact that undermines the generality of modernization and individualization theories. Secondly, the process of change is temporarily uneven, colored by dominant family systems while at the same time illuminating inter-continental paths of change. Thirdly, the fact that the driving forces are always external, and that social movements are a far more important factor than previously estimated. The last point gives rise to hope for the future and maybe it is the enormous variety in how Family has been done and is being done that makes him end the book with the following sentence: 'But in the end, the best bet for the future is on the inexhaustible innovative capacity of human-kind, which eventually surpasses all science' (p. 315).

On our part, we find his illustration and argumentation regard-ing the uneven fertility rate and its possible consequences to be his most important contribution both theoretically and politically. Here he illuminates how the change in fertility rate affects the power bal-ance between countries and continents, placing the family not only on the political but also the theoretical agenda. Family is accordingly not just 'gender stuff' but stuff for Social Theory.

We would characterize the book as a thick description with its solid collection of empirical data. As such it is a very impressive and solid work. But we are surprised that he emphasizes cultural and socio-psychological factors so strongly, while not paying any attention to the material livelihood of different families, regionally, nationally or by social class. For instance, religion is seen as a powerful influence, while the clan society is not discussed. Is it not the hierarchy and power monopoly of old men in the clan societies that determine the role of women and men, and not the various – later emerging – inter-pretations of Islam?

The book triggers a lot of reactions and questions; as such it pro-vides a great starting point for anyone who would like to take the analysis one step further with the help of more recent concepts and results from gender research.

References

Almqvist, Carl Jonas Love (1990 [1839]) *Det går an: En tavla ur livet.* Stock-holm: Wahlström & Widstrand.

Boserup, Ester (2007 [1970]) *Woman's Role in Economic Development*, new ed. with a introduction by Nazneen Kanji, Su Fei Tan and Camilla Toulmin. London: Earthscan.

Fridlizius, Gunnar (1979) 'Population, enclosure and property rights', *Econ-omy and History*, vol. XXII:1. Lund: Ekonomisk-historiska institutionen.

Göransson, Anita (1988) *Från familj till fabrik: Teknik, arbetsdelning och skikt-ning i svenska fabriker 1830–1877.* Lund: Arkiv förlag.

Hajnal, John (1965) 'European marriage patterns in perspective', in Glass, V.D. and Eversley, D.E.C. (eds.) *Population in History*. London: Edward Arnold.

Hajnal, John (1982) 'Two kinds of preindustrial household formation systems', *Population and Development Review*, 8, 3.

Matović, Margareta (1984) *Stockholmsäktenskap: Familjebildning och partnerval i Stockholm 1850–1890*. Stockholm: Liber.

Solheim, Jorun (2012) 'Den nordvesteuropeiske modellen. Familie og hushold i historisk og komparativt perspektiv', in Ellingsæter, Anne Lise and Widerberg, Karin (eds.) *Velferdsstatens familier: Nye sosiologiske perspektiver*. Oslo: Gyldendal Akademisk.

Therborn, Göran (2004) *Between Sex and Power: Family in the World, 1900–2000*. London: Routledge.

Weiner, Mark S. (2013) *The Rule of the Clan*. New York: Farrar, Strauss and Giroux.

Winberg, Christer (1977) *Folkökning och proletarisering: Kring den sociala strukturomvandlingen på Sveriges landsbygd under den agrara revolutionen*, 2 ed. Lund: Cavefors.

ERIC HOBSBAWM

Retreat of the Male

The family is a subject on which, for obvious reasons, there is no shortage of public or private views. Google records 368 million items under the word 'family', as against a mere 170 million under 'war'. All governments have tried to encourage or discourage procreation and passed laws about human coupling and decoupling. All the global religions (with the possible exception of Buddhism) and all the 20th-century ideologies have strong convictions on these matters. So have masses of otherwise politically inactive citizens, as the rise of electoral support for religious fundamentalism indicates. It has been plausibly argued that 'moral issues' (i.e. abortion and homosexual marriage) won George W. Bush his second term in office.

The passion with which these opinions are held is almost always inversely correlated to knowledge of the facts, even in the holder's own country: most of the public discourse on the relations between men, women and their offspring is both unhistorical and deeply provincial. Göran Therborn's comparative survey of the world's family systems and the ways in which they have changed (or failed to change) in the course of the past century, the result of eight years of intensive thought and research, is a necessary corrective in both respects. Thanks to its global perspective and unique accumulation of data, it should from now on be the standard guide to the subject. In addition, it makes available the sometimes surprising results of a generation of demographic, ethnographic and sociological researches recorded in a bibliography of more than forty pages. How

Eric Hobsbawm's review of Göran Therborn's *Between Sex and Power: Family in the World, 1900–2000* (London: Routledge 2004) was originally published in *London Review of Books*, vol. 27, no. 15, 4 August 2005. Republished here with kind permission.

many people knew, for example, that up to the middle of the 20th century by far the highest rate of divorce ever recorded – up to 50 per cent – was to be found among nominally Muslim Malays, that there is less gender bias in domestic work in Chinese cities today than in the USA, that the highest divorce rates in the second half of the 20th century were to be found among the main protagonists of the Cold War, the USA and Russia, or that the most sexually active Western people are the Finns? It is far from common knowledge that the two or three decades of the mid-20th century 'were *the* age of marriage and of intra-marital sexuality in modern Western history' – in 1960, 70 per cent of American women aged between 20 and 24 were married, as against 23 per cent in 2000.

Therborn, whose previous books include *European Modernity and Beyond: The Trajectory of European Societies, 1945–2000* (1995), is here particularly concerned with three themes, all of them involving changes both in family values and in actual practice, although the text does not always make it easy to follow them. (Therborn's Scandinavian commitment to ending 'humanity's long patriarchal night' is not an analytical asset.) Two of these themes – the decline of patriarchy and growth of birth control – are unproblematic, unlike the third, clumsily described as 'the role of marriage, and non-marriage, in regulating sexual behaviour, and sexual bonding in particular'.

Despite some common global developments, notably the spread of birth control, the world's family patterns have not converged; the process of 'family change … has been neither evolutionary nor unilinear'. The world in 1900 was divided broadly into five family systems – the European (including the New World settlements), the sub-Saharan African, the East Asian, the South Asian and the West Asian/North African – belonging to the two major branches which the social anthropologist Jack Goody has taught us to recognise, the African and the Eurasian. Therborn prefers a 'geocultural' division to one based on religion, since, as he sees it, geoculture generally prevails. Hindu and Muslim family practices in North India are similar but markedly distinct from Hindu practices in South India, and African Christianity has had to make substantial practical concessions to African polygyny. The South East Asian and Creole American are 'interstitial systems'. In the former, 'the rigid patriarchies of Confucianism, Islam and Catholicism were mellowed by Buddhist insouciance in family matters'; and in the latter, European conquest created the curious combination of rigid patriarchy among rulers, mass miscegenation, and an uprooted non-marital family pattern among the conquered indigenous and the imported slave populations. The imperial conquest of the Western hemisphere, Therborn suggests, produced the first sudden transformation of family structure before the 20th century.

Among Creole Americans male power was macho rather than institutional, but for the great majority of family systems up until the 20th century it was patriarchal, even in the minority of matrilineal systems. It rested on the power of older males over the young of both sexes and on the institutionalised superiority of men over women, though Europe, South-East Asia and Africa proved less unfavourable to women than elsewhere. The West European family, we are reminded, 'was by far the least patriarchal in a very patriarchal world'. Unexpectedly, women also benefited in the only region of systematic mass polygamy, south of the Sahara, thanks perhaps to the fact that the African family was essentially non-nuclear ('kin was always more important than spouse') and to the early public recognition that sex is a legitimate human pleasure. Patriarchy also rested on the overwhelming prevalence of marriage, not necessarily indissoluble, even in South-East Asia and Africa, where weddings are not central rites of passage.

Therborn holds plausibly that, unlike social structures of power and production, 'family systems do not seem to possess an intrinsic dynamic – their changes are exogenous': i.e. in the absence of any push from outside, they will reproduce themselves. Of course, the ways in which human groups earn their living – both limitations and opportunities – have always led to adjustments in marriage (by abstention or varying the age of partners) and in child-bearing (by varying the birth-rate or infanticide). The very earliest 18th-century demographers regarded it as almost axiomatic that in any year the number of marriages varied inversely with the price of corn. More generally, the long-established 'West European marriage system' that prevailed west of the historic line from Trieste to St Petersburg, the original 'Iron Curtain', assumed that marriages would lead to new households ('neo-locality'), which required the new couple to have initial resources – in agrarian societies, access to land. But, Therborn argues, in settled regions like those of medieval and early modern Western Europe this required systems of land transfer between generations by inheritance. This, he suggests, is what led to the characteristic 'Western' marriage system (later exported to settler societies overseas): late marriages at variable ages, a high proportion of the never-married, and 'a combination of ... non-hierarchical sexual informality ... with a strongly normative sexual order'. On the other hand, in Africa, where the majority of subsistence farming, not to mention, in some parts, commerce, was carried out by women, marriage was more than elsewhere a crucial form of labour supply.

What are the outside impulses that lead to changes within the family of unparalleled historical rapidity? Somewhat unexpectedly, what Therborn feels obliged to explain is the long delay in the 18th and 19th centuries before the rapid decline and fall of Western patriarchy in the 20th. Would we not have expected industrialisation to weaken it by severing the place of work from the place of residence, proletarianisation to deprive fathers of power both because they had no property to transmit and because they were now clearly themselves dependent on the owners of land or capital? Did urbanisation not weaken authority as such? Indeed, had male dominance not appeared to retreat, at least among the poor, in the era of 'proto-industrialisation' (what used to be known as the putting-out system)?

In fact, the rise of industrial capitalist society protected and reproduced patriarchy, not least because up until the rise of corporate business it was not, and could not yet be, a system operating primarily, let alone uniquely, by market rationality (in many countries this is still the case). The patriarchal family was not only 'a heavy social anchor' but an essential mechanism of economic enterprise. Moreover, as 19th-century British industrialisation shows, a prosperous industrial capitalism was to turn its proletarians into a manufacturing working class, very probably class-conscious, but also increasingly composed of males functioning as the primary bread-winners of their family. This became 'the normative aspiration of the European working classes'.

Perhaps some of Therborn's surprise is due to what he sees as the priority of anti-patriarchal argument over changes in actual behaviour, although he shows that ideas were not translated into national state action before the 20th century. He dates the argument back to the emergence in the 18th-century Scottish Enlightenment of the idea that the position of women in society was an indicator of social progress, though this did not yet mean equal rights of the sexes. Possibly, it had links to radical Protestantism which, with (atheistic) socialism, Therborn sees as the major 19th-century challengers to patriarchy. While the American and French Revolutions were not concerned with the liberation of women, this was to be a central element in socialist and Communist ones. Hence, in the 20th century he sees the major 'broad ideological currents behind determined thrusts into the fortress of patriarchy' as, in order of importance: the revolutionary socialist/Communist movement (notably via the vast effects and influence of the Russian Revolution); the non-Western 'nationalist developmentalists' (notably in Turkey); feminist women's movements, which he does not think were of major significance outside the Anglo-Saxon regions; and 'a secularised liberalism mainly of Protestant Christian or Jewish – seldom Catholic – provenance'.

From a global point of view it makes obvious sense to insist, with Therborn, that 'international Communism played a crucial, if not overwhelming role' at all the major leaps forward in the 20th-century retreat of patriarchy – World War One, the aftermath of World War Two and the great turn from the mid-1960s to the 1980s. However resistant actual family behaviour was to the imposition of Lenin's model of egalitarian modernism or Ataturk's westernisation, the massive 20th-century changes between the Balkans and the China Seas could hardly have happened but for the impact of revolutionary supercharged state power. Though Therborn antedates its death, the best expert in the field (Karl Kaser) holds that it was the decades of Communism that put paid to the traditional Balkan *zadruga*, the ultra-patriarchal extended family.

In the West the decline and fall of patriarchy, far greater than elsewhere until the last third of the century, was based on indigenous dynamics. The impact of organised ideology and state power – the latter chiefly concerned, until the unexpected post-1945 'baby boom', with encouraging childbirth – was therefore less significant and less necessary. Compulsory primary state education for girls as well as boys and the prohibition of child labour, both of which raised the costs of children to parents, were the main ways in which state action directly affected the family. The modern model was pioneered not in the core countries of capitalist development, but on its margins – among (non-Catholic) white settler societies, in Australasia and the North American Midwest and West, but especially in Scandinavia. (Therborn warns us against simple and unilineal models of the relations between economic and cultural transformation, apart from the patent economic correlation of variations in the age of marriage and family planning.)

The general Western pattern appears to be that ideas favouring modernity spread within societies from secularised and educated (middle-class) elites and 'progressive' political movements, and outwards by the imitation of influential models of modernity abroad. The progress of birth control in Sicily, analysed in a beautiful study by Jane and Peter Schneider, is an excellent example. Even so, except for the mass decline in child-bearing from 1880 onwards, ideology and legal change ran far ahead of change in actual family and sexual behaviour until the 1960s. This did not become dramatic until the last third of the 20th century even in the West. In fact, the last third of the 20th century saw the most rapid and radical global change in the history of human gender and generational relations, though it has not so far penetrated very deeply into the rest of the world. Therborn is better at recording and monitoring this unprecedented revolution in human behaviour in the developed capitalist countries, and the corresponding upheavals in the post-Communist regions, than in analysing its causes and its relation to the extraordinary acceleration of socio-economic growth and transformation of which it is a part.

Somewhat unexpectedly, his conclusions about the state of the family at the end of the last quarter-century of behavioural revolution are undramatic, not to say trite. Humanity is likely to continue to carry on with varieties of the old family ('the modal pattern of long-term institutionalised heterosexual coupling'), only – at least in the post-1968 West – in a less standardised bourgeois form. Some recent developments are worrying, notably the 'commodification' of sexual and personal relations, but none is 'necessarily fatal or even threatening to the existing institutional set-up. They only indicate that the future will have its problems too.' Such statements are surprising, because they are at variance both with Therborn's own analysis and with some of the evidence to which he draws incidental attention.

He has himself formulated the problem lucidly: family systems are held in balance. When they are disturbed by internal contradictions or – in this case – exogenously, a given set of social arrangements is destabilised. The disruption may or may not be managed by re-equilibrating, restabilising mechanisms. If it isn't, 'there arises the need for a second phase of change … a phase of setting a direction of change and of organising the institution anew.' But if this does not succeed 'there will be a shorter or longer period of anarchy, after which the institution in question will either change (including disappear) or relapse into its previous form.' It can hardly be denied that the developments surveyed by Therborn amount to a historically sudden and spectacular disruption of the long-lasting norms and arrangements by which genders and generations were linked in societies, at least since the invention of agriculture. When the number of extra-marital births in developed countries rises, in 40 years, from 1.6 to 31.8 per cent (Ireland), 1.4 to almost 25 per cent (Netherlands), 3.7 to 49 per cent (Norway), or when, as in Canada, the mean number of children per woman falls from 3.77 to 2.33 in the single decade of the 1960s, we are clearly facing a revolution in social and personal behaviour. One might have expected a less superficial enquiry into the consequences of this extraordinary disruption. The only aspect Therborn considers seriously is the strictly demographic, which is likely to reduce Europe from holding a quarter of the world's population in 1900 to a fifteenth in 2050.

Here Therborn's own strong identification with the Scandinavian ideals of progressive gender and sexual emancipation gets in the way of his analysis, skewing his view of the family's historic social functions. It is perhaps no accident that the book's index contains more references to 'divorce' than to 'children', to 'sexuality' than to 'inheritance', far more to 'marriage' than to all these put together and none to any form of 'adoption' or other constructed forms of kinship. His book considers marriage primarily as a sexual order, separate from though intertwined with the social order, which incidentally allows him to open it to same-sex partnerships. For him this comes before its other functions ('a choice deriving from early 21st-century experience'): as an arrangement for procreation and bringing up children, as a mechanism for social exchange and integration into wider communities, and as an establisher of social status of age-groups and householding. Curiously, he seems to show little interest, at least in this context, in the parent-child or tri-generational unit as a medium of material and cultural transmission and as a system of social support within and between generations, or with the married couple as an income-generating unit.

Is it still adequate since the 1970s, as economic inequality rises sharply within developed capitalist societies, to see the decline of 'the housewife family' from its mid 20th-century zenith as entirely 'driven not – as later in many poor countries – by poverty but by a new life-course priority, of independent income and of a career'? Incidentally, Therborn's own findings suggest that marriage as a sexual order is historically a social norm or ideal rather than a description of reality, except insofar as in some systems it forces all women into formal marriage as virgins and makes (heterosexual) sex virtually impossible for them outside it. Quite apart from the Creole zone, 'the classical area of centuries of massive coupling outside the norms of the Church and of the law', he observes the historic informality of the sexual order in sub-Saharan Africa, in parts of which the frequency of marital sex runs a clear second to non-marital sex, and in some regions of Europe, e.g. in the Austrian Alps and north-west Iberia, with their 'historically accepted proletarian or minifundist deviants from the law of the Church' and, he might have added, from the celibacy of the priesthood.

Therborn's own data suggest a less complacent view of the situation created at the start of the 21st century by the earthquake shaking the traditional family. Probably the basic trend of the 20th century – essentially, the emancipation of women from their age-old position of social and institutional inferiority to men – still prevails, but he also observes that 'where fathers and husbands do not rule, phallocracy or asymmetrical male sexual power may dominate the sociosexual order, as in popular Creole societies or in the swollen slum cities of Africa.' Or, as he notes in the post-Communist context, 'while the power of fathers and husbands does not seem to have increased, that of pimps certainly has.' In the very period of the most dramatic collapse of traditional standards of sexual morality and behaviour, the male-dominated family has been reinforced by strong religious revivals, 'often with intense patriarchal preoccupations'. Strongest though this is in Islam, it is far from clear that the victories of US Christian fundamentalism are as 'Pyrrhic' as Therborn suggests. Indeed, at present it looks as though under George W. Bush it is about to score further victories in 'the first and so far the only country to see a successful anti-feminist backlash in the area of the European family system'.

Therborn also acknowledges that the supremacy of the ideal which liberal emancipation shares with consumer capitalism – namely, the satisfaction of individual desires, including the sexual – has some aberrant consequences: not merely the fall of Western fertility far beyond replacement rates but the birth of fewer children than women actually want. He does not mention the consequences, especially in a market society, of the novel and rapidly increasing human capacity to manipulate the genetics of our species (cloning etc.). They will inevitably be substantial, unpredictable and almost certainly troubling. The problems created in male-preferring societies in the 1990s, by the combination of birth control and parents' ability to discover the sex of embryos, are already obvious. In 1995, the Chinese sex ratio at birth was 117 boys to 100 girls. I refrain from commenting on Therborn's own prediction that the market will solve this in the long run by raising the scarcity value of girls.

This is a deeply impressive book by a major sociologist, original and mostly persuasive in its historical analysis and remarkable in its survey of the global marital and sexual scene. However, it under-

estimates the actual and potential effect of the recent revolutionary changes in the human family, unprecedented in their scale and
speed, both globally and in the Western societies in which it has
gone furthest. In my view it also underestimates the relationship
between effects on the family of the Western cultural revolution of
the last third of the 20th century and its economic equivalent, the
belief in a theoretically libertarian capitalism which thinks it can
function without the heritage that gave it much strength in the past,
the rules of obligation and loyalty inside and outside the traditional
family, and other proclivities which had no intrinsic connection
with the pursuit of the individual advantage that fuelled its engine.
As neo-liberalism triumphed in economics its inadequacy could no
longer be concealed. In the light of the contents of this book, it may
be suggested that we are also reaching this point in the ideology of
cultural libertarianism.

PERRY ANDERSON
Atlas of the Family

Few topics of fundamental importance have, at first glance, generated so much numbing literature as the family. The appearance is
unjust, but not incomprehensible. For the discrepancy between the
vivid existential drama into which virtually every human being is
plunged at birth, and the generalized statistical pall of demographic
surveys and household studies often looks irremediable: as if subjective experience and objective calibration have no meeting-point.
Anthropological studies of kinship remain the most technical area
of the discipline. Images of crushing dullness have been alleviated,
but not greatly altered, by popularizations of the past: works like *The
World We Have Lost* by the doyen of Cambridge family reconstruction, Peter Laslett, fond albums of a time when 'the whole of life
went forward in the family, in a circle of loved, familiar faces', within
a 'one-class society'.[1] The one outstanding contemporary synthesis,
William Goode's *World Revolution and Family Patterns* (1963), which
argued in the early sixties that the model of the Western conjugal
family was likely to become universal, since it best fulfilled the needs
of industrialization, has never acquired the standing its generosity
of scope and spirit deserved.[2] Family studies are certainly no desert.

---

1. Laslett 1965: 22–23ff. A work subject to one of Edward Thompson's most
devastating reviews: 'The book of numbers', *Times Literary Supplement*, 9
December 1965.
2. Out of the unpromising functionalism of modernization theory, Goode
produced a balanced and intelligent survey of family systems across the world
that treated the USSR – in 1963 – as part of a Western pattern, and omitted
only Latin America and the Caribbean.

From Perry Anderson's *Spectrum* (London: Verso, 2005). Republished here
with kind permission from the author. Originally published in *The Nation*,
30 May 2005.

They are densely populated, but much of the terrain forms a feature-less plain of functions and numbers, stretching away to the horizon, broken only by clumps of sentiment.

Over this landscape, Göran Therborn's *Between Sex and Power* (2004) rises up like some majestic volcano. Throwing up a billowing column of ideas and arguments, while a lava of evidence flows down its slopes, this is a great work of historical intellect and imagination, the effect of a rare combination of gifts. Trained as a sociologist, Therborn is a highly conceptual thinker, allying the formal rigour of his discipline at its best, with command of a vast range of empirical data.[3] The result is a powerful theoretical structure, supported by a fascinating body of evidence. But it is also a set of macro-narratives that compose perhaps the first true example of a work of global history we possess. Most writing that lays claim to this term, whatever other merits it may display, ventures beyond certain core zones of attention only selectively and patchily. In the case of general histories of the world, of which there are now more than a few, problems of sheer scale alone have dictated strict limits to even the finest enterprises.

Therborn, by contrast, by focusing on just one dimension of existence, develops a map of human changes over time that is faithful to the complexity and diversity of the world in a quite new way, omitting no corner of the planet. Not just every continent is included in this history, but differences within each between nations or regions – from China and Japan to Uruguay and Colombia, North to South India, Gabon to Burkina Faso, Turkey to Persia, Norway to Portugal – are scanned with a precise eye. Such ecumenical curiosity, the antithesis of Barrington Moore's conviction that only big countries matter for comparative history, is the attractive product of a small one. Therborn's sensibility belongs to his nationality. In modern

---

3. His first writings – *Science, Class and Society* (1976), *What Does the Ruling Class Do When it Rules?* (1978), *The Ideology of Power and the Power of Ideology* (1980) – lay more on the conceptual side; from *Why Some Peoples Are More Unemployed than Others* (1986) onwards, it has combined both registers, issuing into his major study *European Modernity and Beyond* (1995), now a standard reference.

times Sweden, situated in the northern margins of Europe, with a population about the size of New Jersey, has for the most part been an inconspicuous spectator of world politics. But in the affairs of the family, it has more than once been a pace-setter. That the comparative *tour de force* on them should be Swedish is peculiarly appropriate.

Surveying the world, Therborn distinguishes five major family systems: European (including New World and Pacific settlements), East Asian, sub-Saharan African, West Asian/North African, and Subcontinental, with a further two more 'interstitial' ones, South-East Asian and Creole American. Although each of the major systems is the heartland of a distinctive religious or ethical code – Christian, Confucian, Animist, Muslim, Hindu – and the interstitial ones are zones of overlapping codes, the systems themselves form so many 'geocultures' in which sediments of a common history can override contrasts of belief within them. This cultural backdrop lends its colour and texture to *Between Sex and Power*. The tone of the book recalls aspects of Eric Hobsbawm, in its crisp judgements and dry wit. While Therborn is necessarily far more statistical in style, something of the same literary and anecdotal liveliness is present too. Amid an abundance of gripping arithmetic, novels and plays, memoirs and marriage ads have their place in the narrative. Most striking of all, in a field so dominated by social or merely technical registers, is the political construction Therborn gives to the history of the family in the twentieth century.

What are the central propositions of the book? All traditional family systems, Therborn argues, have comprised three regimes: of patriarchy, marriage, and fertility. Crudely summarized – who calls the shots in the family, how people hitch up, what kids result. *Between Sex and Power* sets out to trace the modern history of each. For Therborn patriarchy is male family power, typically invested in fathers and husbands, not the subordination or discrimination of women in general – gender inequality being a broader phenomenon. At the beginning of his story, around 1900, patriarchy in this classical sense was a universal pattern, if with uneven gradations. In Europe, the French Revolution had failed to challenge it, issuing into the ferocious family clauses of the Code Napoleon, while subsequent industrial capitalism – in North America as in Europe – relied no less on patriarchal norms as a sheet-anchor of moral stability. Confucian and Muslim codes were far more draconian, though the 'minute regulations' of the former set some limits to the potential 'blank cheque' for male power in the latter (*Between Sex and Power*, p. 63). Arrangements were looser in much of sub-Saharan Africa, Creole America and South-East Asia. Harshest of all was the Hindu system of North India, in a league by itself for repression. As Therborn notes, this is one of the very few parts of the world where men live longer than women, even today.

By 2000, however, patriarchy had become 'the big loser of the twentieth century', as Therborn puts it, yielding far more ground than religion or tyranny. 'Probably no other social institution has been forced to retreat as much' (p. 73). This roll-back was not just an outcome of gradual processes of modernization, in the neutral scheme of structural-functional sociology. It was principally the product of three political hammer-blows. The first of these, Therborn shows, came in the throes of the First World War, when full legal parity between husband and wife was first enacted in Sweden, and then, in a more radical series of measures, the October Revolution dismantled the whole juridical apparatus of patriarchy in Russia, with a much more overt emphasis on sexual equality as such. Conduct, of course, was never the same as codification. 'The legal revolution of the Bolsheviks was very much ahead of Russian societal time, and Soviet family practices did not immediately dance to political music, however loud and powerful' (p. 85). But the shock wave in the world at large of the Russian example was, Therborn rightly emphasizes, enormous.

The Second World War delivered the next great blow on the other side of the world, again in contrasted neighbouring forms. In occupied Japan, MacArthur's staff imposed a Constitution proclaiming 'the essential equality of the sexes' – a notion, of course, that has still to find a place in the American Constitution – and a Civil Code based on conjugal symmetry. In liberated China, the victory of Communism 'meant a full-scale assault on the most ancient and elaborate patriarchy of the world', obliterating all legal traces of the Confucian order (p. 93). Finally, a third wave of emancipation was unleashed by the youth rebellions of the late sixties – when the revolt of May 1968 erupted in France, the country's High Court was still upholding the French husband's right to forbid his wife to move out, even if he was publicly maintaining a mistress – that segued into modern feminism. Here the inauguration by the UN of an International Decade for Women in 1975 (also the ultimate outcome of a Communist initiative, in the person of the Finnish daughter of one of Khruschev's Politburo veterans) is taken by Therborn as the turning point in a global discrediting of patriarchy, whose last legal redoubt in the US – in Louisiana – was struck down by the Supreme Court as late as 1981.

The rule of the father has not disappeared. In the world at large, West Asia, Africa and South Asia remain the principal hold-outs.

Islam itself, Therborn suggests, may be less to blame for the resistance of Arab patriarchy than the corruption of the secular forces once opposed to it, abetted by America and Israel. In India, on the other hand, there is no mistaking the degree of misogyny in caste and religion, even if the mediation of patriarchal authority by market mechanisms has its postmodern ambiguities. Surveying the 'blatant instrumentalism' of the matrimonial pages of a middle-class Indian press, in which 'more than 99 per cent of ads vaunt socio-economic offers and desires' he wonders: 'To what extent are parents the "agents" of young people, in the same sense as any money-seeking athlete, musician or writer has an agent?' (p. 109). At the opposite extreme is Euro-American post-patriarchy, in which men and women possess equal rights, but still far from equal resources – women enjoying not much more than half (55–60 per cent) the income and wealth of men.

In between these poles come the homelands of the Communist revolutions, which did so much to transform the landscape of patriarchy in the last century. The collapse of the Soviet bloc has not seen any restoration here, whatever other regressions it may involve ('the power of fathers and husbands does not seem to have increased', though 'that of pimps certainly has', p. 127). Therborn ventures the guess that in both Russia and Eastern Europe, the original revolutionary in this respect here may prove Comunism's most lasting legacy. In China, on the other hand, there is much further to go, amid more signs of recidivist urges in civil society. Still, he points out, not only is gender inequality in wages and salaries far lower in the PRC than in Taiwan – by a factor of three – but patriarchy proper, as indicated by conjugal residence and division of labour, continues to be weaker.

The first part of Therborn's story is thus eminently political, as he remarks, this is logical enough, since patriarchy is about power. His second part moves to sex. In questions of marriage, Europe diverged from the rest of the world far earlier than in matters of patriarchy – or more precisely, Western Europe and those of its marchlands affected by German colonization in the Middle Ages. In this zone a unique marital regime developed already in pre-industrial times, combining late monogamy, significant numbers of unmarried, and Christian norms of conjugal duty, contradictorily surrounded by a certain penumbra of informal sex. The key result was 'neo-locality', or the exit of wedded couples from parental households. Everywhere else in the world, Therborn maintains that the rule was universal marriage, typically at earlier ages, as the necessary entry into adulthood. (He does not make it clear whether he thinks this applies to all pre-class societies, where such a rule might be doubted.)

Paradoxically, however, although patterns of marriage might be thought to have varied more widely around the world than forms of patriarchy, Therborn is much briefer about them. Polyandry is never mentioned, the map of monogamy is unexplored, nor is any taxonomy of polygamy offered, beyond a tacit distinction between elite and mass variants (the latter peculiar to sub-Sahara). The baseline of his tale of marriage is set by a contrast between two deviant areas and all other arrangements. The first of these is the West European anomaly, with its subsequent overseas projections into North America and the Pacific. The second is the Creole, born in plantation and mining zones of the Caribbean and Latin America with a substantial black, mulatto or mestizo population, where a uniquely deregulated sexual regime developed.

Some startling figures emerge from Therborn's comparison of these. If sexual mores in Europe first became widely relaxed in aristocratic circles of the eighteenth century, flouting of conventional norms reached epidemic proportions among the lower classes of many cities in the nineteenth, if only by reason of the costs of marriage. At various points in the latter part of the century, a third of all births in Paris, a half in Vienna, and over two-thirds in Klagenfurt, were out of wedlock. By 1900 such figures had fallen, and national averages of illegitimacy become quite modest (Austrians still outpacing Afro-Americans, however). Matters were much wilder in the Creole system, readers of Garcia Marquez will not be surprised to learn. 'Iberian colonial America and the West Indies were the stage of the largest-scale assault on marriage in history' (p. 157). In the mid-nineteenth century between a third and a half of the population of Bahia never tied a knot; in the Rio de la Plata region, extra-marital births were four to five times the levels in Spain or Italy; around 1900 as many as fourth-fifths of sexual unions in Mexico City may have been without benefit of clergy.

These were the colourful exceptions. Throughout Asia, Africa, Russia and most of Eastern Europe, marriage in one form or another was inescapable. A century later, Therborn's account suggests, much less has changed than in the order of patriarchy. Creole America has become more marital, at least in periods of relative prosperity, but remains the most casual about the institution. In Asia, now mostly monogamous, and sub-Saharan Africa, still largely polygamous, marriage continues to be a universal norm – with pockets of slippage only in the big cities of Japan, South-East Asia and South Africa; but the age at which it is contracted has risen. If divorce of one kind or another has become nearly universal as a legal possibility, its practice is much more restricted – in the Hindu cow-belt, virtually zero. At the top end of the scale, in born-again America and post-Communist Russia, any wedding guest is entitled to be quizzical: half of all marriages break up. But with successive tries at conjugal bliss, the crude marriage rate has not fallen in the US. Globally, it would seem, the predominant note is stability.

In one zone, however, Therborn tracks a major change. After marrying as never before in the middle decades of the century, West Europeans started to secede from altar and registry in increasing numbers. Sweden was once again the vanguard country, and still remains well ahead even of its Scandinavian neighbours, not to speak of lands further south. The innovation it pioneered, from the late sixties onwards, was mass informal cohabitation. Thirty years later, the great majority of Swedish women giving birth to their first child – nearly 70 per cent – were either cohabiting or single mothers. Marriage might or might not follow cohabitation. What now became a minority option, in one country after another – the UK, France, Germany – was marriage before it. In Catholic France and Protestant England alike, extra-marital births jumped from 6–8 to 40–42 per cent in the space of four decades.

Manifestly, the sexual revolution of the sixties and seventies lay behind this spectacular transformation. Therborn notes the arrival of pill and IUD, as facilitating conditions, but is more interested in consequences. What did it add up to? In effect a double liberation: more partners and – especially for women – more pleasure. In Finland, women had bedded an average of three men in the early seventies, six in the early nineties; by then the gap in erotic satisfaction between the sexes had closed. In Sweden, the median of lovers more than trebled, a much greater increase than for men. 'More than anything else', Therborn concludes, 'this is what the sexual revolution has brought about: a long period for pre-marital sex, and a plurality of sexual partners over a lifetime becoming a "normal" phenomenon in a statistical as well as in a moral sense' (p. 210).

How far does the US conform to the emergent European pattern? Only in part, as its different religious and political complexion would lead one to think. Europeans will be astonished to learn that in 2000 about a fifth of American eighteen- to twenty-four-year-olds claimed to be virgins on marriage. Only 6 per cent of American couples cohabited. Over 70 per cent of mothers at first birth are married. On the other hand, the US has nearly twice as many teenage births per cohort as the highest country in the EU, and an extra-marital birth rate higher than the Netherlands. Without going much into race or region, Therborn describes the American system as 'dualist'. But from the evidence he provides, it might be thought electoral divisions are reflected in sexual contrasts, blue and red in the boudoir too.

In the last part of his book, Therborn moves to fertility. Here the conundrum is the 'demographic transition' – the standard term for the shift from a regime of low growth, combining lots of children and much early death, to one of high growth, combining many children but fewer deaths, and then back to another one of low growth, this time with both many fewer deaths and fewer children. There is no mystery about the way medical advances and better diets led to falling rates of mortality in nineteenth-century Europe, and eventually reached most of the world, to similar effect, in the second half of the twentieth century. The big question is why birth rates fell, first in Europe and North America between the 1880s and 1930s, and then for the majority of human race from the mid-1970s onwards, in two uncannily similar waves. In each case, 'a process rapidly cutting through and across state boundaries, levels of industrialization, urbanization, and levels of income, across religions, ideologies and family systems' (p. 236) slashed fertility rates by 30–40 per cent in three decades. Today, the average family has no more than two to three children throughout most of the former Third World.

What explains these gigantic changes? The first nations to experience a significant fall in fertility were France and the United States, by 1830 – generations in advance of all others. What they had in common, Therborn suggests, was their popular revolutions, which had given ordinary people a sense of self-mastery. Once the benefits of smaller families became clear in these societies, neo-locality allowed couples to make their own decisions to improve their lives before any modern means of contraception were available. Fifty years later, perhaps triggered initially by the onset of a world recession, mass birth control began to roll through Europe, eventually sweeping all the way from Portugal to Russia. This time, Therborn's hypothesis runs, it was a combination of radical socialist and secular movements popularizing the idea of family planning, together with the spread of literacy, that brought lower fertility as part of an increasingly self-conscious culture of modernity. This was birth control from below.

In the Third World, by contrast, contraception – now an easy technology – was typically propagated or imposed from above, by political fiat of the state. China's one-child policy has been the most dramatic, if extreme example. Once lower birth rates became a general goal of governments committed to modernization, it was family systems that then determined the order in which societies entered the new regime: East Asia in the lead, North India and Black Africa far in the rearguard. Here too it was a sense of mastery, of human ability to command nature – not always bureaucratic in origin, since the better-off societies of Latin America moved more spontaneously in the same direction – that powered the change. Its consequences, of which we can still see only the beginnings, are enormous. Without it, the earth would now have some two billion more inhabitants.

In Europe and Japan, meanwhile, fertility has moved no less dramatically in the opposite direction, falling below net reproduction rates. This collapse in the birth rate, from which the US is saved essentially by immigration, promises rapid ageing of these nations in the short run, and, if unchecked, virtual extinction of them in the long run. There is now a growing literature of public alarm about this prospect, what the French historian Pierre Chaunu denounces as a 'White Death' threatening the Old World. Therborn eschews it. Negative rates of reproduction in these rich, socially advanced societies do not correspond to any birth-strike by women, he suggests, but rather to their desire to have both two to three children and careers that are the equal of men's, which the existing social order does not yet allow them to do. In denying themselves the offspring they want, European parents are 'moving against themselves' (p. 284ff), not with the grain of any deeper cultural change.

Between Sex and Power ends its narratives with four principal conclusions. The different family systems of the world reveal little internal dynamic of change. They have been recast from the outside, and the history of their transformations has been neither unilinear nor evolutionary, but rather determined by a series of unevenly timed international conjunctures, of markedly political character. The result has not been one of convergence, other than in a general decline of patriarchy, due more to wars and revolutions than to any 'feminist world spirit'. In the South, the differential pace of changes in fertility continues to shift the distribution of global population further towards the Subcontinent and Africa, and away from Europe, Japan and Russia. In the North, European marriage has altered its forms, but is proving itself supple and creative in adapting to a new range of desires: conventional jeremiads notwithstanding, it is in good shape. Predictions? Serenely declined. 'The best bet for the future is in the inexhaustible innovative capacity of humankind, which eventually surpasses all social science' (p. 315).

In due course, an army of specialists will gather round *Between Sex and Power*, like so many expert sports fans, to pore over its multitudinous argument. What can a layman say, beyond the magnitude of its achievement? Tentatively, perhaps only this. In the architectonic of the book, there is something of a gap between the notion of a family system and the triad of patriarchy, marriage and fertility that follows it. In effect, the way these three interconnect to form the *structure* of any family system goes unstated in the separate treatment accorded each. But if we consider the trio as an abstract combinatory, it would seem that logically – as the order in which Therborn proceeds to them itself suggests – patriarchy must command the other two, as the 'dominant', since it will typically lay down the rules of marriage and set the norms of reproduction. There is, in other words, a hierarchy of determinations built into any family system.

This has a bearing on Therborn's conclusions. His final emphasis falls, unhesitatingly, on the divergence between major family systems today. After stressing continuing worldwide dissimilarities between fertility and marital regimes, he concedes that 'the patriarchal outcome is somewhat different' (p. 306). His own evidence suggests this is an understatement. For what it shows is a powerful process of convergence, far from complete in extent, but unequivocal in direction. But if the variegated forms of patriarchy are what historically determined the main parameters of marriage and reproduction, would not any ongoing decline of them across family systems towards a common juridical zero-point imply that birth rates and marriage customs are eventually likely to converge, in significant measure, at their own pace too? That seems, at any rate, a possible deduction side-stepped by Therborn, but which his story of fertility appears to bear out. For what is clear from his account is that the astonishing fall in birth rates in most of the underdeveloped world has been the product of precisely a collapse in patriarchal authority, as its powers of life and death have been transferred to the state, which now determines how many are born and how many survive.

What then of marriage? Here certainly contrasts remain greatest. In speaking of 'the core of romantic freedom and commitment in the modern European (and New World) family system', Therborn implies this remains specific to the West. But while the caste system or the shariah plainly preclude extempore love, does it show no signs of spreading, as ideal or realization, in the big cities of East Asia or Latin America? The imagination of urban Japan, he shows, is already half seized with it. Not, of course, that the aeration of marriage in Western Europe, with the advent of mass cohabitation, has so far been replicated anywhere else. But here a different sort of question might be asked. Is it really the case that the negative rates of reproduction that have accompanied this pattern are as unwished for as Therborn suggests? He relies on the discrepancy between surveys in which women explain how many children they expect, and those they actually have. But this could just mean that in practice their desire for children proved weaker than for a well-paid job, a satisfying career, or more than one lover at time. Voters in the West regularly say they want better schools and health care, and in principle expect to pay for them, and commentators on the Left often pin high hopes on such declarations. But once such citizens get to the polling booth they tend to stick to lower taxes. The same kind of self-deception could apply to children. If so, it would be difficult to say European marriage was in such good shape, since there would be no stopping place in sight for its plunge of society into an actuarial abyss.

Therborn resists such thoughts. Although *Between Sex and Power* pays handsome homage to the role of Communism in the dismantling of patriarchy in the twentieth century, it displays no especially Marxist stance towards the family. Engels would have not shared the author's satisfaction that marriage was flourishing, however ductile the forms it has adopted. In expressing his attachment to them nevertheless, Therborn speaks with the humane voice of a level-headed Swedish reformism that he understandably admires, without himself having ever altogether coincided with it. In looking on the bright side of the EU marital regime, he is consistent with the case he has made in the past for its welfare states too, surviving in much better condition than its critics or mourners believe.[4] It is in the same spirit, one might say, that he insists on the persistent divergence of family systems across the world. Uniformity is the one condition every part of the political spectrum deplores. The most unflinching neo-liberals invariably explain that universal free markets are the best of all guardians of diversity. Social Democrats reassure their followers that the capitalism to which they must adjust is becoming steadily more various. Traditional conservatives expatiate on the irreducible multiplicity of faiths and civilizations. Homogeneity has no friends, at least since Alexandre Kojeve. But when any claim becomes too choral, a flicker of doubt is indicated. It scarcely affects the magnificence of this book. In it, you can find the largest changes in human relations of modern times.

2005

References

Goode, William (1963) *World Revolution and Family Patterns*. London: Free press of Glencoe.

Laslett, Peter (1965) *The World We Have Lost*. London: Methuen.

Therborn, Göran (1984) 'The prospects of labour and the transformation of advanced capitalism', *New Left Review* 145.

Therborn, Göran (2001) 'Into the twenty-first century', *New Left Review* 10.

Therborn, Göran (2004) *Between Sex and Power: Family in the World, 1900–2000*. London: Routledge.

---

4. 'The prospects of labour and the transformation of advanced capitalism' (Therborn 1984), still a basic text; for a striking political vision of the world two decades later, see 'Into the twenty-first century' (Therborn 2001).

SECTION III
Global Modernities

IMMANUEL WALLERSTEIN

Empire: Dangerous Slippage of a Concept

We have all been long aware that concepts in the human and social sciences have multiple, often contradictory, meanings in practical usage. One of the most widely discussed is the concept of 'liberal/ liberalism'. In order to understand the arguments of someone who uses this concept, we have to discern what definition the author is using for it.

We are unfortunately not always as aware about this multiplicity of usages. I would contend that we tend to be relatively unaware that the concept 'empire/imperial/imperialism' is just as subject to definitional multiplicity as is 'liberal/liberalism'. Because we are less aware, we tend not to engage in discerning the definitional frame of the utilizer. This has important negative consequences for the diagnosis and prognosis of our analyses.

Göran Therborn, for example, has written very impressively on the consequences for the ethnic composition of major cities in East-Central Europe of the decline of various nineteenth-century imperial systems and their replacement by independent sovereign states operating on a claim to ethnic priority of the supposedly original inhabitants.

But does it follow that we can then use the same concept to compare the presumed decline of the United States today with that of ancient Rome? I think not. I think doing so lumps together apples and oranges. Nonetheless, such a comparison is a widespread usage in the beginning of the twenty-first century.

For the large number of scholars who use the concept, such a comparison seems to be self-evident. We usually think of an empire as a structure (certainly political for all, but in addition cultural for some) in which one state and/or one ethnic group dominates other states and/or ethnic groups. So, if one is anti-imperialist, one is seeking to undermine the reign of the imperial power. And 'decline' refers to the diminishing ability of the imperial power to impose itself on those previously dominated.

I wish to resume briefly what seem to me the two radically different usages of the concept of 'empire'. It is something that I have elaborated previously in multiple writings about what I term 'world-systems analysis'. On the one hand, there exist historical systems of three varieties: mini-systems and two kinds of world-systems – world-empires and world-economies.

All historical systems have lives. That is, they are not eternal but rather each has three historical moments: their coming into existence; their 'normal' functioning under rules they have established and enforce; their inevitable structural crisis when their normal rules no longer maintain the system in relative equilibrium.

We are currently living in the third phase, that of the structural decline of the modern world-system (or capitalist world-economy) that has had a life of 500 or so years. There have existed within the modern world-system 'empires' that have been one of the institutional bulwarks of the normal functioning of the system. These empires have indeed been in decline and this has contributed to the growing chaotic situation that constitutes part of the process of the structural decline of the system.

If, however, we shift our optic from the analysis of the modern world-system to the millennial development of historical systems, we must assess the picture over at least 5 000, perhaps 10 000 years. In doing that, we are looking at something radically different from the life of a single historical system. The following picture emerges: For most of this period, all three kinds of historical systems have existed, but not co-existed. The world-empires have been the strong form. The world-empires have emerged, expanded to their ecological/political limits, and then began to recede.

In the process of expansion, they have absorbed both mini-systems and world-economies. In the process of receding, both mini-systems and world-economies have found the space to re-emerge. The story of world-systems in this optic has been that of a millennial rise and fall of world-empires.

In this usage and this optic, ancient Rome or Han China or the Mughal Empire were all world-empires. One can legitimately engage in a comparative analysis of these world-empires. One cannot compare anyone of them to empires within a world-economy, which include Great Britain or the United States during the last 500 years.

If one continues in this optic, the pattern of a zigzag between expanding and receding world-empires did not continue forever. Somehow, during the long sixteenth century, the world-empire lost its characteristic of being the strong form. Instead, a particular world-economy, that located primarily in northwest Europe and parts of the Americas, replaced the world-empire as the strong form, was able to expand its geographical and political strength so that, over time, it absorbed mini-systems and world-empires until its purview included the entire globe.

The fact that the modern world-system, a world-economy, became global in coverage was a total novelty in the millennial development of historical systems. But this meant that after a certain point, the modern world-system no longer had space in which to expand. And this fact alone undid the mechanisms by which the modern world-system had been constantly regaining its moving equilibrium. The result was structural decline, but one of a more serious kind than any previous decline.

I shall not review here what I believe have been the immediate triggers for the structural decline of the modern world-system, nor the nature of the political struggle that is taking place about the successor system to the capitalist world-economy. I have done this extensively elsewhere. I wish to remain on the question of the appropriate comparison of declines.

If one tries to compare the decline of the US empire within the modern world-system with that on ancient Rome, one is diverted into a meaningless comparison. This diversion however makes it more difficult to perceive what is actually going on – the transition from the capitalist world-economy to some alternative system or systems.

If then significant numbers of people across the globe do not focus of the nature of the transition and the necessary moral judgments and political tactics that ought to ensue, the chance that there will be a largely egalitarian, largely democratic outcome is reduced to a significant degree. This is the reason why understanding the large gamut of meanings that the concept of empire may be utilized is not simply an argument between users of the concept but a critical determinant of the outcome of our present transition to a new world-system (or world-systems). We cannot simply leave the concept unexamined in the greatest detail and with the most careful attention. No analysis of the current world situation should be written in which the word 'empire' is not to be found in the index, as though it were a self-evident idea.

HABIBUL HAQUE KHONDKER

Entangled Globality

Global–Regional Interface in Asia

Nearly half a century ago, Gunnar Myrdal (1898–1987), a Swedish economist with considerable 'sociological imagination' characterized social transformation in Asia as 'Asian Drama' (Myrdal 1968). The post World War Two development challenges in the assorted Asian countries such as India, Pakistan, and Indonesia were viewed in light of contemporary modernization and development theories. Myrdal was not optimistic about the development prospects of India, for example, observing the weakness of the state (what he called 'soft state'), and the bottlenecks caused by the forces of tradition. This chapter aims to understand the new Asian drama through the theoretical frames provided by Göran Therborn, a famous Swedish sociologist. One of the central features of Therborn's opus is that he takes a global focus that incorporates a specific consideration of the regions. This is an important and useful corrective to an over-globalized focus of many writers. Therborn (2006) saw to the fact that the discussions of globalization and globality do not undermine region by subsuming it under the overarching dynamics of the global. In his own empirical works, Therborn has taken on such projects as social inequality, family and urbanization, staples of sociology with special attention to the regional variation within a global framework. Not many sociologists have the good fortune to earn praise by historians. Therborn's *Between Sex and Power* (2004), a study on family systems across cultures, received accolades from one of the most distinguished historians of the twentieth century, Eric Hobsbawm (2005).

One of the central contributions of Therborn (1977; 1978) is his theory of the rise of democracy, which he links to the dynamics of class struggle. Framing his discussion in the nominal Marxist tradition, Therborn, in fact, provides a critical elaboration of the theory of democracy from a handmaiden of the bourgeoisie view to the struggles of the working class with a far reaching emancipatory potential and true to a more enlightened understanding of democracy. The historical discussions of John Markoff (1996; 1999) on the origins, spread of democracy and its institutionalization (or lack of) around the world provide empirical support for Therborn's theoretical claims. In the present chapter, while we draw upon all these important ideas of Therborn, the central argument of this chapter is a consideration, and hopefully elaboration, of his other important contribution, a theorization of entangled modernity, which also provides a launching ground of his theory of globalization with a keen sense of empirical realities of the nations, regions and continents. Like his historically grounded views of multiple routes to modernization, Therborn's globalization theory is also nuanced and veers towards a theory of *globalizations*.

Asia is in the middle of a paradigm shift. Three of the ten leading economies in gross income are in Asia, which includes China as number two and Japan as number three, according to the World Bank data.[1] The economic transformations in Asia were in the making for sometime, largely unacknowledged. The Asian countries with large population have posted high GDP growth rate in the last five years. Economic growth has been slow in Japan and Iran, the latter due to continued economic sanctions. Table 1 illustrates this trend.

Socio-economic transformations in several parts of Asia can be examined in terms of their regional specificities. For example, since the late 1970s, East and Southeast Asian regions have seen spectacular economic development under soft authoritarian political systems that led to high growth economies, a rising middle class and a class of super rich. In West Asia – Asian part of what is popularly known as Middle East – saw spectacular economic growth in certain countries thanks to rising prices of fossil fuels that led to a dramatic change in social indicators whereas rest of that region remains mired

---

1. See http://databank.worldbank.org/data/download/GDP.pdf.

Table 1: Economic growth in the most populous countries of Asia

Country	Population (millions)*	2000–2009	2009–2013
Bangladesh	160.4	5.9	6.2
China	1 372	10.9	8.7
India	1 314	7.6	6.9
Indonesia	256	5.3	6.2
Iran	78.5	5.4	1.7
Japan	126.9	0.9	1.6
(South) Korea	50.7	4.4	3.7
Malaysia	30.8	5.1	5.7
Nepal	28	3.7	4.2
Pakistan	199	5.1	3.1
Philippines	103	4.9	6.1
Saudi Arabia	31.6	5.9	6.6
Sri Lanka	20.9	5.5	7.4
Thailand	65.1	4.6	4.2
Turkey	78.2	4.9	5.9
Vietnam	91.7	6.8	5.8

* The population data is drawn from Population Reference Bureau 2015: http://www.prb.org/pdf15/2015-world-population-data-sheet_eng.pdf

Source: http://data.worldbank.org/news/ release-of-world-development-indicators-2015.

in deprivations. The political drama unfolding in West Asia presents as a contrasting foil against which the experiences of East Asia can be seen. The transformation in the Asian regions is both spectacular and daunting giving way to new challenges and paradoxes for the social scientists. Is it possible to discover an overarching global theoretical frame that would make sense of developments in the various regions of Asia, which are geographically as well as politico-economically diverse? Or should we pursue each region as a case following its own regional specificities?

Drawing upon Therborn's contributions, this chapter argues that it would be of immense value to focus on the regional and sub-regional entities while not neglecting the overarching global framework, the nature of entangled modernity and the class dynamics of democracy in Asia. The main arguments of this chapter are two folds. First, Asia has been touted to become the center of economic gravity in the twenty-first century globalized world. Yet, Asia is rarely understood as a totality. In the late 1980s when East and Southeast Asian economies were undergoing rapid economic growth and social modernization defying the predictions of the economists and development experts, they labeled these countries as 'Asian Tigers'. The definition of the economic transformation was limited to four relatively small Asian economies: Hong Kong, Taiwan, South Korea, and Singapore. Asia is rarely taken as a whole in any study. While 'Asian Miracle' dazzled some writers in the late 1980s and early 1990s especially, because of the rapid economic growth of the 'Asian Tiger' economies, they neglected remarkable but gradual transformation taking place in South Asia. Now while the world attention is riveted on India and China, significant foundational changes are taking place in West Asia.

While the world attention was focused on the Asian Tigers, China and India, the two large Asian countries were neglected and not even considered as contenders for Tiger status; no one predicted that in a space of less than two decades they would emerge as important economic powers. Developments in the Peoples Republic of China were seen through the prisms of Cold War ideology, socialist growth was not recognized, let alone appreciated in a world tinged with ideological blinders. Yet, remarkable social modernization took place in China in terms of basic literacy, health care, schooling and housing and infrastructure that paved the way for the miracle growth in the post-Mao period in the late 1970s. India, too, often touted as having the so-called Hindu growth rate in the 1970s and 1980s experienced slow but steady growth accompanied by a Green revolution in agriculture and since 1980s a pro-business stance of the government (Rodrik and Subramanian 2004). The growth was lopsided and transformation slow, the large number of graduates left engineers, scientists unemployed who unable to find employment in their own country took the route of overseas employment in effect created a potential for subsequent back-office status of India in the 1990s and in the first decade of the 21st century. The Indian experiment of democracy with development resulted in sluggish economic growth yet it laid the basis of a long-term political stability.

India provides a good example of entangled modernity rooted in India's historical experience. In the words of Pundit Nehru, one of the founders of modern Indian and a champion of Indian democracy: 'Foreign influences poured in an often influenced that (Indian) culture and were absorbed. Disruptive tendencies gave rise immediately to an attempt to find a synthesis' (Nehru 1994: 62). India was an ocean where multiple streams of influences converged. 'Iranians, Greeks, Parthians, Bactrians, Scythians, Huns, Turks (before Islam), early Christians, Jews, Zorastrians; … came, made a difference, and were absorbed. India, was, according to Dodwell, "infinitely absorbent like the ocean"' (Nehru 1994: 73). India's success lies in its historical trajectory of tolerance and inclusion. The Muslims ruled in a society dominated by heterodox communities where religion was not featured as a prominent social or cultural theme. The indigenous multiculturalism, a syncretic culture was an asset on which entangled modernity was built.

The entangled modernity in India was a product of her historical experiences of colonialism as India became exposed to the ideas of modernity, not only through Western education but also western institutions and cultural encounters. Changes took place not only in the class structure and a national consciousness; changes took place in cultures, aesthetics and ideology as well. The shift in historical studies from a nation-centered focus to a discourse of circulations, connections, convergence and differences brought out by comparative studies, as illustrate in the writings of Sunil Amrith (2013) or Andrew Sartori (2008) provide a newer, albeit somewhat complex but more nuanced understanding of global modernity. The position of Roland Robertson contra Anthony Giddens is vindicated as far as the sequence of globalization is concerned. For Giddens, globalization is a consequence of modernization; while Robertson (1992)

argued that globalization can be traced to a much longer historical process and predates modernization. For Prasenjit Duara, '[t]he
early modern period is simultaneously the period when expanding
and accelerating circulations bring parts of the world closer to each
other through exchange of knowledge, technologies and ideas ...'
(Duara 2015: 7). The idea of entangled modernity, I would argue,
can be conceived as 'entangled globality' or just globality on the
ground that modernity has always been global. The distinction
between modernity and globality, thus, remains only in the fact that
while modernity is space-centric and rooted in specific geo-cultural
setting, globality transcends moorings in specific geo-cultural settings, thus phrases such as 'de-territorialization' and 'transnational',
'multi-local' become the defining features of globality.

For Arif Dirlik (2007), 'The globalization of modernity needs to
be comprehended not just in the trivial sense of an originary modernity reaching out and touching all, even those who are left out of
its benefits ... but more importantly as a proliferation of claims
on modernity. So-called traditions no longer imply a contrast with
modernity, as they did in modernization discourse. Nor are they the
domain of backward-looking conservatism, except in exceptional
circumstances – such as the Taliban. They are invoked increasingly
to establish claims to alternative modernities (but only rarely to
alternatives to modernity). They point not to the past but, taking
a detour through the past, to an alternative future.' They have even
taken over from socialism the task of speaking for those oppressed or
cast aside by capitalist modernity and politics to different possibilities of the future (Dirlik 2007: 90–91).

In tracing the historical debates over Chinese national education
(*guoxue*) in the context of the global – national nexus, which began
in the last decade of the Ming period, Dirlik (2011) quotes Wang
Guowei, one the protagonists of 'Western' education. For Wang,
'In learning there is no new and old, Chinese or Western, useless
or useful' (quoted in Dirlik 2011: 7). Another writer of the period,
Zhang Zhidong wanted: 'Chinese learning for substance, Western
learning for function' (quoted in Dirlik 2011: 7). The rhetoric of
the last decade of the nineteenth century is reminiscent of the same

in the last decade of the twentieth century, when Deng Xiaoping, the Paramount leader of China favored: 'Democracy with Chinese characters'.

Entangled modernity, a term that Therborn borrows from Shalini Randeria, (originally used in German) involves a multidisciplinary approach that considers not only a time orientation but also an interplay of social institutions, culture and social conflicts (Therborn 2003: 294). This goes against the Eurocentric conceptualization of modernization from Max Weber to Anthony Giddens. One of the underlying assumptions in the writings of the classical sociologists was that modernity is a universal process and that it was only a matter of time when the peoples around the world who live according to their cultural traditions, collective norms or civilizational heritage will all be amalgamated into a modern man/woman and societies will embrace the universal ideals of democracy and capitalism. In other words, the march of progress will lead to the universal victory of liberalism. Such views can be distilled from Hegel to Fukuyama. The pessimists, such as Samuel Huntington had a more realist view of clashing civilizations, no matter how arbitrary his conceptualization of 'civilizations' were. Therborn's distinction between 'globality' and 'universality' is useful in the conceptualization of 'modernity'.

> Globality has two basic meanings: finitude and connectivity, both planetary. Universality, by contrast, denotes unlimited extension. Because of its modes of historical generation, modernity has to be seen as a global phenomenon, rather than a universal one. As such, it should be the study object of a global history and a global social science. A global approach to social phenomena means focusing on global variability, global connectivity, and global inter-communication. It also implies a global look at processes of change, of continuity and discontinuity. To capture the actual globality of modernity, the latter had better be seen in the plural, as constituting a set of 'multiple modernities', ... The emphasis on entangled modernities is meant to highlight, not just the co-existence of different modernities but also their interrelations, current as well as historical. (Therborn 2003: 295.)

Therborn's views of entangled modernity can be contextualized in various historical and geographical settings. The views of the first

Indian Prime Minister, and a visionary of Indian modernity, Pundit Jawaharlal Nehru, traced Indian history as sedimented by layers of cultural and institutional influences. Indian historians have traced the entangled history by recounting the admixtures of historical experiences and enmeshed institutional developments. In the realm of ideas, Kris Manjapra (2014) has explored the cultural and intellectual connections that linked Germany and India from the late nineteenth to the mid twentieth century. India and Germany sought to challenge an Anglo centric world. Indian physicist Satyendra Nath Bose and German physicist Albert Einstein collaborated in the 1920s to develop Bose-Einstein condensate and Bose-Einstein statistics. The particle 'boson' is named after Bose. Bose, a polyglot, translated Einstein's papers of relativity from German to English for the Indian scientific community. From science to arts and humanities many such collaborations and interconnections took place. Nobel Laureate Tagore visited Germany to recruit German professors for Visva Bharati, the university he set up in a rural town. Such connectivity and intercultural entanglement began with Max Muller and other keen students of oriental affairs. Syed Mujtaba Ali, a Bengali writer and a disciple of Tagore went to Germany in 1929 and studied German literature in Berlin and Bonn. Ali, a Goethe specialist and a polyglot spent rest of his life teaching at various colleges before joining the Tagore's University and wrote novels and stories of his sojourn in Germany and elsewhere. Such illustrations of entanglements signaled a cultural globalization based on cosmopolitan worldview. Similar developments took place at the experiential level of many Indians who never left India.

Following Therborn's taxonomy of multiple routes to modernity, we highlight the two, namely colonial modernity where modernity came 'out of the barrels of guns' (Therborn 2003: 299); and the reactive modernity, which I would like to view as *modernity by choice* as it is revealed in the historical experiences of China and Japan. True, the push for modernity in the case of China or more so for Japan came with colonial incursions, best illustrated by the well-known forays of Commodore Perry from 1853 to 54. Even before there were, at least twenty-five times, attempts were made privately or officially to establish contacts with Japan (Holcombe 2011: 215). Hence, there are clear evidences of reactive modernity since the Japanese officials knew the fate of China during the Opium war in 1842. Yet, it would be useful to recount the Japanese interest in acquiring Dutch knowledge of medical sciences and military sciences in the early eighteenth century during the Tokugawa period (Holcombe 2011: 213). Even in the twentieth century, there are several examples of globalization by choice. Most of the Newly Industrializing Economies in East and Southeast Asia and later China and India pursued the strategy of inviting and negotiating with neo-liberal globalization. While for the smaller nations it was a conscious drive to economic globalization keeping certain arenas sealed off from the global influences. For example, Singapore sought to be the Switzerland of Asia, followed an open, market-friendly economic policy, and adopted English as the lingua franca, yet promoted Confucian values to maintain political order and social harmony. A preference for indigenous political system unaffected by the call for universal human rights and liberal democracy was a feature of most of the Tiger economies. Malaysia's simultaneous 'look East' policy for economic development and anti-Western rhetoric championed by Mohamed Mahathir, in the 1980s and 1990s were conscious effort to partake in a selected version of global modernity.

While partaking in the process of global modernity in a robust manner, the leadership in the 'Tiger Economies' invested a great deal of ideological energy in the discourse of Asian values showing how Asian high economic growth performers were 'different' from the West. In the revitalized binaries, the West was (re)created. One writer captures that debate succinctly as follows:

> The category of Asian values was born, during the 1990s, from the attempt of the political-governmental elites of some South-East Asian countries to characterize their identity on the international scene in opposition to individualistic values, considered dominant in Western societies. Indeed, those that refer to Asian values believe they can discern some arguably typical traits in them, such as: the embodiment of the traditional cardinal virtues of Confucianism; the primacy of collective on individual interests; the care for order and stability; the

continuity between generations; the openness to sacrifice; and the deferment of instant gratification. Asia, therefore, would be governed by the principles of social harmony and the respect for authority and family; while the West is depicted as a place in which community values are eroded by the spread of rampant individualism, where the proliferation of rights is not compensated by a hierarchy of community duties and constraints. (Fornari 2007: x.)

Acceptance of Western science, technology, education and popular culture unquestioningly, and rejecting their political views and cultures, an ambivalent position took shape. Such ambivalence was deeply rooted in the discourses of coloniality and postcoloniality. The colonial modernity cannot be simply viewed as a one-way imposition as viewed by the Marxist-oriented Dependency theorists. Immanuel Wallerstein, the founder of the World Systems theorist, envisaged 'development by invitation' as a strategy for the periphery to move into semi-peripheral status. The problem with Marxist colonial history and the Dependency theory was that they denied any agency to the subjects. Interesting, Marx's position was more ambivalent when it came to the impact of colonialism, especially with regard to India. The interplay between the local traditions and the western tradition of modernity evolved in a delicate interplay. Ideas and institutions clashed and influenced each other and a distinct Indian modernity evolved, thus modernity was not just an imposed burden. Therborn himself makes us aware of this entangled process and cautions us against the overgeneralizations of both modernization theories and their nemesis Dependency/World-Systems theories. The cases of modernity of China and Japan illustrate, what Therborn calls, reactive modernity, or I would call: modernity by choice by leveraging on the ideas and institutions of modernity assembled from the wide world.

China's modernity was also built upon a conscious design that started in the first decade of the twentieth century that resulted in the Republican revolution of 1911. China provides a civilizational continuity unmatched in other cases. China experienced centuries of civilizational continuity. The waves of modernity reached Chinese shores as Europeans came to seek new markets and raw materials.

Here colonialism exposed its ugly face in the imposition of opium trade and commodity production. The growth of Chinese cities such as Shanghai was linked to the new political economy. Hong Kong was a trading outpost (Mills 1942) as was Singapore in the colonial trade route (Buchanan 1972; Wong 1978).

The spread of modern education began in Asia by the missionaries and the beginning of higher education with setting up of new western style university system in Peking and Shanghai and Hong Kong. It was in Hong Kong from where Dr. Sun Yat Sen, the future father of modern China was trained in medicine after secondary education in Hawaii, US. Many prominent wealthy Chinese families sent their children both sons and daughters to overseas for western education. In fact, Sun Yat Sen's wife too was educated in Wesleyan College. Modern education had a variety of multiplier effects. It created a new class, consciousness and a sense of identity as a people. The entangled nature of Chinese modernity was revealed in the ideological crosscurrents. Both India and China were exposed to an ensemble of modernist ideas that included the communist ideas.

The tale of Manabendra Nath Roy, or M.N. Roy – an assumed name – for which he is known, an anti-colonial revolutionary went to Indonesia and Japan to raise weapons and support for the anti-colonial struggle and failing to achieve his objectives ended up at Palo Alto, California in 1916 to be a guest of Dhanagopal Mukherji, a student at Stanford University and an erstwhile young revolutionary from India. Dhanagopal Mukherji's life is no less cosmopolitan. He met his bride, a fellow graduate at Stanford and lived in a social circle that included the former president of Stanford University. Mukherji became an award winning children's book writer in the US (Tathagatananda 2010). It was through Mukerji's girlfriend Roy was introduced to his future bride, Evelyn Trent, a Marxist who provided Roy an education in Marxism (Manjapra 2010: 32). Trent helped transform Roy from ant-colonial nationalist to a communist. Together they went to Mexico where Roy was eventually elected as the first General Secretary of the Socialist Party of Mexico in December 1918. From Mexico the Roys went to Germany on their way to Moscow where Roy met Lenin and 'differed with him on the role of the local bourgeoisie in nationalist movements' (Nath 2001). By 1926 Roy was elected as a member of all four official policy making bodies of the Comintern – the presidium, the political secretariat, the executive committee and the world congress eventually assumed membership at the Comintern (Nath 2001). In 1927, Stalin sent him to Canton, China to promote socialism. Roy in his late years was considered as a humanist philosopher.

Whereas most Indian communists were schooled in England, Chinese communists went to France to get full flavor of western modernity and were indoctrinated with communist ideologies. One of the founders of Chinese communist party, Chen Duxiu (1879–1942) upon his return from France to China launched a magazine 'La Jeunesse Nouvelle ("New Youth" or Xin Qingnian in Chinese), and for the first issue, he also wrote an article on "The French and Modern Civilization"' (Holcombe 2011: 238–219). This journal was aimed for the young people and was published in French. Similarly, upon return to India in 1915, Gandhi in 1919 launched a weekly magazine in English titled Young India, ostensibly aimed for the young people in India. While European education helped Asians literacy in modernity, the new periodicals helped create a discourse in modernity. The ideological conversion was not as dramatic as it looks, it was the interplay between the new Western ideas and the indigenous thoughts, the encounters and conversations that often took a circuitous routes since there were local resisters and conservatives who were deeply suspicious of modern ideas. The new luddites were also products of an incomplete conversation. An entangled modernity was the result of the complex dialogue and encounters. The newspapers helped form an imagined community in both these large Asian nations.

Japanese modernizers at the onset of the Meiji reforms in the late nineteenth century, for example, Fukuzawa Yukichi (1835–1901) wanted Japan to 'leave Asia' culturally from the ranks of the Asian nations and to join the civilized nations of the West (Holcombe 2011: 220). Fukuzawa's modernist ideas were formed after this trips to Europe and North America. The Meiji modernizers embarked on a linear trajectory of modernity, which in course of time became entangled in the mid twentieth century when a new wave of modernization was imposed by the occupied forces in the aftermath of Japan's defeat. A nation that managed to escape colonialism for centuries was reduced to a virtual colony of the US under the command of the Allied Forces. Yet the consequence of this historical irony has been an entangled globality for Japan. As the first industrial country outside the Western world, Japan did leave other Asian countries behind becoming the second largest economy for a while.

The entangled globality in West Asia or the Middle East is manifested not just in the debates over tradition and modernity and the extent of institutional transformations of these societies. Modernity in the Muslim West Asia has been relatively recent and more entangled as religious worldviews presented a formidable challenge to modernist ideas. The debates that took place in Indian sociological circles in the 1950s and 1960s between tradition and modernity were replayed in Southeast Asia in the 1980s and 1990s and in the Gulf region in the beginning of the twenty-first century.

South Asia or East Asia and the Middle East have followed different trajectories of modernity underpinned by their different historical and politico-economic formations. Societies are inter-connected but their tryst with modernity varies from context to context. Even in Europe, which viewed from outside looks like a homogenous entity presents interesting diversity in their differential routes to modernity (Therborn 1995). The looming doubts over the future of the European Union may be an aspect of that historical legacy. Therborn's view of entangled modernity opens a new vista and presages the formulation of entangled history of which can be easily accommodated in what we view here as entangled global modernity.

Therborn seeks to define modernity as a dimension of time not certain ways and practices, which he thinks – I might add, correctly – gave rise to Eurocentric or North Atlanticist hubris. But one could do both, giving priority over the temporal dimension yet not falling into truly multiple modernities. Rather than pursuing ideas such as modernity with Chinese characters or Indian characteristics, it is plausible to claim that the modern institutions in the context of local traditions and culture assume somewhat different features but remains recognizable as modernity, if disassembled. For example, one of the features of modernity has been the march of women towards greater equality vis-à-vis men. The rights gained cannot be reversed. Similar arguments can be made with regard to universal adult franchise. Many of these irreversible processes accompanied by a determined emphasis on education is found all over the continent of Asia. In the Middle East or West Asia, it may be of some value to understand democratic transition more as a societal phenomenon where a march towards equality between gender and decline of authoritarian patriarchy is clearly visible. The new technology, especially the information technology is another factor that has contributed to the egalitarian trends. Yet the new media has also been contentious which reflects the embedded contradictions in the forces of globality. When in 2011 a number of countries in the Middle East and North Africa (MENA) experienced protests that came to be known as the 'Arab Spring', many commentators concluded – somewhat prematurely – that the whole region will be engulfed in social upheavals that would remove the old regimes much like the East Europe in the 1990s. Few, however, cautioned of such generalization stressing the specificity of the nations (Khondker 2011).

The idea of entangled modernity is particularly relevant to understand two seemingly disparate modes of social transformation. The changes in East and South Asia, India and China are creating opportunities for new formulations of democracy and capitalism in West Asia economic and educational developments have created a new ethos of social equality. The emergence of a national bourgeoisie in the West Asia dependent both on the state as well the global capital is not in the offing. Here state, rather than the class, is the main actor in the interface of globality. In the words of Ehteshami, 'Globalization has been pouring into the deep geopolitical grooves of this complex regional system in which culture, force, and economy form the pillars on which nation-states have been building their competitive and comparatives advantages' (Ehteshami 2013: 67).

The growing economic relationship between Saudi Arabia and China or the growing economic and cultural relationships between the United Arab Emirates and China and India are clear signs of an increasingly entangled globality, a process that would be reinforced by the declining influence of the North-Atlantic nations as the sole arbiters of an entangled globality, yet their role as reference points in the Asian dram is likely to remain unchallenged.

References

Amrith, Sunil (2013) *Crossing the Bay of Bengal: The Furies of Nature and the Fortunes of Migrants.* Cambridge: Harvard University Press.

Buchanan, Ian (1972) *Singapore in Southeast Asia: An Economic and Political Appraisal.* London: G. Bell and Sons Ltd.

Dirlik, Arif (2007) *Global Modernity: Modernity in the Age of Capitalism.* Boulder, CO: Paradigm Press.

Dirlik, Arif (2011) 'Guoxue/national learning in the age of global modernity', *China Perspectives* 1, pp. 1–13.

Duara, Prasenji (2015) *The Crisis of Global Modernity: Asian Traditions and a Sustainable Future.* Cambridge: Cambridge University Press.

Ehteshami, Anoushiravan (2013) *Dynamics of Change in the Persian Gulf.* London: Routledge.

Fornari, Emanuela (2007) *Modernity Out of Joint: Democracy and Asian Values in Jürgen Habermas and Amartya K. Sen.* Aurora, CO: The Davies Group Publishers.

Hobsbawm, Eric (2005) 'Retreat of the male', *London Review of Books*, 27, 15, 4 August, pp. 8–9 (also included in this volume).

Holcombe, Charles (2011) *A History of East Asia: From the Origins of Civilization to the Twenty-First Century.* Cambridge: Cambridge University Press.

Khondker, Habibul (2011) 'Many roads to modernization in the Middle East', *Society*, 48, 4, pp. 304–306.

Manjapra, Kris (2010) *M.N. Roy: Marxism and Colonial Cosmopolitanism.* New Delhi: Routledge.

Manjapra, Kris (2014) *The Age of Entanglement: German and Indian Intellectuals Across Empire.* Cambridge, Mass: Harvard University Press.

Markoff, John (1996) *Waves of Democracy: Social Movements and Political Change.* Newbury Park, CA: Pine Forge Press.

Markoff, John (1999) 'Where and when was democracy invented?', *Comparative Studies in Society and History* 41, pp. 660–690.

Mills, Lenox (1942) *British Rule in Eastern Asia.* Hong Kong: Oxford University Press.

Myrdal, Gunnar (1968) *Asian Drama: An Inquiry into the Poverty of Nations*, 3 vols. New York: Pantheon Books.

Nath, Ramendra (2001) *M.N. Roy's New Humanism and Materialism*. Patna: Buddhiwadi Foundation.

Nath, Ramendra (nd.) 'Manabendra Nath Roy (1887–1954)', in *Internet Encyclopedia of Philosophy*.

Nehru, Jawaharlal (1994) *The Discovery of India*. Delhi: Oxford University Press.

Population Reference Bureau (2015) http://www.prb.org/pdf15/2015-world-population-data-sheet_eng.pdf (accessed on 18 January 2015).

Robertson, Roland (1992) *Globalization*. London: Sage.

Rodrik, Dani and Subramanian, Arvind (2004) *From 'Hindu Growth' to Productivity Surge: The Mystery of Indian Growth Transition*. NBER Working Paper no. 10376.

Sartori, Andrew (2008) *Bengal in Global Concept History: Culturalism in the Age of Capital*. Chicago: The University of Chicago Press.

Tathagatananda, Swami (2006) 'Dhan Gopal Mukherji and the face of silence', *Prabuddha Bharati*, January and February (two parts).

Therborn, Göran (1977) 'The rule of capital and the rise of democracy', *New Left Review* 103.

Therborn, Göran (1978) *What Does the Ruling Class Do When it Rules?* London: Verso.

Therborn, Göran (1995) *European Modernity and Beyond: The Trajectory of European Societies, 1945–2000*. London: Sage.

Therborn, Göran (2003) 'Entangled modernities', *European Journal of Social Theory*, 6, 3, pp. 293–305.

Therborn, Göran (2004) *Between Sex and Power: Family in the World 1900–2000*. London: Routledge.

Therborn, Göran and Khondker, Habibul H. (eds.) (2006) *Asia and Europe in Globalization: Continents, Regions and Nations*. Leiden: Brill.

Wong, Lin-Ken (1978) 'Singapore: Its growth as an entrepot port, 1819–1941', *Journal of Southeast Asian Studies* 9, pp. 50–84.

World Bank (2015) http://data.worldbank.org/news/release-of-world-development-indicators-2015 (accessed on 17 January 2015).

GABRIELLA ELGENIUS

The Principles and Products of the Identity Market

Identity, Inequality and Rivalry

This chapter explores the principles and products of the identity market and associated power relations through a closer look at collective rituals, ceremonies, commemorations, holidays and festivals (religious or national) in Europe. In view of Therborn's significant scholarly contributions about structures of inequality in the modern world within different nation-building arenas (see e.g. Therborn 1995, 2002, forthc.; Bekker and Therborn 2012), collective rituals are here analysed as 'power scripts' exposing related power struggles and inequalities. The following arguments are proposed for the purposes of this chapter: (a) Collective rituals constitute 'symbolic repertoires' (Spillman 1997) that make claims about identities through the (re-) production of values and norms. (b) Identity products, rituals and symbols, correspond to identity claims that, in turn, are embedded in official history narration. (c) Through closer inspection claims about identity and history expose 'rival claims', identifiable through patterns of collective and national symbolism called 'symbolic regimes' (traced alongside the establishment of symbols and rituals as these are adopted, modified, abolished during pivotal times of nation-building) within which appear 'rival clusters' of rituals and counter-rituals in clusters of symbolism and counter-symbolism, (Elgenius 2011a, 2011b, 2015). (d) Collective rituals are therefore intimately connected with official political memory and the choice of some histories at the expenses of others to reproduce and justify domineering structures (Connerton 1989). Structures of inequality are thus embedded in all aspects of ceremonial development such as with the conceptual

tools of membership (Bhambra 2016), history narration, ritualization of official memory and access to these processes as well as access
to actual participation (Elgenius 2014, 2016a). In general terms, the
working classes, women and ethnic groups gained access to collective rituals in Europe at a later stage than to other social institutions
(Gillis 1996) and the history of access to the ceremonial field and
related contestations remains a significant function of social change
and the democratisation of social and national memory. The various
cases below are drawn from different socio-political, socio-economic
and historical contexts and shed light on the arguments proposed in
various forms and guises.

The nexus of principles and products of the identity market is
thus one closely associated with political and economic power and
includes the competition over history and heritage resources. Below
a brief outline of the main identity producing principles in terms of
self-reference, differentiation and recognition, before turning to the
products these principles generate. In Therborn's writings, the basis
for collective ritual expression in Europe is derived from Christianity,
commemoration of war, and social class, the latter seemingly offering
a lighter ritual baggage and symbolic repository than do the others.

Identity principles: differentiation, self-reference and competitive recognition

The principles of identity construction refer to the construction
of cognitions, norms and values connected to processes of *identity
enculturation* and identities as continuously produced and reproduced, constructed and reconstructed:

> The process of identity formation may be seen as composed of three
> crucial moments: by differentiation, by the settlement of self-reference
> or self-image, and by the recognition of others. (Therborn 1995: 229.)

Identity formation relies on these three main and simultaneous processes that generate a set of structural counterparts of boundaries,
rights, means, actions and opportunities (1995: 228) and generate

the prerequisites for identity products. Boundary making is multi-referential by nature (Turner 1969) simultaneously oppositional and relational (Cohen 1995) by references to the in-group and to the out-group, 'others', 'otherness' and 'outside-ism'. Some boundaries are blurred, others bright and in different ways associated with ambiguity or clarity (Alba 2005). In times of uncertainty, boundaries are embellished and provide an opportunity for 'national architects and entrepreneurs' to produce for the identity market. Identity products, such as the public rituals in Europe, brighten communal boundaries. In general terms; all communities depend on the manipulation and embellishment of symbolic and ritual elements as they authenticate and reproduce boundaries. These play a vital role in enforcing and reviving official history, heritage, memory and visualization of togetherness, commonality and uniqueness of the group. The nationalist discourse becomes integral to every-day-life situations (by Billig defined as banal nationalism) and enables more extreme forms of the extensive flagging of boundaries (1995).

With the above in mind, boundaries are drawn around social distinctions imposed by ethnic majorities on diverse groups. Building on Barth (1969) and Merton's theory of reference groups (Merton 1957) Therborn argues that boundaries define groups by settling on self-reference and self-image as 'key movements of differentiation' and 'the supply and demand of reference images, and for positive and negative recognition' (1995: 232). The processes of self-reference, differentiation and recognition are therefore not easily separated, with or against the boundary making of others. There is a wealth of examples of identity- or recognition-politics, historically or contemporary. Everything else being equal, as Therborn observes, 'the less value the present appears to provide, the more important the past, the more important ethnicity' (1995: 231). Seemingly the same applies to nations-to-be and related nation-building processes within and without nations. Identity politics on behalf of ethnic minorities and diaspora communities follow similar patterns with the formation of organisations and campaigns for recognition, being positioned in between different spaces of identity-politics – the first space of the majority and the third space of hybrid and cosmopolitan mixtures

(Hutnyk 2010; Van Hear 2015; Vertovec 2010). Civil society activity in the diaspora is therefore suitably analysed as relational and processual phenomena. Diaspora civil society making is developing in relation to the majority and other minorities as a space for protection and group *elevation* and as a struggle for recognition against *devaluation*. In the context of permanent settlement of ethnic groups, linking ethnicity to social class is therefore integral for the analysis of diaspora activism (Elgenius 2016b).

Products of and rivals on the identity market: making 'we' of public rituals

Therborn analyses the power scripts of public rituals in Europe, within the contexts of main 'steering projects' post-1945: the formation of the European Union in Western Europe and the influence of socialism in Eastern Europe. In *European Modernity and Beyond: The Trajectory of European Societies, 1945–2000* he explores the central connections between collective identity, the role of collective memory and collective rituals. The route towards European modernity appears with regards to such connections as one of rival narratives and contestations – without the boundaries of modernity necessarily contested. Public rituals are boundary creating and 'have their architects, their entrepreneurs and their builders, who vary in their competitiveness on the imperfect identity market' (Therborn 1995: 229). Rituals help authenticate boundaries through cultural codes, symbolic forms and communicative action between those who belong and those who do not and are therefore significant empirical variables through which we may understand collective identities:

> A collective identity is not just an identity held in common in their souls by an aggregate of individuals. As a rule it is also a public thing, manifested in and sustained by public rituals. (Therborn 1995: 223.)

Commemorative practices are heavy repositories of symbolic capital and legitimises heritage and cultural memory through the dramatization and performativity of national history. For Connerton, 'commemorative ceremonies prove to be commemorative only in so far they are performative; performativity cannot be thought without a concept of habit; and habit cannot be thought without a notion of bodily automatisms' (1989). The dramatization of cultural memory turns the latter into personal, cognitive and socially habits. Spillman argues that history and memory are culturally reproduced within broader discursive fields of meaning and that ceremonies, commemorations and rituals constitute symbolic repertoires of national identity claims (1997: 9). Developing Shil's (1988) distinction between the norm-producing centres versus the periphery, she highlights the imperial and unequal dimensions associated with ritual production and as ways by which cultural centres promote value systems and norms. Cultural centres are defined by their closeness to value production whereas peripheries are recipients of norms and values. For this chapter on public rituals in Europe, the distinction centre-periphery is central and exposes related hierarchies and political relations: 'memory is as central to modern politics as politics is central to modern memory', argues Gillis (1996) too. Politics and rivalry are therefore intimately connected to collective identities and by default central to ceremonial life, building on historical narratives and heritage traditions (see Berger 2014) that have come to serve and justify social hierarchies with the aim to enforce bonds, motivate action, confer honour and justify authority (Cerulo 1995). Political memory and official histories are visible also through other collective identity products such as national flags (Eriksen and Jenkins 2007), capital cities, statues, city squares, museums or academies. When explored in clusters of nation-building the patterns of identity productions contain important clues also about existing power relations.

The public rituals in Europe also speak of common origins and trajectories. Eyeing around for rituals and ceremonies in Europe, Therborn argues that these are to be found in three main clusters based on Christian values, connected to the European wars and the commemorations of the fallen or associated with demonstrations of social class for equality. We return to these ritual foundations in various cases below, drawn from different socio-political, socio-economic and historical contexts in order to shed light on the complex nexus of collective identity, ritualization, memory creation, contestation and underlying rivalry.

The Church and the Nation

Therborn argues that 'the collective identity of Europeans is still more than anything else a religious, a Christian identity. The latter is not primarily an embrace of Christian theology as participation in the great Christian holidays' (1995: 234). Christian rituals besides Christmas and Ester also include christenings, confirmations and burials and from this perspective, the main basis for collective identity and boundary creation in Europe. True, the European public calendar is in effect a Christian one evolving around annual public and private rituals. Given, Christianity's originally central role in European ceremonial life and control over values and norms, life and death, it is especially interesting that the Church's exclusive role in public life was increasingly challenged with the nationally inspired celebrations (public national holidays and national days) that came to constitute a younger strata of rituals in Europe – a process that commenced after the French Revolution and the forming of modern nations characterized by mass-participation and citizenship. In effect, these were imagined as the union of *one* people and *one* state, expressed via the aspirations of one dominant culture asserting itself. These new ritual and national contexts officially negated inequalities in the public sphere and made people, at least, ritually equal (Kapferer 1988).

A unique case of ritual contestation was made on behalf of the French Republic attempting to institutionalise a revolutionary calendar with rituals, public celebrations around statues, parades, processions and commemorations (Hutchinson 2009) echoing the ideological rationale of liberty, equality, brotherhood of the Revolution – removing hereby the religious and royal references (Alter 1994) dominating public life. The republicans replaced Virgin Mary with Goddesses of Reason and transformed churches into temples of the nation, most notably the Cathedral of Notre Dame that became the Temple of Reason and the Panthéon a temple *aux grands hommes la patrie reconnaissante* (Ozouf and Furet 1989). However, most of the revolutionary initiatives rendered unsuccessful according to Ozouf (1988) who argues that the exclusive control of the Catholic Church over public rituals and public space in France was nevertheless challenged. This also marked the transition of ceremonial change with the institutionalisation towards a *national* day in France with the celebrations of 14 July. The former also called Bastille Day commemorated the storming of the prison Bastille in 1789, at the time a symbol of despotism and arbitrary rule. As a national day 14 July did not take on a mass-character before the first formal celebrations in 1880 used to justify the violent reality of the revolution that brought about the first French Republic. Hundred years later it had been drained of its original and violent meaning and memory producers could attempt to make something suitable of this. Therefore, the celebration of Bastille Day 14 July was in a ceremonial proclaimed the Day the Republic received its New Testament in 1880. The religious references do not stop here. A republicanised *Pater Noster* was also recited: 'Our father, who art in the nation's *Élysée*, glory be thy name. May Liberty, Equality, and Fraternity reign through thee on earth, and may the will of our forefathers of 1789, that man should be his own master, be done. Give us this day our Liberty, and forgive us our sins against the Republic.' (Amalvi 1996: 134). Now, the enemies of the Third Republic were less convinced and contested the emerging national day celebrations as 'revolutionary saturnalia' and treasonous: 'Christianity celebrates the holidays of its God, its heroes, its saints, and its martyrs; the monarchy had its splendid national calendar: Tolbiac, Bouvines, Taillebourg, Marignano, Arques, Ivry, Rocroi, Fontenoy, Marengo, Austerlitz, Jena, Algiers, Sebastopol, Magenta. The Republic celebrates cowardice, treason, and murder' (Amalvi 1996: 129). Nevertheless, despite its origin, Bastille Day or 14 July survived as a ceremonial initiative and became the public national holiday of the Republic.

Strikingly, and with regards to the other national days in Europe the majority of national days appear from the mid 19th century onwards with the age of nationalism when national communities began to celebrate their alleged distinctiveness and hereby challenging the exclusive control of the Church. The majority of European national days appear close to the period of mass-production of invented traditions (1870–1914) as defined by Hobsbawm (1992). For comparison, out of 42 national days in Europe only 11 were introduced before 1870 (many with a religious focus that was later nationalised), 6 appear during 1870–1914 and 25 are introduced after 1914 mainly as days of Independence. This supports the argument that a new tradition had been invented by the end of the 19th century (Elgenius 2011a). The struggle between the rulers of the Church and the nation were fought ceremonially too and demonstrates how nations gained increased significance as the basis for collective identities in the ritual sphere e.g. with the increasing popularity of national day celebrations and commemorations.

Self-identity depends on 'othering' and the traces of a collective identity in Europe resting on Christianity is rather illusive in view of incompatible and rival imaginations of competing nations and nationalisms. As mentioned, identity products of nations (national days but also flags, anthems etc.) form clusters of symbolism – *symbolic regimes* – and provide clues about nation building when explored systematically. For the nations of Europe, the main identity products appear as pre-modern (pre-1789), modern (*ca.* 1789–1914) and post-imperial (*ca.* 1914–) *symbolic content.* Thus, whereas some nations e.g. via their flags or national days are represented by pre-modern religious and monarchical imagery others reproduce the symbolism linked to the ideals of the modern age. As a rule, post-imperial symbolism introduced post-1914 point towards a (suitable) past often long before the post-1914 formation (Elgenius 2005[1], 2011a, 2015). Nations and national identities and their products, it seems, collect its symbolic capital from a rich repository of the past. (There are some notable exceptions for younger formations where the past simply is too contested and therefore look towards the future.) With this in mind, nations and appear as layered and their formations on-going and visible through the adoption of public rituals, identity related symbols and products. These help us analyse collective

1. With gratitude to my supervisors Göran Therborn and Anthony D. Smith.

identities and scrutinize the processes of identity-, community- and nation-building.

War commemorations and dividing memories

Identity products generated by competing nationalism leads us to the second basis for a collective identity in Europe, with the evidence provided by public rituals devoted to commemorating the fallen. Public ceremonies of the war dead were institutionalised after the two world wars and emerged also with the aesthetics of mass politics (Mosse 1975) to inspire the living (Smith 2003). The unprecedented losses of the First World War brought about the public honouring of the fallen – a way by which sacrifice was democratised. In Britain, war commemorations were perceived as a measure to dampen resentment, as 'the government feared that Bolshevism might gain a foothold in Britain. Therefore, it was felt that everything possible should be done to use the victory to work up patriotic feeling' (Mosse 1990: 95). Traditionally, war monuments had commemorated kings, emperors or generals but public war iconography started to pay attention also to unknown soldiers. Examples are the Cenotaph in Whitehall and the Unknown Soldier's tomb in Westminster Abbey (London); *Le Tombeau du Soldat Inconnu* at *Arc de Triomphe* (Paris); the tomb to the unknown solder at the *Vittorio Emmanuele* Monument (Rome), and the Unknown Soldier by the neoclassical guardhouse (Berlin) in a defeated Germany. In Belgium a blinded veteran selected the unknown solder, in Italy a bereaved mother placed white flowers on an unknown coffin and in Romania a war orphan pointed to one of ten coffins and stated '*This is my father*' (Inglis 1993: 11).

The war cemeteries were easily distinguished from civilian ones as they turned the war dead into comrades and members of the nation. Remembering the fallen is another example of how national rhetoric and symbolism merge with Christian iconography (Moriarty 1991). The cross remained, the most common symbol on memorials after the First World War. Interestingly, the burial of the Unknown Soldier involved also Westminster Abbey in Britain where the body of the Unknown Soldier was carried through procession in London in 1920, having been selected from the cemeteries on the Western Front (King 1998). Christian imagery remains essential to commemorations of the war dead in Europe, and involves religious services and religious codes.

Originally, victory days these remembrance ceremonies transformed into commemorations of the fallen. Commemorations of the fallen in states with competing nationalities is especially noteworthy as they have turned into de facto national days as exemplified with the commemorations of war dead in Britain (Remembrance Sunday) and Belgium (Armistice Day). Having said this, in recent years, remembrance days are increasingly contested as glorifying war, as military and male by nature. The design of e.g. Remembrance Sunday in Britain has been significantly modernised to combat its appearance of being an exclusive occasion. Steps were therefore taken towards the modernising a ceremony steeped in protocol, the process of recognising and including that losses had been suffered by inclusion of the established faith communities in Britain, other than Christian, previously excluded. Representations at the Cenotaph today include also representatives of faith communities whose members lost their lives in the two world wars. Members of the Commonwealth have been invited for some time. The First World War Pardon Association representing those shot for cowardice and desertion was first invited in 2000. An initiative to formally acknowledge the contributions of all the women who worked for the war effort lead to the construction of a monument to 'Women in the Second World War' unveiled in 2005 alongside the ceremonial route of the Cenotaph – after sixty years post-Second World War. Actually, a monument to the animals that died alongside the British, Commonwealth and Allied Forces had been unveiled a year before in 2004 (Park Lane, London).

Europe clearly demonstrates a ritual pattern in terms of war commemorations, but as rituals they point to a divisive history in more ways than one.

Social class and May Day

Social class constitutes a third basis for the politics of recognition for collective identities in Europe expressed through the May Day (1 May) as a 'ritual of class, community, struggle and union' (Hobsbawm 1984: 78). Hobsbawm's study on the transformation of labour rituals describes new forms of ritualization developing spontaneously around May Day meetings and the red flag as a symbol of revolution. As part of the politics of recognition, May Day originated with the struggle for the eight-hour working day in 1886 in North America (Haverty-Stacke 2008) but was celebrated across Europe by the 1890s (and after the 1889s proclamation of the Second International). May Day asserted and defined the 'new class through class organization' (Hobsbawm 1984: 80) with the liturgy of the future (Pederson and Reiter 2016). In terms of ceremonials the latter is especially significant, in comparison to the previously discussed public rituals in Europe that are firmly anchored in the past, the labour movement had a comparatively small 'ritual baggage' as its legitimacy was derived by class-based identification.

As highlighted by Therborn, in terms of official history narration (or the important role of elite sponsorship for ritual making) only three European countries had made May Day a public holiday before the Second World War: working class history did not constitute a priority for official history narration and the history of inequality would contradict the national one based on the imagination of the 'horizontal brotherhood' (Anderson 1991). Interestingly, May Day was introduced as a public holiday in three different – we may even say contrasting political regimes – the USSR introduced May Day in 1917, Germany in 1933 and Sweden in 1938, assumingly with different agendas. After the Second World War, May Day became a main working-class holiday in most European countries in Europe and developed stable traditions in Sweden, Norway and Denmark, Austria, Belgium, Italy and Germany. In Britain, however, the labour movement was closely tied to local events and in the Netherlands May Day rivalled by the royal imagery of Queen's Day, the Queen's official birthday on 30 April and the day before May Day.

May Day celebrated universal ideals beyond nations and provided shape and form to the working class in a similar fashion that religious or national rituals provided shape to religious national groups, movements and causes. Undeniably, official group narration was a male business as per the ritual patterns above too. Moreover, even class-based identities were unable to escape nationalisation and took different forms in Europe over time and have not remained unchallenged either. The continued success of May Day demonstrations depends on revitalization, re-appropriation and the combination of protest and celebration (Pederson and Reiter 2016). (Cf. success-factors associated with national day popularity Elgenius 2011a, 2014.) The decreased significance of May Day demonstration are thus linked to the loss of character as a day of struggle and protest. In recent years, with the financial crises various anti-austerity demonstrations were unleashed in the wake of austerity (Pederson et al. 2016) For Therborn, the future of May Day events depend on the extent to which they come to include internationalist multiculturalism with global visions of sharing privilege and giving a voice for marginalised groups.

In terms of ritual equality, May Day seemingly also depend on modernisation and inclusion – the recognition of diversification of the working classes, narration of marginalisation and discourses of solidarity to survive over time. This is especially interesting in view of recent May Day findings that middle-class participants outnumber working-class protesters (see Pederson et al. 2016; Wahlström 2016). This has something to tell us about the changing dynamics of political engagement and the exclusive understanding of solidarity in the contexts of identity.

Concluding reflections

For the purposes of this chapter, rituals, ceremonies and commemorations, have been analysed as dramatizations of values and provide groups with 'a definite shape and force, both by projecting certain images and by enabling people to come together in ways which seem directly to express the solidarity' (Breuilly 1993: 64). By default, public rituals will therefore manifest structures of inequality and contestation, through underlying group narrations, participation in and access to these. Since the discourse of nationalism is promoted as *one* of social solidarity and the rhetoric of solidarity, in turn, is based on nationalist claims (Calhoun 2007) of dominant groups. The heterogeneity of nations is seldom reflected in ceremonial contexts. In some ways public rituals are exclusive and divisive by nature, and their design rather contradictory to fulfil their Durkheimian functions. With regards to the popularity of ritual products such as national days, research indicates that modernization, democratisation and inclusion figure as paramount for survival over time as has been mentioned. Seemingly, ethnic groups, women and working classes were invited into public rituals at a later stage than they gained the right to vote or gained access to education – and were not perceived as contributors to history narration or ritual making. Although May Day demonstrations stand out as challenging dominant structures, these also have to relate to discourses of solidarity and membership with the selection of some narratives over others. To this discussion of public rituals Therborn's significant work on national capitals (Therborn 2002, forthc.; Bekker and Therborn 2012) could preferably be added. National capitals are in a similar fashion to public rituals key manifestations and representations of power with the structuring of social relations as 'power scripts' of architecture, monumentality and functionality.

The rituals in Europe are here understood as narrative processes that in Bhaba's (1993) terms resembles the construction of narratives in novels, films, or indeed, in history books. In order to achieve a coherent master narrative, nations rely on narrators' and narrative texts that cannot accommodate contradictions (exclusion of marginalised groups or repressed issues or the misrepresentations of enemies) if they are to tell a story that makes sense of *one* group with a well-defined origin. Thus, all narratives of group history and heritage presuppose both ambivalence and contestation between told and untold histories. Public rituals therefore have much to tell us about underlying structures of inequality related to discourses of group boundaries, 'heritage' or 'history' whether based on religion, nation or class. Studying community rituals, their origins, developments and designs, help us explore many aspects of collective identities and related discursive elements of community, solidarity, cohesion and identity branding. With regards to the identity market, the production of symbolic measures by the European Commission is of interest. The European Commission looked to the nation for inspiration when it introduced a European flag, a European anthem and a Europe Day (Shore 2000, 1993) – to raise awareness among Europeans about their heritage. The EU flag, for instance, in representing the whole of Europe were devised to steer away from the symbolism of European ancestry linked to Christian imagery, heraldic designs or images related to republicanism associated with many European flags. Instead, the EU flag was devised to be multi-national, multi-ethnic and inclusive – as it displayed a circle of twelve gold stars on a blue background denoting the union. Given the complexity of history in and of Europe, its rival histories and narratives, it would be a challenge to find meaningful, uniting and non-contested symbols. The European entourage of symbolism have also been associated with controversy in several contexts.

For the purposes of this chapter, the symbolic repertoires underlying the public rituals of Europe have been explored in terms of main foundations for collective identity: Christianity, war and social class. Christian rituals, war commemorations and class-based demonstrations negotiate at their core different power relations, structures and dimensions of inclusion. Collective rituals based on religion, wars (competing nationalisms) or social class merge, from this perspective, in Europe's ritual life. The ritual patterns of Europe also fundamentally challenge the notion of a collective identity through a history of rival narratives within Christian branches (also in relation to other world religions in Europe) between the enemies of competing nationalisms and world wars deeply embedded in the symbolism of nations and states. The nations of Europe do not share the wars or the fallen – visible through the practices and foci of commemorations excluding former enemies and marginalized contributions or sacrifices within. Moreover, the cultural legacies of imperialism, racial hierarchies and inequalities raise further questions about boundary making, ways of perceiving and being perceived, being representation in and access to the imagined community (Anderson 1991) and begs the question 'whose imagined community' (Chatterjee 1993, 2004). Nations are marked by cultural differences and the heterogeneous histories of contending peoples. Bhambra (2016) therefore argues for the need to historicize conceptual tools as central dimension of identity and membership. For instance, in the recent British referendum on EU membership in June 2016 and the campaign and win for the Leave Campaign, exposed the entrenched discriminatory patterns with regards to 'citizenship' in relation to 'in' and 'out'. British citizens were stripped of their membership or citizenship and turned into 'immigrants' on the basis of racial hierarchies that reproduce injustices of the past along the lines of imperial modes of governance. Similar modes of exclusion are also found in the context of social class in the public sphere, as understandings of being 'British', 'English' or 'working class' is equated with being 'white'. Thus, there is a need to consider the role of race, ethnicity and the historical legacies of exclusion, with reference to both theoretical and empirical dimensions of identity politics and public rituals underpinning collective identities in Europe.

References

Alba, R. (2005) 'Bright versus blurred boundaries: second-generation assimilation and exclusion in France, Germany and the United States', *Journal of Ethnic and Racial Studies* 28, 20–49.

Alter, P. (1994) *Nationalism*, 2nd ed. London: Edward Arnold.

Amalvi, C. (1996) 'Bastille Day: From Dies Irae to holiday', in Nora, P. (ed.) *Realms of Memory: The Construction of the French Past*, vol. 3 *Symbols*. New York: Columbia University Press, pp. 117–162.

Anderson, B. (1991) *Imagined Communities: Reflections on the Origin and Spread of Nationalism*. London: Verso.

Aronsson, P. and Elgenius, G. (eds.) (2015) *National Museums and Nation-building in Europe 1750–2010: Mobilization and Legitimacy, Continuity and Change*. London: Routledge.

Bekker, S. and Therborn, G. (eds.) (2012) *Capital Cities in Africa: Power and Powerlessness*. Cape Town: HSRC Press.

Berger, S. (2014) *The Past as History National Identity and Historical Consciousness in Modern Europe*. Basingstoke: Palgrave.

Bhabha, H. (ed.) (1993) *Nation and Narration*. London: Routledge.

Bhambra, G. (2016) 'Viewpoint: Brexit, class and British "national" identity', *Discover Society*, 5 July. Available at http://discoversociety.org/2016/07/05/viewpoint-brexit-class-and-british-national-identity/.

Billig, M. (1995) *Banal Nationalism*. London: Sage Publications.

Breuilly, J. (1993) *Nationalism and the State*. Manchester: Manchester University Press.

Calhoun, C. (2007) *Nations Matter: Culture, History and the Cosmopolitan Dream*. London: Routledge.

Cerulo, K. (1995) *Identity Designs: The Sights and Sounds of a Nation*. New Jersey: Rutgers University Press.

Chatterjee, P. (1993) *The Nation and its Fragments: Colonial and Postcolonial Histories*. Princeton: Princeton University Press.

Chatterjee, P. (2004) 'Whoose imagined community?', in Chatterjee, P., *The Politics of the Governed: Reflections on Popular Politics in Most of the World*. New York: Columbia University Press.

Cohen, A. (1995) *The Symbolic Construction of Community*. London: Routledge.

Colley, L. (1992) *Britons: Forging the Nation, 1707–1837*. New Haven, CT: Yale University Press.

Connerton, P. (1989) *How Societies Remember*. Cambridge: Cambridge University Press.

Durkheim, E. (1976) *The Elementary Forms of the Religious Life*, 2nd ed. London: George Allen.

Elgenius, G. (2005) *Expressions of Nationhood: National Symbols and Ceremonies in Contemporary Europe*. PhD thesis, The London School of Economics and Political Science (LSE). Published open access: http://etheses.lse.ac.uk/638/.

Elgenius, G. (2011a) *Symbols of Nations and Nationalism: Celebrating Nationhood*. Basingstoke: Palgrave Macmillan.

Elgenius, G. (2011b) 'The politics of recognition: Symbols, nation-building and rival nationalisms', *Nations and Nationalism*, 17, 2.

Elgenius, G. (2014) 'A formula for successful national day design', special feature: National Celebrations, *Bibliotheca Nova*, no. 1, 92–107.

Elgenius, G. (2015) 'National museums as national symbols: A survey of strategic nationbuilding; nations as symbolic regimes', in Aronsson, P. and Elgenius, G. (eds.) *National Museums and Nation-building in Europe 1750–2010: Mobilization and Legitimacy, Continuity and Change*. London: Routledge, pp. 145–166.

Elgenius, G. (2016a) 'What makes national events successful? The 200 Jubilee of the Constitution as a *Super-17 May*', in Aagedal, O. et al., *Kunsten at Jubilera*. Oslo: KIFO.

Elgenius, G. (2016b) 'Ethnic bonding and homing desires: The Polish diaspora and civil society making', in Jacobsson, K. and Korolczuk, E. (eds.) *Civil Society Revisited: Lessons from Poland.* Oxford: Berghahn Books.

Eriksen, T. H. and Jenkins, R. (eds.) (2007) *Flag, Nation and Symbolism in Europe and America.* Abingdon: Routledge.

Gillis, J.R. (ed.) (1996) *Commemorations: The Politics of National Identity.* Princeton: Princeton University Press.

Haverty-Stacke, D. (2008) *America's Forgotten Holiday: May Day and Nationalism, 1867–1960.* New York: NYU Press.

Hobsbawm, E. (1984) *Worlds of Labour. Further Studies in the History of Labour.* London: Weidenfeld and Nicolson.

Hobsbawm, E. and Ranger, T. (eds.) (1992) *The Invention of Tradition.* Cambridge University Press (Canto ed.).

Hutchinson, J. (2009) 'Warfare and the sacralisation of nations: The meanings, rituals and politics of national remembrance', *Millennium*, 38, 2, 401–417.

Hutnyk, J. (2010) 'Hybridity', in Knott, K. and McLoughlin, S. (eds.) *Diasporas: Concepts, Intersections, Identities.* New York: Zed Books, pp. 59–62.

Immerfall, S. and Therborn, G. (eds.) (2010) *Handbook of European Societies: Social Transformations in the 21st Century.* New York: Springer.

Inglis, K. (1993) 'Entombing unknown soldiers: From London and Paris to Baghdad', *History and Memory*, 5, 2, 7–31.

Kapferer, B. (1988) *Legends of People, Myths of State: Violence, Intolerance and Political Culture in Sri Lanka and Australia.* Washington DC: Smithsonian Institution Press.

King, A. (1998) *Memorials of the Great War in Britain: The Symbolism of Politics of Remembrance*, series: The Legacy of the Great War. Oxford: Berg.

Moriarty, C. (1991) 'Christian iconography and First World War memorials', *Imperial War Museum Review*, no. 6, pp. 63–75.

Mosse, G. (1975) *The Nationalization of the Masses: Political Symbolism and Mass Movements in Germany from the Napoleonic Wars Through the Third Reich.* New York: Howard Fertig.

Mosse, G. (1990) *Fallen Soldiers: Reshaping the Memory of the World Wars.* Oxford: Oxford University Press.

Nora, P. (ed.) (1996) *Realms of Memory: The Construction of the French Past*, vol. 3, *Symbols*. New York: Colombia University Press.

Ozouf, M. (1988) *Festivals and the French Revolution.* Cambridge, MA: Harvard University Press (original title: *La fête révolutionaire, 1789–1799*).

Ozouf, M. and Furet, F. (eds.) (1989) *The French Revolution and the Creation of Modern Political Culture*, vol. 3, *The Transformation of Political Culture 1789–1848*. Oxford: Pergamon Press.

Peterson, A. and Reiter, H. (eds.) (2016) *The Ritual of May Day in Western Europe: Past, Present and Future*. Farnham: Ashgate.

Peterson, A., Wahlström, M., Wennerhag, M., Christancho, C. and Sabucedo, J.M. (2012) 'May Day demonstrations in five European countries', *Mobilization*, 17, 3, 281–300.

Shore, C. (1993) 'Inventing the "people's Europe": critical perspectives on European Community cultural policy', *Man*, 28, 4.

Shore, C. (2000) *Building Europe: The Cultural Politics of European Integration*. London: Routledge.

Smith, A.D. (2003) *Chosen Peoples: Sacred Sources of National Identity*. Oxford: Oxford University Press.

Spillman, L. (1997) *Nation and Commemoration: Creating National Identities in the United States and Australia*. Cambridge: Cambridge University Press.

Therborn, G. (1995) *European Modernity and Beyond: The Trajectory of European Societies, 1945–2000*. London: Sage.

Therborn, G. (2002) 'Monumental Europe: The national years: On the iconography of European capital cities', *Housing, Theory and Society*, 19, 1.

Therborn, G. (forthc.) *Cities and Power. Worldwide Perspectives*. Forthcoming book.

Turner, V.W. (1969) *The Ritual Process*. London: Routledge & Kegan Paul.

Van Hear, N. (2015) 'Spheres of diaspora engagement', in Sigona, N. et al. (eds.) *Diasporas Reimagined: Spaces, Practices and Belonging*. Oxford: Oxford Diasporas Programme.

Vertovec, S. (2010) 'Cosmopolitanism', in Knott, K. and McLoughlin, S. (eds.) *Diasporas: Concepts, Intersections, Identities*. New York: Zed Books, pp. 63–68.

Wahlström, M. (2016) 'Why do people demonstrate on May Day?', in Peterson, A. and Reiter, H. (eds.) *The Ritual of May Day in Western Europe: Past, Present and Future*. Farnham: Ashgate.

ZHANNA KRAVCHENKO, LISA KINGS
& SVEN HORT

Power Ideology and Transformations of Space

Leningrad/St Petersburg and Stockholm Contrasted

> It is normal in modern times that a younger generation of schol-
> ars finds it more promising to try different paths than those
> trodden by an older one.
>
> 'Afterword' to *Transformations of the*
> *Swedish Welfare State*, Therborn 2012: 289.

During the first decade of the new millennium in particular, Göran
Therborn was a tremendous source of inspiration to those of us
researching space and urban development at Södertörn University,
the newly established Swedish Harvard in Flemingsberg, metropolitan Stockholm. Perhaps he is not aware of it? Though formally based
at SCASSS in Uppsala, between his many trips abroad he visited us
once, and on that occasion spoke about patriarchy. However, from
the late 1990s onwards Therborn had started to look into the rise of
national capital cities as symbolic representations and sites of power
focusing on architecture, iconography, nomenclature and urban layout. We are still waiting for the final outcome of this global project. However, already in 2003 Therborn's 'Monumental Europe: The
national years: On the iconography of European capital cities', first
published 2002 in *Housing, Theory and Society* was translated into
Swedish and printed in the journal *Arkiv* (no. 90).

At the same time, a new cohort of researchers at Södertörn began
investigating metropolitan life and urban development around the
Baltic Sea where new-old capitals had recently seen the light of day.

On the one hand, the establishment of the Baltic and East European Graduate School provided fertile ground for novel approaches to social transformation in the Far North in aftermath the Soviet Empire's fall. On the other hand, the sudden crisis faced by Sweden's capital in the 1990s made possible the formation of a research group interested in the mechanisms behind the emerging killing fields of inequality in the very center of welfare and modern social policies: homelessness, racial and residential segregation, stigmatized and medialized suburbs, unemployment, urban decay, welfare protest movements as well as policy responses from the powers of the day (cf. Pred 2000). The role of traditional social movements in urban civil society took on a special meaning (Kings 2011 and 2010; also Papakostas 2012; Olofsson 1987). Apart from those of Therborn the works of Mike Davis (2006; 1990), Norbert Elias (2000; 1965), Marco d'Eramo (2003) and Gunnar Olofsson (2000, 1999; also Gough and Olofsson 1999) were instrumental in challenging received wisdom in this field of social and spatial action and research (cf. Aidukaite and Frölich 2015; Lindström 2014).

Parallel trajectories, divergent (hi)stories?

Inspired by Therborn's early work on symbolic representations of urban spaces this article analyses urban planning by exploring conceptualisations of space in two European cities: Stockholm and Leningrad/St Petersburg. Planning processes are often treated as passive instruments of politics or capital, while symbolic aspects of planning in fact carry significant weight as they provide relevant representations of spaces in addition to economic and political goals and means of spatial development. This study examines the unfolding of underpinning ideological principles embedded in main documents for city planning to link commonalities and differences in socio-political contexts to their spatial organisation. In line with Brown (2001), Therborn (cf. also Le Galès and Therborn 2010), and Marcuse and van Kempen (2000), our point of departure is a comparative approach which takes into account the parallel processes of continuity and change in specific national surroundings. With this approach we also want to challenge the underlying notion especially evident in East/West comparisons, where one geographical entity is seen as being at an earlier stage of development and should with time, follow its antipode. Such a view establishes a deterministic relationship between time and space, where space becomes subordinated by time and geography is restricted by history. Following Massey we see the need to address space as the simultaneity of difference that cannot be annihilated by time (2005: 90).

Since this study is focused on transformation of ideas about space over time in cross-national perspective, we used city plans as 'books of ideas' and not mere policy documents or drama stories (Mandelbaum 1990). The central point of each plan are highlighted and connected to ideas and conceptions of different but dominant ideologies, power regimes and 'subjectivities' (cf. Therborn 1981; also the exchange between Abercrombie et al. 1983 and Therborn 1984). More precisely, we examined sections that define goals and targets of plans, their formulation, and degree of precision and order of appearance of goals and targets with the aim to capture the overarching ideology embedded in representation of space. Therefore, details on how the plans were developed, which agencies and actors were involved, and what power relations were constructed were excluded from the analysis. Such an approach is not common among researchers because the process of conceiving of space is not formally separated from the process of institutionalizing and enacting plans. Nonetheless, general plans are not *meant* to serve as 'daily blueprints'. Because a large part of planning coordination and urban management occurs spontaneously between various organizations, the content of the representations of space contained in plans can be analytically distinguished from the role of agency in the planning process.

Using general city (master)[1] plans of Leningrad/St Petersburg (1966 and 2005) and Stockholm (1952 and 1999), henceforward

---

1. Although the term 'master plan' is used more often in relation to this type of documents, this study uses 'general plan' as a category that is semantically close to categories used in respective languages: '*генеральный план*' in Russian and '*generalplan*' in Swedish (before 1987). Unless otherwise stated all translations from Russian and Swedish is ours (ZK and LK).

GPG 1966, StPL 2005, and GPS 1952 and ÖPS 1999 respectively, we illuminate how normative perceptions related to ideological paradigms are placed into a spatial dimension and how social and economic targets are translated into questions of space. St Petersburg is a city that during its rather short (by European standards) history has acquired both imperial and socialist heritage and has gone through an extreme form of rapid ideological, organizational and economic transformation since the abrupt fall of the Soviet Union, recently re-inventing itself as a 'world city' (Golubchikov 2004). Stockholm, which still to some extent can be seen as a physical manifestation of 20th century social democratic politics has gone through a more timid but nonetheless significant form of reconstruction (cf. Hall 1999). The analysis compares two moments in the history of both countries – the period of 1950–1960s and the early 2000s in order to explore how national and global moral-spiritual processes are reflected in different localities across time. The selected countries have experienced significant systemic shifts, albeit of a different magnitude, over the last decades (cf. Therborn 1992). This provides an opportunity to reveal different nuances of the transformation of planning ideals in countries with different balance of power relations, political-institutional arrangements and patterns of socio-spatial inequalities. Otherwise, fundamental theoretical and methodological concerns have been addressed elsewhere (Kings and Kravchenko 2013; also Kravchenko 2008).

Suffice to say, the two cities selected as case studies have experienced different approaches to planning throughout their history but they belong to the few cities that had general (usually twenty-year) development plans throughout their modern history. St Petersburg has evolved from the imperial capital of the Russian Empire and a second-tier yet culturally esteemed Soviet city to a rejuvenated capitalist '*metropolia Russia*'. The history of city planning in St Petersburg/Leningrad accounts for five general plans: 1935/39, 1948, 1966, 1987 and 2005. This study analyses the last four decades of the city's history with two nodal points – the 1960s (both previously classified documents for the general plan that were accepted in 1962 and the publically available version of the plan from 1966)[2] and the 2000s. In Russia, the general plan is defined as a guiding document for city developers, which outlines the trends of the use and management of city's space but does not elaborate on exact details of these trends. Usually plans include specifications of prospect transport development; infrastructure (heat, energy, water and gas supply, sanitary services); industry construction and development; housing construction and development; business construction and development; recreation construction and development; and development of protected territories (national parks) and constructions (e.g. UNESCO heritage).

Stockholm has a long history of different approaches to urban governance stretching from the time it was a small merchant city during the mid-1200s, becoming the capital of Sweden during the 1600s (the period when the country became in its self-image a great power, or semi-periphery, in Europe) to a laboratory of social democratic interventions during the 1900s. The history of city planning in Stockholm's accounts for three general plans: the first one is dated 1952 and was applied for development planning until 1991, the next one was enacted in 1999, and the most recent one was officially accepted in 2012 after a long period of public debate. Since 1987, it became compulsory to develop overarching plans for city development in Sweden and they changed their name from general to 'outline plans' (*översiktsplaner*). All documents are in open public access. The general/outline plan determines the fundamental physical characteristics of the city space, for instance prescribing *where* new housing districts would appear. It acts as a guiding document with the objective of being 'flexible'. It is running only throughout a period of five years, when adjustments can be introduced. The general plan is complemented by binding detailed city plans, which embrace smaller areas and determine more precise targets for city development, such as *when* and at *what cost* residence estates will be built.

---

2. Considering the fact that general city plans were not publically available during the Soviet period, three versions of the text of the plan were examined in order to capture representations targeted at both professional and general public.

Space: goals, objectives and principles

In the Soviet Union, urbanization was viewed as an integral element in the process of socioeconomic and cultural development. It was seen as a two-stage development: *concentration* and accumulation of the 'achievements of the material and spiritual production' in large cities, and then *dissemination* of these achievements to other peripheral towns and rural settlements, giving new impulse for increasing the potential of the centres (Kogan 1982: 9). This duality was expected, on one hand, to stimulate differentiation between different regions, cities, and even city districts, and, on the other hand, to gradually eliminate these differences and increase equality among them. This idea of translating progress from the centre to the periphery fits very well into the conception of centralized planning as such, defining the archetype of Soviet governance.

By the end of the communist era many of the problems confronting Soviet planners on the ground were not essentially different from those being faced in the West (French 1995). Among the significant specific challenges that were formulated in academic discussions was the need to develop planning legislation, to reconsider the technocratic approach, and to establish the relationship between agents within the public sector and between the public and the private sectors (Golubchikov 2004). Reforms of the 1990s promised a *new* impulse for urban development as a result of opened opportunities for local self-government and private initiative, and new ideological prospects. All these processes were mirrored in the history of the transformation of Leningrad/St Petersburg and its plans.

The Swedish social democratic welfare state originated in distrust against possibilities of the market to organize a society that served the public good and the role of cities and further urbanization was a central issue in the creation of the new welfare state (Hort 2014). In contrast to the socialist-communist ideal that perceived the notion of democratization of ownership as essential, the social democratic perception and practice was based on commodification of space, though strictly controlled by centralized planning. During this time centralized planning involved shared responsibility between

state and local authorities of public funds, co-operative ownership of apartment blocks, state aid for construction and production (Franzén 1986; Franzén and Sandstedt 1981). This meant that
the involvement of private actors to a large degree was limited to
the production of housing. During the 1980s, public control in city
planning decreased, and possibilities for private actors to influence
the city planning process increased. Internal processes of ideological
transformations and external processes of globalization and Sweden
entering the European Union (1995) accompanied this process.
Although the current restructuring of the Swedish welfare state in
favor of market expansion in the era of global capitalism and neoliberalism cannot be compared with the drastic transformation that
has occurred in Russia, the new conditions for city planning follow,
to some extent, similar patterns.

The following empirical presentation includes a general overview
of each plan – as already mentioned GPG 1966, GPS 1952, ÖPS
1999 and StPL 2005 – as well as a description of central themes identified in them, focusing especially on the ideal of equality in the first
time period, and the ideal of the 'European/global city' in the contemporary period. Detailed analyses of these themes are provided in
four following separate sections below starting with the bigger one
of the two Baltic cities and its second post-war plan.

Plan Leningrad 1966

The first Soviet/Russian case in this study dates to the mid-1960s,
when it became clear that the first post-World War II plan (1948)
outgrew its usefulness, and the Khrushchev Thaw signified a new
stage in the city's development, allowing the formulation of new
priorities different from the demands of the early post-war reconstruction period. Once completed, the new plan provided general
guidelines for future detailed plans for the city's 16 districts in the
form of 5-year plans during the next quarter of the century (cf.
Ruble 1990).

The structure of the plan concerned six major issues 1) the size
of the population, 2) housing construction, 3) social infrastructure,

4) territorial development, 5) transport and plumbing and heating installations, and 6) suburban areas. The Leningrad plan did not have a separate section outlining guiding norms and principles. As several years later the main architect of the plan emphasised, there were two main general goals: to limit population growth and move the city closer to the sea (Kamenskii 1972). Our analysis highlights that these two goals had a common denominator, improving the living and housing standards of the population.

The first goal was common for large metropolitan areas in the Soviet Union (including the capital city of Moscow), frequently motivated by the problem of high density of population as a negative factor for the quality of living. More importantly, it was dictated by poor housing conditions and the fact that housing construction was financed on the residual basis and the government was unable to meet the demands with adequate supply generating the housing shortage. In contrast to the focus of the Stockholm plan on expanding the labour force, decreasing the density of population was so important that the drafters of the Plan chose to prohibit construction of any new industries, educational or research institutions. The emphasis was made on creating housing and service facilities for the residing population: '[The general plan] is a grand programme of further development and reconstruction of the city that will provide the best *conditions for work, life and recreation*, high satisfaction of their everyday needs' (GPG 1966: 6, emphasis added).

A substantial increase of housing provision – from 25.8 to 50 million square metres – was planned to be located in large yet compact prefabricated housing districts, on empty territories within the existing borders of the city, taking natural conditions and work possibilities and computing into account. In this project, micro districts (*mikroraiony*) became the basic planning unit for the construction, aiming to create comprehensive infrastructure of accommodation and social amenities, complemented by a system of public transport, or in the words of the plan author(s): 'The planning structure of the micro district provides for a comfortable, within 500 meters, allocation of services; functional zoning of territories (housing, schools, preschools, garden, and sport center) and isolation of buildings from negative [environmental] effects of public transport. [...] School becomes one of the core planning elements and determines the size of the micro districts, informed by the normative idea that children should not be deprived of family influence [which occurs if they are forced to spend a lot of time commuting between school and work]' (PGP 1964: 67).

The strong emphasis on the development of the social infrastructure and development of collective consumption was made in the presentation of future development of social infrastructure for the planned period 1966–90. One of the main ideological premises of the planned economy was the inevitable increase in wellbeing as a result of 'decreased working time, increased free-time and increased need for recreation' (GPG 1966: 11). Therefore, the development of public services was symbolically important and the Plan specified exact numbers of various facilities per 1 000 inhabitants (places in preschool and school, hospitals; working places at shops, and square meters of sports facilities): 'All facilities planned for everyday use are recommended to be allocated close to dwellings [...] or partly inside dwellings. The overall territory [allocated for such facilities] will amount to ten sq. meters per dweller' (PGP 1964: 67, 69). Although the territorial development was limited to the city borders that were formed before 1966, the increase in capacity of public transportation was planned as a key element in implementing the key principle of social settlements, i.e. short distance between the work place and place of residence.

The second goal of bringing the city closer to the Gulf of Finland had three premises: an aesthetic – creating an impressive architectural composition; a practical – developing sea transportation route further – and a social – giving residents the opportunity to enjoy the sea view and various recreational facilities. The objective of improving the living standards by means of developing suburban areas mainly as residential districts, natural reserves and healthcare institutions was pronounced. Apart from that, integration of the surrounding region – the Leningrad *oblast* – into the general layout of the city would contribute to creation of a joint labour force and connecting the centre and periphery into a *coherent* territory.

Plan Stockholm 1952

During the 1940s the late urbanisation process in Sweden conveyed serious challenges for the city planning and became an essential part of the ambitious project of a welfare state. The expansion of Stockholm, the renewal and demolition of older housing accommodation was essential for attracting the labour force for an intensified industrialisation. The development of the city was dramatic, and the extensive planning was aimed to avoid mistakes that had been revealed in cities where urbanisation had started earlier (GPS 1952: 114). From the 1940s, the character of state interventions changed: sporadic and supporting measures that were gradually introduced during two preceding decades developed into an overreaching practice of urban planning (cf. Hort 1992). The 1952 plan is as an illustrative example of this new practice. It took seven years to complete and contained a total of 500 pages divided into four different parts: 1) conditions, 2) norms and principles, 3) the plan, and 4) a timeline for realization. Two major issues were central for the formulation of the plan's main goals: continuous population growth and housing provision.

The social democratic plan underlined that further industrialization and economic development were in need of allocating the labour force. Since the location of industries was strongly linked to large urban areas, it was essential to provide the labour force with attractive residential conditions in the city in terms of standards of living, affordability and availability for all, and means of transportation (GPS 1952: 113). A special attention was paid to 'socio-psychological environment', facilities for personal development and social adaptation of coming generations of citizens: 'The size of the population within the borders of Stockholm city is not a precondition but an effect of planning. The size of the population depends on the one hand on the standard of how upcoming residential area will be built, and, on the other hand, how sanitation of the inner city will be carried out' (GPS 1952: 28). In other words, the plan did not project the future development of population, but considered it to be in direct relation to how comfortable the future city environment was to be.

City expansion was realized foremost through new construction of housing districts on unexploited land in the outskirts of the city. The new ideal for the suburbs was the so-called 'residential area', planed as a holistic concept with a neighbourhood centre, public space, green space, and recreational area, in contrast to the old inner city, where the living space were often scattered (GPS 1952: 115–124). These areas were to be organized as functional units, which also included detailed plans of housing complements and collective consumption, even industry ('ABC'). Somewhat later suburban Vällingby – the home of for instance Lisbeth and Olof Palme and their children – became the obvious showcase.

The calculations of provisional norms for construction required formulation of standardized every day routines still far from the nowadays famous family-friendly gender equality welfare policy: 'The youngest and the oldest rarely go further than one block away [from home], and according to research by the department of parks and recreation children in the city centre rarely go more than 200–300 meters to play. The married housewife has little opportunity for mobility especially during the period when small children are at home' (GPS 1952: 124). A new kind of city was to be erected, where the vibrancy of the metropolitan inner city with access to culture and work would be combined with peaceful green environment and good conditions for raising a family. An enlarged network of public transport and increased possibilities for private car traffic would connect the city's different parts and reduce long and time-consuming commutes.

In the section 'Norms and Principles' (Chapter 6 in GPS 1952), where an extensive discussion of the aim and the preconditions of planning are presented, it is made clear that planning cannot be limited to technical and economic efficiency. The physical wellbeing of inhabitants, personal development and social adjustment is contrasted against technological and economic development and must, according to the plan, be joined together in a holistic vision: 'The influence of the present on the future will be so much stronger if in our planning we narrowly adapt our solutions to the needs of today or tomorrow. Our vision of the future will therefore always constitute a weighty condition in planning' (GPS 1952: 46, English in the original[3]).

Plan Stockholm 1999

Urban development and housing policy had a central role in the shaping of the Swedish welfare state. The physical development demanded extensive coordination of efforts to bring together laws, policy areas, regulations, and public subsidies to accomplish the 'social-democratic city'. When the 1999 plan was launched during a non-social-democratic city government but initiated by the previous SD-majority, several preconditions for planning had changed since the 1950s and 60s: above all, the prospects and the support for a centralized city planning had decreased both in the academic and public debate, something that is evident throughout the plan itself. As a result, the plan of 1999 had a less extensive format and its content was of a more general nature. The plan was divided into two broad sections: the first one comprised conditions and strategies for outline planning, while the second provided guiding principles for land use, development of settlements, construction, green areas and areas of cultural-historical value. The overreaching goals included: 1) using the advantages of the Stockholm region, 2) meeting the demand for transformation and dynamism, 3) develop and make use of the quality and character of the city, 4) promoting employment, welfare and social balance, and 5) to ensure a sustainable society (ÖPS 1999: 16).

The 1999 plan is significantly different from the general plan of 1952. The first three established goals are implicitly intertwined and emphasise the unique place Stockholm takes among other European cities that is especially described in terms of the beauty and cultural heritage of the city but also – to a lesser extent – the possibilities for a comfortable everyday life for its inhabitants. It promotes the idea of increasing its attractiveness for tourists by arranging large-scale international events and spectacular architectural innovation.

---

3. The 1952 general plan for Stockholm includes a 19 pages long summary in English.

The role of Stockholm in the 'new' post-Soviet Baltic Sea region was especially accentuated: 'changes in Eastern Europe result in the fact that earlier historical relations and economic connections with the Baltic countries and Russia can be rediscovered, grown and strengthened' (ÖPS 1999: 14–15). Intensification of relations with the rest of Europe through Swedish membership in the European Union was directly mentioned through the launching of the 'European city' concept and its actions for developing sustainable cities. Related to the engagement in EU – and OECD as well – for the future of urban environment and the development of European sustainable cities was a focus on cultural, esthetical and environmental aspects. But the need for 'flexibility' is also of special concern.

Economic growth and the different strategies to increase the attractiveness of the city to achieve this goal have gained an extended focus. The social aspect, which in the earlier plan was central, has a more peripheral position. The issue of residential segregation is put forward as a concern, though the focus on good and affordable housing for all prominent in the earlier plan does no longer characterise the strategy for future development and building. Instead of promoting common standards, the plan stresses the existence of and wishes to satisfy the diverse requirements of citizens from different social groups. It distinguishes special interests of citizens with precarious patterns of residence – homeless, young, divorced with children, etc. – in need of affordable housing, those who have means to acquire higher standards of living; and those who are situated in the immigrant-dense areas. As a way of meeting these diverse demands, the construction of new high-quality (and high-cost) housing should initiate 'chains of migration' (*flyttkedjor*) within the city – those who can afford the new expensive housing would vacate their old residence for the less privileged (ÖPS 1999: 32–34).

A striking difference between the main principles for production of urban space is demonstrated by the abandonment of the idea of the possibility to steer city development by means of planning in general: '[...] physical planning is not a means of governing in the sense that it can force a development in a desired direction or guarantee that measures in fact will be realized. Those driving forces in the society, those 'many invisible hands' that are decisive for city's vitality, as well as changes in business, technology and international economy, are situated outside the sphere of competence of both state and individual communes' (ÖPS 1999: 5). 'Globalization', 'open and active planning', 'future scenarios' are the new concepts that have been introduced and illustrate the new 'cultural turn' in contemporary, 'post-modern', urban planning also in Stockholm.

Plan St Petersburg 2005

During the forty years that followed after the first discussed second post-war Leningrad plan, the city did not simply change its name; the strategy of urban development had undergone a drastic reconsideration, which was reflected in the most recent general plan from 2005. First, the plan was discussed and accepted at the level of the city's Legislative Assembly in the form of a law for the first time in the city's history. Previously, the city development was not regulated by local laws but by subordinate regulations. According to Vladimirov (2003), the socialist command system of administration did not require more comprehensive regulation mechanisms. The new approach to city planning included other social and economic actors, such as municipalities and private entrepreneurs, and required an explicit legislative framework and technocratic presentation.

Second, objectives and priorities were revised in light of new social, political and economic realities. The plan begins with two general goals: 1) to ensure stable improvement of the living standards of all groups of the population with orientation toward 'European standards'; 2) integration of the city into Russian and world economy as a multifunctional city that provides a high quality environment for living and production; strengthening the role of the city as a centre in the Baltic Sea region and North-Western Russia.

Two important aspects in interpreting the desired living standards can be mentioned here: the idea of restricting the size of the city's population was abandoned, and the persistent references to European standards in formulating indicators for development of housing, social and healthcare provision as well as recreation facilities was not accompanied with references to what those standards actually constitute. The projected growth of population by incoming migration was justified by the need to compensate for negative demographic tendencies – decrease in fertility, increase in mortality and outgoing migration – and to ensure adequate supply of labour force. Housing provision is prioritized as one of the most urgent and effective means of reaching this goal: 'An increase in the quality of life of citizens of St Petersburg with the aim to achieve average European standards, above all things, in terms of providing them with housing space no less than 35 sq. metres per person by 2025; increase in the number of organizations of social sphere (healthcare, education, sports, social protection, etc.) up to the standard level of the Russian Federation and average European level' (StPL 2005, section 2.1 'Goals of the Territorial Planning').

Similar to the earlier references to the standards of living of socialist settlements, the recurring ideal of European standard is very abstract and somewhat *ad hoc*: what is defined as prospective outcomes in the plan is to be considered an international standard. An important innovation into the concept of city space is the recognition and embracement of diversity, both in terms of the above-mentioned standards of living, economic practices and overall territorial organization. Extensive plans of renovating and transforming dilapidated and crowded housing as well as constructing new housing of high quality still focused on large prefabricated housing districts. However, individual construction is expected to grow substantially: by 2025 the share of housing space produced in the form of one-family houses was expected to be larger than the share of apartment estates (3.7 and 3.3 sq. hectares respectively). Although all neighbourhoods irrespective of forms of construction were planned to be integrated into the city's infrastructure, 'diversification of residential environment and used [construction] materials, construction forms and planning solutions in accordance with the diversity of urban conditions' was also expected to satisfy diverse needs of various social groups (StPL 2005, section 2.2 'Targets of the Territorial Planning').

St Petersburg's special status both as an 'Open European city' attractive for international tourism and investments, and as an important national megapolis became a veritable refrain throughout the whole plan. Creating a new façade of the city oriented towards the Baltic Sea region and the European Union aimed to integrate it into the international system of economy and politics, especially as a nodal point for shipping and land routes. As a consequence, the emphasis was made on the development of new business areas. Territorial planning was expected to follow projections for economic development which is no longer planned and aimed to be diversified, as means of increasing the city's attractiveness to new investors and new inhabitants.

Bringing power ideologies to life

We started this study scrutinizing how the process of city planning can be viewed as a part of a larger urban project in a Lefebvrian sense (Lefebvre 1991; cf. also Franzén 2004). Differences in the presentation of the plans as well as in the levels of their specificities make the comparison a challenge. It is, nevertheless, possible to conclude that the change in the political and ideological environment had a direct and predictable effect on the way representations of space in the planning documents and what directions of space transformation were accepted. The comparative analysis reveals a set of important similarities and differences.

First, although the intensive construction of socialism in Russia and social democracy in Sweden were underpinned by the same strong focus on equality, homogeneity and social cohesion, the general planning objectives were specified sometimes very differently, with the most contrasting understanding of the role of the population size for the future equality project. Soviet ideology of space conceived of urbanization as initially uneven, and therefore, distribution and location of industries and labour force was supposed to be controlled in order not to allow 'old' urban areas (like Leningrad) to continue growing (Seniavskii 2003). In Sweden, the production of spatial ideology was integrated into the project of welfare state construction with a much stronger emphasis on redistribution, through social security 'from the cradle to the grave', as a key instrument in equalization of life-chances and opportunities (Khakee 2003; cf. also Khakee, Elander and Sunesson 1995).

The idea about encompassing state responsibility for citizens' welfare was equally important for both approaches, but, while Soviet planners could expect a direct coercion in the process of implementation of their objectives, Swedish planning scenarios were to be realised in a more open manner, though under strict supervision and in co-operation with private actors. The significant and pronounced retreat of the idea of equality that followed transformations in both countries in the late 1980s and early 1990s undermined the *distribution* of resources as a mechanism for achieving wellbeing. Letting go of the notion of providing for equality through spatial organization also precludes the possibility of imposing norms of social conduct. Nevertheless, the conviction that space can and should be planned was reflected in the degree of precision with which the planning indicators were presented in the earlier plans' allowing for subsequent *control* of their realization. This approach would be incompatible with recent orientation in the later plans' toward *flexibility* in methods and attraction of capital interested in participating in dynamic creation of space.

The planning strategy aimed at unifying and equalising the physical environment in Soviet Russia has on a broad range been criticized for producing a poor aesthetic culture (Cooke 1997), failure to solve the problem of housing shortage, and strengthening rather than eliminating inequalities in access to housing (Bessonova 1992). In Sweden, especially the neighbourhoods built during the Million Dwellings Programme (*Miljonprogrammet*) launched in relation to the 1952 plan have been criticised for being too uniform, too large scaled and even as 'no-go' areas reserved for society's least privileged in both professional, academic and public debates (Hall and Vidén 2005; also Hedin et al. 2012). Although these are valid and important observations, a less often discussed element of the spatial organization embedded in the planning is the normative censure of the everyday life. In Sweden, it was rooted in the notion of the Swedish 'people's home' (*folkhemmet*)[4] and the conception of the city as an

4. A social democratic idiom from 1930s for the expanding welfare state.

organism with the division between 'the others' and 'us'. The city planning and housing policy has also been a way of trying to discipline and normalize *the others* through residence patterns. The objective of equality in this sense included perceptions of 'sameness' and thereof contained excluding practices (Molina 1997). In Russia, the regulation of everyday practices was grounded in the subjection of the domestic realm, the strong normative notions of good and bad practices (and not only bad taste as Buchli (1997) asserted). It is not only the space that is allocated when the city's economic and political structure takes shape, it is also the activities (child raising, consumption, leisure, etc.) that are expected to be carried out in that physical environment. The sanctioning of individual behaviour is realised by making deviant practices uncomfortable or impossible, the disciplining policy that was developed and successfully employed decades earlier (Meerovich 2008). The critique of city planning in Sweden and Soviet Russia during this time follows the line of a more general critique of post-war modernistic planning as such (cf. Jacobs 1961). This also emphasises the common influences with regard to spatial representations in different systemic worlds.

Second, as the rhetoric of both contemporary plans aspires to create a comfortable urban environment, equality, no longer a prerequisite of successful economic development and an end-goal, is still present in the planning discourse and considered to be a result of innovative marketing and investments, *adjustment* to the demands and opportunities of the market. This finding is not surprising in the light of recent global socio-economic, cultural, political, and spatial restructuring which made cities and urban regions into denationalized platforms for economic and symbolic power in the new global economy (Castells 1996; Friedmann 2002; cf. also Therborn 2011). It is especially important to note that political, economic and social changes that accompanied these parallel ideological shifts did not have to be equally drastic. While the Russian transformation was dramatic, the retrenchment of the Swedish welfare state was more subtle but nevertheless undeniable.

In the last two decades both St Petersburg and Stockholm employed various strategies to enable and enhance their competitive-

ness in the global arena, which can be related to the global phenomenon of the 'entrepreneurial city' (Golubchikov 2010; Harvey 1989).
Both cities are also involved in the inter-regional cooperation for
instance through the EU Strategy for the Baltic Sea Region comply-
ing with the EU efforts in urban/regional development (European
Commission 2008). The specific feature of this strategy is that while
promoting spatial homogenization and coherence, it supports urban/
regional entrepreneurialism that consequently leads to competition
and expected 'trickle-down effect' where the outcome are expected to
benefit a classless 'all of society'.

Formulation of standards for further development – the European
city, the global city – are open to interpretation depending on
national preconditions, but are largely based on external models. Earlier research has related the construction of the ideal of the 'European
city', with its local idiosyncrasies, to the oppositional concept of the
'American city', with its uniformity (Molnar 2010), referring both
to the aesthetical but also to the social and historical distinctiveness.
St Petersburg is being reinvented and re-established among other
European cities, though not without the ambiguities of international post-politics (sanctions, etc.), while for Stockholm the notion
of 'European city' is developed for stimulating marketing strategies
and capitalizing on the 'local idiosyncrasies' in an era of global competition between cities. Instead of competing, the current plan for
St Petersburg is struggling to ascertain commonalities in order to
overcome the past separation from the European community. The
shift that took place in both environments, exemplified by the notion
of the European city, unveils a normative perception of the commodified urban space, which is in strong contrast to the earlier focus
on the inhabitants and the living standards of the urban users. The
principle of centralized top-down steering has been replaced by the
globalized agenda-setting approach which only can be realized at the
local level.

The power ideology of economic and political restructuring
has changed the understanding of planning practice as means of
transforming the fabric of urban space, restricted planners' room
of manoeuvre and simultaneously increased the state's needs for

planning legitimation. While in the earlier plans space was conceptualised as 'plannable', a means of centralised manipulation of social development toward a desired direction, the contemporary plans transfer some of the control over space to the market and underscore the need for continuous flexibility and adjustment. As a result, space in general becomes conceptualised as 'unplannable', not subjected to direct top-down control, instead the formulation of the spatial representations and organisation of the planning process becomes open to other actors, creating new conditions for reformulating what planning is without centralised state or city government control. The subsequent unpredictability of the representations of space needs to be incorporated into the plans. In reaction to this challenge, the plan for St Petersburg include a special projection for which laws would need to be passed by the city's legislation bodies in order to structure relationships between different actors (government, investors, entrepreneurs, citizens, etc.). The 1999 Stockholm plan became less precise in its orientation creating opportunities for regular revisions and adjustments without reconsideration of the overall concept. Social engineering within the capitalist economy of today is as well as in other systems based on ideological prerequisites should not be overlooked. General city plans are much more similar in promoting global neo-liberal goals than in projecting equality goals, the killing fields of inequality a reality also in the two Baltic cities of the Far North.

Concluding remarks: global neighbours, local/regional competitors

Eagerly looking forward to the final Therbornian global city analysis we end by a few preliminary remarks (Therborn forthc.; cf. also Therborn 2016). The way space is organised in social figurations or survival units determines the several important aspects of its materiality, including location, use and value of economic resources, density, propinquity and cohesion of the population, exercise of public and private practices, and power manifestation and protest. Modern urban life takes place in a more or less planned society on the planet of slums; the logic behind any planning is authoritative, constituted through a set of power relations that manifest themselves spatially in both material and immaterial ways. In theoretical discussions by urban sociologists, city space often appears as a backdrop of social actions and experiences, a location for various economic, social, and political processes (Gans 2002). However, public policymakers who formulate targets and provide instruments for solving social problems in specific urban environments also formulate conceptual definitions of these problems and map their role in urban space. Ideas about the appropriate forms and use of space play a crucial role in the process of public governance. Although attempts to control and plan social life do not always result in the anticipated outcomes, official perceptions of space impose specific normative structures in which social life operates.

In contemporary urban development neoliberalism is usually presented by politicians in the public debate as the only alternative for post-industrial society where different forms of interventions and regulations are designed to create the best condition for expanding market adaptation and appropriation. Here, we do not discuss whether all change in planning ideas took the form of neoliberalism, but concentrate on the fundamental principles that tend to follow the trend to extend 'market discipline, competition, and commodification throughout all sectors of society' (Brenner and Theodore 2002: 3). In our analysis of city planning in St Petersburg and Stockholm this becomes most evident through the relocation in conceptualizations of space – from plannable to unplannable – during the two time periods. The critique of disciplining aspects of the former centralist bureaucratic conceptualization of space is comprehensive in the scientific literature, but '[...] the disciplining order of the market or of non-state social forces is more rarely subjected to the same attention, hiding its power behind the love affair with chaos' (Massey 2005: 112). The shift in conceiving of space signifies the abandonment of the ideas that presented an alternative to market-based societal development. In line with the notion of globalization, this illustrates the totemic resonance of neoliberal ideology and its influence on urban planning.

This, of course is not the same as to imply that homogenization of the ideological underpinnings of urban planning leads to the same outcomes in any national context – this deserves a study of its own – but the analysis of changes in city planning in two cities, St Petersburg, Russia, and Stockholm, Sweden, testifies to a certain convergence to a uniform post-industrial, in other words neoliberal, 'global' city order – at least in the Far North around the Baltic Sea. There is no single modernity in sight – regional variation will prevail.

References

Abercrombie, Nicholas, Hill, Stephen and Turner, Bryan S. (1983) 'Determinacy and indeterminacy in the theory of ideology', *New Left Review* 142, pp. 55–66.

Aidukaite, Jolanta and Frölich, Christian (2015) 'Struggle over public space: grassroot movements in Moscow and Vilnius', *International Journal of Sociology and Social Policy*, 35, 7–8, pp. 565–580.

Bessonova, Olga (1992) 'The reforms of the Soviet housing model. The search for a concept', in Turner, Bengt, Hegedus, József and Tosics, Iván (eds.) *The Reform of Housing in Eastern Europe and the Soviet Union*. London: Routledge.

Brenner, Neil and Theodore, Nik (2002) 'Cities and geographies of actually existing neoliberalism', in Brenner, Neil and Theodore, Nik (eds.) *Spaces of Neoliberalism: Urban Restructuring in North America and Western Europe*. Oxford: Blackwell publishing.

Brown, Kate (2001) 'Gridded lives: Why Kazakhstan and Montana are nearly the same place', *The American Historical Review*, 106, 1, pp. 17–48.

Buchli, Victor (1992) 'Khrushchev, modernism, and the fight against petit-bourgeois consciousness in the Soviet home', *Journal of Design History*, 10, 2, pp. 161–176.

Castells, Manuel (1996) *The Information Age: Economy, Society and Culture. Vol. 1, The Rise of the Network Society*. Malden, Mass.: Blackwell.

Cooke, Catherine (1997) 'Beauty as a route to the "radiant future": Responses of Soviet architecture', *Journal of Design History*, 10, 2, pp. 137–160.

Davis, Mike (1990) *City of Quartz: Excavating the Future in Los Angeles*. London: Verso.

Davis, Mike (2006) *Planet of Slums*. London: Verso.

D'Eramo, Marco (2003) *The Pig and the Skyscraper: Chicago: A History of our Future*. London: Verso.

Elias, Norbert (2000) *The Civilizing Process*. Oxford: Blackwell.

Elias, Norbert and Scotson, John (1965) *The Established and the Outsiders: A Sociological Enquiry into Community Problems*. London: Frank Cass & Co.

European Commission (2008) *Green Paper on Territorial Cohesion*, COM 616, October. Retrieved 21 June 2010, http://ec.europa.eu/regional_policy/consultation/terco/paper_terco_en.pdf.

Franzén, Mats (1986) 'Urban sociology: the Swedish case', in Himmelstrand, Ulf (ed.) *The Social Reproduction of Organization and Culture*. London: Sage.

Franzén, Mats (2004) 'Rummets tvära dialektik. Notater till Henri Lefebvre' ['The Reversed Dialectics of Space. Notes on Henri Lefebvre'], in Sernhede, Ove and Johansson, Thomas (eds.) *Urbanitetens omvandlingar: kultur och identitet i den postindustriella staden*. Göteborg: Daidalos.

Franzén, Mats and Sandstedt, Eva (1981) *Välfärdsstat och byggande: Om efterkrigstidens nya stadsmönster i Sverige* ['Welfare State and Construction: On New City Design in Sweden After the World War II']. Lund: Arkiv förlag.

French, Antohny R. (1995) *Plans, Pragmatism and People: The Legacy of Soviet Planning for Today's Cities*. Pittsburgh, Pa.: University of Pittsburgh Press.

Friedmann, John (2002) *The Prospect of Cities*. Minneapolis: Univ. of Minnesota Press.

Gans, Herbert J. (2002) 'The sociology of space: A use-centred view', *City and Community*, 1, 4, pp. 329–339.

Golubchikov, Oleg (2004) 'Urban planning in Russia: Towards the market', *European Planning Studies*, 12, 2, pp. 229–247.

Golubchikov, Oleg (2010) 'World-city-entrepreneurialism: Globalist imaginaries, neoliberal geographies, and the production on new St Petersburg', *Environment and Planning A*, 42, 3, pp. 626–643.

Gough, Ian and Olofsson, Gunnar (1999) 'Introduction: New thinking on exclusion and integration', in Gough, Ian and Olofsson, Gunnar (eds.) *Capitalism and Social Cohesion: Essays on Exclusion and Inclusion*. London: MacMillan.

'GPG' (1966) *General'nyi plan razvitiia Leningrada* ['General plan of the development of Leningrad'], by Kamenskii, Valentin Aleksandrovich and Naumov, Aleksandr Ivanovich. Leningrad: Stroiizdat.

'GPS' (1952) *Generalplan för Stockholm 1952* ['General plan for Stockholm 1952']. Stockholm: Stockholms stadsplanekontor.

Hall, Peter (1999) *Cities in Civilization: Culture, Innovation, and Urban Order*. London: Phoenix Giant.

Hall, Stefan and Vidén, Sonja (2005) 'The million homes programme: A review of the great Swedish planning project', *Planning Perspectives*, 20, 3, pp. 301–328.

Harvey, David (1989) 'From managerialism to entrepreneurialism: The transformation in urban governance in late capitalism', *Geografiska Annaler*, 71, 1, pp. 3–17.

Hedin, Karin, Clark, Eric, Lundholm, Emma and Malmborg, Gunnar (2012) 'Neoliberalization of housing in Sweden: Gentrification, filtering and social polarization', *Annals of the Association of American Geographers*, 102, 2, pp. 443–463.

Hort, Sven E.O. (1992) *Segregation – ett svenskt dilemma?* Stockholm: Finansdepartementet (Långtidsutredningen, appendix 9).

Hort, Sven E.O. (2014) *Social Policy, Welfare State, and Civil Society in Sweden*, vols. I & II. Lund: Arkiv förlag.

Hort, Sven, Kings, Lisa and Kravchenko, Zhanna (2016) 'Still awaiting the storm? The Swedish welfare state after the latest crisis', in Schubert, Klaus, Villota, Paloma de and Kuhlmann, Johanna (eds.) *Challenges to European Welfare Systems*. Cham: Springer.

Jacobs, Jane (1961) *The Death and Life of Great American Cities*. New York: Random House.

Kamenskii, Valentin Aleksandrovich (1972) *Leningrad: general'nyi plan razvitiia goroda* ['Leningrad: The General City Development Plan']. Leningrad: Lenizadt.

Khakee, Abdul (2003) 'Den post-socialdemokratiska staden är här' ['The post-social democratic city is here'], *Plan. Tidskrift för samhällsplanering*, 57, 1, pp. 40–43.

Khakee, Abdul, Elander, Ingemar and Sunesson, Sune (eds.) (1995) *Remaking the Welfare State: Swedish Urban Planning and Policy-making in the 1990s*. Aldershot: Avebury.

Kings, Lisa (2010) 'In defence of the local', in Hort, Sven E.O. (ed.) *From Linnaeus to the Future(s) – Letters from Afar*. Växjö: Linnaeus University Press.

Kings, Lisa (2011) *Till det lokalas försvar: Civilsamhället i den urbana periferin*. Lund: Arkiv förlag.

Kings, Lisa and Kravchenko, Zhanna (2013) 'Giving up on great city plans? Transforming representations of space in Sweden and Russia', *Laboratorium* 3, pp. 43–65.

Kogan, Leonid Borisovich (1982) *Sotsial'no-kul'turnye funktsii goroda i prostranstvennaia sreda* ['Socio-cultural Functions of the City and Spatial Environment']. Moskva: Stroiizdat.

Kravchenko, Zhanna (2008) *Family (versus) Policy: Combining Work and Care in Russia and Sweden*. Stockholm: Acta Universitatis Stockholmiensis.

Lefebvre, Henri (1991) *The Production of Space*. Oxford: Basil Blackwell.

Le Galès, Patrick and Therborn, Göran (2010) 'Cities', in Immerfall, Stefan and Therborn, Göran (eds.) *Handbook of European Societies*. New York: Springer.

Lindström, Jonas (2012) *Drömmen om den nya staden: Stadsförnyelse i det post-sovjetiska Riga*. Lund: Arkiv förlag.

Mandelbaum, Seymour J. (1990) 'Reading Plans', *Journal of American Planning Association* 56, pp. 350–356.

Marcuse, Peter and Kempen, Ronald van (eds.) (2000) *Globalizing Cities: A New Spatial Order?* Oxford: Blackwell.

Massey, Doreen (2005) *For Space*. London: Sage Publications.

Meerovich, Mark (2008) *Nakazanie zhilishchem: Zhilishchnaia politika v SSSR kak sredstvo upravleniia liud'mi, 1917–1937*. Moscow: RosPEn.

Molina, Irene (1997) *Stadens rasifiering: Etnisk boendesegregation i folkhemmet*. Uppsala: Uppsala universitet; Kulturgeografiska institutionen.

Molnar, Virag (2010) 'The cultural production of locality: Reclaiming the "European city" in post-wall Berlin', *International Journal of Urban and Regional Research*, 34, 2, pp. 281–309.

Olofsson, Gunnar (1987) 'After the working class movement? What is new and what is social in the new social movements', *Acta Sociologica*, 31, 1.

Olofsson, Gunnar (1999) 'Embeddedness and integration', in Gough, Ian and Olofsson, Gunnar (eds.) *Capitalism and Social Cohesion: Essays on Exclusion and Inclusion*. London: MacMillan.

'ÖPS' (1999) *Översiktsplan 1999 Stockholm* ['Outlineplan 1999 Stockholm']. Stockholm: Strategiska avdelningen, Stadsbyggnadskontoret.

Papakostas, Apostolis (2012) *Civilizing the Public Sphere*. London: Palgrave.

'PGP' (1964) *Proekt general'nogo plana Leningrada 1958–1980* ['Project of the General Plan of Leningrad 1958–1980']. F. 386, op. 3-3, No. 35.

Pred, Allan (2000) *Even in Sweden: Racisms, Racialized Spaces, and the Popular Geographical Imagination*. Berkeley: University of Clifornia Press.

Ruble, Blair A. (1990) *Leningrad: Shaping a Soviet City*. Berkeley: University of California Press.

Seniavskii, Alexandr (2003) *Urbanizatsiia Rossii v XX veke* ['Urbanization of Russia in the Twentieth Century']. Moskva: Nauka.

'StPL' (2005) *O general'nom plane Sankt-Peterburga i granitsakh zon okhrany ob'ektov kul'tunogo naslediia na territorii Sankt-Peterburga* ['On the General Plan of St Petersburg …']. St Petersburg Law No. 728-99, 21 December, with attachments.

Therborn, Göran (1981) *The Ideology of Power and the Power of Ideology*. London: Verso.

Therborn, Göran (1984) 'The new questions of subjectivity', *New Left Review* 143, pp. 97–107.

Therborn, Göran (1992) 'The life and times of socialism', *New Left Review* 194, pp. 17–32.

Therborn, Göran (2002) 'Monumental Europe: The national years: On the iconography of European capital cities', *Housing, Theory and Society*, 19, 1.

Therborn, Göran (2011) 'End of a paradigm: The current crisis of the idea of stateless cities', *Environment and Planning* A, 43, pp. 272–285.

Therborn, Göran (2012) 'Afterword: Social change, scholarly change and scholarly continuity', in Larsson, Bengt, Letell, Martin and Thörn, Håkan (eds.) *Transformations of the Swedish Welfare State*. London: Palgrave MacMillan.

Therborn, Göran (2016) 'Introduction', *International Journal of Urban Sciences*, 19, 1, pp. 1–6.

Therborn, Göran (forthc.) *Cities of Power: The Urban, the National, the Popular, and the Global*. London: Verso.

Vladimirov, V.V. (2003) *Regional'noe gradostroitel'noe planirovanie* ['Regional City Planning']. St Petersburg: Limbus Press.

Zukin, Sharon (1995) *The Culture of Cities*. Oxford: Blackwell.

BO ROTHSTEIN

Manufacturing Social Solidarity

Designing Institutions for Social Justice

Understanding inequality

Looking out over the world, both the rich industrial nations as well as the less developed countries, it is striking how large differences there are in social, economic and political equality. Measures of political, social and legal rights as well as respect for human rights vary enormously between countries (Bohara et al. 2008; Donnelly 2003). The same goes for measures of economic inequality and measures of social well-being such as poverty, literacy and population health. It is also the case that there is not only variation between countries but also huge variation within countries regarding most measures of social, economic and 'de facto' political equality (Piketty 2015; Pontusson 2005; Jefferson 2012; Norris 2012; Therborn 2013). Another example is the variation in the percentage of children that live in poverty which is much lower in some countries than in others although they have the same level of general prosperity. In fact, some very rich countries have more children living in poverty than countries that are not so prosperous (Halleröd et al. 2013). In addition, in all democracies, possibilities to influence public policy vary systematically with social class and economic resources. Moreover, the overall development within most of the rich capitalist market oriented countries is that inequality has increased over the last two or three decades (Piketty 2014; OECD 2011; Therborn 2013). Social solidarity, understood as a practice that increases equality in equal treatment by the state and in overall life chances is thus something that varies a lot both between and within countries. From a normative perspective on social justice, all this is certainly problematic but from an empirical social science perspective, this variation can be used for explanatory purposes to answer the following question: What makes some societies more prone to social justice than others?

The normative starting point for this article is based on the results from several empirical studies showing that for a vast majority of people, human well-being would be improved if political and social inequality would decrease (Radcliff 2013; Wilkinson and Pickett 2009; Hall and Lamont 2009). The problem is how this can manufactured given a) available knowledge and b) resources? This article is an effort to summarize the policy relevant results of a large amount of both philosophical and empirical research into this problem since it is my firm believe that both types of research are needed for answering the question of how to 'manufacture' social solidarity.

A second point of departure for this article is that the level of solidarity in a country is not culturally determined. For example, the Nordic countries are not more egalitarian and less corrupt than Italy, the UK, Kenya, Brazil, Hungary or the US because there is something special with the Nordic culture. This is an often heard argument, for example, John Roemer argues that the reason the Nordic countries developed more extensive system of redistribution is due to the educational and cultural homogeneity of their population (Roemer 2009). The problem is that his argument is empirically unsubstantiated and from what is known from the historical research about history of class structure in the Nordic countries, inaccurate. For example, Finland had very low levels of education well into the first decades of the 20th century and a severe conflict between the Finnish and Swedish speaking population (Uslaner and Rothstein 2016). Moreover, the country endured a gruesome civil war in 1918 in which, as a percentage of the population, more people were killed than in the Spanish Civil War during the 1930s. The broad based political support for redistribution was instead constructed 'from above' by the universal (or near universal) design of the policies (Rothstein 1998). The same broad based support for universal type of social policies can be found in the UK for the National Health Service (Klein 2010) and in the United States for Social Security (Béland 2005). It is thus the institutional design of the programs, not the specific national culture that determines the type of a country's social policies. In political terms, designing institutions is thus the sophisticated equivalent to designing policies (Tsebelis 1990). This is because institutions (understood as formal rules and 'standard operating procedures' in organizations) have a large impact on what future agents come to understand as being in their interest and/or being in line with their social norms. To be more precise, if increased social justice is the goal, thinking about how to design the institutions that deliver the policies is of the outmost importance.

What should social solidarity be about?

Anyone who is interested in a more equal and just society needs to be in possession of a correct understanding of 'the nature of the problem'. To achieve this, one has to answer three questions. The first is the 'what is it' question, namely what should equality be about? The second is the 'how to get it' question, that is, what can be expected from (the vast majority of) humans when it comes to their propensity for solidarity. The third question is about strategy, namely how to make social solidarity politically (electorally) sustainable.

The first question – equality of what? – has turned out to be complicated (Sen 1979). In an era of 'conspicuous consumption' and increased individualism and social heterogeneity, it is difficult to argue that the government has a responsibility to equalize all or even most forms of consumption. First, consumption cannot be an end in itself and secondly, we should reward ambition and maybe also talent. The best answers to the question 'equality of what' have been given by liberal right-based philosophers such as John Rawls, Amartya Sen and Martha Nussbaum (Rawls 1971; Sen 2010; Nussbaum 2001). They differ in certain important respects, but they agree that equality should be about guaranteeing access to a specific set of goods and services that are important for people in order for them to be capable to realize their various potentials as human beings. The central term for Rawls is 'primary goods', and for Sen and Nussbaum 'capabilities'. The terminology implies that the problem is not to equalize economic resources or social status as such, but to ensure all individuals a set of *basic resources* that will equalize their chances to reach their full potential as humans. Standards are access to high quality health care and education, basic food and shelter, equality in civil and political rights, equal protection under the laws, basic social services and social insurance systems that support people that for various reasons cannot generate enough resources from their own work, support for persons with disabilities, etc. The set of such capabilities enhancing goods and services can of course vary, but it is important to realize that equality, as a politically viable concept, has to be about specific things.[1] There is simply no way we, by political means, can equalize the ability to be a skilled musician, to be creative, to be loved, to be an outstanding researcher, a good parent or a first rate ballet dancer. What *is* possible to do by political means is to increase the possibility for those who happen to have ambitions in these (and many other) fields to realize their talents even if they have not entered this world with huge endowments. This can be done by giving them access to a certain bundle of goods and services that are likely to enhance their capabilities of reaching their full potential as human beings.

One implication from this that is very important is that *equality should be about individuals, not collectives* such as classes, groups, clans or tribes whether these are based on social class, occupation, kinship, religion, gender, ethnicity, sexual orientations or any other form of collective categorization. One reason for this is that many of these community belongings or identities are floating and that branding individuals (especially children and young people) into such collectives by administrative means can result in gross violations of their human rights (Okin and Cohen 1999; Talbott 2005; Neier 2002). A second, and more important argument, is that there is no guarantee that the majority in groups like these will not oppress or exploit individuals that are put under their surveillance or, even worse, jurisdiction (Talbott 2005; Rawls 2005). In sum, arguments for increased equality should not be based on utilitarian group theory but on theories about individual rights.

---

1. Increased equality in the work life and in the family is for sure also important, but for reasons of space, I leave this out.

It should be emphasized that the idea of giving all citizens equal access to a set of primary goods or basic resources that will increase the likelihood that they can fulfil their potential as human beings is in itself problematic. The reason is that while some 'basic resources' are mostly procedural (equal protection under the laws, civil and political rights), others are substantial (health care, education, social services, social insurance schemes). The substantial type is problematic because the majority's preference for whatever set of such primary goods/basic resources can be seen as very controversial for various minorities. Even such a, usually uncontroversial, 'primary good' as access to secondary education has been contested by ethnic-religious groups (e.g. the Amish group in the United States) as a threat to the survival of their culture since it dramatically increases the risk that their children/daughters will leave their communities. The problem is of course that the children deprived of such education will have to forsake many roads in life in which they may have realized their potential. There seems to be no perfect solution to this problem other than that this calls for a fair amount of tolerance and respect for human rights in the implementation of any set of 'primary goods' policies.

Reciprocity is the main template for human behaviour

When striving for a more equal society, it is important to start from a correct understanding of 'human nature', especially if you want your reforms to have a lasting (sustainable) impact. Ideas about the 'basic human nature' have had a long history in the social sciences that has now, I believe, finally been resolved mostly by experimental research (Fehr and Fischbacher 2005; Henrich et al. 2001; Gintis et al. 2005; Bicchieri 2006; cf. Ostrom 1998). To make a long story short, the idea of man as a 'homo economicus' has simply been refuted by this type of research. The results from laboratory-, fieldwork-, and survey research speaking against man as a utility-maximizing rational agent is by now overwhelming. Self-interest is for sure an important ingredient when people decide how to act, but it is far from as dominating as has been portrayed in neo-classic economics. Moreover, it would be impossible to create solidaristic or cooperative institutions of any kind (including democracy, the rule of law and respect for property rights) if individual utility-maximizing self-interest would be 'the only game in town'. The reason is that such individuals would always fall for the temptation to 'free-ride' and if a majority do this, such institutions would never be established and if they existed (for some other reason) they would soon be destroyed. If all agents act out of the template prescribed in neo-classic economic theory, they will sooner or later outsmart themselves into a suboptimal equilibrium. Also known as a 'social trap' this is situation where all agents will be worse off because even if they know they would all gain from cooperation, lacking trust that the others will cooperate, they will themselves abstain from cooperation (Rothstein 2005b).

However, this new experimental (and to some extent field) research does not present humans as benevolent altruists (Henrich and Henrich 2007; Bicchieri and Xiao 2009). True, there is altruistic behaviour, but it is usually restricted to very small circles of family and close friends. Or it is simply too rare and also too unpredictable for building sustainable systems for solidarity at a societal level. This lesson is important since it tells us that trying to mobilize political support for increased equality by referring only to peoples' altruistic motives is likely to fail (Svallfors 2007). What comes out from this research is instead that *reciprocity is the basic human orientation*. The central idea here is that people are not so much motivated 'from the back' by utility-based calculations or culturally induced norms. Instead, human behaviour is to a large extent determined by forward looking strategic thinking in the sense that *what agents do, depends on what they think the other agents are going to do* (Gintis et al. 2005). Experimental studies show that people are willing to do 'the right thing' but only if they can be convinced that most others are willing to do the same (Bicchieri and Xiao 2009). Thus, the idea of reciprocity recasts fundamentally how we should understand and explain human behaviour. Instead of looking backwards to what causes variation in utility-based interests or culturally induced norms, the important thing is to understand how people's forward looking perceptions about 'other people' are constructed. Historical experiences and 'collective memories' certainly play a role here, but research also shows that people update their perceptions based on new information (Boyd et al. 2010).

Regarding the prospect for solidarity, results from research show that most people are willing to engage in solidaristic cooperation for common goals even if they will not personally benefit from this materially (Levi 1998). However, for this to happen, three specific conditions have to be in place. First, people have to be convinced that the policy is morally justified (substantial justice). Secondly, people have to be convinced that most other agents can be trusted to also cooperate (solidaristic justice), that is that other agents are likely to abstain from 'free-riding'. Thirdly, people have to be convinced that the policy can be implemented in a fair and even-handed manner (procedural justice) (Levi 1991; Rothstein 1998). For the first issue, the work from the philosophers mentioned above will come in handy. The second requirement, which is as important for generating support for solidarity for policies for increased equality, has to be resolved *by institutional design* where knowledge from research in policy implementation and public administration in general are needed. For example: It is not difficult to argue that universal access to high quality health care and sickness insurance qualifies as a 'primary good' in the above mentioned sense. However, if a majority cannot be convinced that a) most people will pay the increased taxes required for producing these goods, or that b) the good will not be delivered in a manner that is acceptable, fair and respectful, they are not likely to support this policy (Rothstein et al. 2011). If the health personnel are known to be corrupt, unprofessional or disrespectful, support for this policy will dwindle. The same goes for sickness insurance. People are likely to support insurance for people that are ill, but if perceptions of misuse or overuse (that is, 'free-riding') become widespread, support will decline (Svallfors 2013; Rothstein 2011). In other words, *solidarity is conditioned on the institutional design of the systems that are supposed to bring about the policies that will enhance equality*. This has been formulated in the following words by John Rawls:

> A just system must generate its own support. This means that it must be arranged so as to bring about in its members the corresponding sense of justice, an effective desire to act in accordance with its rules for reasons and justice. Thus, the requirements of stability and the criterion of discouraging desires that conflict with the principles of justice put further constraints on institutions. They must not only be just but framed so as to encourage the virtue of justice in those who take part in them. (Rawls 1971: 261.)

The central idea in this quote is how Rawls specifies that for making a solidaristic system sustainable, we have to be aware of the existence of a 'feed-back mechanism' between people's support for just principles and their perceptions of the *quality of the institutions* that are set up to implement these principles (Kumlin 2004). Recent empirical research strongly supports Rawls argument in the sense that individuals' perceptions of forms of unfairness (or inefficiency) in the public services influences political views about support for social solidarity. Using survey data for 29 European countries that includes questions about the fairness of public authorities (health sector and tax authorities) as well as questions about ideological leanings and policy preferences, Svallfors (2013) has shown the following: Citizens that have a preference for more economic equality but that lives in a country where they perceive that the quality of government institutions is low, will in the same survey indicate that they prefer lower taxes and less social spending. However, the same 'ideological type' of respondent but who happens to live in a European country where he or she believes that the authorities that implement policies are basically just and fair, will answer that he or she is willing to pay higher taxes for more social spending. This result is supported in a study using aggregate data about welfare state spending and quality of government for Western liberal democracies (Rothstein et al. 2011) – the higher the quality of government the more countries will spend also when they control for variables that measures political mobilization and electoral success from left parties. To summarize my interpretation of these studies – citizens that live in a country where they perceive that corruption or other forms of unfairness in the public administration is common are likely to be less supportive of the idea that the state should take responsibility for policies for increased social justice even if they ideologically support the goals such policies have. The most likely reason is that they will believe that their solidarity will not be reciprocated.

It is important to realize that reciprocity also has a dark side. History and many contemporary events as well as experimental evidence show that 'ordinary people' are willing to engage in the most horrible atrocities to other people (again, also if they do not personally benefit from their actions) if they are convinced that those 'other people' would otherwise harm them. However, bad reciprocity also exists in less dramatic (and horrible) circumstances. Distrust in other agents or in the institutions may lead to a vicious circle that can break any system or policy set up to increase solidarity. Again, Rawls did clearly see this problem between institutional design and support for justice (which has sadly been neglected by most of his followers in political philosophy):

> For although men know that they share a common sense of justice and that each wants to adhere to existing arrangements, they may nevertheless lack full confidence in one another. They may suspect that some are not doing their part, and so they may be tempted not to do theirs. The general awareness of these temptations may eventually cause the scheme to break down. The suspicion that others are not honoring their duties and obligations is increased by the fact that, in absence of the authoritative interpretation and enforcement of the rules, it is particularly easy to find excuses for breaking them. (Rawls 1971: 240.)

It is clear that Rawls pointed to the problem of reciprocity in the form of trust in others ('confidence') and that he argues that it is the existence of institutional arrangements that can handle 'free-riding' and other forms of anti-solidaristic and opportunistic behaviour that are needed to avoid that systems based on principles of justice break down.

Thus, we arrive at the conclusion that regarding justice, the basic nature of human behaviour – reciprocity – can go both ways. On the one hand, the idea of reciprocity stands against the cynicism about human nature that has been central to interest-based theories that has dominated most economic approaches in the social sciences (Ostrom 1998, 2000). On the other hand, reciprocity is also in conflict with a naïve idea about human nature as genuinely benevolent, which many equality-enhancing policies have been built on. Instead, reciprocity tells us that if we through the design of institutions can make people trust that most other agents in their society will behave in a trustworthy and solidaristic manner, they will do likewise. If not, they will defect, even if the outcome will be detrimental to their interests.

That reciprocity can go in different directions is also what we see if we take just a simple look at most of the rankings of countries' performance that have now become abundant. The level of corruption, to take just one example, shows staggering differences between countries (Rothstein 2011). This particular 'social bad' also serves as a good example of why reciprocity is a better starting point for understanding human behaviour than its rivals. If we relied on cultural explanations, we would have to say to our sisters and brothers in, for example, Nigeria that the extremely high level of corruption in their country is caused by their corrupt culture. Or if we started from interest-based explanations, we would be unable to explain why the huge variation of corruption exists without relying on either genetic or cultural explanations. However, if we base our explanations on the idea of reciprocity, the explanation for the high level of corruption in, for example, Pakistan is that the institutions in place makes it reasonable for most people to believe that most other agents will be engaged in corrupt practices, and thus they have no reason not to engage in these practices themselves (Rothstein 2010). Simply put, it makes no sense to be the only honest policeman in a thoroughly corrupt police force. It is important to underline that, contrary to what is taken for granted in neo-classical economics, we have absolutely no reason to believe that societies (or any group of agents) are able to produce the type of institutions that they would prosper from. A quick look at available measures shows that a vast majority of the world's population live under either deeply or fairly corrupt public authorities (Holmberg and Rothstein 2012). This, it should be added, turns out to have devastating effects on their prosperity, social well-being and possibility to launch policies that will increase equality.

Enters social trust

A central conclusion is thus that reciprocity, as the baseline for human agency, can go in two directions. One will result in more solidaristic cooperation for increased equality and thereby increased human well-being. The other one is exactly the opposite resulting in all sorts of bad outcomes such as high levels of corruption, discrimination, civil strife, massive exploitation and ethnic cleansing even in democratic societies (Mann 2005). Given what is known from the record of human history, it is not advisable to be naïve in these matters. We should never forget that even societies known for their high level of civilization have shown themselves to be capable of the worst imaginable forms of atrocities.

The most important thing we need to know is then what it is that makes reciprocity turn bad or good. Theory and research gives a reasonably clear answer to what determines the direction reciprocity will take society, namely the level of social or generalized interpersonal trust. Simply put, if most people in a society believe that most other people in that society can be trusted, they have good reasons to support policies that are based on solidarity and thereby will increase equality as it has been specified above. However, if they believe that most people should not be trusted, the outcome will be the opposite (Svallfors 2013; Rothstein 2011).

As with corruption, research on social trust (and the related concept of social capital) has increased tremendously since the mid-1990s. This is in part because empirical research shows that high levels of social trust at the individual level is connected to a number of important factors such as tolerance towards minorities, participation in public life, education, health, and subjective well-being. At the societal level, high trust societies have more extensive and generous social welfare systems (Rothstein and Uslaner 2005). However, how to understand a concept like social trust is not easy; obviously when asked in surveys, most people do not really know if most other people in their society can be trusted. One interpretation is that social trust is an expression of optimism about the future (Uslaner 2002). Another interpretation is that when people answer the survey question if they believe (or not) that most other people can be trusted, they are in fact answering another question, namely that they are making an evaluation of the moral standard of the society in which they live (Delhey and Newton 2003). Both interpretations should be seen as answers to the central question for the way in which reciprocity will turn, namely what people believe about what other people will do if they try to engage in some collaborative effort with them. Again, the notion of reciprocity says that what people do depends on what they think other people will do, and this is likely to be determined by how they think about other people's trustworthiness, which of course can be seen as how they interpret the general moral standing of their society. For the case of creating a more equal society, the results are quite clear. Although not a perfect correlation, societies with more interpersonal trust have more political, economic and social equality, including gender equality (Rothstein 2005b). It is important to note that I am here referring to what is known as generalized trust, that is, trust in people in general of whom there is no way to have anything that comes close to perfect information. This is different from particularistic trust which refers to trust in small groups of friends, clans or (social and professional) cliques. Such inward or group-based trust can often lead to severe social conflicts that are detrimental to human well-being (Mann 2005).

An important result from recent research is that people from cultures where interpersonal trust is very low do not keep their low social trust when they have moved to a society where interpersonal trust is high. Instead, they update their trust in other people based on new information of how trust-relations operate in their new society (Dinesen 2011). Most important for the issue discussed here is how they perceive the trustworthiness of other agents in their new society and especially how they perceive the fairness of the public institutions that exist in their new society (Dinesen 2011). This shows that propensity for social solidarity is not culturally determined but can be influenced by institutional design.

Political institutions, social trust and social justice

How then, can generalized trust be generated? Again, recent empirical research gives a reasonably clear answer to this question. A high level of generalized trust is caused by what has been called high quality government institutions, especially the institutions that implement public policies (Stolle 2003). The central basic norm for these institutions is impartiality. This implies that things like discrimination (whether based on ethnicity, gender, class, etc.), corruption (in its many forms), clientelism, nepotism and political favouritism are very rare or non-existent when public officials or professionals implement public policies. Social trust is thus not generated 'from below', for example from civil society or voluntary associations, but 'from above', by how people perceive the fairness and competence of government institutions (Rothstein 2011). Thus, *designing institutions that implement public policy is to create (or destroy) social trust.* The reason for this effect is that when people make up their mind if most people in their society can be trusted, they make an inference from how they perceive the authorities. If the local policeman, schoolteacher, social insurance administrator, judge or doctor cannot be trusted (because they discriminate against people like you, or ask for bribes, or give preferential treatments to some groups, etc.), then it is reasonable to assume that neither should you trust 'people in general' in your society. And vice versa, if they are known to be honest, impartial, competent and fair, then it is likely that this will spill over to 'people in general'. Moreover, if the public authorities are known to be engaged in the type of 'bad' practices mentioned above, then many people will come to think that in order to get what they need in life (immunization to their children, building permits, employment in the public sector, etc.) most people will have to be engaged in these kinds of bad practices, and thus they should not be trusted (Rothstein 2011) The empirical evidence from both experimental and survey research gives a very strong support for this theory of how social trust is generated 'from above' (Rothstein 2013).

For social policy and many other policies that are intended to cater to increased equality in the above-mentioned sense, this has a number of implications regarding institutional design. The most important is to strive for universal systems and avoid, as much as possible, all systems that are directed to supporting specific groups and/or entail bureaucratic discretion (Rothstein 2002). Universal programs, like for example universal child allowances, universal pre-schools and schools, universal pensions, universal health care, are to be favoured instead of specific programs directed to specific groups like 'the poor', to certain minorities, or to women, etc. The reasons for universalism are fivefold: First, universal systems entail a minimum of (if any) bureaucratic discretion. Thereby, not only corruption, but all forms of bureaucratic intrusions connected to needs-testing can be avoided. Secondly, since universal programs in principle cater to 'all', they will include the middle class and thereby almost automatically secure a political majority and thereby make the program politically sustainable. Programs that are built solely on interest group mobilization will always be vulnerable to interest-based counter-mobilization. Universal programs also avoid an 'us and them' division of society. Thirdly, universal programs avoid the problem of stigmatization of specific groups and individual 'stereo-type-threat' that was mentioned above. Fourth, although they give benefits also to 'rich' people, universal programs turn out to be very redistributive, more so than programs which 'take from the rich and give to the poor'. The reasons are that the benefits are usually nominal in money or costs of services, but taxes are either proportional to income or progressive (Korpi and Palme 1998; Rothstein 1998). Even when universal programs are income-related, such as for example many pension systems in more developed countries, there is usually a 'cap' which makes them redistributive. Fifth, universal programs, especially when it comes to services like education or elderly care, will usually be of high quality since the need to keep the more well-to-do people 'on board' will make it difficult for politicians to lower the quality of the services if they want to stay in power. In sum, universal programs have the capacity to 'generate their own support' as stated by John Rawls above.

Admittedly, there are policies when universal institutions will not work. It is difficult to have a universal policy for active labour market policy since each unemployed person is different and will need different types of support in order to find a new job. The same goes for much of social assistance to dysfunctional families since each decision of whether or not to take a child into custody must be based on a professional judgement of the specificities of the particular case. In these areas, it is important to try as much as possible to use other means to ensure impartiality and fairness in how decisions are made in the implementation process. High quality training for professionals and civil servants, systems for accountability and control, possibilities to appeal, are but a few such possibilities.

Conclusions

The result from using the constructive theory approach for the problem of how to increase social solidarity can be summarized in one sentence. *High quality of government institutions will increase the level of social trust, which will make reciprocity turn into solidarity, which in turn will increase the possibility for creating sustainable social solidarity.* The most counterintuitive result from this analysis is perhaps that in order to support the 'needy', 'poor', or 'discriminated' one should avoid policies that are directed specifically at these groups. Because of their lack of interest in the implementation issues and also research about public opinion about support for policies for social justice, many well-known political philosophers have failed to see this. The issues about how people perceive the fairness, impartiality and justice in the implementation of policies for social justice have been greatly underestimated. When striving for increased social solidarity, universal policies are much more likely to be implemented in ways that are considered fair, impartial and just than are policies that are targeted to specific groups. Moreover, it is countries that 'taxes all' and 'supports all' through universal programs that succeeds in redistribution while countries that 'taxes the rich to give to the poor' fail to do so. The logic is quite simple; services and benefits intended 'for the poor' are likely to be 'poor' services and benefits thereby increasing stigmatization of the group one wants to support. If the 'middle class' is left out of the system for social solidarity, there will neither be an electoral majority for policies for social solidarity nor enough taxes to pay for such policies. To paraphrase Rawls, such a system for social justice will be unable to generate its own support.

References

Atkinson, Anthony B. (2015) *Inequality: What Can Be Done?* Cambridge, MA: Harvard University Press.

Béland, Daniel (2005) *Social Security: History and Politics from the New Deal to the Privatization Debate*. Lawrence: University Press of Kansas.

Bicchieri, Christina (2006) *The Grammar of Society: The Nature and Dynamics of Social Norms*. New York: Cambridge University Press.

Bicchieri, Chistina and Xiao, Erte (2009) 'Do the right thing: But only if others do so', *Journal of Behavioral Decision Making*, 22, 2, 191–208.

Bohara, Alok K., Mitchell, Neil J., Nepal, Mani and Raheem, Nejem (2008) 'Human rights violations, corruption, and the policy of repression', *Policy Studies Journal*, 36, 1, 1–18.

Boyd, Robert, Gintis, Herbert and Bowles, Samuel (2010) 'Coordinated punishment of defectors sustains cooperation and can proliferate when rare', *Science*, 328, 5978, 617–620.

Delhey, Jan, and Newton, Kenneth (2003) 'Who trusts? The origines of social trust in seven societies', *European Societies*, 5, 2, 93–137.

Dinesen, Peter Thisted (2011) *When in Rome, Do as the Romans Do. An Analysis of the Acculturation of Generalized Trust of non-Western Immigrants in Western Europe*. Aarhus: Aarhus University, Department of Political Science.

Donnelly, Jack (2003) *Universal Human Rights in Theory and Practice*, 2nd ed. Ithaca: Cornell University Press.

Fehr, Ernst and Fischbacher, Urs (2005) 'The economics of strong reciprocity', in Gintis, Herbert, Bowles, Samuel, Boyd, Robert and Fehr, Ernst (eds.) *Moral Sentiments and Material Interests. The Foundations for Cooperation in Economic Life*. Cambridge, Mass.: The MIT Press.

Gintis, Herbert, Bowles, Samuel, Boyd, Robert and Fehr, Ernst (eds.) (2005) *Moral Sentiments and Material Interests. The Foundations for Cooperation in Economic Life*. Cambridge, Mass.: The MIT Press.

Hall, Peter A. and Lamont, Michèle (eds.) (2009) *Successful Societies: How Institutions and Culture Affect Health*. New York: Cambridge University Press.

Halleröd, Björn, Rothstein, Bo, Daoud, Adel and Nandy, Shailen (2013) 'Bad governance and poor children: A comparative analysis of government efficiency and severe child deprivation in 68 low- and middle-income countries', *World Development* 48, 19–31.

Henrich, Joseph et al. (2001) 'In search of Homo economicus: Behavioral experiments in 15 small-scale societies', *American Economic Review*, 91, 2, 73–78.

Henrich, Natalie and Henrich, Joseph Patrick (2007) *Why Humans Cooperate: A Cultural and Evolutionary Explanation*. Oxford: Oxford University Press.

Holmberg, Sören and Rothstein, Bo (eds.) (2012) *Good Government: The Relevance of Political Science*. Cheltenham: Edward Elgar.

Jefferson, Philip N. (ed.) (2012) *The Oxford Handbook of the Economics of Poverty*. Oxford: Oxford University Press.

Klein, Rudolf (2010) *The New Politics of the National Health Service (6th ed)*, 3. ed. London: Longman.

Korpi, Walter and Palme, Joakim (1998) 'The paradox of redistribution and strategies of equality: Welfare state institutions, inequality, and poverty in the Western countries', *American Sociological Review*, 63, 5, 661–687.

Kumlin, Staffan (2004) *The Personal and the Political: How Personal Welfare State Experiences Affect Political Trust and Ideology*. New York: Palgrave/Macmillan.

Larsen, Christian Albrekt (2007) 'How welfare regimes generate and erode social capital: The impact of underclass phenomena', *Comparative Politics*, 40, 1, 83–110.

Larsen, Christian Albrekt (2008) 'The institutional logic of welfare state attitudes', *Comparative Political Studies*, 41, 2, 145–168.

Levi, Margaret (1991) 'Are there limits to rationality', *Achives Européennes de Sociologie*, 32, 1, 130–141.

Levi, Margaret (1998) *Consent, Dissent, and Patriotism*. New York: Cambridge University Press.

Neier, Aryeh (2002) *Taking Liberties: Four Decades in the Struggle for Rights*. New York: Public Affairs.

Norris, Pippa (2012) *Democratic Governance and Human Security: The Impact of Regimes on Prosperity, Welfare and Peace*. New York: Cambridge University Press.

Nussbaum, Martha C. (2001) 'The enduring significance of John Rawls', *The Chronicle of Higher Eduction: The Chronicle Review*, 20 July.

OECD (2011) *The Causes of Growing Inequality in OECD Countries*. Paris: OECD Publishing.

Okin, Susan Moller and Cohen, Joshua (1999) *Is Multiculturalism Bad for Women?* Princeton, N.J.: Princeton University Press.

Ostrom, Elinor (1998) 'A behavioral approach to the rational choice theory of collective action', *American Political Science Reveiw*, 92, 1, 1–23.

Ostrom, Elinor (2000) 'Crowding out citizenship', *Scandinavian Political Studies*, 23, 1, 3–16.

Piketty, Thomas (2015) *The Economics of Inequality*. Cambridge, MA: Harvard University Press.

Pontusson, Jonas (2005) *Inequality and Prosperity: Social Europe vs. Liberal America*. Ithaca, New York: Cornell University Press.

Radcliff, Benjamin (2013) *The Political Economy of Human Happiness*. New York: Cambridge University Press.

Rawls, John (1971) *A Theory of Justice*. Oxford: Oxford University Press.

Rawls, John (2005) *Political Liberalism*, expanded ed. New York: Columbia University Press.

Roemer, John E. (2009) 'The prospects for achieving equality in market economies', in Salverda, Weimer, Nolan, Brian and Smeeding, Timothy M. (eds.) *The Oxford Handbook of Economic Inequality*. Oxford: Oxford University Press, 693–708.

Rothstein, Bo (1998) *Just Institutions Matter: The Moral and Political Logic of the Universal Welfare State*. Cambridge: Cambridge University Press.

Rothstein, Bo (2002) 'Sweden: Social capital in the social democratic state', in Putnam, R.D. (ed.) *Democracies in Flux: The Evolution of Social Capital in Contemporary Society*. Oxford: Oxford University Press.

Rothstein, Bo (2005a) 'Is political science producing technically competent barbarians?', *European Political Science*, 4, 1, 3–13.

Rothstein, Bo (2005b) *Social Traps and the Problem of Trust*. Cambridge: Cambridge University Press.

Rothstein, Bo (2010) 'Happiness and the welfare state', *Social Research*, 77, 2, 441–468.

Rothstein, Bo (2011) *The Quality of Government: Corruption, Social Trust and Inequality in a Comparative Perspective*. Chicago: The University of Chicago Press.

Rothstein, Bo (2013) 'Corruption and social trust: Why the fish rots from the head down', *Social Research*, 80, 4, 1009–1032.

Rothstein, Bo, Samanni, Marcus and Teorell, Jan (2011) 'Explaining the welfare state: Power resources vs. the quality of government', *European Political Science Review*, 3, 2.

Rothstein, Bo and Uslaner, Eric M. (2005) 'All for all: Equality, corruption and social trust', *World Politics*, 58, 3, 41–73.

Sen, Amartya (1979) *Equality of What?* Stanford, CA: The Tanner Lecture of Human Values.

Sen, Amartya (2010) *The Idea of Justice*. London: Penguin.

Stolle, Dietlind (2003) 'The sources of social capital', in Hooghe, M. and Stolle, D. (eds.) *Generating Social Capital: Civil Society and Institutions in a Comparative Perspective*. New York: Palgrave/Macmillan.

Svallfors, Stefan (ed.) (2007) *The Political Sociology of the Welfare State: Institutions, Social Cleavages, and Orientations*. Stanford, Calif.: Stanford University Press.

Svallfors, Stefan (2013) 'Government quality, egalitarianism, and attitudes to taxes and social spending: A European comparison', *European Political Science Review*, 5, 3, 363–380S.

Therborn, Göran (2013) *The Killing Fields of Inequality*. London: Polity Press.

Tsebelis, George (1990) *Nested Games: Rational Choice in a Comparative Perspective*. New York: Cambridge University Press.

Uslaner, Eric M. (2002) *The Moral Foundation of Trust*. New York: Cambridge University Press.

Uslaner, Eric M. and Rothstein, Bo (2016) 'The historical roots of corruption: State building, economic inequality, and mass education', *Comparative Politics*, 48, 2, 227–248.

Wilkinson, Richard G. and Pickett, Kate (2009) *The Spirit Level: Why More Equal Societies Almost Always Do Better*. London: Allen Lane.

ERIK OLIN WRIGHT

The Capitalist State
and the Possibility of Socialism

The most fundamental challenge facing Marxist theory today is developing an account of a socialist alternative to capitalism that is strategically relevant for anti-capitalist struggles in the 21st century. The issue here is both the ambiguities in formulating a coherent and compelling concept of socialism itself in the face of the historical experience of the 20th century as well as the difficulty in developing a plausible strategy for challenging capitalism in ways that would help bring socialism, however it is defined, about. The theory of the state bears on both of these issues: the state is one of the central structures that contributes to the reproduction of capitalism and obstructs transformative struggles, and the state would have to play a central role in the successful construction of a socialist alternative.

In this essay I will explore some of the ways Göran Therborn's book, *What Does the Ruling Class Do When it Rules?*, can contribute to meeting this challenge. The book was published in 1978, at the apex of the wave of innovative theoretical work in Marxism that began in the mid-1960s. It constitutes the most systematic attempt to give analytical rigor to the idea that in capitalist society the state is a *capitalist state* rather than simply a *state in capitalist society*. While this idea has a long pedigree in the Marxist tradition and had been given renewed attention a few years earlier in a debate in *New Left Review* between Ralph Miliband and Nicos Poulantzas (Poulantzas 1969; Miliband 1970 and 1973; Poulantzas 1976), no one had deeply explored the theoretical implications of this claim nor attempted to develop as elaborate a conceptual map of the class character of the capitalist state.

The book was written in a period of considerable optimism and self-confidence on the left. The developed capitalist economies were floundering in the midst of stagflation and seemed incapable of overcoming their internal crises. The radical upsurge of the 1960s and early 1970s had stimulated new thinking and theoretical vigor, especially within the Marxist tradition. And in spite of the horrific defeat of the Allende regime in Chile, the prospects for significant advance of the left through electoral politics seemed real. In discussing the idea of a ruling class, Therborn could still with some optimism explore 'how it can be overthrown' (*What Does the Ruling Class Do When it Rules?*, p. 135). The result was that at the end of the book, after writing about both the possibilities and the contradictions of strategies being pursued by working class parties in Europe, Therborn could write: 'These and many other contradictions and problems still have to be overcome – and they will be overcome one way or another. But in order to tackle them in the right way, it is far better to prepare for them in advance' (p. 283).

In the second decade of the 21st century, it is difficult to muster this kind of self-confidence that the contradictions facing anti-capitalist strategies 'will be overcome one way or another'. In what follows I will argue that it may be possible to navigate the deep contradictions facing any strategy for transcending capitalism, but to do so requires, once again, new thinking on the relationship of the state to the problem. I will begin by reviewing the central arguments of *What Does the Ruling Class Do When it Rules?* I will then indicate how, with some modification, Therborn's framework can help open an agenda for engaging the strategic problem of challenging capitalism.

The central arguments of the book

The class character of state power and state apparatuses

The title of Therborn's book asks the question, 'What does the ruling class do when it rules?' The answer to the question is this:

> When we say that a class holds state power we mean that what is done through the state positively acts on the (re-)production of the mode

of production, of which the class in question is the dominant bearer. (p. 144.)

What then does the ruling class do when it rules? Essentially it reproduces the economic, political and ideological relations of its domination. This rule is exercised through state power, that is to say, through the interventions or policies of the state and their effects on the positions of the ruling class within the relations of production, the state apparatus and the ideological system. (p. 161.)

Power, in this formulation, is defined in terms of the capacity to generate effects in the world.[1] *State* power, then, is the capacity of the state to produce effects through its actions, where the state itself is defined as: 'a separate institution which concentrates the supreme rule-making, rule-applying, rule-adjudicating, rule-enforcing and rule-defending functions of that society' (p. 144). To be a *ruling class* is to identify the class-character of the 'rules' in all of those functions. The rules are not class neutral; they contribute to reproducing the class relations of the mode of production. Insofar as rule-making/applying/adjudicating/enforcing/defending contribute to the maintenance and promotion of a given mode of production, the dominant class in that mode of production can be identified as the ruling class: 'To take and hold state power signifies to bring about a particular mode of intervention of the special body invested with these functions' (p. 145).

The class character of state power is indicated by the effects of what the state does: State power has a class character to the extent such effects promote and protect the class relations of a mode of production. The class character of the state apparatuses is defined by organizational properties of the state that make those effects possible. The basic idea here is that while 'state power is exercised through the state apparatus' (p. 35), the ability of states to actually generate effects

---

1. This view of power, Therborn argues, is sharply different from the dominant approach in sociology which he refers to as the '*subjectivist* approach' that 'seeks to locate the subject of power' (p. 130). In contrast, the Marxist approach 'starts not from "the point of view of the actor" but from that of the on-going social process of reproduction and transformation' (p. 131).

that maintain and promote given class relations depends to a significant extent on the properties of these apparatuses. The state apparatus 'provides a filter determining the modality of state economic and ideological interventions'. Different organizational forms, then, infuse these filters with a different class content, excluding interventions that would undermine the position of dominant classes and favoring interventions that would maintain or promote those classes.[2] Some forms of state apparatuses would simply be unsuitable for the exercise of state power on behalf of certain classes.

The major innovation in the book is to go beyond these very general formulations about state power and state apparatuses, and attempt to identify the specific mechanisms in the state apparatuses themselves that contribute to the class character of carrying out these functions in different modes of production. Therborn pursues this conceptual task through a systematic exploration of the variation in the properties of the state in feudalism, capitalism and socialism; the specificity of the properties of the state connected to any given mode of production comes from contrasts with other modes of production. The resulting analysis combines an elaborate analytical framework that identifies the relevant structural elements of state apparatuses with extensive empirical discussions of historical variations in the machinery of the state in different times and places.

While Therborn insists throughout his analysis that his proposed conceptual menu of the class character of state apparatuses should be treated as provisional and subject to revision, he also insists that it is not a speculative philosophical analysis based on some purely logical understanding of feudalism, capitalism and socialism. He wants the claims about the class character of apparatuses to be empirically grounded: the categories are meant to be theoretical abstractions from empirical observations of actually existing societies rather than pure thought experiments. This is fairly straightforward for his investigation of capitalism and feudalism. It is much more precari-

---

2. Claus Offe usefully elaborates this idea of filter mechanisms by referring to them as generating *negative selections* with built-in *class biases*. Negative selection identifies the mechanisms as operating through what they exclude: they make certain kinds of interventions much less likely than others. Class bias identifies the content of what is excluded. See Offe 1974.

ous for the investigation of socialism given the highly contentious disagreements even within Marxism over the historical meaning of states that proclaimed themselves to be socialist. Therborn insists that the USSR, China, Cuba and other countries that called themselves socialist were, when he wrote the book, actually socialist. Just as capitalist states can be organized as liberal democracies or authoritarian fascist regimes, so too, Therborn argues, can socialist states be authoritarian or democratic. While Therborn clearly endorses radical democracy, he does not see this as a necessary ingredient of socialism itself. This is a controversial position, and as we will see in the second half of this essay, has important implications for the way we think about challenges to capitalism. Democracy is more central to socialism than it is to capitalism since without democracy it is hard to see what it means for the working class as such to 'exercise power'. It is for this reason that I prefer to characterize the USSR and other authoritarian command-economies as instances of a *statist mode of production* rather than socialism. In any case, in *What Does the Ruling Class Do When it Rules?*, Therborn treats the states that called themselves socialist in the mid-20th century as appropriate empirical cases for building his conceptual map of variations in the class character of state apparatuses.

To conduct this investigation, Therborn creates an elaborate inventory of structural elements of state apparatuses involved in determining the inputs to the state, the transformation of those inputs by the internal practices of the state, and the outputs of the state. Two examples of these structural elements will help clarify Therborn's strategy of analysis: the determination of *appropriate tasks* for state activity, and the *acquisition of necessary material resources* for state actions.[3]

---

3. In total, Therborn distinguishes twelve structural elements in state apparatuses. Three are connected to inputs (which he refers to as tasks, personnel recruitment, and energy or the acquisition of resources); three are connected to transformation (handling of tasks, patterning of personnel, utilization of resources); five are connected to outputs (foreign policy tasks, domestic policy tasks, inter-state personnel relations, domestic personnel relations, outputs of material resources); and finally one is referred to somewhat cryptically as the effects of technology. A summary list of these elements can be found on pp. 118–119.

First, every state, regardless of what it does, needs to distinguish between activities that are the legitimate business of the state and activities which are not. This is basically the problem of the relationship between the public and the private. In capitalism, there is a fairly sharp distinction between public and private spheres: 'The issues with which the bourgeois state is concerned are ... defined by the characteristic *distinction between the private and public spheres:* the state occupies itself only with the latter' (p. 63). While the precise boundary between the public and private is often contested, and have certainly shifted in the course of capitalist development, nevertheless,

> Generally speaking, the private sphere has extended to the choice of occupation and place of work, the choice of marriage-partner, and the ideological convictions, consumption habits and life-style of the individual. In other words, it has comprised the labour market, capital accumulation, the bourgeois nuclear family, and the whole field of bourgeois 'individualism'. (p. 66.)

This sharp demarcation of public and private spheres acts as a class-based filter mechanism on state actions which protects the core class relations of capitalism, making it much more difficult for state interventions to undermine the private property and the power of the capitalist class.

In contrast to capitalism, 'Under feudalism the state is "privatized"' (p. 67). This doesn't mean, Therborn argues, that the state in feudalism is literally the private property of the king. Rather, in feudalism there is 'a fusion of this institution with the appropriation of the means of production (land) by individual lords, of whom one rose to the position of king.' This fusion tends to reproduce the power of the feudal ruling class by making it less likely that state actions will undermine the capacity of feudal elites to coercively appropriate surplus from peasants.

In socialism, there is a 'politicization of all spheres, including "private life"' (p. 118). This doesn't imply that individual autonomy and choice is continually subjected to intrusive state regulation, and it certainly 'is not the equivalent to the absorption of the private sphere by a public bureaucracy' (p. 69). Rather, it means that the precise boundary of personal autonomy is subjected to public deliberation. While the filter mechanism in the public/private demarcation of capitalism protects private property and promotes the power of capitalists, the politicization of the private sphere in socialism, Therborn argues, helps to secure the power of the working class.

A second example of class mechanisms inscribed in state apparatuses concerns the ways in which states acquire the necessary resources to pay for state actions. In capitalism this is accomplished mainly through taxation: 'funds needed for public purposes are provided by regular and compulsory levies on private individuals and business enterprises' (p. 85). Public budgets require a capacity to transfer income from private accounts. Under feudalism, in contrast, 'the state budget depended above all on the size of the royal domain and on the degree of exploitation to which its attached peasants were subjected' (p. 86). In a sense the private accounts of the king were directly the source of public budgets. Finally, in socialism, 'Revenue is drawn principally from public enterprise and is directly bound up with the global planning process and the pricing of goods' (p. 86). The state divides the publicly generated surplus into a part used to fund state functions and a part used for other purposes.

As in the example of the public/private demarcation, these three different ways of acquiring revenues for state activities act as class-biased filter mechanisms on state actions, favoring actions that tend to reproduce the class relations of capitalist, feudal and socialist societies respectively. In capitalism, because state revenues depend upon taxes extracted from private economic activity, the state is forced to pay attention to the impact of its tax and spending policies on private incentives, especially the incentives of capitalists to invest. In feudalism, in order to have a secure source of revenues, the state is forced to be concerned with the size of the royal estates and the degree of exploitation of its peasants, thus reproducing feudal class relations. And in socialism, the dependency of the state on surpluses generated by public enterprise means that there is pressure for state actions to attempt to strengthen the class solidarity and mobilization within the working class that is a crucial source of productivity in a socialist economy.

Complications and contradictions:
moving from modes of production to social formations
and from structural forms to historical contingency

The analytical framework Therborn develops to specify the class character of state power and state apparatuses is formulated at the level of abstraction that Marxists refer to as the mode of production. Analyzing state power and state apparatuses at that level of abstraction gives the analysis a somewhat functionalist cast: the exercise of state power reproduces the class relations of a mode of production and the state apparatuses are structured in such a way as to facilitate these reproductive effects. This comes close to explaining the form of the state by the functional requirements of reproducing a given mode of production.[4]

Therborn resolutely rejects such functionalist reasoning by insisting that there is no guarantee that these functional requirements are actually fulfilled. Actual states are riddled with contradictions, both in their internal organization and in their relationship to the broader society. Such contradictions can significantly interfere with any smooth functional reproduction of class relations.

There are three main sources of such contradictions.

First, actual societies never consist of a single mode of production. The state thus always faces the problem of how different kinds of relations of production with their associated class relations are connected and interact within concrete social formations. This opens the possibility of a variety of different forms of disjuncture between state and economy, especially in periods of transitions from one kind of economic structure to another:

> These well known cases of disjuncture between state and economy provide glimpses of a number of areas of complexity. Not only do several different classes and modes of production coexist; they also inter-penetrate one another in many ways, giving rise to hybrid forms and special transmutations. (p. 149.)

---

4. For a sustained and rigorous elaboration of the functionalist explanations embodied in the idea of base and superstructure, see Cohen 2000.

Second, the state consists of many apparatuses – it is really a system of apparatuses rather than 'an' apparatus – and this creates the potential for tensions and disjunctures among different apparatuses:

> It follows that, although the variance between state power and the state apparatus is limited by the fact that they express the class relations of the same society, at any given moment significant disjunctures appear between the two. The possibilities of variance are substantially increased by the coexistence within a particular state system of several apparatuses, in which different sets of class relations may have crystallized. These disjunctures have a fundamentally destabilizing effect … (p. 35.)

Third, there are potentially significant time lags between the changes in the class relations of a society and the organizational properties of the state apparatus. In Therborn's words, state apparatuses are a 'materialized condensation' of class relations and 'tend to manifest [those relations] with a particular rigidity' (p. 153). This rigidity is part of the reason state apparatuses can robustly support a given set of class relations. But rigidity also means that there can be significant changes in class relations and class power in a society that are not instantaneously reflected in the class character of state apparatuses. The tasks which the state is called upon to execute 'basically derive from the changing totality in which it operates'. This changing totality may involve new configurations of class forces and problems. There is thus the potential for a significant contradiction between the form of class domination currently embodied the state apparatuses and the task execution required of state actions:

> But the successful organization of class domination in the state apparatus itself generates new problems of government, administration, judicatures and repressions – problems which call into question the existing organizational forms domination. This contradiction between domination and execution, which may take diverse forms has to be resolved in one way or the other, and it thus becomes an internal force for change within the apparatus. (p. 47.)

Taken together, these three kinds of contradictions imply that the state should not be regarded as a smoothly operating machine for the reproduction of class domination, but as contingently functional and contested system. The functionalist side of this argument shows how the distinctive class character of the state apparatuses of the state imposes limits on state policies in ways that tend to maintain and promote the position of dominant class in society; the analysis of contradictions and disjunctures helps make sense of why those limits may break down and new possibilities emerge.

The problem of challenging and transcending capitalism

Towards the middle of the book, Therborn explains why Marxist theory seeks to understand the class character of the state:

> It does so in order to discover the characteristic social structures and relations which are promoted and protected above all others by the material force of the state; and in order to determine the conditions under which they may be changed or abolished ... There then arises the question of how this class rule is grounded and maintained and how it can be overthrown. (p. 132.)

This is a fundamental point, also reflected in one of Marx's most famous aphorisms, the eleventh thesis on Feuerbach: 'The philosophers have only interpreted the world, in various ways; the point is to change it.' The point, of course, is not merely to change the world, but to change in a very particular way: challenging and transcending capitalism by constructing an alternative economic structure in which the working class controls the means of production and capitalist class domination and exploitation is eliminated. This is broadly what is understood as the transition from capitalism to socialism.

One of the crucial issues in the theory of transcending capitalism concerns the role of the state in impeding or facilitating this transition. In *What Does the Ruling Class Do When it Rules?*, Therborn frames the problem of the transition from capitalism to socialism in a fairly traditional Marxist way. His most explicit statement occurs in a discussion of disjunctures between the class character of state power (again: the effects of state interventions on class relations) and state apparatuses. Therborn notes that historically there are many instances in which the class character of state power and the class character of state apparatuses do not coincide. 'The transition from feudalism to capitalism raises just this question in a number of instances' (p. 149). He cites the case of England on the eve of the English Civil War and Russia before the Bolshevik Revolution as instances where the 'state apparatus was still fundamentally feudal' even though 'little remained of feudal relations of production', and thus state power no longer promoted or maintained feudal relations. 'In fact,' Therborn writes, 'in most countries other than France, such disjunctures seem to have been the rule rather than the exception' (p. 149). He then states,

> Similar [disjunctures] may be found in the transition from capitalism to socialism, *with the important qualification that here a decisive change in the state apparatus precedes the transformation of relations of production.* The NEP period in the USSR, when maintenance of a new socialist state apparatus was combined with the fostering of both capitalist and petty-commodity production, is probably the clearest example of such a phenomenon. (p. 149, italics added.)

The italicized phrase reflects a critical asymmetry in traditional Marxist understandings of the transition between feudalism and capitalism and the transition from capitalism to socialism. In the former, capitalist relations emerge within feudalism, and for a long period these societies are characterized by an articulation of these two modes of production. The feudal state, especially in the form of the Absolutist State, thus superintends a social formation within which feudal relations are gradually eroded as capitalist relations expand and deepen. The destruction of the feudal character of that state apparatus comes at the end of the process of erosion of feudalism, not at the beginning. In contrast, in the transition from capitalism to socialism, 'a decisive change in the state apparatus precedes the transformation of relations of production'. Therborn discusses the Russian and Cuban revolutions as instances in which 'these revolutions initially fostered peasant petty-commodity production and even capitalist enterprise, at the same time as they brought about a more or less complete smashing and transformation of the bourgeois state apparatus' (p. 152). As a result of this successful transformation of the class character of the state apparatuses, 'the proletarian character of the state apparatuses secured for [the working class] a decisive position of strength from which to ... embark upon socialist construction' (p. 152). In short: in the transition from feudalism to capitalism, capitalist relations of production develop within feudalism and then the class character of the state is transformed; in the transition from capitalism to socialism, the class character of the state is transformed, and then socialist relations of production can develop alongside remnants of capitalist relations.[5]

This is the standard Marxist model. It underwrites the classical revolutionary vision which sees seizing the state and rapidly transforming its fundamental structures as a necessary condition for the development of socialism. This was an inspiring vision for anti-capitalists throughout much of the 20th century, but it no longer seems credible to many (perhaps most) people today, even if they are resolutely anti-capitalist. There are two basic issues in play here. First, it is very hard to construct a convincing scenario for developed capitalist countries in which anti-capitalist forces would be able to seize state power in a way that would make possible 'a more or less complete smashing and transformation of the bourgeois state apparatus'. One might envision over an extended period of time a democratization of the state through a heterogeneous process of changes in particular apparatuses and the creation of new kinds of quasi-state apparatuses that undermined the unity of the state; what is difficult is to imagine is the ruptural transformation of the state that the standard Marxist model sees as necessary for setting in motion 'socialist construc-

---

5. Marxists often also argue that within capitalism the *forces of production* gradually have a more and more social character, while the relations of production continue to generate the private appropriation of the surplus generated using those forces of production. This 'contradiction' between the forces and relations of production is one of the conditions which makes the transformation of the relations possible. Nevertheless, that transformation of capitalist class relations only occurs after the seizure of state power and transformation of state apparatuses.

tion'. Second, the historical evidence from the 20th century does not provide much confidence that even if it were possible to smash the bourgeois state apparatus, the result would be human emancipation through the broad, democratic empowerment of the working class. If, then, a revolutionary rupture in the capitalist state is actually a necessary condition for socialism, this suggests that socialism simply is not possible.

There is, however, an alternative model of the transition from capitalism to socialism which is constructed around the possibility of socialist relations emerging within capitalism and eroding its dominance. Even though Therborn does not envision such a possibility, his framework for understanding the complex, contradictory configurations of the class character of state power and state apparatuses is congenial to this model of socialism as a destination and the process of getting there. The model can be distilled into four basic arguments.

1. SOCIALISM AS ECONOMIC DEMOCRACY. There is no agreement among anti-capitalists, even among Marxists, about how to define socialism. Do markets play a significant role in a socialist economy, or does socialism imply comprehensive planning? Is socialism based on state ownership of the means of production, or are there a variety of social forms of ownership in a socialist economy? What does it really mean to say that the working class controls the means of production in socialism? Is socialism the only post-capitalist alternative to capitalism?

One way of approaching these issues is to focus on the way power is organized within economic relations, particularly over the allocation of the social surplus and control of the process of production. This, I would argue, is the most fundamental line of demarcation between economic structures (or modes of production in traditional Marxist terminology). Invoking power, of course, opens up a Pandora's box of theoretical issues. I will adopt a deliberately stripped-down concept of power: power is the capacity to do things in the world, to produce effects. This is what might be called an 'agent-centered' notion of power: people, both acting individually and collectively, use power to accomplish things. In particular, they use power to allocate investments and control production.

At first glance this definition of power might seem like the kind of subjectivist concept of power that Therborn criticizes. This is not correct. While I have specified the concept in terms of agents using power to accomplish things in the world, this does not imply that their actual capacity to do so is at attribute of the agents themselves rather than the structure in which they are embedded. Capitalists use their economic power to allocate investments, but they can only do so because of the ways in which the relations of production enable them to do so. People wield power, they use it for particular ends which are in part their subjective purposes, but the power they wield is structurally determined and a property of the social relations in which they act.

With this broad definition of power, we can then distinguish three kinds of power that are deployed within economic systems to allocate the surplus and control production: *economic power*, rooted in control over the use of economic resources; *state power*, rooted in control over rule making and rule enforcing over territory; and what I will term *social power*, rooted in the capacity to mobilize people for cooperative, voluntary collective actions.[6] Expressed as a mnemonic slogan, you can get people to do things by bribing them, forcing them, or persuading them. Every complex economic system involves all three forms of power, connected in different ways.

Different economic structures can be distinguished on the basis of which of these forms of power is most important for determining the use of the social surplus and the control of production. In particular, capitalism can be distinguished from two post-capitalist economic structures in these terms:[7]

---

6. There is a sense, of course, in which all power is 'social'. I am using the expression *social power* in a narrower sense here to refer to power that is embedded in the capacity of people to make choices within social interactions.
7. This is not a complete theoretical specification of the differences between these three types of economic structure, but only their differentiation in terms of power relations. For a fuller discussion, see Wright 2010: 111–123.

– Capitalism is an economic structure within which the means of production are privately owned and the allocation and use of resources for different social purposes is accomplished through the exercise of economic power. Investments and the control of production are the result of the exercise of economic power by owners of capital.

– Statism is an economic structure within which the means of production are owned by the state and the allocation and use of resources for different social purposes is accomplished through the exercise of state power. State officials control the investment process and production through some sort of state-administrative mechanism.

– Socialism is an economic structure within which the means of production are socially owned[8] and the allocation and use of resources for different social purposes is accomplished through the exercise of 'social power'. In effect this is equivalent to defining *socialism as pervasive economic democracy.*

This definition of socialism differs from the one adopted by Therborn in *What Does the Ruling Class Do When it Rules?* For Therborn, socialism is not an ideal-type abstraction; it is a theoretical characterization of the kind of economic system socialists empirically struggle to create: '... socialism is that which socialists are fighting to realize in history' (p. 277). It was on this basis that he argued that the Soviet Union and China were empirical examples of socialist economic structures and socialist states, even if the regimes in these societies had many undesirable characteristics. If socialism were

---

8. Social ownership should be distinguished from state ownership. Social ownership of economic resources means that these are owned in common by everyone in a society, and thus everyone has the collective right to decide on the distribution of the net income generated by the use of those resources and the collective right to dispose of those resources. Under conditions of deep and pervasive democracy, state ownership becomes one way of organizing social ownership.

the only possible economic structure that could replace capitalism, then this might be a reasonable solution to the problem of giving some empirical grounding to the discussion of socialism and the socialist state. But if this is not the case, then the situation becomes much more ambiguous, for while socialists might be fighting for an alternative to capitalism in which workers become the dominant class, the unintended consequences of their struggles could result in something quite different. Socialists could fight for socialism, but nevertheless produce authoritarian statism and still, for purposes of legitimation, call this 'socialism'.

Because of these considerations, I will adopt a definition of socialism as an alternative to capitalism that is not an abstraction from empirically observable cases of post-capitalist societies. This does not mean, however, that this concept has no empirical grounding. The existence of relations of production embodying social power is part of real structures of actually-existing capitalist economic systems. The theoretical extrapolation that these could constitute the dominant relations of a future economy is therefore not simply an affirmation of normative ideals.

To understand this proposition, we need to turn to the second element in the model: the idea that economic systems are complex combinations of heterogeneous relations of production.

2. ECONOMIC STRUCTURES AS COMPLEX ECONOMIC ECOSYSTEMS. The definitions of capitalism, statism and socialism I have proposed are ideal types. In the world, actual economies are complex forms of combination of these three types. They are *ecosystems of economic structures* that vary according to how these different forms of power interact and intermix.[9] To call an economy 'capitalist' is thus shorthand for a more cumbersome expression such as 'an economic ecosystem combining capitalist, statist and socialist power relations within which capitalist relations are dominant'. The idea of

---

9. This formulation is similar to the idea of 'articulation of modes of production', but has a bit more empirical flexibility since some of the different forms in an ecosystem may not be full-fledged 'modes of production' in the traditional Marxian meaning of that concept.

economies as ecosystems dominated by particular relations of production can be used to describe any unit of analysis – firms, sectors, regional economies, national economies, even the global economy. These power relations also interpenetrate within individual units of production, so particular enterprises can be *hybrids* operating in the economic ecosystem that surrounds them. The possibility of socialism thus depends on our ability to enlarge and deepen the socialist component within the overall economic ecosystem and weaken the capitalist and statist components.

This way of understanding the complexity of economic structures is familiar in the case of the ways capitalist relations emerge within feudal societies. As Therborn writes: 'Mercantile capital not only coexisted with feudalism within the social formation; it also entered into the reproduction of the feudal mode of exploitation itself, connecting the economic units of the latter with one another' (p. 46). What is less familiar is the idea that socialist relations of production can emerge as a salient feature of the economic structure of capitalist economies. But what does this mean concretely? What are instances of socialist relations of production within capitalism?

Here are a few examples:

– Worker-owned cooperatives in which the means of production are owned by the workers and production is governed through democratic mechanisms.

– The social and solidarity economy in which production is oriented to meeting needs and governance is organized in a variety of democratic and quasi-democratic ways.

– Community land-trusts in which land is taken out of the market, its use specified through the conditions of the trust, and the trust itself is governed by some kind of community-based board.

– Peer-to-peer collaborative production of use-values such as Wikipedia and Linux.

– State production of public goods when the priorities for public goods production are set through robust democratic processes.[10]

All of these examples, in different ways, embody some aspects of socialist relations of production insofar as social power plays a significant role in the organization of economic activities, but of course, these examples also often take a hybrid form in which features of capitalist relations are also present.[11] Worker-owned cooperatives often have some employees, for example. Capitalist corporations may pay some of their employees to participate in peer-to-peer collaborative production – Google pays some of its software engineers to contribute to the development of Linux, even though Linux itself is an open-source, free software system. Enterprises in the social and solidarity economy sometimes get grants from private foundations and philanthropists whose resources come from capitalist investments. The articulation of the capitalist and socialist elements in this complex array of social forms is messy, ambiguous and contradictory. Nevertheless, these all constitute ways of organizing economic activities in which social power plays a significant, and in some cases, dominant role.

3. ERODING CAPITALISM. If one accepts the idea that capitalist societies contain a variety of noncapitalist forms of economic organization, including socialist and proto-socialist forms, then there is at least the possibility that these socialist relations and practices could expand and deepen over time, even in an economy in which capital-

---

10. In my proposed typology of economic structures, the direct state provision of public goods can be an instance of either statism or socialism or a hybrid depending upon the extent to which the state itself is democratically subordinated to social power. The state's production of use values, including public goods, can be viewed as one of the *pathways of social empowerment* when it is the case that the exercise of state power is itself effectively subordinated to social power through robust mechanisms of democratic rule. For an elaboration of these issues, see Wright 2010: 131–134.

11. Details of these examples and many others can be found in Wright 2010, chapter 7. For an extended discussion of the complex hybridity of these forms, see Wright 2010, chapter 5.

ism is dominant. The could occur both within capitalist firms, if the socialist elements become stronger over time, and within the broader ecosystem of capitalism, if *social*ist economic organizations (i.e. organizations built around the exercise of social power) occupied an ever greater economic space. The first of these involves, for example, an increasing role for workers' assemblies and other forms of worker-governance within capitalist firms, along with increasing worker-ownership of the assets of the firms and participation on boards of directors. The second involves the development and spread of a wide range of economic organizations that operate on non-capitalist principles. The growth of the social/solidarity economy in some parts of the world and the development of novel forms of peer-to-peer collaborative production mediated by the Internet would be examples. Over time, then, if these socially-empowered relations and practices developed sufficiently, the cumulative effect of such expansion could be a gradual erosion of the overall dominance of capitalism. Capitalism would continue to exist, but in a more restricted domain of economic activities and without being able to impose definitive constraints on the other economic forms within the economic ecosystem.

4. THE CAPITALIST STATE AND THE EROSION OF CAPITALISM. It is one thing to observe that capitalist societies contain all sorts of non-capitalist forms of production, including forms that have in some sense a socialist character, and quite another to imagine that these quasi-socialist forms of production could expand in ways that seriously eroded the dominance of capitalism. Here, then, is the critical, problem: On the one hand, it is implausible that socialist relations of production to expand to the point of undermining the dominance of capitalism within the economic ecosystem without the support of the state, but on the other hand if socially-empowered forms of economic activity were seriously encroaching on capitalism in ways that threatened capitalist dominance, the capitalist class would use the capitalist state to neutralize the threat. This, after all, is precisely what the capitalist state is designed to do: to reproduce the dominant relations of production in the face of threats. So the question: how can the capitalist state simultaneously reproduce capitalism and

facilitate conditions that in the long-run undermine the dominance of capitalism?

If the class character of the capitalist state meant that it was a functionally-integrated coherent machine preoccupied with the long-term reproduction of capitalism, then the prospects of non-capitalist forms of economic organization ever eroding capitalist dominance would indeed be dim. Therborn's account of state power and state apparatuses argues, however, that the capitalist state should not be analyzed in such strongly functionalist terms. More specifically, there are three elements of his analysis that open a space for a more contradictory relationship between the capitalist state and the development of potentially corrosive alternatives to capitalism: heterogeneity in the class character of different state apparatuses; concessions, compromises, and contingent functionality; and temporal inconsistencies in state actions.

Variability in the class character of state apparatuses

Even if the state is properly described as a 'capitalist state' by virtue of the class character of state as a whole, as was explained in the summary of Therborn's framework, Therborn stresses that this does not imply that there is no variability in the class character of specific apparatuses within the state:

> Although the state is, in a fundamental sense, always one, the level of integration of its apparatuses varies considerably, and it should not be taken for granted that they share a common class character. For the state is the concentrated expression of a highly complex set of class relations, which are refracted in disjunctures of varying profundity between the different apparatuses. Within limits imposed by the general nature of the state, it is especially probable that the class character of its diverse apparatuses will vary with the link between the tasks of the apparatus and the concerns of classes rooted in the mode of production. (p. 41.)

Therborn goes on to clarify this point by saying 'It may thus be expected that ... the welfare apparatus, whilst remaining bourgeois, would be affected by its close relationship with the working class' (p. 41–2). Different apparatuses within the state are thus likely to coexist 'in which different sets of class relations may have crystallized' (p. 35). Therborn is careful to add the qualifier that that these variations occur 'within limits imposed by the general nature of the state' (p. 41) and that 'the state is, in a fundamental sense, always one' (p. 35). Still, he leaves open the question of how wide or narrow those limits are. In particular, the class heterogeneity of apparatuses opens the possibility that certain apparatuses will be at least partially amenable to protecting and promoting noncapitalist economic relations, not merely capitalist relations.

Of particular relevance in assessing the variability in the class character of different state apparatuses is the problem of democracy. The more robustly democratic are the forms of accountability of particular apparatuses, the less purely capitalist is the class character of that apparatus. Even ordinary parliamentary democracy has always had a contradictory class character: while it may be true, as Marxists generally claim, that the rules of the game of electoral democracy have the general effect of constraining and taming class struggles over the state in ways that support capitalist dominance, it is also true that to the extent elections involve real democratic competition, they introduce potential tensions in the class character of legislative bodies. In times of crisis and popular mobilization, those tensions can loosen the limits of possibility for new forms of state initiatives.

Demands for deepening and revitalizing democracy can thus be thought of as demands for diluting – not eliminating, but diluting – the capitalist character of the state apparatuses. This is not simply a question of the democratic accountability of ordinary state machinery, but also of the wide variety of parastatal commissions and organizations that interface with all modern states.[12] Deepening democracy is also not simply a question of democratization of centralized national states, but of local and regional state apparatuses as well. Struggles over the democratic quality of the local state may be especially important in terms of thinking about ways in which state initiatives can enlarge the space for noncapitalist economic initiatives.

---

12. For a discussion of the principles of democratic deepening that extend beyond the boundaries of ordinary state apparatuses, see Fung and Wright 2003.

Concessions, compromises, and contingent functionality

While the class character of state power is defined by Therborn in terms of the reproductive effects of the state on class relations, the actual actions of the state are the result of struggles, not a smooth response to functional needs: 'state power is exercised not according to a pre-established functionalist harmony, but in and through the struggle of antagonistic classes. In this process it may be necessary to have recourse to concessions and compromises whereby, for instance, the state goes against the logic of capital accumulation without break-ing it' (p. 146). Concessions and compromises can be short-lived and reversed, or they can create more or less institutionalized alterations in social relations. This also opens the possibility – not explicitly dis-cussed by Therborn – that some concessions and compromises could directly or indirectly create more secure spaces for the development of noncapitalist relations, including relations of a distinctly socialist character. Such possibilities could be relatively durable if they became 'crystallized' in particular state apparatuses, giving those apparatuses a class character in tension with the state as a whole. One can imagine, for example, that under some circumstances, apparatuses of the local state responsible for community development and poverty alleviation could become closely connected to local social movements in ways that were particularly supportive of the social/solidarity economy and worker cooperatives.

Temporal inconsistencies and disjunctures

The final element in Therborn's analysis of the state that suggests that there are situations in which the capitalist state would toler-ate, and even encourage, economic practices rooted in social power, concerns temporal inconsistencies between the relatively short-term reproductive effects of state actions and the long-run dynamic con-sequences. The reproductive effects of state actions on the dominant relations of production that define the class character of state power are the result of actions that mainly respond to immediate condi-tions and challenges. This why, for example, the feudal state facili-tated merchant capitalism even though in the long run the dynamics of merchant capitalism was corrosive of feudal relations: 'Mercantile

capital not only coexisted with feudalism within the social formation; it also entered into the reproduction of the feudal mode of
exploitation itself, connecting the economic units of the latter with
one another' (p. 46). Mercantile capitalism helped solve immediate
problems for the feudal ruling class, and this is what mattered.

Similarly, in the middle of the twentieth century the capitalist
state facilitated the growth of a vibrant public sector and public regulation of capitalism associated with social democracy. Social democracy helped solve a series of problems within capitalism – it helped
reproduce capitalism – while at the same time expanding the space
for various socialist elements in the economic ecosystem: the partial
decommodification of labor power through state provision of significant components of workers material conditions of life, the increase
in working class social power within capitalist firms and the labor
market, and the democratic regulation of capital to deal with the
most serious negative externalities of the behavior of investors and
firms in capitalist markets (pollution, product and workplace haz-
ards, predatory market behavior, market volatility, etc.).

The fact that this array of state actions contributed to the stability of mid-twentieth century capitalism is sometimes taken as an
indication that there was nothing non-capitalist about these policies,
and certainly that they could not in any way be considered corrosive
of capitalism. This is a mistake. It is entirely possible for a form of
state intervention to have the immediate effects of solving problems
for capitalism, and even strengthening capitalism, and nevertheless
set in motion dynamics that have the potential to erode the dominance of capitalism over time. Indeed, it is precisely this property of
social democratic initiatives that eventually lead to the attacks on the
affirmative state under the banner of neoliberalism as the capitalist
class came to see the expansive affirmative state as creating progres-
sively suboptimal conditions for capital accumulation.[13]

The question for capitalism in the twenty-first century, then, is
whether or not this kind of temporal disjuncture is still possible

---

13. I prefer the term 'affirmative state' to 'welfare state' as a way of characterizing the expansive role of the state in neutralizing the harms of capitalism,
since the term 'welfare state' is often taken as referring to a narrow range of
issues concerned with individual insecurity.

within the capitalist state. Are there arrays state interventions which could solve pressing problems faced by capitalism but which, nevertheless, also have the potential long-run consequence of expanding the space in which democratic, egalitarian economic relations can develop?

Prospects for the future

The world in the first decades of the 21st century looks very different from the period in which social democracy flourished. The globalization of capitalism has made it much easier for capitalists to move investments to places in the world with less regulation and cheaper labor. The threat of such movement of capital, along with a variety of technological and demographic changes, has fragmented and weakened the labor movement, making it less capable of resistance and political mobilization. Combined with globalization, the financialization of capital has led to massive increases in wealth and income inequality, which in turn has increased the political leverage of opponents of the social democratic state. Perhaps the decades of the so-called Golden Age were just an historical anomaly, a brief period in which favorable structural conditions and robust popular power opened up the possibility for the relatively egalitarian, social democratic model of encroaching on the absolute dominance of capitalism. Before that time capitalism was a rapacious system, and under neoliberalism it has become rapacious once again, returning to the normal state of affairs for capitalist economic ecosystems. Perhaps in the long run the dominance of capitalism is just not erodible. Defenders of the idea of revolutionary ruptures with the capitalist state have always claimed that the dominance of capitalism could not be mitigated by reforms and efforts to do so were a diversion from the task of building a political movement to overthrow capitalism. Therborn, at the time of writing *What Does the Ruling Class Do When it Rules?*, certainly adopted the language of 'overthrow' as a way of thinking about a socialist future.

But perhaps things are not so dire. The claim that globalization imposes powerful constraints on the capacity of states to raise taxes, regulate capitalism, redistribute income and foster noncapitalist forms of economic activity is a politically effective claim because people believe it, not because the constraints are actually that narrow. In politics, the limits of possibility are always in part created by beliefs in the limits of possibility. Neoliberalism is an ideology, backed by powerful political forces, rather than a scientifically accurate account of the actual limits we face in making the world a better place. While it may be the case that the specific policies that constituted the menu of social democracy in the Golden Age have become less effective and need rethinking, the capitalist state remains an internally contradictory structure facing temporally inconsistent conditions for the reproduction of capitalism.

There are two trends that suggest some grounds for optimism about future possibilities for the kinds of state initiatives that could potentially foster long-term erosion of capitalist dominance.

First, global warming is likely spell the end of neoliberalism. Even aside from the issue of mitigating global warming through a conversion to non-carbon emitting energy production, the necessary adaptations to global warming will require a massive expansion of state-provided public goods. The market is simply not going to build sea walls to protect Manhattan. The scale of resources needed for such state interventions could easily reach the levels of the major wars of the twentieth century Second World War. Even though capitalist firms will profit enormously from such public good production – just as they profit from military production in times of war – the financing of such projects will require substantial tax increases and an effort ideologically at rehabilitating the affirmative state. If these processes occur within the framework of capitalist democracy, then this reinvigoration of the affirmative state will open up more space for broader, socially-directed state interventions.

The second trend with which the capitalist state will have to contend in the course of the 21st century is the long-term employment effects of the technological changes of the information revolution. Of course, with every wave of technological change there is speculation about the destruction of jobs leading to a widespread marginalization and permanent structural unemployment, but in previous waves, economic growth eventually created sufficient jobs in new sectors to overcome deficits in employment. The forms of automation in the digital age, which are now penetrating deep into the service sector, including sectors of professional services, makes it much less likely that future economic growth will provide adequate employment opportunities through the capitalist market. The magnitude of this problem is further intensified by the globalization of capitalist production. As the twenty-first century progresses, these problems will only get worse and will not be solved by spontaneous operation of market forces. The result is increasing precariousness and marginalization of a significant portion of the population. Even aside from social justice considerations, this trend is likely to generate social instability and costly conflict.

These two trends taken together pose major new challenges to the capitalist state: the need for a massive increase in the provision of public goods to deal with climate change, and the need for new policies to deal with broad economic marginalization caused by technological change. This is the context in which popular mobilizations and struggles have some prospect of producing new forms of state intervention which could underwrite the expansion of more democratic-egalitarian forms of economic activity coexisting with capitalism within the economic ecosystem.

More specifically, consider the following scenario.

The necessity to deal with adaptations to climate change marks the end of neoliberalism and its ideological strictures. The affirmative state embarks on the needed large scale, public works projects and also takes a more intrusive role economic planning around energy production to accelerate the shift from carbon-based energy. In this context, the broader range of roles for the affirmative state is back on the political agenda, including the state's responsibility for jobs and the problem of increasing marginalization and economic inequality. But full employment through capitalist labor markets seems increasingly implausible.

One approach to responding to these challenges is unconditional basic income (UBI), a policy proposal that is already being given increased public discussion in the first decades of the 21st century.[14] The design is simple: every legal resident receives a monthly income, without any conditions, sufficient to live at a culturally respectable, no-frills standard of living. It is paid for out of general taxation and paid out to everyone regardless of their moral worth or economic standing. Of course, for people with well-paying jobs taxes would increase by more than the UBI they receive, so their net income (wages + UBI − taxes) would decline. But for many net contributors, it would still be the case that the existence of a UBI component to their income would be experienced as a stabilizing element that reduces the risks they face in the labor market.

UBI is a possible form of state intervention that responds to the difficult challenges confronting the capitalist state in the face of the decline of acceptable employment opportunities within capitalist markets. From the point of view of the reproduction of capitalism, UBI would accomplish three things. First, it would mitigate the worst effects of inequality and poverty generated by marginalization, and thus contribute to social stability. Second, it would underwrite a different model of income-generating work: the self-creation of jobs to generate discretionary income for people. UBI would make a wide range of self-employment attractive to people even if the self-created jobs did not generate enough income to live on. One can imagine, for example, that more people would be interested in being small farmers and commercial gardeners if they had a UBI to cover their basic costs of living. And third, UBI would stabilize the consumer market for capitalist production. As a system of production, automated production by capitalist firms inherently faces the problem of not employing enough people in the aggregate to buy the things produced. UBI provides a widely dispersed demand for basic consumption. For these reasons, UBI may become an attractive policy option for capitalist elites, especially in the context of the exhaustion of neoliberalism as an ideology in the face of a rehabilitated affirmative state.

If UBI is an attractive solution to problems facing capitalism, how can it also contribute to the erosion of capitalism? A central feature of

14. For discussions of unconditional basic income, see Parijs 1995; Ackerman, Alstott and Parijs 2006.

capitalism is what Marx referred to as the double separation of workers – separation from the means of production and from the means of subsistence. Unconditional basic income reunites workers with the means of subsistence, even though they remain separated from the means of production. A tax-financed unconditional basic income provided by the state would thus enable workers to refuse capitalist employment and choose, instead, to engage in all sorts of noncapitalist economic activities, including those constructed through social power. Worker cooperatives, for example, would become much more economically viable if the members of the cooperative had a basic income guaranteed independently of the commercial success of the cooperative. UBI would also help solve credit market problems currently faced by worker cooperatives by making capital loans to cooperatives more attractive to banks: such loans would suddenly become less risky since the income stream generated by a cooperative would not need to cover the basic standard of living of its members. Unconditional basic income thus expands the space for sustainable socialist – socially empowered – economic relations.

Furthermore, the same technological developments that create the problem of marginalization also, ironically, may contribute to a more robust space for the expansion and deepening of economic activities organized in a more democratic, egalitarian and communitarian manner. One of the material conditions of production that helps to anchor capitalism is the increasing returns to scale in industrial production: when the unit costs of producing hundreds of thousands of something is much lower than producing only a few, it is very difficult for small scale producers to be competitive in a market. The hallmark of the industrial era of capitalist development is massive returns to scale. The new technologies of the 21st century are, in many sectors, dramatically reducing the returns to scale, making small scale, localized production more viable. Basically, the amount of capital needed to buy sufficient means of production to be competitive in the market declines in a digital world. This, in turn, is likely to make cooperatives and social/solidarity economy enterprises and worker cooperatives more viable as well, since they operate more effectively at a relatively small scale oriented to local markets. To use classical

Marxist terminology, the changing forces of production expand the possibilities for new relations of production.

Other state policies, many of which could be organized at the local level, could further stabilize a dynamic noncapitalist sector. One of the obstacles to many varieties of social production is access to physical space: land for gardens and farms, workshops for manufacturing, offices and studios for design, performance spaces for the performing arts, and so on. These could be provided as public amenities by local states interested in creating favorable infrastructure for these more democratic-egalitarian forms of economic activity. Community-land trusts can underwrite urban agriculture. Publicly provided or subsidized makerspaces and fablabs with 3D printers and other digital manufacturing technologies can underwrite physical production. Educational institutions could also provide training specifically around issues of cooperative management and social production.

The combination of a UBI facilitating the exit of people from the capitalist sector of the economy, new technologies facilitating the development of noncapitalist forms of production, and a congenial local state to provide better infrastructure for these initiatives, means that over time the sector of the economy organized through social power could develop deeper roots and expand in as yet unforeseen ways.

All of this would occur, it is important to stress, within capitalism, and thus inevitably these noncapitalist forms of production would have to find ways of positively articulating to the imperatives of capitalism. Many inputs to the noncapitalist sector would be themselves produced by capitalist firms; producers in the noncapitalist sector would purchase some of their consumption, perhaps most, from capitalist firms; and the state's production of public goods would also often involve contracts with capitalist firms. Even after this new configuration stabilized, the state would still be superintending an economy within which capitalism remained prominent, and almost certainly dominant. But the dominance of capitalism would be reduced insofar as it imposed much weaker constraints on the ways people gain their livelihoods and open new possibilities for on-going struggles to enlarge the scope of social power within the economy.

There is, of course, nothing inevitable about this trajectory. There is certainly no guarantee that a basic income would ever be instituted, or if it were instituted, that UBI would be accompanied by the kinds of state initiatives to create supportive infrastructure for the expansion of democratic, socially empowered forms of economic activity. There is also certainly no guarantee that an unconditional basic income would be used by its recipients to construct socially empowered economic structures. UBI can also be used purely for individual consumption. As Philippe van Parijs argues, UBI redistributes 'real freedom' to people and thus enables beachcombers and couch potatoes as well worker cooperatives and the social economy. The specter of parasites exploiting those who work is one of the potent moral arguments against UBI, and such arguments could certainly block political efforts for UBI, or at least result in adding undesirable conditionalities to the program.[15] What's more, an unconditional basic income sufficiently generous to set in motion a dynamic expansion of noncapitalist economic activities would be costly, although by no means beyond the fiscal capacity of capitalist states, and so it is likely that if a UBI were to be passed it would be set at a level below the culturally respectable standard of living. This would also undermine its dynamic effects.

For these reasons, the prospects for eroding capitalism, aided by unconditional basic income and other interventions of the capitalist state, depends in significant ways upon political mobilization and struggles over the state. If the limits of possibility inscribed in the capitalist character of the state are so narrow as to prevent state actions that have the effect of facilitating the growth of these kinds of noncapitalist economic processes, then the prospects are remote. But if, as Therborn suggests, the class character of different appa-

---

15. There are many possible conditions that could be appended to a basic income proposal: for example, there could be 'social contribution' requirements in which a person would have to provide evidence of some productive contribution in order to receive a basic income; or there could be means testing, so only people below a certain income or wealth level can receive a basic income. Some conditionalities would destroy the positive dynamic effects of a BI; others would simply weaken those effects.

ratuses can vary quite a bit, if the democratic class struggle can in some circumstances dilute the dominance of the capitalist character of some state apparatuses, and if disjunctures between present problem-solving and future consequences is possible, then it is possible that a significant growth of the space for economic activity built around democratic, egalitarian and communitarian values could be possible.

References

Ackerman, Bruce, Alstott, Anne and Parijs, Philippe van (2006) *Redesigning Distribution: Basic Income and Stakeholder Grants as Alternative Cornerstones for a More Egalitarian Capitalism*. London: Verso.

Cohen, G.A. (2000) *Karl Marx's Theory of History: A Defense*, expanded edition. Oxford: Oxford University Press.

Fung, Archon and Wright, Erik Olin (2003) *Deepening Democracy: Innovations in Empowered Participatory Governance*. London: Verso.

Miliband, Ralph (1970) 'The capitalist state – Reply to Nicos Poulantzas', *New Left Review* 59.

Miliband, Ralph (1973) 'Poulantzas and the capitalist state', *New Left Review* 82.

Offe, Claus (1974) 'Structural problems of the capitalist state: Class rule and the political system. On the selectiveness of political institutions', in Beyme, Klaus von (ed.) *German Political Studies*, vol. 1. London: Sage, pp. 31–54.

Parijs, Philippe van (1995) *Real Freedom for All: What (if Anything) Can Justify Capitalism?* Oxford: Clarendon Press.

Poulantzas, Nicos (1969) 'The problem of the capitalist state', *New Left Review* 58.

Poulantzas, Nicos (1976) 'The capitalist state', *New Left Review* 95.

Therborn, Göran (1978) *What Does the Ruling Class Do When it Rules?* London: Verso.

Wright, Erik Olin (2010) *Envisioning Real Utopias*. London: Verso.

Contributors

RISTO ALAPURO, professor emeritus, sociology, Helsinki University, Finland. Author of numerous articles and books including *State and Revolution in Finland* (1988).

PERRY ANDERSON, teaches history at UCLA. Editor of *New Left Review* 1962–1982; 2000–2003. Founder of New Left Books/Verso. *The Indian Ideology* (2014) is his latest book. Regular contributor to *London Review of Books*.

ROBIN BLACKBURN, professor of sociology, Essex University, UK. Editor *New Left Review* 1982–1999 and board member of Verso publishing house. Author of *Age Shock: How Finance is Failing Us* (2006) among other books.

CHANG KYUNG-SUP, professor of sociology, Seoul National University, Korea. Author and co-editor (with Ben Fine and Linda Weiss) of *Developmental Politics in Transition: The Neoliberal Era and Beyond* (2012). Guest editor of *Korean Journal of Sociology* 2015 (December).

GABRIELLA ELGENIUS, associate professor of sociology, Göteborg University, Sweden and fellow Nuffield College, Oxford. Author of numerous articles and books on nationalisms and national celebrations and symbols.

ANITA GÖRANSSON, economic historian, professor emerita of Göteborg and Linköping universities. Visiting professor at Uppsala University. Founding editor, *Kvinnovetenskaplig tidskrift*. *Från familj till fabrik: Teknik, arbetsdelning och skiktning i svenska fabriker 1830–1877* (1988) was her PhD-dissertation.

ANNA HALLBERG, poet and literary critic at *Dagens Nyheter* in Stockholm, Sweden. The poem included in the opening pages of this book will be part of a collection of her latest poems to be published by Bonniers (Spring 2017).

ERIC HOBSBAWM, historian, passed away in 2014. Latest book, *Viva la revolución: On Latin America* (posthumous 2016).

SVEN E.O. HORT, professor emeritus, social welfare, Seoul National University. Teaches sociology at Linneaus University, Sweden. Deputy editor *European Societies* (2011–2014). Taught at European Humanities University, Minsk and Vilnius (2005–2009).

PER H. JENSEN, professor of social policy at the Centre for Comparative Welfare Studies, Aalborg University, Denmark. His most recent article (with Barbara Fersch) is 'Institutional entrepreneurs and social innovation in Danish senior care' (*Administration & Society* 2016).

HABIBUL HAQUE KHONDKER, professor, Zayyad University, Abu Dhabi, UAE. Among his publications are *Asia and Europe in Globalization* (2006) co-edited with Göran Therborn.

LISA KINGS, lecturer in social work at Södertörn University. *Till det lokalas försvar: Civilsamhället i den urbana periferin* (2011) is her PhD-dissertation in sociology from Stockholm University. Editor of Swedish journal *Arkiv: Tidskrift för samhällsanalys*.

ZHANNA KRAVCHENKO, lecturer in sociology at Södertörn University, Sweden. Contributor to *And They Lived Happily Ever After: Norms and Everyday Practices of Family and Parenthood in Russia and Central Europe* (2012), which she also co-edited with Helen Carlbäck and Yulia Gradskova. Editor of *Arkiv: Tidskrift för samhällsanalys*.

ALIAKSEI LASTOUSKI, associate professor, Polonsk State University, Belarus. PhD in sociology from Belarusian Academy of Sciences, Minsk.

ÅSA CRISTINA LAURELL, professor of social medicine at the Universidad Autónoma Metropolitana Xochimilco, Mexico. Main work on social and health policy and workers health. Secretary of health in Mexico City 2000–2006.

LENA LAVINAS, professor, economics, Federal University of Rio de Janeiro, Brazil. Most recently with Birgitte Fritz editor of *A Moment for Equality in Latin America* (2015).

GUNNAR OLOFSSON, professor emeritus in sociology, Linnaeus University, Sweden. Recent books on Greek migration, professions and higher education in Sweden.

BO ROTHSTEIN, professor in political science, Nuffield College, Oxford University, UK. Author and editor of numerous books and articles on corruption, inequality and the quality of government.

ANDERS STEPHANSON, professor, history, Columbia University, New York. One of the editors of *The 60s Without Apology* (1984), author of *Manifest Destiny: American Expansionism and the Empire of Right* (1995). A collection of essays are forthcoming on Verso.

IMMANUEL WALLERSTEIN, senior research scholar at Yale University since 2000; founder and director of the Fernand Braudel Center for the Study of Economies, Historical Systems and Civilizations at Binghamton University, 1976–2005; president International Sociological Association, 1994–1998.

KARIN WIDERBERG, professor of sociology at the University of Oslo, Norway. Founding editor, *Kvinnovetenskaplig tidskrift*. Her main research fields are theory of science and methodology, understandings of gender (in general) and the role of the welfare state.

ERIK OLIN WRIGHT, professor, sociology, University of Wisconsin-Madison, US. Past president of American Sociological Association (2011–12). *Understanding Class* (2015) is his most recent book.

NIKOLAY ZAKHAROV, lecturer in sociology at Södertörn University, Sweden. PhD from Uppsala University. Kandidat Nauk, Lomonosov University, Moscow. Author of *Race and Racism in Russia* (2015).

ELISABETH ÖZDALGA is professor of sociology and research associate at the Swedish Research Institute in Istanbul. Her previous positions have been at Middle East Technical University and Bilkent University in Ankara. Her publications are related to religion and politics in late Ottoman society, modern Turkey and the wider Middle East.

Arkiv Academic Press

Arkiv Academic Press is an imprint of the Swedish publishing house Arkiv förlag. For up-to-date information on distribution and available titles, please visit:

www.arkivacademicpress.com

Published books

Ericka Johnson, *Situating Simulators. The Integration of Simulations in Medical Practice* (paperback 2012 [original edition by Arkiv förlag 2004])

Olof Hallonsten (ed.), *In Pursuit of a Promise. Perspectives on the Political Process to Establish the European Spallation Source (ESS) in Lund, Sweden* (paperback 2012)

Rebecca Selberg, *Femininity at Work. Gender, Labour, and Changing Relations of Power in a Swedish Hospital* (paperback 2012)

Sven E O Hort (birth name Olsson), *Social Policy, Welfare State, and Civil Society in Sweden.* Volume I: *History, Policies, and Institutions 1884–1988* (hardcover & paperback 2014, 3rd enlarged edition [1st edition by Arkiv förlag 1990])

Sven E O Hort (birth name Olsson), *Social Policy, Welfare State, and Civil Society in Sweden.* Volume II: *The Lost World of Social Democracy 1988–2015* (hardcover & paperback 2014, 3rd enlarged edition [1st edition by Arkiv förlag 1990])

Lisa Lindén, *Communicating Care. The Contradictions of HPV Vaccination Campaigns* (paperback 2016)

Gunnar Olofsson & Sven Hort (eds.), *Class, Sex and Revolutions. Göran Therborn – A Critical Appraisal* (paperback 2016)

www.ingramcontent.com/pod-product-compliance
Lightning Source LLC
Chambersburg PA
CBHW020450270326
41926CB00008B/554